MY VIEW FROM THE CORNER

★ ★ ★ ★ ★ ★ ★ ★ ★ ★ ★ ★ ★ ★ ★ ★ ★ ★ ★

A LIFE IN BOXING

★ ★ ★ ★ ★ ★ ★ ★ ★ ★ ★ ★ ★ ★ ★ ★ ★ ★ ★

ANGELO DUNDEE

·········· *with* ··········

BERT RANDOLPH SUGAR

New York Chicago San Francisco Lisbon London Madrid Mexico City
Milan New Delhi San Juan Seoul Singapore Sydney Toronto

2 3 4 5 6 7 8 9 10 11 12 13 14 15   WFR/WFR   1 9 8 7 6 5 4 3 2 1 0

ISBN 978-0-07-162847-1
MHID   0-07-162847-9

McGraw-Hill books are available at special quantity discounts to use as premiums and sales promotions or for use in corporate training programs. To contact a representative, please e-mail us at bulksales@mcgraw-hill.com.

To Helen Dundee:
You are a rare and wonderful woman. Thank you for being everything
that a wife and mother should be. You are my last fighter
and the greatest fighter I ever had.

—Angelo

Contents

Foreword

Muhammad Ali

I first heard of Angelo in 1957. I was watching him on Friday Night Fights; he was working in the corner with Willie Pastrano, Luis Rodriguez, and others. I said to myself, "One day I'm gonna meet that man." I liked his style.

After winning the Olympics in Rome, I turned professional. I eventually went to Florida to meet that man named Angelo Dundee. Before that I went to train with Archie Moore, and he was so strict. He told me that to be in his camp, I had to wash dishes, keep the place clean, and do other work. I didn't like that type of camp.

So, I went to see Angelo. He wasn't bossy. He didn't tell me what to do. He let me set my own pace. I turned pro under him but soon gained a controversial image. In Miami, I joined Islam, and the news got out that I was a Muslim.

In those days, Elijah Muhammad told us that the white man was the Devil, and I believed him. It made me very controversial. Angelo Dundee paid no attention to all that talk, all that bad publicity. He never said I was wrong, he never asked why I joined the Muslims, he never said anything about it.

That is one reason I stayed with him. Of course, he was a great trainer, too! But through all those days of controversy, and the many that followed, Angelo never got involved. He let me be exactly who I wanted to be, and he was loyal. That is the reason I love Angelo.

Muhammad Ali

ONE

Fifty-Plus Years in the Fight Game: How Did I Get Here?

Here I am after more than fifty years in boxing—almost sixty, but who's counting?—and with all those wonderful moments pressed somewhere in the pages of my memory, I don't know where to start. Finally, after looking at it every which way, I decided to start with a tale of two of the most unforgettable characters I've ever met: Muhammad Ali and Willie Pastrano. But it's not the kind of story you'd expect.

The story goes back to 1952, when I took two fighters to New Orleans to appear on a local show. As luck would have it, the two fought on the same card as two youngsters trained and managed by Whitey Esenault, a New Orleans legend known as "Mr. Whitey." After the fights were over, Esenault approached me and asked if I'd be interested in working with his two kids. "Ange," Esenault said, "I got these two kids. They're both under-age and can only fight six-rounders here, but they're something special. If I sent them to you, would you work with them?" Would I? Having seen the two, both of whom had won their fights and showed promise, I hastily accepted Esenault's generous offer.

The two boys, and I do mean boys, were Ralph Dupas and Willie Pastrano, two sixteen-year-old kids who had grown up a couple of houses from each other in the French Quarter, Ralph the oldest of the two by six weeks. Their entry into boxing was as dissimilar as their backgrounds similar, Ralph having been a tough, hard-nosed street brawler, while Willie, in his own words, having been a five-foot, two hundred–pound butterball who was "a fat little coward who ran from even the slightest suggestion of a fight." Ralph, after watching Willie in action, or inaction, took his friend, then called "Fat Meat," to Esenault's gym over at the St. Mary's Catholic Youth Organization (CYO) to learn how to defend himself—and, not incidentally, to lose weight. The lessons took, and Willie soon followed his neighbor's lead into boxing.

The two arrived at the 5th Street Gym in Miami Beach soon afterward, looking weary and tired and carrying all their gear in paper bags and their records in newspaper clippings. Dupas, having doctored his birth certificate so that he was able to turn pro at the age of fourteen, had a gaudy 24–2–3 record; Willie, entering the pro ranks later, had a more modest one of 5–0–1.

Now, training fighters is like trying to catch fish. It's not the strength but the technique; you've got to play the fish nice and easy and go with what's there. And what was there in these two kids was that "something special" Whitey had first seen.

Over the next few weeks I added to their meager gear, giving them headguards, new trunks, and new jockstraps. And these two works in progress repaid me in kind, putting in the time and effort as they trained under my guidance. That is, Ralph did, taking to training. Willie took to something less. See, each fighter is different; they're all individuals. And if you listened to Willie's quote book you could tell he was an individual— one not given to training. Every day, as he climbed the steps to the gym, he would mutter, "I'm on my way to hell." Willie also wanted to invent a roadwork pill. According to Willie, "You get up in the morning, take the pill, have breakfast, then a deep breath, and look around, and you've done five miles on the road." He even said his ambition was to make enough money so he could "dynamite the gym."

Soon the two began appearing on my brother Chris's Tuesday night cards at the Miami Beach Auditorium and were adopted as hometown heroes. Here's Chris's genius in developing the two: he changed the amount of time of the rounds in their fights from three to two minutes so the two could fight eight two-minute rounds instead of the six three-minute rounds they had previously been limited to. Now, fighting eight-round bouts, they both kept busy. Ralph, fighting as a lightweight, had fifteen fights in 1952 and twelve more in '53, both in Miami Beach and New Orleans; he won twenty-four times and rose as high as number nine in *The Ring* ratings. Willie, fighting as a welter, won seventeen in '52 and '53 and also rose in the ratings.

Willie was a particularly clever fighter who had become known as "Will o' the Wisp." He also was becoming known for something else. For Willie worked his hands as though he was outlining the form of a beautiful woman—which was only fair because that seemed to be all that was on Willie's mind.

Willie's motto was "Show me a guy who doesn't have sex with his girl at least four times a week, and I'll show you a girl that can be had." And Willie was always in search of girls who could. Not only that, he didn't care who knew it, believing it paid to advertise. One time columnist Jimmy Cannon said to him, "Willie, you must be a good dancer the way you move around the ring," following with the question, "What's your favorite dance?" Willie came back, "the horizontal tango," and wouldn't you know it, Willie's quote appeared in the paper the next morning.

A member of the you-can't-take-it-with-you-so-why-not-wear-it-out-while-you're-here school of thought, Willie was always out in search of two-legged wildlife, his out-of-the-ring nocturnal antics including things you wouldn't find on French postcards. Once, during a sit-down interview with British sportswriter Dick Curry, Willie went into such graphic detail recounting his various sexcapades that a shocked Curry had to excuse himself to, as they say over there, go out to regurgitate.

The combination of sex and fighting has long been one of boxing's greatest controversies, old-timers believing it to be a no-no that would sap a fighter's strength, especially before a fight. Veteran trainer Freddie Brown once told me that his fighter, Tony Janiro, was a real chick magnet: "Coulda been a champion, but sex was his problem. That's what ruined him. For the first four, five rounds, no trouble . . . but the next four, five . . . no strength." And former lightweight champion Ike Williams was quoted as saying, "I did it once, and I got the hell whipped out of me."

Others, however, have come down on the opposite side of the question—and the blanket. One of them was Carmen Basilio who, when asked about sex before a fight, said, "It's not bad for the married guys 'cause they're at home. They're in bed early, and they get their sleep and get up and do their roadwork. It's those young guys who are single. They go out all night trying to pick up some bimbo and they're not going to get up and do their roadwork. That's where the lack of conditioning comes from. It's not about the sex." And Evander Holyfield, when asked about prohibiting sex before a fight, just laughed and said: "Managers, yes; fighters, no." In other words, to quote Casey Stengel, "It ain't the sex that'll kill you; it's the chasing after it."

Still, the prevailing feeling among trainers is that while abstinence not only makes the heart grow fonder, it also makes their fighters meaner sons of bitches when they climb into the ring ready to take their frustrations out on their opponent. Former light-heavyweight champion Bob Foster gave voice to this belief, saying, "You can't see your wife for two and a half months. I was a mean SOB when I was training. . . . I didn't like my sparring partners . . . I didn't like my trainers . . . I didn't like nobody."

Now when it comes to the question of sex before boxing, I've got to tell you I keep business and personal life separate. It's never been my style to get involved with my fighter's personal life. I learned my lesson very early on when I had a four-round fighter who came to me one day and said, "That wife of mine, what a pain in the ass she is. . . ." Distracted, I just said, "Well, you know how women are . . ." and left it at that. Wouldn't you know it, the fighter went home and told his wife, "Angie thinks you're wrong, . . ." and I lost him. So whenever a fighter tries to say something to me about his private life, I just say, "Look, do me a favor, will ya? Go over and hit the light bag."

Even with Willie, who apparently never met a gal with a headache, I tried not to be judgmental and allowed him some leeway as long as it didn't impair his performance in the ring. Hey, fighters are human beings. After all, as Charlie Goldman said, "One of the troubles with fighters today is that they don't start till they're interested in females." And while Willie may have been younger and just stumbled over them, you've got to try to be understanding. So I just kept a polite noninterest, figuring if he hadn't destroyed himself by now it wasn't for want of trying.

A trainer's job has been described as one part motivator, one part strategist, one part physical culturalist, one part cut man, one part psychiatrist, and one part father figure. Nowhere in that job description will you find the term *babysitter*. So while I tried to be only minimally involved in my predicament-prone fighter's life and lifestyle, I brought aboard my pal Lou Gross to handle some of those duties. It was his job to superintend Willie, to make sure he wasn't making the rounds instead of fighting them.

One time Lou was up in the Catskills making sure that Willie was not out chasing Miss Wrong. And Willie, who always liked his girls a little on the zaftig side, had made a play for the rather heavyset telephone operator at the summer resort, always saying things like "Hiya, Sweetie" when he passed her desk. It so happened that Lou had wandered away from the room they were sharing to purchase a cigar, and when he got back he noticed the switchboard lit up like a Christmas tree, with no one behind the desk. Hurrying up to the room, he found Willie in bed with the telephone operator.

(Another example of the pitfalls of babysitting is what befell Charlie Goldman, who babysat Oscar Bonavena after his fight with Ali. Seems that Charlie awoke the next morning not only to find Bonavena gone, having departed for his home in Argentina, but also to discover he was missing his radio, which Bonavena had taken with him as a souvenir.)

Maybe that was the reason I usually shared a room with my Don Juan–wannabe on the road. And the reason I was in the hotel room that afternoon to receive a telephone call. But more about that later . . .

By the end of 1953 both Willie's and Ralph's careers continued, as Howard Cosell would say, apace, and their futures looked bright. But by 1958 both seemed to have hit a wall, Ralph losing to Joe Brown in his bid for the lightweight title and Willie, having added several notches to his belt, growing from a welterweight to a heavyweight where he decided to fight for larger purses with some moderate success against the bigger guys.

Willie had been over to London twice to meet and beat Dick Richardson and Brian London, promoter Jack Solomons always preferring to stage international bouts with Americans versus Brits where the British fighter had "the slightest chance of winning." The crowds also liked Willie's style of fighting, sort of a throwback to the "sweet science" of their fistic forebears with lots of movement and defense. Now Solomons was bringing Willie back for a rematch with Brian London, the former British and Empire heavyweight champ who was in line to fight Henry Cooper in another shot at the title. London knew he couldn't let Willie fight his fight from the outside, there being no way in hell he could match Willie's speed nor catch him, so he had to bore his way in, trying mightily to make the fight into a brawl.

It was during one of those push-me-pull-you attempts to get inside in the fourth round that Willie came away with a cut. I don't know if it was from a clash of heads, an elbow, or a punch, but what I did know was that Willie had a nasty gash over his left eye. I had my work cut out for me as I tried to stop the flow of blood around the cut and applied a coagulant and then carefully covered the cut with a thick layer of Vaseline. As the bell rang for the fifth round, the referee, John Hart, came over to the corner and said, "Remove the Vaseline so I can see the cut." "What are you talkin' about?" I screamed. "If I remove the Vaseline I may open the cut again." Unmoved, Hart repeated the request: "I want to examine the cut." Adamant, I hollered back, "Well go ahead and examine the cut, but I ain't removing the Vaseline." That did it. The next thing I knew Hart was waving his hands in the air to signal that the fight was over, the first time in his fifty-nine-bout career that Willie had been stopped. As they said on "The Sopranos," "Whaddya gonna do?"

Ask any fight fan how long the period between rounds is and they'll tell you sixty seconds. Ask any trainer and he'll tell you it's more like forty, forty-five seconds by the time he gets in and out of the ring—that is, unless you have a fighter like former light-heavyweight great Tommy Loughran, who always managed to wind up in his own corner at the end of a round, saving at least ten seconds. Take away the time placing the stool down, wiping your fighter's face off, washing his mouthpiece out, and tending to his cuts and bruises, and it's somewhere in the neighborhood of twenty to twenty-five seconds. Maybe less.

The cornerman is no mere spectator. As I've said many times, when I see things, I see things, and in those twenty to twenty-five seconds I've got to communicate details that caught my eye and try to implement everything I've seen, providing quick recaps of what's going on and projections of what needs to be done in the form of instructions—not just armchair chatter or feel-good-isms, but solid guidance. It's no time for panic or bile-inducing moments. That's not what my fighter is looking for. He's looking for me as the ring general to calmly and quickly deliver instructions that will help him win the fight.

But any trainer is only as good as the guy on the stool. It's a twosome, a blend, and the fighter must pay attention and heed the instructions given. Or, at least, attempt to. I can't abide eye-blinking boredom or disinterest or inattentiveness. Too many times a fighter lets his attention wander and doesn't focus on what the cornerman is saying. I've seen fighters looking away from their cornermen, almost as if they were counting the house or trying to find a friend in the audience—and I even saw one fighter, Jorgé Paez, blowing kisses to the round-card girls. Such inattention is enough to drive cornermen nuts. One who went "boxinglistic" every time his fighter seemed not to be paying attention was Al Braverman, whose solution was "to rip his chin off till he looked you straight in the eye . . . then you know he's listening."

(Talk about listening to *your* corner and no one else, Al Weill, who was known in fight circles as "the Westkit" because he always wore a vest—which, most times, served as a menu of what he had eaten that day, splotched as it was with food stains—used to tell the story of having a good prospect named Marty Fox who was fighting Unknown Winston in Hartford. For eight or so rounds Fox was stabbing Winston to death with his jab. But the referee, hearing the boos of the crowd and sensing that the two were stinking out the joint, waved for him to go in and fight. And wouldn't you know it, as Weill said, "The damned fool did what the ref told him and was knocked out." Another time, Chickie Ferrara, who in the words of the crowd, "knew what's all about it," was in the corner of a fighter who was going against an opponent Ferrara had once trained. Ferrera's fighter scored a knockdown, and the opponent, so used to looking to Chickie for advice, heeded his motion to stay down, and stay down he did, for the full ten-count.)

Sometimes the help given by the corner is so simple it goes unnoticed. Take, for example, Ray Arcel's little trick of cleaning off his fighter, wiping his gloves, greasing him nice and smooth, and putting his hair back in place before sending him out of the corner for the next round. Now the opponent figures, "What the hell's going on? I thought I was beating this guy, and he looks like he's stepping out of the pages of *GQ* magazine." It was a subtle bit of applied psychology.

Or that help from the corner can come in the form of between-round advice, although some of what is said in the corner sounds as though it came straight out of an old B movie script, such as the advice Charlie Goldman said he got back in his fighting days from his trainer, Jack "Three-Fingered" Dougherty. According to Charlie, Dougherty's advice before every round went something like this: "G'wan, quit fiddlin' around . . . go in there and knock the bum out." Similar boilerplate advice was given by Jack Dempsey's manager-trainer, Doc Kearns, who always exhorted Dempsey before every round to "Pull up your socks and go in there and slap that guy down," even though Dempsey never wore socks. And then there are those cornermen who always seem to be using the same stock line to their well-beaten fighters: "He ain't hitting you . . ." almost as if they were reenacting that old joke where the trainer tells his fighter that the opponent isn't hitting him and the fighter looks back through swollen eyes to say, "Well then, you'd better keep your eye on the referee 'cause somebody is."

More times than not the cornerman has to resort to something more to motivate his fighter. Not a talk-'em-off-the-ledge plea, but something that motivates them to reach beyond their limits—whatever is necessary to make them respond, to energize them. I once trained a heavyweight named Johnny Holman out of Chicago whose manager had given up on him and sent him down to me in Miami Beach to see if I could do something with his reluctant dragon. It was amazing how little Holman expected of himself. Slowly I was able to get him to the point where he began to believe in his abilities. It was then, because of the efforts of my brother Chris, that we were able to line up a match with former heavyweight champion Ezzard Charles, who had had two tough title fights with Rocky Marciano only the year before. Now Big John had three speeds: slow, stop, and wait-a-minute, and all three were on display in the early rounds as Charles continued to dig to his body, causing him to pick up his leg every time he was hit. It began to look as if he was going to take a walk, his spirit wilting along with his efforts. After one particularly disappointing round I decided to resort to mind games, trying some psychology.

Remembering that Holman had told me that his dream was to buy a house with shutters and a television set, I got in his face and shouted, "What the hell are you doing in there, Johnny? What's the matter with you? Don't you want your new home? You hear me, Johnny . . . this guy's taking away your house from you . . . he's taking away those shutters from you . . . he's taking away that television set from you." And with that Big John finally began fighting—not *against* Charles so much as *for* his house, shutters, and television set. And ended up winning.

Then there are those times when short of tendering up burnt offerings the trainer has to resort to something more dramatic to motivate his fighter, even resorting to theatrics. And nobody did it better than Teddy Atlas, Michael Moorer's trainer. To rouse his battler out of his impersonation of a sleepwalker, Teddy resorted to such tactics as sitting on the stool between rounds of Moorer's fight with Evander Holyfield and shouting, "Ya wanna trade places?" Another time, between rounds against Franz Botha, Atlas went over to the referee Mills Lane and asked Lane to come to the corner with him. When the two arrived back in the corner Teddy said to Moorer, "See, here's the referee, and I told him that if you didn't start to do something I'm gonna stop the fight." And in Moorer's fight against Vaughn Bean, Teddy produced a cell phone out of nowhere and, trying to build some giddyup in the reluctant warrior, told him, "I've got your son on the other end, and he wants to talk to his daddy." (Meanwhile, down at the bottom of the steps, assistant trainer Lou Duva was successfully blocking the way, preventing a Nevada State Athletic Commission official from coming up the stairs to warn Atlas that such goings-on were taboo, telling the official that Teddy was "just calling out for pizza.") And, not incidentally, all three calls to arms worked; Moorer responding to each and every ruse to make him come on and win.

When verbal exhortations fail, sometimes physical ones are needed. Like the time Willie was defending his newly won light-heavyweight title against Terry Downes and after seven rounds began shaking his head and moaning about something or other he had done the night before that I could only guess at. Coming back to the corner he let out one giant sigh and lamented, "Why has God forsaken me?" Knowing full well it wasn't God who had directed his activities the night before, I answered, "God ain't gonna help you tonight; you've got to do it on your own," and mushed him in the puss and slapped him on the rump to propel him out of his corner at the bell. With that Willie lunged at me in an effort to hit me in retaliation, and I hollered, "Don't get mad at me . . . I ain't takin' your title. . . . There's the chump over there you should be mad at. . . . He's takin' your title, sucker. . . ." And wouldn't you know it, it worked; Willie came back to knock Downes down and out. (Carmen Basilio might have had the best answer for those who seek the help of God. When he was asked why he crossed himself after a fight but not before, he said, "God ain't gonna help you if you can't fight!")

In a similar manner to my almost to-do with Willie, Gil Clancy once slapped Emile Griffith to waken him from one of his sleep-induced trances, and Emile turned on Gil, threatening to hit him. Seeing Emile draw back his glove, Clancy cried out, "Not me . . . him!" pointing across the ring at Emile's opponent, an order Emile fulfilled to the fullest, hitting and beating the party of the second part. And one of the best stories I ever heard in this vein was from Whitey Bimstein, who had Fred Apostoli in a 1940 match with Melio Bettina. Apostoli returned to the corner after taking a beating and asked Whitey, "What's the matter with me? I can't fight!" Bimstein didn't say a thing; he just hauled off and hit Apostoli in the puss and hollered, "Now get out of there and do your stuff." Apostoli went out in the next round and beat the bejabbers out of Bettina. When he returned to his corner he said to Bimstein, "That's what I needed. Sock me again . . . but hard! Get me mad!" P.S.: Apostoli won the fight.

Then there are times more drastic action must be taken, as when your fighter comes back to the corner plumb tired out, weary in mind and body, and unable to muster up the energy for another round. Or worse, in a daze and unsure of where he is. One method of reviving him is to drop ice down his pants. Another, massage his legs. Then there's the tactic Bimstein used to use of twisting his fighter's ears till the fighter came around. And there were always smelling salts—or there were till state athletic commissions began banning their use. However, such a ban didn't stop trainers Ray Arcel and Freddie Brown in Larry Holmes's corner during his title fight against Gerry Cooney. When Holmes, exhausted from the heat and the effort, plopped down on the stool after the eighth round, the two veterans, using some fancy sleight of hand, administered smelling salts to Holmes. Brown furiously waved an oversized towel in front of Holmes while Arcel, under cover of the towel, deftly waved the smelling salts under Holmes's nose behind the flapping towel and—voilà!—Holmes was reenergized and went back into battle to wear down his challenger.

A cornerman will go to any extreme to help his fighter, from stretching his ass to keep the referee or doctor from getting too close to look at a cut to handing his fighter schnapps, as Panama Lewis did to Aaron Pryor between rounds of his fight against Alexis Arguello. But perhaps the most drastic measure I ever heard of for reviving a fighter was one I heard from trainer Whitey Bimstein. There once was a fight back in the '20s at the old Commonwealth Club in Harlem between one of the top lightweights of the era, Willie Jackson, and a hard-hitting Brit by the name of Sid Marks. Seconds into the fight Marks landed a thunderous right to Jackson's chin and Jackson went down, the first of five times Jackson was hammered to the canvas in the opening round. And five times Jackson arose, more rubbery-legged and glassy-eyed than the time before. At the end of the round, according to Whitey, Jackson's trainer, Doc Bagley, collected his fighter, half dragging, half carrying his groggy charge back to the corner. Bagley tried everything he could to bring his fighter back to some sort of fighting life, but nothing worked. In desperation, Bagley took a book of matches out of his pocket, lit them, and, moving the flame up and down Jackson's back, awakened him from his stupor. And wouldn't you know it, Jackson came back in dramatic fashion to fight to a draw.

It just goes to show you, trainers will do anything to help their fighters. Well, almost anything . . .

Even before the fight with Brian London, it was becoming obvious that Willie was fighting at the wrong weight. Granted, his style made great demands of his opponents, but his lack of pop also made great demands of Willie in the heavyweight division. In short, he was out of his depth, a feather duster in amongst howitzers. And with Willie constantly complaining, "I'm not gonna make it . . . not making any bread," we decided to bring him down to the light-heavyweight level where the talent was sparser and his chances for money and a title shot better. But that would require Willie having to make 175 pounds. And keep it.

Going back to John L. Sullivan, who had to boil off several pounds of bloat before every fight, weight has always been a problem for fighters. Or, as trainer Whitey Bimstein put it, "Some of them lunatics put on a pound every time they take a breath."

It's a take on the old saying, "You are what you eat." Old-time trainer Jimmy August used to say that "if your fighter is a little fellow you may have to watch the amount he puts away closely. If your fighter is a heavyweight you can turn him loose at the table and let him go to town." Then he added, "Give him as much steak as he can hold, but be sure to surround it with plenty of green stuff . . . salads, vegetables, they give him the roughage which helps him digest proteins easier."

All those guidelines sound wonderful, but fighters can still overeat and gain weight—which might be somewhat like saying the biggest cause of divorce is marriage. Take Rocky Marciano, for example. A champion in the ring, he was one of the champion eaters outside. His trainer, Charlie Goldman, would make it a ritual to eat at the same table as Rocky, getting the same small portions of meat and greens as his fighter. And more than occasionally, to ensure that the Rock didn't overindulge, Charlie would reach over and take some of Marciano's portion off his plate for himself. Marciano was also, according to Goldman, the champion between-meals snacker. As Charlie told me, "The only arguments me and Rocky ever had was over his eating between meals. I'd go up to his room and under his pillow I'd find a bunch of bananas he was hiding from me."

However, it's not just food that can cause a problem; it can also be what they drink. Trainer Whitey Bimstein, watching his charge Tommy "Hurricane" Jackson take on the look of someone going down in quicksand for the last time, found that Jackson had had five Coca-Colas right before the fight. And he found that Jackson was also a serial snacker, downing candies, cookies, and cakes in the dressing room. Lou Duva, upon first taking over the reins of Evander Holyfield, found Holyfield's room cluttered with all the junk food money could buy and threw it all away, telling him to go out and buy vegetables and meats. And Willie can also be added to this list of those who would eat or drink anything they could swim with—and sometimes not swim with. In fact, I never understood why, when we returned to New Orleans for a fight, Willie would all of a sudden get homesick and have to visit his mother. Little did I know that she hid bottles of Barq's root beer, Willie's favorite, in the toilet tank for her "starving" son.

Water can also be a problem, as 60 percent of all body weight consists of fluids. Harry Wills, the great heavyweight of the early twentieth century, used to go on a monthlong diet, what he called a "waterfast," losing fifty-five to sixty-five pounds. But that was nothing compared to what trainer Ray Arcel had to do with Charley Phil Rosenberg, a robust little bantamweight who ballooned up to as much as 155 pounds between fights. Arcel would have to trim thirty-seven pounds off his fighter in just two months to bring him down to the 118 limit for bantams. And short of amputation of a limb, the only way for Arcel to do so was to boil him in a spa and deprive him of water. Whenever Rosenberg would plead with Arcel for just a gargle to wet his lips, Arcel would momentarily gratify him but would watch his Adam's apple closely to make sure nary a drop of drink had gone down. Others have monitored their fighters' intake of water by having them sip it through a straw, squeezing the straw if necessary to make sure they didn't drink too much.

And then there's the problem of eating when out of town. One of the reasons a fighter will lose a fight he should have won in a strange city is because he can't find a restaurant that serves the same kind of food and cooking he's been getting at home. Maybe that's the reason trainer Emanuel Steward always cooks for his fighters, both at home and on the road.

Willie experienced all of these problems in keeping his weight at 175. On the road I'd have to constantly remind him of the difference between "light and heavy spaghetti," making sure he watched what he ate. I mean, Willie would gain weight just walking past a bowl of pasta. However, it was less the food than the water and other liquids he drank; Willie never met a water fountain he didn't stop at. He also, I found to my surprise, liked milk, lots of it. One day, watching him swill down his milk, I became suspicious of just what it was with Willie and milk. I asked him for a sip, and he pulled the glass back, saying, "You won't like it, it's warm." "But I like warm milk," I lied as I grabbed the glass. And wouldn't you know it, Willie had laced the milk with Dewar's Scotch. That was *his* mother's milk!

To ensure that Willie stayed close to 175, I took on Lou Gross to monitor Willie when I wasn't around. And although Lou had cards printed up that read "Trainer," he was really a caretaker, a male nanny for Willie. He would watch what Willie ate, when he ate, and how much he ate. Lou took to pasting little Mary Poppins–esque Post-its on the refrigerator and everywhere, reading: "A word to the wide is sufficient" and "Don't live beyond your seams." Anything he could do to make sure Willie didn't overdo it.

For 175 was 175 was 175 was 175 . . .

And so it was that after being frustrated for years in his quest for fame and fortune, Willie finally got his shot at a title, the 175-pound light-heavyweight title then owned by Harold Johnson. Now Willie wasn't the originally scheduled opponent but instead a substitute for a substitute. The original opponent, Mauro Mina, had pulled out because of a detached retina, and his replacement, Italian champion Giulio Rinaldi, had likewise excused himself because of a twisted ankle. Higher-ranked Henry Hank had taken a pass because of a torn shoulder, and others ahead of Willie in the rankings, such as Eddie Cotton, Doug Jones, and Gustav Scholz, had already fought and lost to Johnson. But because champions set the calendar and the fight was slated for June 1963 at the Las Vegas Convention Center, the date had to be kept, and an opponent, any opponent, had to be produced. As luck would have it, after all the dominoes had fallen, that opponent was Willie.

(Here it must be noted that this was how Jimmy Braddock got his chance against Max Baer for the heavyweight title. Baer, who had a contract with Madison Square Garden for a certain date, threatened to pull out of the contract if the Garden couldn't produce an opponent for the contracted date. And the Garden, after sifting through the then-threadbare list of potential challengers, came up with the only fighter deemed worthy and available: James J. Braddock. And, if you saw the movie *Cinderella Man*, you know the rest of the story.)

It made no difference how Willie got there, he was there, fighting for the light-heavyweight championship of the world. And although a five-to-one underdog, Willie, never believing it was a mismatch, disposed of the supposed unfair disadvantage by stutter-stepping, deking, and going left-hand crazy, jabbing the bejabbers out of Johnson, keeping him off balance, and tying him into knots. Before the fifteenth and final round, with the fight sill in doubt, I made one final impassioned "Win one for the Gipper" speech. Expressing the urgency of the situation, I cried, "Willie, you win this one and you're the champ. . . . These are the three most important minutes of you life, Willie. . . . Don't blow it, son." And with that, Willie went out and, with a high purpose, closed the show, winning the round and a close split decision. Afterward, many, including Philadelphia promoter Russell Peltz, told me that Willie had "stolen" the fight. But to me, it was a case of who you were going to believe, the storytellers or your own eyes. I mean, they raised Willie's hand at the end, so he won the fight and the title.

And, bless his heart, afterward Willie said, "When Angie talked to me in the corner, I listened. . . . I can't tell you how many times he talked me into winning fights I did not think I could win."

Two months earlier Ralph Dupas had won the vacant junior-middleweight title after spending most of his career in two lower weight divisions. So finally, after eleven years of hard labor, Whitey's two boys had made good on his prophecy that they were "something special."

I have always loved Louisville, Kentucky—friendly people, great fight fans, wonderful hotels, and excellent Italian restaurants. Who could ask for anything more?

One of the first times I visited Louisville, I had come with Willie for a fight against Johnny Holman, the same Johnny Holman I used to train. Figuring Johnny couldn't catch Willie with a taxicab, we decided to take it easy the afternoon before the fight. At lunchtime, Willie went back to the room at the Sheraton Hotel to watch an interview he had taped the day before on local TV, and I went off to lunch. My lunch was one of my favorites: cheese and celery, tagliatelle alla crema, veal pizziola, along with Frascati wine and grappa. Willie's was a light lunch, in keeping with his diet. And please, I had pleaded with him, no milk.

After my sumptuous lunch—which I didn't dare mention to Willie—I returned to our room at the Sheraton. "Our room" I say because I shared the room with Willie to make sure he didn't sneak out for any pleasurable purpose. I had no intentions of losing him to some outside temptation so close to a fight.

It was about 2:00 or 2:30 in the afternoon when the phone rang. Willie was caught up in whatever it was that was on TV and ignored the ringing, so it fell to me to pick up the phone. "Hello, this is Angelo Dundee," I said. And what to my wondering ear should I hear from the earpiece but a rush of words that went something like: "Hello, my name is Cassius Marcellus Clay. . . . I'm the Golden Gloves champion of Louisville. I won the Atlanta Golden Gloves. . . . I'm gonna be the Olympic champion and the champion of the whole world. . . ." and on and on, the number and the names of titles he had and would win flying by so fast I could barely keep track. Then he said, "I'm downstairs and want to come up and talk to you and Mr. Pastrano. . . ." I was, if that's possible, stunned and at a loss for words. Seeing me standing there holding the phone at arm's length and staring blankly, Willie looked up from the TV set and said, "Who is it?" All I could think of saying was, "Some nut . . . he wants to come up and meet us. . . . He sounds like a nice kid. Want to talk to him?" Or somesuch. Willie, by this time bored with whatever it was he was watching, nodded and said, "Sure, send the sucker up. It'll break the monotony. TV's lousy anyway."

"Well, Mr. . . ." and here I paused, hoping he'd help me out with his name. He did, filling in the blank with "Mr. Cassius Marcellus Clay," then politely added, "Mr. Dundee." "Well, Mr. Clay," I said, "I can give you about five minutes or so. Willie has to take a nap." "Thank you, sir," came back the voice. Then a pause and, "Is it OK if I bring my brother up, too?" Again I turned to Willie for his approval. "He has his brother with him," I said. Willie, game for anything, said, "What the hell, send 'em both up."

Within seconds, Mr. Cassius Marcellus Clay and his brother were knocking on the door. I opened it, and almost before I had said "Hello," the young Cassius had entered and introduced himself and his brother, whose name I found out was Rudy. Politely he said, "I've seen you on TV, Mr. Dundee. . . . I saw you with Carmen Basilio," even telling me I had the nickname of being a "Mr. Cutman" because of my work with Carmen. Then he went on without taking a breath to tell me he had seen the Holman-Charles fight and several others and on and on and on, almost as if my face was as known to him as one you'd see in the mirror in the morning, made so by television.

Then he turned to Willie. "And the fight I really enjoyed most was when Mr. Pastrano beat Al Andrews in Chicago. . . . You sure do have one sweet left hand, Mr. Pastrano." Appearing to look modest, Willie smiled, eating it up.

But that merely served as the prologue. For young Cassius continued to ask rapid-fire questions like "How many miles do your fighters run?" "Why do they run?" "What do they eat?" "Do they eat once a day, twice a day, three times a day?" "What do they do prior to a fight?" "How long do they stay away from their wives?" etc. And always, after asking the questions, he would stand there, politely listening to the answers, taking it all in while his brother Rudy just stood there, over on the side, holding a bust made of clay—although I wasn't sure of what. The discussion ranged far and wide and well past the five allotted minutes, lasting almost three and one-half hours.

But while the youngster may have left the room filled with answers to his questions, he had left me with an appreciation of his thirst for information. See, he was a student of boxing, someone who had studied the sport. And somehow I knew, just knew, that our paths would cross again. I didn't know when or where, but I just knew.

But I'm getting ahead of my story. . . .

TWO

My Apprenticeship with Brother Chris

The road to becoming a trainer is not a straight line but a winding one that takes many different turns, many different routes. In my case, it was a particularly roundabout path. Following the bread crumbs back to the beginning, I was born Angelo Mirena in Philadelphia, Pennsylvania, in 1921, the eighth of nine children born to Angelo and Philomena Mirena. Really, it was South Philly, sort of a city within a city filled with Old World Italians, many of whom, hardworking first-generation Italians with a working unfamiliarity with English, spoke only their native tongue.

But whether I call it Philadelphia or South Philly, the so-called City of Brotherly Love was a city of brotherly, sisterly, motherly, and fatherly love for me growing up. For the Mirena family was a caring, warm, loving family, numbering, by the time I and my younger sister came along, just nine—Pop, who worked for the railroad, Mom, the homemaker, and seven Mirena *bambinos* and *bambinas*, two having perished in the diphtheria epidemic of 1917. The remaining members of *la familia* were, in order: Joe, the oldest, followed by Chris, Mary, Frankie, Jimmy, myself, and Josephine.

And with Joe and Chris having left the roost to make their way in the world, there were just seven of us clustered around the dinner table at 829 Morris Street every night for Mom's delicious Italian meals—Mondays, meat and potatoes served in a big pot; Tuesdays, spaghetti and meatballs; Wednesdays, greens; Thursdays, pasta; Fridays, fish; Saturdays, grab bags featuring sandwiches; and Sundays, ah Sundays, a large traditional Italian meal that defied you to finish even the third course. All served with vino made by Pop. And woe to any of us who showed up late for dinner, Pop always warning us, "When food is on the table, show your mother the respect to be there to eat it." In other words, *mange*. And *mange* we did; families coming from Calabria could eat anything.

And here, just for purposes of accuracy, I must tell you that though our name was Mirena, somewhere along the way it had been Mirenda, with a *d*, but the *d* had somehow disappeared. And because Pop never mastered the English language, he sometimes would write our name with a large, looping *a* at the end, which came out looking like an *o*. So some of us were Mirena, with an *a*, while others were Mireno, with an *o*. And I'm sure I had relatives back in the old country whose name was Mirenda with a *d*.

But Mirena or Mireno or even Mirenda, how did I come by the name Dundee? Well, my oldest brother, Joe, who was twenty-one years older than yours truly, harbored dreams of boxing professionally. But like a lot of fighters who didn't want their parents to know, Joe took another name to keep his little secret from Pop. The name he selected was Dundee, a name worn by two fighting brothers out of Baltimore, Joe and Vince, both of whom became champions. Only it wasn't their given name; their real name was Lazzaro.

The original was a great featherweight champion out of New York way back in the first two decades of the twentieth century: Johnny Dundee. But that wasn't his real name either. His name was Guiseppe Carrora. But Carrora wasn't hiding behind his boxing name, Dundee, to keep his boxing activities from his parents. Instead, it was his manager, Scotty Monteith, who changed it, saying the name Carrora sounded like "carrots" and that if Carrora continued to use his real name "people will start throwing vegetables at you." And so it was that Monteith suggested that Carrora change his name, taking, as Monteith advised him, "the name of my hometown in Scotland, Dundee." And so Johnny Dundee it became, a thrilling fighter who fought some 335 pro bouts, exciting his fans by bouncing off the ropes and throwing punches with both hands. One of those who saw Johnny Dundee in action was young Joe Mirena, who decided then and there to adopt his name in tribute to the all-time great known in those days before political correctness as "the Scotch Wop."

And although my brother Joe's career lasted only about nine fights, the name he wore in the ring became the name of a line of another Dundee fighting clan, this one from Philadelphia—my brother Chris first and then yours truly adopting this fitting fighting name.

But, as a kid, I really didn't care what my name was—Mirena, Mireno, Mirenda, or Dundee—I just merrily went on my way, doing things any kid does. There were football games to be played, movies to go to, visits to make to the local firehouse where the firemen called me "Tootsie" for some strange reason, and even, with the Mason Hall AC Gym over on Seventh and Morris, a chance to watch boxing. The only thing I didn't do was run errands, my mother realizing early on in my errand-running days that I would stop and talk to anyone and everyone and never come back. So she assigned that all-important task to my brother Jimmy.

To help make ends meet all the kids pitched in, taking part-time jobs. I had a variety of jobs; my résumé, which read like the Philadelphia Yellow Pages, included blocking hats, shining shoes, making sandwiches at Pat's King of Steaks, and working behind the counter at Bruno's on the corner—where I was fired for giving some customer a dozen and a half eggs instead of the dozen she asked for. In the meantime, in between time, I attended Southern High, the same school heavyweight champion Tim Witherspoon went to, where I took commercial courses, learning such things as typing, a skill that would come in handy later on. (I even took Italian, a language I spoke every day, and wouldn't you know it, I failed!)

After graduation I had no idea what I wanted to do. So, looking for something, anything, that would give me a steady job with long-term possibilities, I applied for a job at the Philadelphia courthouse as a typing assistant to the court reporter. But I stayed there only a short time before taking a job with a naval aircraft factory in Philadelphia as a clerk typist. However, the factory relocated to Johnstown, a sixty-minute drive away—that is, if you drove, which I didn't. So I had to hitch a ride every day with my coworkers to and from the plant. Guess my work was satisfactory because, in a very short time, I was promoted to the position of inspector, a position I knew would serve me well after the outbreak of World War II.

I won't bore you with details of World War II or my career in the Air Corps. I'm sure you've read about the war; it was in all the newspapers of the time. We won, but not because of anything I did. I had had dreams of servicing B-17s, the airplanes that were bombing the bejabbers out of the enemy. But no, those bureaucratic geniuses who could screw up a two-car parade decided to assign me to organizational duties and even tried to make me a spy behind enemy lines in Italy. Great, a spy. Hell, I failed Italian in high school. What was I going to do behind enemy lines? Order pasta in pidgin Italian?

The only thing I got out of the war was the experience, if you could call it that, of working corners in some of the service boxing tournaments. As luck would have it, I met up with my brother Jimmy over in England, and the two of us, known as "Chris Dundee's kid brothers"—Chris was by this time known as the manager of former middleweight champion Ken Overlin—were thought of as "experienced" fight men. Hell, what we knew about boxing could be written on the back of a picture postcard with more than enough room left over for a stamp and a beautiful picture of the English countryside. Nevertheless, after studying a few books on the functions of cornermen, or "seconds" as they were called over there, the two of us worked the corners of several tourney boxers, nearly drowning the poor guys we were supposed to be spritzing with water as we overenthusiastically sponged them down. And God forbid a fighter ever needed our help over and above a sponge bath. We were totally at sea. Equally at sea as a boxer was Angelo Mirena, who won a few fights but not sure how.

Working corners, no matter how ineptly, brought me into contact with several important figures in the world of boxing, including heavyweight champ Joe Louis, then over in England touring the bases for the USO and giving exhibitions, and Marcel Cerdan, the great French middleweight, also entertaining the troops. But the most important chance meeting I had during my tour of duty was with a Canadian boxing writer named Eddie Borden. I didn't know it at the time, but it would turn out to be one of the most important run-intos of my life.

The war was finally over. And like a lot of returning veterans I had absolutely no idea what I was going to do with the rest of my life. I had no great ambitions, no fantasies; I was just, like any twenty-five-year-old kid, trying to figure out what I was going to do with my life. The job at the naval aircraft factory was still open, so I went back to being an aircraft maintenance inspector. However, a funny thing had happened to the industry during my absence: the technology had advanced radically, and no longer was I working on prop-engine planes as I had before the war; rather, I was working on jets. I was completely lost, my skills now obsolete.

But stuff happens, doors open, and you fall into something. It was at this point in time that Lady Luck, in the form of Eddie Borden, stepped in. For Eddie, the same Eddie Borden I had first met in England, was now an editor for *Boxing and Wrestling News*. And he had suggested to my brother Chris that maybe, just maybe, Chris could use me in his New York office where he was managing fourteen fighters. As I was to hear afterward, Eddie had said something to Chris along the lines of, "You couldn't do better than use your own flesh and blood. Angie is a nice kid; give him a chance; he'll do OK." And even though I was to learn later that Chris had really wanted my older brother Jimmy instead of me but that Jimmy couldn't take the job because he had married and settled down in Philly, I was flattered and excited to get the call from Chris.

Sure, I could have stayed in South Philly like so many of my *paisanos*. But I decided to roll the dice. If it didn't work out, I could always go back.

Romantic writers of the time were calling the postwar years the "boom years." But you couldn't prove it by me. Hell, my brother was going to pay me only seventy-five dollars a week. But I also got my own adobe hacienda—a room to sleep in and a closet to hang my clothes in at his offices in the Capitol Hotel in exchange for my serving as his gofer—as in go-fer coffee, go-fer errands, and go-fer whatever it is I need you fer. I jumped at the chance. It was my escape into the world of boxing.

Chris's office was Room 711 of the Capitol Hotel, kitty-corner from Madison Square Garden. The narrow room was so small that, to steal a line from Milton Berle, you couldn't get in unless you were born there. It had a cot at one end and two desks at the other—the cot I slept in and one of the desks I worked at, typing up press releases and the names and records of fighters on the backs of their publicity photos and taking phone calls and messages for Chris.

I really didn't know Chris from the man in the moon. You see, I was the last of five brothers, and Chris was fifteen years older than me and had left home when I was just a toddler. Going out into the world to make it on his own, he had hustled any way he could—shining shoes, selling newspapers, and hawking candy and gum on trains—going anywhere and everywhere chasing the buck.

Somewhere along the way he had followed the lead of our oldest brother Joe, who had been a fighter, and turned his talents to training and conditioning fighters. Working with one of the great trainers of the time, Al Lippe, Chris was in the corners of such great Philly fighters as Tommy Loughran and Benny Bass. By the age of twenty-one he had become a manager, guiding Midget Wolgast to the flyweight title and Ken Overlin to the middleweight title. By the time I came aboard, he had gone from

Philly to Norfolk and then to New York and had a stable of fourteen fighters, most notably Jackie Cranford, a heavyweight; Georgie Abrams, a middleweight; and Tommy Bell, a welterweight.

Now there were times Chris's left hand didn't know what his right hand was doing. He always seemed to have twenty-eight balls in the air, two of which were his own, and he ran as if he was afraid of dropping the wrong two. It was not unusual to find him working every night of the week. Contemporaries tell of the time he had Eddie Dunne boxing Steve Belloise up at the White Plains County Center and Georgie Abrams facing Ernie Vigh over at the Bronx Coliseum on the same night. How he did it, nobody ever knew, but Chris showed up in both fighters' corners although the arenas were miles apart.

I knew, with all the work Chris did and all the work there was to do, working in Room 711 at the Capitol Hotel would be an exciting and exhausting time. And I dove into it.

Evenings, if all my work was finished, belonged to me. Time to experience that all-new world called New York. No, not the world I could see from the windows of Room 711, but the world surrounding the Capitol Hotel, a world that extended from about Forty-sixth Street up to Fifty-first, along Eighth and Ninth Avenues and over to Broadway, encompassing Madison Square Garden, Stillman's Gym, coffee shops, eateries, bars, and anything a young man in search of New York life could ever need or want. There one could find Jack Dempsey's Restaurant over on Broadway between Forty-ninth and Fiftieth or The Neutral Corner or Ringside Bar over on Eighth, or the Garden Cafeteria just across the street from the hotel, or any number of inexpensive Chinese restaurants over on Ninth. There may have been other worlds out there, like the so-called Great White Way, with its playhouses over on Forty-second featuring shows like *Annie Get Your Gun*, but the world I would come to know and love was this one, the world Budd Schulberg called "show business with blood," a little twenty-block radius on the island of Manhattan, the world of boxing.

New York could be a terrifying, unforgiving city for some, but to me it was an adventure. Sure, I was a streetwise kid from the streets of South Philly, but any comparison with the streets of New York begins and ends right there. New York could be, as one of the songwriters of the day, Lorenz Hart, called it, "a wondrous toy." And for me it was. Even on seventy-five dollars a week.

I'd wander around, sometimes over to Jack Dempsey's Restaurant, which advertised "Come in, Fellows, here's where you'll meet the writers, the managers, the fighters. Mingle with those you know and who know you," and mingle I did with fight people who knew me as "Chris's kid brother," which was an open sesame. Other times I'd go over to Toots Shor's gin joint just off Sixth Avenue, hoping to find someone who might stake "Chris's kid brother" to a drink or dinner. (There was a time, however, when publicist Irving Rudd invited me to go with him to Toots's and stuck me with the bill.) And then there were times when trainer Charlie Goldman and I would go round to all the cheap joints on Ninth Avenue, especially the inexpensive Chinese restaurants, which suited me just fine, they being Charlie's favorites and I having scratch *dinero*—nada, nothing, zilch.

One day I would be chatting with legendary trainer Ray Arcel while waiting for Chris's early-morning eye-opening coffee over at The Garden Cafeteria. Another day I'd be standing next to trainer Chickie Ferrara at the back of Stillman's Gym watching the action, or sitting at a table over at The Neutral Corner, just down the block from Stillman's on the southwest corner of Fifty-fifth and Eighth, in the company of some of the greatest trainers of all time. And everywhere I went I was given special entry into the trainers' small fraternity as "Chris's kid brother."

It was at the Neutral, as its regulars called it and where they would gather between 3:00 and 5:00 every afternoon—locked out of Stillman's for two hours because training sessions at the gym were held from noon to 3:00 and 5:00 or 5:30 to 7:00 to accommodate those fighters who held daytime jobs—or at The Garden Cafeteria earlier in the morning, where I was privy to some of the greatest stories of all time, told by some of boxing's greatest storytellers. As they sat at the Neutral sipping their ten-cent beers and chewing on their ten-day-old cigars or at The Garden Cafeteria nursing their coffees, they talked and talked and talked, holding nothing back, their experiences, their advice, and their tall tales all told in a gleeful mangling of the English language with tortured syntax and marvelously invented words—like calling a particularly gangly fighter a "noctopus," or the opposite number in a fight a "nopponent," or their ring "stragedy." Depending upon those in attendance, it matched anything the fabled Algonquin Round Table had to offer with the likes of Ray Arcel, Charlie Goldman, Freddie Brown, Whitey Bimstein, Bill Gore, and others, the Mt. Rushmore of trainers, all swapping stories. I would gladly have paid for the privilege of sitting in their company. That is, if I had anything to pay with.

With boxing going on every night of the week—except God's and boxing's day of rest, Sunday—at New York–area arenas like Eastern Parkway, Sunnyside, St. Nick's, the Garden, Ridgewood Grove, etc., and others out of town or in such "faraway" places as White Plains, almost every conversation around the trainers' table invariably began with a "How'd ya make out last night?" There always seemed to be work for them, whether it was the "fair money" worked for in fights "on top" of the card, or "hard" or "short" or "small" money for fights on the undercard or "underneath," many working four-round fights in the hopes of finding the next big thing.

After a short answer to how "we" or "I" did the previous night or nights—most fighters not even being mentioned in trainerspeak—the talk soon turned to tales brimming with nostalgia, the trainers arranging their stories and memories in a thousand different ways. It mattered not what really happened in their stories—that was beside the point. It was how they told the stories, their half-told or unfinished tales proof of their teller's authenticity.

Memory being what it is, by the third time I had heard the same story I thought I was there. As best I can remember some of them, they usually started with the obligatory out-of-town horror story, Whitey Bimstein or someone complaining about fights where, if his warrior was beating the bejabbers out of the local kid, the rounds were strangely shorter, and vice versa if the local boy was pummeling his kid.

The stories would than veer off, sometimes to past stories, now growing gray with time, other times to new ones that had just been relayed to one of those at the table and were now being recycled for the benefit of the rest of us. One I remember was about Jack Dempsey's Restaurant, where at one time he had hired the man he had defeated, Jess Willard, as a barkeep. As the story went, Jack was pushing his "Jack Dempsey Special Label, the Whiskey with a Punch." However, Willard refused to serve it, saying when someone ordered it, "That junk?" Soon thereafter, Jack and Jess parted company.

Another trainer, I think it was Whitey, told the story of welterweight Tony Janiro who, after winning an eight-round bout on the Rocky Graziano–Billy Arnold card, passed by the seat of Harry Truman, then the vice president of the United States. After a handshake, a few photo ops, and a "Nice to meetcha," Janiro continued on his way back to the dressing room unaware who it was he had just "meetcha'd." There his proud manager asked him how it felt to shake hands with the vice president. The duly impressed Janiro incredulously asked, "You mean that man is the vice president of Madison Square Garden?" "Naw, ya dope," replied his manager, "he's the vice president of the United States." "Gee," said the openmouthed Janiro, "I didn't know that."

And no matter where the discussion went, it always came back to stories about Madison Square Garden. About the assortment of wiseacres who sat somewhere up in the first tier, midway between Eighth and Ninth Avenue on the Forty-ninth Street side of the house, hollering, "Ya got the wind wit' ya . . . now throw a punch" or "Waltz him around again, Willie" in slow fights or shouting incitements to murder for their favorite, as in "Moider da bum" or somesuch, many insensitive to the goings-on. But the stories I remember most were those of the fighters and the ring announcer, Harry Balough, a small, foppish man in a tuxedo and slicked-down, brilliantined hair who invested everything he said with a verbal flourish, as when he introduced the fighters and then added, "May the better participant's hand be extended in the token of victory." Another at the table would chime in with the tale of the time, during a bond-drive fight during the war, when a bevy of pretty girls passed among the fans with collection cans, Balough announced, with his usual pomposity, "Ladies and gentlemen, several beautiful volunteers will be going through the crowd tonight shaking their little cans collecting for Navy Relief. . . . So give till it hurts." And then there was time Balough announced the fact that "Gladys Goodding will now play 'The Star-Spangled Banner,' " and with that a voice from the upper reaches of the balcony could be heard to holler, "Gladys Goodding sucks!" Unfazed, Balough grabbed the microphone again and, with an importance that matched the moment, intoned, "Nevertheless, Miss Goodding will still play the national anthem for you."

But as entertaining as the stories were, it was the experiences of each that made the greatest impact on my still impressionable mind—like those of little Charlie Goldman, one of the most lovable of men, who stood only about five feet one with a derby resting atop his head and a chewed cigar clenched in his mouth. Charlie had befriended me almost from the moment I came to New York—probably something about two short men feeling taller when they hang out with other men their size. But whatever the reason, he took me under his wing and introduced me to several things, not the least important of which were the cheap joints over on Ninth

Avenue, which suited me just fine, what with barely two nickels to rub together to my name. Charlie also introduced me to his many "nieces," those lovely young things hanging on his arm, although Charlie had no actual nieces I knew of. But one of the most memorable introductions was one Charlie made on the day he said, "Ang, I want you to see this guy. Not too tall, slightly balding, stiff shoulders, two left feet, and he throws punches from his behind. But, oh, how he can punch." And so it was that Charlie, who always believed that finding a prospect was like "putting a quarter in one pocket and taking a dollar out of the other," took me down to the Twenty-third Street CYO where he had kept this prospect under wraps lest anyone should see him—less because they might steal him out from under Charlie's nose than because they might disparage him to his face. The description was perfect; the boxer he had been describing was a young Rocky Marciano. As I walked into the CYO gym, Charlie was having him do an exercise where he bent his knees completely down, almost touching the floor with his butt, and then came up punching. And this boxer called Rocky would do it and end up with a left hook or a right hand every time. There were tales told that Charlie taught his young protégé balance in the swimming pool or by tying his shoelaces together. I think that was pure bull. But he did sculpt Rocky, changing almost everything but his dynamite right hand, which Charlie called his "Suzi-Q." And, in the process, he was to make Rocky Marciano into one of the greatest fighters of all time.

How could you not love it? Here I was in New York making friends with everyone, from the table waiters at the local restaurants to the fabled trainers. Listening and learning, I was, as the old saying goes, "as happy as a pig in slop."

The center of the boxing world was not, as one would have thought, Madison Square Garden. Instead it was a walk-up gym at 919 Eighth Avenue called Stillman's Gym—or as imaginative writers would have it, "the Mecca of Mayhem," "the Emporium of Sock," or, in the immortal words of A. J. Liebling, "the University of Eighth Avenue."

The gym was run by a crusty, acid-tongued tyrant named Lou Stillman, whose given name was no more Stillman than mine was Dundee, having been named for the gym rather than the other way around. As the story goes, right after World War I two millionaires, wanting to do something to combat juvenile delinquency and give convicted men a chance to put their lives back together, established the Marshall Stillman Movement, named after a dear departed relative. They then sponsored a gym in Harlem as an alternative place for these men to spend time, the gym being named the Marshall Stillman Athletic Club for lack of a better name. Their first step was to hire someone to run the gym that carried their family's name, and the man they hired was thirty-two-year-old Lou Ingber. But almost from the start the inhabitants of the Marshall Stillman A.C. began calling Ingber "Mr. Stillman," and, tired of correcting each and every one of them, Ingber found it easier to change his name.

By the late 1920s the Marshall Stillman Movement and the Marshall Stillman A.C. had gone their separate ways, the movement having decided to get out of the boxing business. And so the A.C. became Stillman's Gym, which was only fair because everyone called it that anyway.

By the time I came to New York the gym, having by now moved from Harlem to Eighth Avenue near the old Madison Square Garden, occupied the top two floors of a three-story building between Fifty-fourth and Fifty-fifth Streets, on the west side of Eighth. The entrance was directly under a sign reading: "World's Leading Boxers Train Here Daily." And in smaller letters, "Boxing Instruction—See Jack Curley." Climbing up a long flight of dark stairs, those seeking admission came upon the gatekeeper of the gym, one Jack Curley, who, with no-nonsense eyes, admitted them into the mother lode of boxing once they plunked a half-dollar into his outstretched palm. Or, if he recognized them as a member of the boxing fraternity, he let them in on sight. It was said that Curley "wouldn't let Jesus Christ in without paying fifty cents" if He wasn't a member of the fraternity.

The gym itself was a sight for sore eyes, possessing all the charm of an unmade bed, which it resembled. It was decorated, if that's the proper word, in early floor-to-ceiling grime, the windows a monument to dirt and grit, never opened and so caked with layer upon layer of filth that even the pigeons had given up trying to look in. And the floor was encrusted with spit, much of it coming from Lou Stillman himself despite the sign hanging over his desk reading "No Spitting." Then there were the smells, the redolent odor—one part sweat, one part liniment, and two parts old jockstraps. To me, they were the most wonderful sights and smells in the world.

An unapologetic Stillman took pride in his gym's appearance, saying, "The golden age of prizefighting was the age of bad food, bad air, bad sanitation, and no sunlight. I keep the place like this for the fighters' own good. If I cleaned it up, they'd catch a cold from the cleanliness." A fight manager once asked Stillman to open the windows, it being at least 90 degrees outside and hotter than hell in. "Look," Stillman hollered at him in his normal dictatorial manner, "don't tell me the place needs air. Take your fighter and get the hell outta here!"

One story had it that Stillman had once cleaned up his gym, even going so far as to remove the dirt and grime caking the walls and painting them. But the fighters, showing their attachment to the old-shoe familiarity of what they considered their second home, preferred it as it was, the filthier and smellier the better. And so it remained, even though Stillman gave a wink to cleanliness by posting a sign that read: "Wash your clothes, by Order of the Athletic Commission," which few fighters did, many even wearing them, including their jockstraps, after their workouts.

A few boxers had escaped to open-air training camps—like Madame Bey's or Dr. Bier's—but most had returned, preferring the stuffy confines and stale air of Stillman's. One who did was former featherweight champ Johnny Dundee, who said, "Us guys been brought up in da slums. From de time we wuz little punks we didn't know what fresh air was. Why that stuff is liable to kill us." Another who had trained outdoors and returned, Tami Mauriello, complained that "the boids singin' drives ya nuts . . . there's nothin' to do at night but listen to da lousy crickets."

The barnlike two-story room that was Stillman's Gym was dominated by two regulation-sized rings, both illuminated by bright lights to make up for the light unable to fight its way through the begrimed windows. Ring number one, as it was called, was reserved for the headliners, the who's who in boxing. Perched atop his stool underneath a big clock sat Lou Stillman orchestrating the comings and goings of the fighters. Finally, after checking his list twice, without benefit of a microphone he would announce in a voice that sounded as though he had just gargled with ground glass that so-and-so would be fighting in ring number one and that somebody-or-other would be in ring number two. (One writer had the chutzpah to describe Stillman's voice as having the quality of "the racket made by sanitation workers emptying garbage cans" and for his effort was threatened with permanent disbarment from the premises for life by the injured Stillman.) Ring number two, sitting side by side with ring number one, was for some of the most well-unknown boxers of the day, the wannabes, the maybe gonnabes, and those whose fame had lasted only as long as their last fight.

At the sound of the three-minute bell the participants in the two rings began their workouts, their trainers leaning over the ropes or standing down the stairs below the ring watching. Also watching, or not watching as the case may be, was a gallery of members in good sitting—managers, matchmakers, publicity men, and plain old paying customers, some there to soak up the atmosphere and others just to pass the time of day with newspapers draped over their faces.

And, oh, the characters. One of them, "Sellout Moe" Fleischer, the promoter over at Ridgewood Grove, had his own way of dealing with those unschooled paying customers who got in his way, hitting them over the head with his shoe and saying to the poor souls, "Goddamn ceiling's falling down . . . better move over, pal." And then there was Izzy Grove, better known as "Yussel," who had perfected the talent of spitting BBs through his teeth, unerringly at that, at unsuspecting targets who hadn't the foggiest notion of what it was that just stung them nor where it came from. He drove everyone nuts with those damned BBs.

But most of those around the rings would spend more time schmoozing than watching—and if they were watching anything it was their coat, which had a habit of walking despite the sign reading, "Watch your coat." The noise and ruckus made by them in pursuit of deals and jokes often muted the sounds made by the fighters.

The number of paying customers normally rose and fell depending upon who was training that day. When a heavily promoted fighter appeared and the word spread, the joint would be jammed. Perhaps the biggest day in the life of Stillman's came with the first New York appearance of the most ballyhooed fighter in the history of boxing ballyhoo: Primo Carnera. According to Stillman, more than two thousand of Carnera's Italian fans and fellow countrymen, along with the usual curiosity seekers, crowded Eighth Avenue, all the better to witness the man billed as "the Ambling Alp," and forcing the cops to come and clear the area.

Toward the rear stood a bank of pay phones—beneath a sign warning against the use of slugs. Not just ordinary pay phones, mind you, but six or seven phones that served as the offices of many of the managers congregated at Stillman's who had listed their phone numbers in *The Ring*'s "Manager's Directory" as COlumbus 5-8700, which just happened to be the number of Stillman's. Most of the time all the phones would be ringing off their hooks, nobody answering—not even the managers' assistants whose job it was to wait for calls. (And no manager would ever admit to waiting for calls that cost less than a dollar.) But in my job as boxing's "gofer," which included being the "phone picker-upper," I tried to answer as many of the calls as possible, calling out the name of the person asked for. And woe to those who were either tardy answering their call or weren't there to answer. For that was when some wisenheimer would take the call intended for someone else and make the deal offered on the phone. Maybe that's why several of the managers had small cubbyholes that served as offices along the back walls of Stillman's—so they could be assured of getting their calls. And why Chris rarely took calls at Stillman's, preferring instead to take them at his office across the street.

Toward the rear wall was what could charitably be called a lunch counter that served, as Charlie Goldman would say, "a cuppa cawfee" and sometimes doughnuts. But, in the words of Rocky Graziano, it was "the only hot dog stand that don't serve hot dogs." And nearby, in the little nooks and crannies that surrounded the lunch counter, could be seen several managers talking through clenched teeth and half-chewed cigars, conspiratorially making deals or haggling with other managers over the terms for this or that fight for this or that fighter—or just retelling the latest boxing gossip.

And farther back were the stairs leading to the second floor, where the fighters would go to loosen up or hit the bags or jump rope. And nobody, but nobody, got in the back if Lou didn't let them. He'd chase them away, hollering, "Get outta here, you two-dollar bum, you!" and then, just for emphasis, he'd spit on the floor—the spittle no doubt improving the appearance of the place.

No, Stillman wouldn't be caught dead calling his gym a "sporting club." It was a gym, pure and simple. But the gym and its sights, sounds, and smells was to serve as my introduction to the world of boxing. It was to be a world I fell in love with on the spot, a world I yearned to become a part of.

That seventy-five dollars a week Chris was giving me? Well, after three weeks it sort of dried up. One week I didn't get a check. So I thought maybe he'd take care of it the next and the next and the next. But it never came. Finally, he got around to telling me I would have to fend for myself.

That meant, in essence, I had to hustle as much as possible to earn a living, any living. I would be at an arena where the fight guys gathered and volunteer to go get the beers. Big sport, right? Nope, short of bread but still hustling. I would also bring coffee to trainers, anyone, trying to scare up work, even taking coffee to the matchmaker at Madison Square Garden, Al Weill, hoping to get an assignment of a four-rounder at the Garden knowing that even if the bout didn't get on I'd still get paid.

Once, carting coffee over from the Garden Cafeteria to Weill, I chanced to walk into his office over on Broadway and found him berating his son, Marty, hollering at the poor kid, "Dumb sucker, how could you put that four-round kid in without asking me?" and so on . . . and on. . . . But most of the time the coffee was welcome as I continued to edge my way in, getting to know the important players and letting them get to know me.

Thankfully, something worked as one trainer, Chickie Ferrara, sort of adopted me. I don't know whether it was because I was "Chris's kid brother" or a fellow *paisano* or just because I looked like a little stray dog waiting for someone to adopt me. But whatever it was, Chickie liked something about me, one time saying, "Hey, Angie, I've been watching you. You've got a nice way with the kids. They like and respect you. Stay in the game; you've got a feeling for it. If you need help, all you gotta do is ask."

And ask I did, and Chickie took me through chapter and verse, teaching me everything there was to know about boxing, every little trick, every little angle, what to do, what not to do, everything. I was his student, he my teacher.

First Chickie allowed me into his fighters' corner as a bucket carrier. To tell the truth, I was more concerned with the bucket than with the fighter, worried that, like Jack and Jill, I would fall down and not so much break my crown as spill the water. A lot of guys get buckets, but they tip them over. They wet newspaper guys; they flood corners; they don't know what the hell they're doing in there. There's much more to it than meets the eye. You've got to know how to handle a bucket—the bottle here, the ice there, and not too much ice, just enough to make sure it's wet enough to get the sponge into it. Little things like that. If you don't do those little things properly, you're in trouble.

After a few of these "keep-your-eye-on-the-bucket" jobs with Chickie, as well as some with Charlie Goldman and Jimmy Wilde over in Jersey, my apprenticeship took on another dimension when Chris told me to go up to the Hamilton Arena up in the Bronx where "you're gonna work with Chickie." That "work" was helping Chickie with his six-round fighter and began in the dressing room when Chickie threw me a couple of bandages and a roll of tape and said, "Wrap this kid's hands." Great, Mr. All Thumbs was going to wrap some poor schnook's hands. But Chickie stayed with me all the time, directing me in what to do—how to lay the gauze long, how to lay the tape on top, how to strap the wrist, the whole megillah. The good news was that the kid won the fight and didn't break his hands. The better news was that Chickie wanted me to work the corner with him some more.

I continued to get work on a regular basis and was now earning the heady amount of twenty-five to thirty-five dollars a week. And afterward, instead of just leaving the arena after the fights were over, I was invited by the rest of the guys to go out to their favorite watering holes where the talk would be boxing, boxing, and more boxing. But, like that old brokerage house commercial that went, "When E. F. Hutton talks, people listen," I kept my mouth shut and listened, my education in the fine art of training still continuing. As I always said, "You watch, you learn." And listen, too.

I don't remember what it was I was delivering for Chris that afternoon, but it was something that took me to the Forrest Hotel over on West Forty-ninth Street. Errand over, I took the elevator down and found myself in the company of a debonair man of small stature wearing a well-fitted gray silk suit, an oyster gray fedora, and a sinister smile. Having read all the out-of-town papers that crossed Chris's desk, I remembered having seen a picture of this man, I didn't know in what context but thought it had something to do with L.A. gangster Mickey Cohen. Anyhow, after a few seconds of trying to recollect where it was that I had seen his picture, I turned to meet his gaze and said to him, "I know you. . . ." In a quiet voice that commanded attention and obedience, he politely responded, "No you don't . . ." in no uncertain terms telling me to look the other way—which was what everyone else in boxing had been doing.

For this was Frankie Carbo, aka "Mr. Gray," a man who had his well-manicured fingernails in every pocket in boxing—and his fingerprints on file at FBI headquarters.

Carbo was no man to be trifled with. A member of the old Murder, Inc., mob, he had been implicated in no fewer than five murders, scuttlebutt having it that he was the "button man" in the offing of mobster Bugsy Siegel. Called "the Underworld Commissioner of Boxing," Carbo ruled the sport, making its fights, controlling its fighters, and enforcing his will, whether by manipulation, shakedown, threat, or strong-arm tactics. In short, you couldn't make a move in big-time boxing without his blessing. And that usually came with a price to be paid. In the words of matchmaker Teddy Brenner, "If you knew better, you didn't mess with him."

But being new to the world of boxing, I didn't know any better. Maybe it was that I was too naive or too green. Or just that brother Chris, running a close second to a clam for the closed-mouth division title, never mentioned a word to me about Carbo or any of his group of associates—all of whom seemed to have wonderful Runyonesque nicknames like "Blinky," "Honest," "Gaspipe," and my favorite, "the Honest Brakeman," 'cause he never stole a train—except to let drop once that he had sold gum and candy on trains with "Blinky," as in Frank Palermo. And all of whom had rap sheets longer than Joe Louis's left.

Carbo and gang were boxing's hidden secret, although it probably was the worst-kept secret in the history of the sport, their very presence at every big fight giving further evidence that they had attached themselves to boxing's soft underbelly. And while everyone could see Carbo & Co. at ringside, few made mention of it or even cast their eyes in their direction for fear they might be turned into blocks of salt. Or worse.

One of those who did look in their direction was artist LeRoy Neiman, who was seated at ringside one night and spotted mobster Frank Costello nearby. Neiman had just begun to put pen to paper to sketch the mob boss when the publicist for the Garden, John F. X. Condon, rushed over and anxiously told Neiman to stop lest he "upset *him*." But Neiman paid Condon no heed, continuing on with his sketching until Costello noticed his efforts and sent one of his gangland gunzels over to ask for the drawing. Unfazed, Neiman turned to Costello's messenger and said, "Tell him he can buy one . . ." and went back to his work in progress. As Neiman tells it, Costello later invited him to lunch and bought the sketch. But Neiman was one of the few, the very few, who dared to look in the direction of those called "the mob," especially Frankie Carbo.

Any such talk about Carbo and his nefarious doings came in the form of rumors, and there were never more rumors than those that swirled around the outcome of the Billy Fox–Jake LaMotta fight in November of '47. Having just come to New York in the summer of that year, I was in attendance the night LaMotta "lost" to Fox, a fourth-round stoppage that left such a rancid odor that even the press smelled it. Dan Parker of the *New York Mirror* wrote, "There has always been larceny in boxing, but it's worse now than ever before." And every time the word *larceny* was employed, the name Frankie Carbo came bobbing to the surface, creating more rumors about his behind-the-scenes maneuverings.

Rumor became the currency of the day. Especially when those in the training fraternity took to analyzing the Fox-LaMotta fight and every other fight that smelled even slightly fishy, studying each and every rumor as scientists would a specimen. And then, when finished discussing the many rumors of the day, they recycled those that had a faint odor from the past.

Thus the trainers' grapevine was constantly revisiting fights such as the Rocky Graziano–Ruben Shank fight. Or, more correctly, the Rocky Graziano–Ruben Shank nonfight, which Graziano had pulled out of because of what he called a "bad back." But that bad back was rumored to have been a yellow streak that had run down his back after he had received a call at Stillman's offering him money to go into the tank against Shank. Rather than take the dive or rat against those he called "certain people," Rocky invented the injury. Another so-called fight revisited was the time Lee Oma had pulled what in the old days was called a "hippodrome" against British heavyweight Bruce Woodcock, flopping to the canvas like a beached fish the first time a Woodcock punch even came close in what the British press labeled, "Oma, Coma, Aroma." Then there was the time Goldie Ahearn, who controlled boxing in Washington, D.C., came running into the dressing room to tell the two featured fighters, Alex Miteff and his current sparring partner, "It's going too fast . . . we've been having too many knockouts. . . . Carry each other!"

There seemed to be hundreds of other stories about fights that were fishy at best; at worst, they were out-and-out flimflams, like the Fox-LaMotta fandango. And whatever the rumor, it always seemed as if Carbo and his henchmen, most notably Frank "Blinky" Palermo, had their fingerprints all over it, making the fights, fixing them, and collecting the money—both from the manager's end and from the betting end as well. There were times their overtures of "offers" were turned down, but those times were rare. Rumor had it that Sugar Ray Robinson turned down two of their offers, one to lose to Jake LaMotta, the other to Rocky Graziano, even though there was talk that, as one writer said, Robinson was "the greatest carrier since Mother Dionne," carrying several of his opponents the full distance for benefit of the boys, as he did against an outclassed Charlie Fusari. Another who turned the mob down was welterweight Billy Graham who, before his title bout with Kid Gavilan, was told by Carbo that he couldn't win unless he gave up 20 percent of his contract to Carbo. Graham didn't and didn't.

Carbo and his gallery of rogues not only had alliances with several managers—it was even rumored that Carbo had cut himself in for a piece of Rocky Marciano's manager Al Weill's piece—but they also operated with heavy hands behind the scenes as the undercover managers of several fighters, the legally licensed managers fronting for those the New York State Athletic Commission deemed "unsavory" and "undesirable."

And if that weren't enough, they also created an auxiliary, the Managers' Guild, to ensure that their will would be served. The guild was a closed shop where so-called uncooperative managers and fighters found themselves shut out of the big fights.

An example of how the guild worked could be seen in the case of lightweight champion Ike Williams. For even though Williams was the National Boxing Association (NBA) champ, he was a free agent, independent of his manager whom he had fired for continually being drunk. But his manager had been a member of the guild. And the firing didn't sit well with the head of the Managers' Guild, Jimmy White, who would not tolerate anyone challenging the guild. "We're going to show everyone just how powerful we are," White trumpeted. "We're going to stop Ike Williams from fighting. And if anybody fights him, we're going to blackball them, too." Suddenly Ike Williams was an untouchable. That is, by all except Blinky Palermo, who approached Williams and told him, "Listen, Ike, you sign with me and I'll straighten you out with the guild." Suddenly doors opened for Williams, courtesy of the Managers' Guild and Palermo. But, in testimony a decade later before the Kefauver Committee—a congressional committee investigating organized crime—Williams testified just what he had found behind those doors: countless offers to throw fights and no payment for title defenses; in two of those defenses, Williams was shortsheeted his entire purse. Williams's plight so infuriated sportswriter Barney Nagler that he asked in print, "Why won't sharks eat managers?" and then answered his own question by writing, "Professional courtesy."

Others sought to defy Carbo and his gang with even more dire consequences than those that befell Williams. Trainer Ray Arcel and promoter

Sam Silverman tried to go it alone, staging Saturday night fights in Boston without Carbo & Co.'s sanction, and all they got for their efforts was being whacked over the head in the normal mob manner, with iron pipes wrapped in newspapers. The threat of the same for anyone else even thinking about not cooperating with Carbo & Co. was enough to bring the entire sport into line.

Everyone, or so it seemed, was cooperating with Carbo and gang, even the sportswriters who were rewarded for looking the other way or for favorable coverage of their fighters; they would find fat envelopes stuffed with pictures of dead presidents on their press-row seats before big fights to thank them for past favors. Bill Gallo of the *New York Daily News*, who has been on the boxing beat for years, remembers the time when he was approached by a manager of one of the top fighters who stuffed a fifty-dollar bill into his jacket pocket. "What's this for?" a startled Gallo asked, pulling the bill out. "Go buy your wife a hat," replied the manager, "She deserves it." To which Gallo said, "My wife doesn't wear hats," and shoved the bill back into the manager's hand. But many a sportswriter's wife was wearing a hat that season. Irving Rudd, the famed publicist called "Unswerving Irving" by Red Smith, said that even Nat Fleischer, the sainted publisher of *The Ring* magazine, "could be gotten to."

But Carbo couldn't have happened without others looking the other way as well, in this case Madison Square Garden's president James D. Norris. Norris, one of the wealthiest men in sports, had amalgamated his holdings, which included ownership of the Detroit Red Wings and the Chicago Blackhawks, together with those boxing interests held by his predecessor, Mike Jacobs, the 20th Century Sporting Club, and formed the International Boxing Club, or the IBC—better known in boxing circles as "Octopus, Inc." The IBC had a stranglehold over not only Madison Square Garden but also the Detroit Olympia, the Chicago Stadium, and other sports arenas in St. Louis, Chicago, Indianapolis, Omaha, and Washington, D.C. The IBC also had a million-and-a-half-dollar TV contract to package Wednesday night fights for Pabst Blue Ribbon beer and Friday night fights for the "Gillette Cavalcade of Sports." To fill those fight nights, he needed fights and fighters. And for that, he turned to Carbo to supply them.

I can't claim that I knew what was going on at the time. Later I would be able to connect the dots. But all I knew then was secondhand, gleaned by way of rumor or partial information that filtered down or from what Chris would say in that closemouthed way of his. And I certainly wasn't prying around, trying to find out. As the new kid on the block, I fully subscribed to the trainers' eleventh commandment: "Thou shalt not stick thy nose into other people's business."

After all, what could I do other than what Carbo had so unsubtly told me to do the first time I met him: look the other way? Jimmy Breslin, who was on the scene back then, best summed up the trainers' arm's-length relationship with the criminal element when he told a writer: "Nobody mentioned them. It was like the hidden, secret sin. That's the business end. Your job is just the fighter. What are you gonna do? Are you gonna make statements and change America? It couldn't be done. I mean, what shot did you have causing trouble?" And so, no matter what I may have heard or suspected, even that my brother Chris may have been doing a little business "with the business end" just to stay afloat, I looked the other way, too.

There was one time, however, when I didn't look away. It was a decade later, and I was in Washington, D.C., with my fighter Jimmy Beecham for a middleweight matchup with Willie Vaughn on a fight card put together by Washington promoter Goldie Ahearn. The two had met twice before, each getting a decision, and this was to be their rubber match. The Uline Arena bout was a crowd-pleaser, but, unfortunately, it ended in a draw, although naturally I thought my guy had won.

Now I wanted to get out of there and go home, back to Miami. But the problem was that it was snowing. No, make that blizzarding. Everything was at a standstill, including the airports, which were socked in. (I've always thought that during the cold war the Russians only had to seed the clouds, not bomb Washington; Washingtonians are unable to do anything in snowy weather.) Anyway, with my flight canceled and nothing else to do, I thought I'd catch a late-night bite and remembered that Goldie's brother, Johnny Goldstein, owned a restaurant where the fight mob always hung out; I decided to go there rather than eat at the hotel.

Catching a cab, seemingly the only one out that night, I directed the driver to the Golden Parrot, right off Connecticut Avenue at DuPont Circle, where I hoped to catch some of the fight crowd and get a sandwich and a bowl of soup or a glass of hot milk or something to warm me up on a cold and blustery night. As I walked into the restaurant I was surprised to find the joint empty, but a friendly Goldie Ahearn greeted me and took me to a table in the back, promising to join me later for a drink. After dinner Goldie returned to share a glass of wine and fight talk before he hurriedly ran off to greet the late-arriving crowd who had finally made their way through the snow. A couple of them paused as they went by to tell me that they thought Jimmy had won the fight, though, after some thought, I was happy with the draw.

I paid my bill, asked the waiter to get me a cab, and began to make my way to the front door when I heard a voice call out, "Hi, Angie, how ya doin'?" I turned and saw three men seated near the door, one of whom I faintly recognized. But when one of the three said, "Frankie thought the other guy won, but I thought Beecham sneaked in," I remembered who the face belonged to: Frankie Carbo, the same Frankie Carbo I had first met in the elevator years before.

"Sit down; have a drink," the face with a name said. But a little voice went off inside my head saying that somehow that wouldn't be a good idea, and so I mumbled something about having a cab waiting outside and beat a hasty retreat with a quick *ciao*.

But apparently I wasn't hasty enough, for two weeks later I got a call from Charlie Goldman. "Angie," he said in a distressed voice, "I've got some bad news for you." And with that, he went on to explain that Carbo had been under surveillance by the authorities and that there were two detectives at the next table at the Golden Parrot that snowy night. "The whole night's friggin' conversation was taped, including yours." Mine? What the hell had I said? *Ciao.* But apparently the New York State Athletic Commission was threatening to take away my license for "consorting" with Carbo. All this for a hello-and-goodbye? Hell, I had met the guy only twice, and now they were threatening to take away my license?

I finally arranged a meeting with the counsel to the Athletic Commission, and although they had found nothing incriminating in my taped conversation, they felt I was guilty by association with the man they were investigating for everything from bribery to criminal infiltration into boxing, fixed fights, and all manner of things up to and including, at least it seemed, dining at the Golden Parrot and talking, albeit momentarily, to yours truly. The counsel believed I was just plain unlucky to have been there that night and just an innocent victim of circumstances. He said that he would inform the State Athletic Commission and the DA's office of my unwitting involvement and recommend that my license not be revoked but advised me to apply the following year for renewal when the investigation would be concluded.

All this for one "hello-goodbye." So, for one year, I would not be able to work in the state of New York, courtesy of Frankie Carbo. But hell, I was already in Miami anyway. Which is another story . . .

Chris was always on the phone—make that phones, most times working two phones, one to each ear, like earmuffs—almost from the moment he walked in the door to the time he left the office for his home in Long Beach at the end of the day. At times he would be talking to promoters who might want his star pupil, Georgie Abrams, and Chris would say something like, "Look, I'd let you have Georgie, but use my kid Tommy Bell and let me see how he is, and then I'll come down there later with Georgie Abrams. Bell's big 'cause he fought [Sugar Ray] Robinson . . . he fought everybody." Other times he would bark detail-thin instructions in my direction for me to jot down, all of which sounded like, "Chicago . . . third week . . . March . . . middleweight . . . Sunnyside . . . February 4 . . . headliner, . . ." but instructions I understood anyway, writing them down as fast as Chris shouted them out in the usual fast-paced chaos that engulfed his office.

On one particular day, the day one of his fighters, Jackie Cranford, was to fight in the Garden, we set a new high in chaos as both Chris and I fielded calls from anyone and everyone seeking free or "house" tickets—called "Chinesees" by Damon Runyon because they had holes in them like Chinese coins. Now, as Chris tried to take care of all the people wedged into Room 711 at the Capitol, the phone kept ringing with all the callers trying to get tix—newspapermen, hangers-on, and just plain friends and friends of friends—all on-the-cuff, of course. And guess who was assigned this wonderful task?

Well, anyway, about 5:00 the frenzy was over, or so I thought, and I was just about to lock up to go see the fight when the phone rang. "Hi. Chris Dundee's office," I answered. The voice on the other end, a pleasant female voice tinged in a syrupy southern drawl, came back with, "Hello . . . this is Jackie Cranford's cousin. I'd like three seats for the fight, please. I'd prefer them ringside." Great, I thought. "Oh, you would, would you?" I responded, by now tired of all the requests for "Chinesees" and tempted, like Chris, to just blurt out, "You wanna ticket? Just go across to the Garden and buy one." But instead I said something to the effect of, "Why, honey chile, we're all out of ringside," giving it my best try at a southern accent. "Look here," the suddenly unsweet voice shot back, "I'm Jackie Cranford's cousin, and I need the tickets for his Auntie Mildred, that's my mother, my sister Frances, and me."

Three free tickets! Chris would shoot me. He hated people putting the arm on him for freebies. He would tell those deadbeats, "Go over to the Garden and buy them yourself," and slam the phone down. Now I had a mind to do the same thing to the syrupy voice on the other end of the phone. And so I shot back, "You're Jackie's cousin, eh? How come he didn't get you tickets?" I was tired of all these requests, and all with some sort of dodge, up to and including, "I'll pay you later." Apparently the southern drawl had had enough too and now asked, "Is Jackie there?" in an icy, aggravated, surely not syrupy tone. "No, Jackie ain't here; I'm here. . . ." "Now listen here," the voice broke in, "I'm Helen Bolton from North Carolina, and Mr. Chris Dundee told me to call for tickets." "Well, doll, this is Angelo Dundee, . . ." and here I stole a line from Chris's handbook and said, "Why don't you buy three tickets?" Then, as an afterthought, I threw in, "And after the fight, come over to Toots Shor's; we're going to be there with your cousin and a writer named Will Grimsley, and he's going to write a story on Jackie and say that we're ready to make a fight with Joe Louis for the championship. . . ."

So what happens? The fighter Chris had been promoting as "the Next Great White Hope" and a possible challenger for Joe Louis's heavyweight crown was thoroughly beaten by Gino Buonvino. And now here we were at Toots's saloon after the fight trying to drink away our miseries. Among those at the "party" were writers posing as Sir Lunchelots, friends of Chris's and Jackie's, and friends of friends. And there were three pretty ladies, one of whom, upon being introduced to yours truly, stared straight through me with an expressionless gaze.

Her name, she said, was Helen Bolton, the same Helen Bolton I had had that little phone to-do with earlier that afternoon. Not only that, the seats she had purchased were an eagle's perch, way up in the rafters. I tried to be nice, especially because she was a strikingly good-looking gal, and asked, "How did you like the fight?" In a deadpan response that would have done Buster Keaton proud, she answered, "Great, I was up so high I only had a minor nosebleed."

That should have been the end of the story and the short-lived acquaintanceship right then and there. But it wasn't. As the Cranford party, if you could call it that, was making somewhat polite conversation to fill the dead-air time, Jackie made the mistake of asking his cousin, "I can't understand what happened tonight. What happened? I mean, I felt great in the first round. . . ." And his cousin, whose name I now knew to be Helen, in her straightforward and honest manner, replied, "Jackie, you just didn't fight." And that was the end of the questioning. And the beginning of my infatuation with this straight-talking, no bullspit—and did I say beautiful?—girl.

Soon we were joined at our table by the man himself, Toots Shor. Now Toots Shor was what might be called a character. The stories about him abound, like the time he was chatting with the discoverer of penicillin, Dr. Alexander Fleming, when the then-manager of the New York Baseball Giants, Mel Ott, came into the restaurant and Toots excused himself with an "Excuse me, somebody important just came in." Or the time Charlie Chaplin complained about the wait for a table and Toots told him, "Just stand there and be funny, Charlie," and walked away. Or when he and Jackie Gleason got into a drinking contest and bet one another who could run around the block faster, each going in a different direction around the block, and Toots came back huffing and puffing to find Jackie at the bar already celebrating, only to find out later that Jackie had taken a cab around the block. Now the great man was seated alongside us drinking from a bag-wrapped bottle produced by Auntie Mildred from out of her purse.

Somewhere during the goings-on I managed to strike up a conversation with the attractive girl I had hardly done a favor for earlier that evening with the "nosebleed" seats and found out she was single and working in New York as a fashion model. I even worked up the nerve to ask for her phone number.

But caught up in work, and hustling for more, it would be another six months before I got around to calling her. After all, boxing was my first calling, and I was working 'round the clock, both at Chris's office and in fight arenas around the area. In fact, I was now training my first fighter, Bill Bossio, a featherweight out of Pittsburgh who was referred to Chris by an old friend, Bill Brennan from Norfolk, where he had promoted fights before coming to New York. And Bossio turned out to be a winner, even headlining in the Garden.

I finally got around to calling her even though I was to find out that in the meantime others had discovered her as well, one of whom was—get this!—Jack Dempsey. But it made, as Helen said in her southern drawl, "no never mind," and we began seeing each other regularly. I don't know, maybe she figured what a handsome guy I was. And I figured she needed glasses. But even though I thought this lovely lady was nine feet tall, what she really needed was flat shoes because she towered over me in heels.

It was, as they say in the movies, the beginning of a beautiful relationship, one that would last a lifetime. And while her mother couldn't quite conceive of an Angelo Mirena from South Philly and a Helen Bolton from North Carolina becoming an "item," it, as they say in the South, "took."

By the beginning of the '50s, the very nature of the sport was changing—and not for the better. Boxing had planted the seeds of its own destruction by televising boxing matches. Now fans were staying at home to watch free televised boxing shows every night of the week—except, again, on Sundays—rather than attending them. And the grass roots of boxing, the small-town and neighborhood boxing clubs where boxers as well as trainers had a chance to earn their spurs and learn their trade, were drying up. First it was Sunnyside Garden; then, like Agatha Christie's ten little Indians, they began going down one by one. By 1952 there was only one small club left for every ten that had existed in the postwar boom year of 1946.

Chris had worked up some figures that showed just how bad it was. The IBC, which had a contract calling for the production of some eighty-plus fights on Wednesday and Friday nights for $1.5 million, lost more than that in live gates. According to Chris's back-of-the-envelope calculations, thirty-three dates in 1946 at Madison Square Garden yielded a total of 406,681 fans and a gross of $2,062,000. Twenty fights in '52 pulled in only 137,381 fans and $435,450, a total loss in revenue of more than $1,600,000.

With its farm system drying up, its small clubs going out of business, the New York boxing scene was suddenly a wasteland. And trainers, who only a few years before couldn't keep up with the work, were now scrambling to find any.

Chris decided it was time for him to look elsewhere; searching for new territory in which to plant his promotional flag, he found it in Miami Beach. And where Chris went, Angie was sure to go.

THREE

Miami Beach and My First Champion

By the beginning of the 1950s the seeds boxing had sown were all but destroying the sport, the hard core of customers getting their fix on a black-and-white screen a little larger than a lunchbox. The appeal of getting something for nothing was keeping them home, away from the live bouts. Even Madison Square Garden, once the mecca of boxing, was little more than a set for virtual TV shows, most of the crowds masquerading as empty seats. Hell, they could have held live fights in a telephone booth for all it mattered because fans were content to stay at home and watch the bouts for free—which is somewhat like eating a ham sandwich with the waxed paper on as far as I'm concerned.

But television was far less interested in building the sport than in building its audience and selling its sponsors' products. John Crosby, writing in the *New York Herald-Tribune*, may have discovered why sponsors were so happy with boxing. One CBS executive, Crosby wrote, decided to try a little experiment one night. Watching the Pabst Blue Ribbon Wednesday night fights over his own network, the executive decided to follow the advice of the between-rounds announcer who sternly advocated that viewers were to visit their refrigerators and repay the kindness of the beer company for bringing them the fights for free. Gulping furiously, he managed to stay up with the announcer, getting a new bottle every time he was told to. The result: the losing fighter was knocked out in the tenth; the executive was flat on his back by the end of the ninth.

Looking for a way to continue building their audience and selling their sponsors' products, TV began looking for rising young stars, prospects who were little more than made-for-TV fighters. One writer even went so far as to compare them to "artificially ripened tomatoes." These kids were thrown into the ring way ahead of schedule and over their heads, long before they had learned the basic ABCs of boxing and not yet ringwise enough to take care of themselves. All of a sudden, a so-called prospect who had been a rugged and ambitious kid became a soft-chinned has-been and little more than an opponent.

Take the case of Chuck Davey, boxing's first made-for-TV fighter. A college graduate, Davey had twice won the NCAA featherweight championship and once the NCAA welterweight title. With ninety-three wins in ninety-four amateur fights, the white, college-educated, and handsome to boot—even sporting red hair, although somewhat sparse on top—fighter was the perfect prospect for TV to tie their kite tail to. Turning pro in 1949, he had won thirty-seven of his thirty-nine fights—the other two draws—with twenty-five knockouts and had become a staple of the Pabst Blue Ribbon Wednesday night fights. Now TV determined he was ready for a shot at the welterweight crown, then held by all-time great Kid Gavilan. The fight was no fight; Gavilan embarrassed and undressed Davey, even turning around to mimic Davey's left-handed stance and continually beating him to the punch—Davey possessing a stylistic quirk that had him bouncing on his right foot three times before throwing a jab, and Gavilan, able to count to three, beat him to the punch time and time again somewhere between the counts of two and three. The fight ended in the tenth round—and with it TV's search for boxing's version of the "American Idol."

But except for a few fighters who continually fought on TV—one writer complaining that he was "fed Ralph 'Tiger' Jones more times on Fridays than fish"—the rest fought in private. Whitey Bimstein complained that at nine-tenths of the boxing shows you might as well be fighting in a telephone booth, only the feature bouts being televised and the fighters in the prelims laboring in private.

Not only that, purses were down across the board, lower than they had ever been. Back in boxing's heyday, the 1920s, principals would get as much as twenty thousand dollars a fight. Now they were lucky to get four thousand dollars or so from TV and 25 percent of the gate, if there was any. And the prelim fighters were getting the same as they got thirty years before, *bubkes*—Madison Square Garden paying $150 for four-rounders, $500 for six, and $1,500 for eight.

Me? I was still hustling. My living was the preliminary kids. I would go with the prelim fighters and make a buck or two. I'd go to Ridgewood Grove and work a corner and make twenty-five bucks and have it in my kick. But even those jobs were few and far between, drying up like the rest of boxing in New York. As Ray Arcel said, "Tough times make monkeys eat red pepper."

My brother Chris, having correctly read the handwriting on the wall, had moved lock, stock, and promotional kit bag down to Miami Beach, where he took over the local promotion at the Miami Beach Auditorium. I still don't know what prompted the move. Some said it was something to do with Blinky Palermo, with whom Chris had a casual friendship. But as far as I knew it was Cy Gottfried, the referee, who brought him down.

I never did know. You see, from the day my father called Chris "a bigga shot," he was always a hero to me. So maybe I saw him through tinted rather than clear glasses. For Chris was an imperfect man in an imperfect world. He could have had dealings with Palermo and the mob, but I knew very little of his business goings-on because, in that closemouthed way of his, he never confided in me. But I prefer to believe, to this day, that Chris merely had what he called "a better idea" and made tracks to Miami Beach on his own counsel.

Anyway, when he left to go to the Beach, he left me with a bunch of fighters but no boxing venues to work them in. After several months of fruitless hustling and making "short bread," I figured it was time to consider my future. And it didn't look like that future was in boxing. Or in New York, for that matter. I even considered going back to my old nine-to-five job at the naval aircraft factory in Philadelphia—or, more correctly, Johnstown. That's how desperate I was.

So I called Chris and told him, "No way New York." The weather was bad, and the work was nonexistent. I told him I'd either come down to Florida to work with him or I would have to go back to inspecting aircraft at the naval factory. That's when Chris told me to come on down.

And so, in October 1951, Angelo Mirena (aka Angelo Dundee), a thirty-something trainer-in-training, was on a train heading south to Florida with two of his fighters in tow—Alex Fimbres, a featherweight, and Bill Neri, a lightweight. They took the crapshoot, too, figuring that even if things didn't work out at least they could get a good suntan. Another of my fighters, Bill Bossio, had been taken over by Al Braverman, who had promised me a percentage of his purses. Unfortunately, Al was the kind of guy who, if you reminded him that a debt was a year old, he'd send it a birthday card and never sent me anything. But, hey, I didn't care. It was a whole new start to my career, such as it was.

There I was again, working on all of Chris's promotions—the boxing shows, the wrestling shows, and even the circus. And for the same seventy-five dollars a week. Talk about upward mobility! And once again Chris conveniently forgot to pay me. When I approached him about my back pay all I got was: "Angie, what are you worrying about? If you want to worry, worry about how bad business is. Look, Angie, I'll take care of you. Don't worry so much." And with that he turned away, shouting over his shoulder, "Listen, Angie, the Continental Restaurant wants twenty tickets for the fight tomorrow night. Will you take care of it?" End of conversation.

Forgetting my pay for the moment, which I did, my brother Chris was one helluva promoter, probably the greatest promoter of all time. If he were around today he'd bury all the other promoters. Let me tell you about his Tuesday night shows at the Auditorium, an arena built by the city of Miami Beach in 1950 for boxing. Always hustling, Chris would feature local talent against what he called "opponents that were always dependable, that could give a good account of themselves and lose." His bouts were always crowd-pleasers, and Chris catered to his patrons, knowing every face and every name. And if he saw a strange face in one of the seats, he would shoo them out. One time Chris noticed that one of his regulars wasn't in his seat and called him to ask why he hadn't shown up. "Chris," the regular said, "I was in the hospital." "Well, why didn't you tell me, I'd have sent you flowers," Chris said, ever mindful of his paying customers. It was a social gathering, and the fans loved it, repaying his efforts by showing up every Tuesday night, almost two thousand strong.

After two years of an uphill battle, Chris finally found the local talent he had been looking for in Bobby Dykes, probably one of South Florida's most popular boxers at the time. The fight crowd also took to Billy Kilgore and adopted both Ralph Dupas and Willie Pastrano as their own. And Miami's Cuban community embraced the imports from Cuba, one of whom, Frankie Otero, became one of Chris's greatest gate attractions. Suddenly the weekly shows at the Auditorium became an overnight success, even if that overnight had taken two years.

If there was one problem in developing homegrown talent it was the lack of training facilities in Miami Beach, the nearest gyms being over across the causeway, in Miami. Unlike Judy Garland and Mickey Rooney, who would always say, "We have a barn, let's put on a show," there was no barn to rehearse in for the big Auditorium show.

That is, until the 5th Street Gym.

To say that the 5th Street Gym was ratty and tatty would be an overstatement. Grungy might have been more like it. But, hey, it was home for me and my family of fighters.

Chris had purchased a second-floor walk-up in a ramshackle old building on the corner of Fifth Street and Washington Avenue that had once been a Chinese restaurant and put me in charge. As a souvenir left by its previous tenants the entire floor smelled like egg-drop soup. My job was to make it into something faintly resembling a gym. And so I got to work, plasterboarding the walls and plywooding the floor. Then I bought bags and a ring and got some seats from a jai alai fronton that cost fifty dollars a row just to haul over. Together with Allie Ridgeway, Jerry and Dave White, and Pat O'Malley, who all chipped in, we put the gym together by putting up speed bags, heavy bags, and the ring. Next I had to have the place painted—although some smart alecks said demolished might have been more like it. For that I turned to a vacationer who came down every winter from Boston and whom I had let train in the gym. Feeling he had to do something for me in return, he volunteered to paint the joint. When it came time to paint the front of the building he asked me what to put on it. And I told him to paint it "5th Street Gym," and that's how the name came into being.

The two flights of stairs leading up to the gym were well worn, so I had them linoleumed. The gym had windows from the left completely across the front that I had painted and left open because, with no air-conditioning, it was hot as hell during the day due to the Miami Beach sun beating down on the building's tin roof. On the right side was a middle room, just an attachment with more plasterboard separating it from the main room, complete with red carpeting for "special" fighters. And, in the back of the gym, just past two speed bags and a wall of posters of Chris's fights and some Schenley whiskey signs covering the holes in the wall, was a door leading to the lockers and two showers, of sorts. That and a landfill of a desk and a locked phone on the left side of the gym for Chris and one pay phone—soon to be disconnected after suffering a severe case of acute indigestion due to an abnormal intake of slugs—were the bare bones of the 5th Street Gym. Chris was very proud of me for the money I *didn't* spend making the gym a reality.

Soon the gym was filled with fighters, many of whom were part of Chris's ongoing import business as he brought fighter after fighter over from Cuba—fighters like Florentino Fernandez, Luis Rodriguez, Doug Vaillant, Ultiminio "Sugar" Ramos, and José Legra among dozens more. There were so many imports that Chris told me to learn Spanish, the only Cuban fighter who spoke English being Rodriguez—and that halting at best. So I came up with a language that could, at best, be called "gym Spanglish," a mélange that was one part Italian, one part Spanish, and one part hand signals. (Lou Duva would say that I "spoke five or six languages—Argentinean, Puerto Rican, Dominican, Mexican, and Cuban." And then he'd add, "But I get upset when he gets me thrown out of the corner for cursing in Italian.") Over and above Chris's imports I also added some of my own, like Ralph Dupas, Willie Pastrano, and Harold Gomes. And later, Lee Canalito.

But no gym was complete without its regulars, those Damon Runyonesque characters who give a gym its flavor. And almost before the last nail was in place, the 5th Street Gym was overrun by many of those who had once formed the nucleus of Stillman's and had moved down to the Beach. Maury Waxman came down to Florida, and I put him to work. I wouldn't let Moe Fleischer retire, same thing. Lou Gross came down to Florida, and I put him to work training fighters. Johnny Burns, former referee, ditto. Same for Duke Stefano, Petey Scalzo, etc. It soon became a gathering of the fight clan, almost a "Hail, hail, the gang's all here" as the 5th Street Gym became Stillman's South.

Like Stillman's, we even had our own gatekeeper, Emmett Sullivan, better known as plain ol' "Sully." Sully was a work of art, an early Picasso. He sat at a table atop the stairs and, through clenched cigar—despite his own sign reading, "No Smoking, This Means You"—mumbled something that sounded like "fifsen." No one was ever quite sure, but they paid their fifty cents, later raised to a buck. No exceptions. That is, unless he recognized you as one of the fight mob. Then he let you just breeze past. One writer, flashing his press card, tried to walk past Sully once, but our Sully was equal to the task and tackled the trespasser, making him pay the entry fee.

It didn't take long before the 5th Street Gym began to take on a used look. The showers began to develop clogs, the mirrors cracks, the paint chips, and the plasterboard holes. And the floor, rickety to begin with, became a trampoline as fighters had to look for good spots to skip ropes and do their shadowboxing lest they fall through the holes. And what the fighters didn't break the termites ate. These termites were extra-strength big brutes who, in gloves, would have been odds-on favorites to beat every fighter in the joint. Those suckers chewed up everything, including Chris's desk and the supports for the ring. To them, it was a never-ending picnic. One time I had to stop a fight fan coming up the stairs, telling him, "You can't come in now, the termites are working. You'd be disturbing them." It was *that* bad.

Every now and then I'd go out and buy some plywood strips, which for some reason termites don't like. And then I'd lay them down on the floor to cover the holes. But that was somewhat like an aging woman of the streets trying to tart herself up. It didn't make any difference; the 5th Street Gym still looked used and down-at-the-heels.

However, we weren't alone in our "appreciation" of the 5th Street Gym. As good neighbors, we thoughtfully shared our fortune with those downstairs. Gottlieb's Bar & Liquor Store, conveniently located directly under the gym, was flooded every time the showers overflowed or a hole developed in the floor. And those in the drugstore downstairs could only watch in amazement as the ceiling swayed every time a fighter upstairs jumped rope or did his exercises, fully expecting it would all come tumbling down—ceiling, fighter, and all.

But even as the waterlogged floor around the showers began to resemble black tar, the termites continued their nonstop handiwork, and the plasterboard walls grew holes made by boxers punching them, I still considered the 5th Street Gym my little slice of heaven, made all the more so by the most wonderful guys in the world: my fighters.

Those early years in Miami Beach were the most wonderful years of my life. I married the girl of my dreams, sweet Helen, got an efficiency apartment in South Beach for seventy-five dollars a month—so small that you needed to open the door just to stretch your arms—legally changed my name to "Dundee," and finally got a driver's license and a car. (Here I was, the same schnook who had given a speech at my high school graduation on "How to buy a car," and I had never owned one till then. And wouldn't you know it, the car was a stick shift and I didn't know how to drive it. So Helen did.) Helen and I would walk over to Lincoln Road for a movie or go fishing from the MacArthur Bridge—I had the fishing pole, and Helen had the drop line. It was wonderful.

At this point in time I was taking opponents over to Cuba on a weekly basis, shuttling back and forth by plane. And the promoters, like Cuco Conde and Oscar Canil, whom I had gotten to know well, wanted me to move there to train their fighters. Even though I considered it, there were a couple of compelling reasons for me not to. First of all, I had more than enough to do in Miami Beach, what with my bride, Helen, and the 5th Street Gym taking all of my time. And second, as the decade wore on, the shadow of Castro loomed over the island and all of professional sports. Knowing that their time in Cuba was coming to an end, the Cuban boxing crowd would give me their jewelry and money to bring back to the States every trip home. One time I was body searched—no, make that cavity searched—but fortunately that was the one time I didn't have anything on me, not even my shorts. Nevertheless, that experience alone gave me more than enough reason not to move again but to stay at home, home now being Miami Beach.

I still had a lot to learn about being a trainer. For even though I had learned at the knees of such greats as Chickie Ferrara, Ray Arcel, Whitey Bimstein, Charlie Goldman, and others, what I didn't know about training could fill a book—a large-sized book at that. I needed hands-on experience. And I was getting that every day at the 5th Street Gym.

The lot of a trainer is not an easy one, the very word *trainer* a catchall covering a complex job. You've got to combine certain qualities belonging to a doctor, an engineer, a psychologist, and sometimes an actor, in addition to knowing your specific art well. The job also comes with a lot of headaches, which aren't included in the job specs. In short, there are more sides to being a trainer than those found on a Rubik's Cube.

Take judging prospects, for instance. Bill McCarney, a fight manager back in the early days of the past century and known to be a great judge of talent, was in a bar one afternoon when he felt a thwack on his back. Whirling around, McCarney saw a somewhat seedy, blue-bearded youngster standing in front of him whom he described as "the toughest egg I ever laid eyes on." The tough-looking egg asked, "Are you McCarney, the fight manager?" "Yes," answered the startled McCarney, still rocking from the get-acquainted tap that had been laid on him. "Well, I'm a fighter, a heavyweight, and I can lick any of these guys around this part of the country," the tough egg said. Then he added, "I'm looking for a manager." "You don't look like no heavyweight to me," came back McCarney. Then he asked, "What's your name anyway?" "Jack Dempsey," answered the back-thwacker. The very idea that someone would call himself Jack Dempsey after the former great middleweight champ so upset McCarney that he told the applicant, "Nothin' doing." And with that he turned his back, both on the fighter and on the millions he would have made handling the future heavyweight champ.

Then there are those prospects you think have everything, but you don't find out till the heat of battle that they are something less than you expected. Whitey Bimstein used to tell the story of a fighter who could hit but when he had his man on the brink of a knockout always seemed to lose him. One night against a very tough opponent, as Whitey told the story, "The guy's eye came up like a grape." After that his warrior refrained from hitting the eye, and the opponent came back, making up lost ground. Before the last round Whitey begged his fighter, "I ain't cruel, but just a touch on the eye would do it." And his fighter said, "I'm sorry, Whitey, but I can't . . . I'm allergic to blood." As Whitey said, "That was one helluva time to find that out."

As I've always said, you learn by watching. And I did, learning some of the tricks of the trade used by the masters. For instance, I was watching Ray Arcel one night when his fighter hit his opponent with a shot to the chops and the opponent went down with a thud.

The referee started the count, tolling off the numbers at a snail's pace. As the count finally reached a torturous and prolonged "five," Arcel showed up at the top of the steps, robe in hand, and put it on his kid, inspiring the ref to quickly pick up the count and count the opponent out. I used the same trick with my fighter, Bill Bossio, who was fighting Pat Marcune at the Garden. Same thing. Bill hit Marcune with an uppercut, and Marcune went down. The referee's counting, turns around, sees me with the robe in hand, and gives Marcune a quick count. You learn from watching other people.

Still, I didn't actually put my training abilities to work until I went to Miami Beach. Then, I put it all together, borrowing old tricks and coming up with new ones. Like when the referee or doctor comes in the ring to examine my guy I "stretch my ass," making it almost impossible for anyone to see the fighter over my shoulder. Or when, in a fight between Florentino Fernandez and one of the Moyer brothers, the doctor came in to examine Florentino between rounds and I said, "You'd better go over and look at the other guy. . . . I think he's got a broken nose." And wouldn't you know it, the doctor did, stopping the fight and awarding Florentino a technical knockout.

There are times, however, when a trainer's mental and verbal sleights of hand fail to work. For instance, when Pinklon Thomas was fighting Mike Tyson I was in Pinklon's corner, and between rounds the Nevada State Athletic Commission's doctor, Flip Homansky, came into the corner. I pushed him away, saying something to the effect of "Get the hell out of here . . . what are you doin' up here?" Homansky, not used to trainers questioning his authority, said, "You can't talk to me that way. . . ." And with that, I fairly shoved him out of the corner and down the stairs; Homansky fled so quickly he almost fell down the steps. After the fight, which Pinklon lost, no amount of help in the corner able to save him, a commission official came up to me and said I couldn't talk to their doctor that way and fined me one thousand dollars. I yelled at him, "He didn't know what the hell he was doin'." With that, he said, "That'll cost you fifteen hundred dollars." Again, I shouted, "That man is a menace to boxing and doesn't know anything." "That'll cost you two thousand dollars," said the humorless official. At two thousand dollars I finally gave in and said, "All right, I'll shut up," my opinion duly noted. And duly penalized.

Another of a trainer's unlisted undertakings is to ride herd on his fighters, making sure they are not only in the best condition for the fight but also in *any* condition for the fight. As with Willie Pastrano and others, that takes the form of watching over them like a shepherd over his flock to make sure they don't stray just before a fight. One of my Miami Beach fighters was Doug Vaillant who, in his own words, claimed a liking for "booze, women, and drugs." Great! So, before a fight out on the Coast I sent Luis Sarria, an assistant trainer who had come over with the flood of Cubans, to watch over him and see to it that Vaillant didn't fall prey to any of his stated pleasures. Unfortunately, when I arrived a couple of days before the fight, I found both of them drunk. When I asked Sarria what happened, he just said, "He got drunk, I got drunk." Two days of sobering up Vaillant and he went on to win the fight, but it was a fight before the fight.

Fortunately, I didn't have too many problems like those. My problems were usually in training, teaching my fighters the ABCs of boxing balance as demonstrable as old-fashioned math; also, I had to teach them defense, counterpunching, and all the other fundamentals. My hope was to get to the point where I could, as Charlie Goldman best said it, "Learn them to do all things right without thinking . . . all they have to think about is what they want to do."

But my real hands-on experience didn't come with those at the 5th Street Gym. Instead, it came with my first champion, Carmen Basilio.

Basilio was a true warrior, one who wore all his marks like a Heidelberg dueling academy graduate with more stitches than could be found on a baseball. He might have looked like a prime prospect for selling pencils on a street corner, but Carmen was everything you wanted a fighter to be. And more.

The first time I saw Carmen was in an eight-rounder in New York when he fought Mike Koballa in 1950. I was working Koballa's corner that night, and he outboxed Carmen to win the decision. In the dressing room afterward, one New York writer, Lester Bromberg, suggested to Carmen that he "should retire." Carmen merely looked at him and, in typical Carmen fashion, sniffed back, "Forget it. . . . I'll be champ." (Years later Howard Cosell confronted that same Carmen before his Chicago fight with Sugar Ray Robinson and told Carmen, "Nine out of ten sportswriters say you'll lose." Carmen merely said, "Well, nine out of ten sportswriters are wrong," and walked away, leaving Cosell to fuffump his way through the rest of his telecast.)

The next time I saw Carmen was two years later when he came down to Miami Beach to face a tough middleweight named Baby Williams. Carmen had come with his two comanagers and no trainer. ("The local promoter was too cheap to give me enough airplane tickets," groused Carmen—the local promoter being Chris, who as usual was trying to squeeze buffaloes off nickels.) So Carmen asked me to work the corner. I figured I'd be the bucket guy and watch the action and learn. Little did I know I was to be *the* guy.

So now I had to get Carmen ready and prepare him. Usually Carmen was his own guy and, not trusting anyone else to attend to him, brought all his own stuff with him in a bag—medications, liniments, wraps, and whatnots, down to the Q-tips. But this time, extending his hands in my direction, he said, "Wrap 'em." And so I wrapped 'em, the first time I had since that night in White Plains when Chickie Ferrara had thrown tape in my direction and told me to wrap some kid's hands. But this was a main-eventer, and, believe me, I was extra careful, barely laying the stuff on Carmen's hands. And when I was finished Carmen, who liked his wraps loose as a goose, felt them, banged them together, and said two of the nicest words I had ever heard other than "check enclosed": "Nice job."

You see, fighters all have their own feelings on how they want their hands wrapped. Some like it tight and strong; some like a grip underneath. There's a variety of ways to wrap hands. And because the hands are a fighter's most precious, and yet fragile, asset, the art of hand wrapping is all important. Muhammad Ali, for example, had trouble with his hands—protruding knuckles and calcium deposits. I'd try to ease the point of the knuckle and do it on each side and cut a hole in the bandage so that all his strength wouldn't be on the point of the knuckle. And sometimes I'd use Kotex and cut a hole in it. I used everything. By the end of his career, I would use sponges with the permission of the other manager. I'd say, "What are you worried about? He won't punch as hard." All just to protect his hands.

That is the real reason you carefully wrap hands, to protect them. It's not, as old stories go, to load them up. I don't how many times I've heard stories about Jack Dempsey's hands being "loaded" in his fight against Jess Willard. All I can say to that is baloney. Ray Arcel, who knew Jimmy DeForest, Dempsey's trainer, told me that DeForest had told him that it was Doc Kearns who circulated the story after Dempsey's career because he was involved in lawsuits with Dempsey and that there was nothing to Kearns's tale of having put plaster of paris on Dempsey's bandages and then sprinkling water on his gloves. DeForest, who had wrapped Dempsey's hands himself, said that, yes, he had sprinkled water on Dempsey's bandages but only after Dempsey complained about the stifling, one hundred-and-ten-degree heat in Toledo that afternoon. Nothing more.

So what happened with Carmen? After the fight, a tough ten-round win over Williams, Carmen said, "Angie, that was the first time in two years I didn't wrap my own hands." "Why?" I asked. "So I wouldn't break 'em," he answered. I was glad he told me after the fight and not before, if you know what I mean.

But Carmen, whose craggy eyebrows were so susceptible to cuts that in later years I would always kid him that he bled at press conferences, on this night got busted up but good by Williams. And I also had to be a "cut-man," what A. J. Liebling called "a short-order plastic surgeon." You've got to be a cool cat when you're working with cuts. You can't get excited. I had learned how to treat cuts by watching Whitey Bimstein, Freddie Brown, Charlie Goldman, and especially Chickie Ferrara, who was always very patient with me, teaching me everything, including how to tie shoes. Each had his own techniques, his own ways of treating cuts. Charlie had all these little bottles in his pocket, everything you ever needed to stop a cut—even magic elixirs, like aromatic spirits of ammonia flavored with spearmint. Freddie used Monsel solution to coagulate the blood. And old-time trainer Doc Bagley used to chew tobacco during a fight, believing that, as he told his protégé Ray Arcel, spit was good for treating cuts. So, on Doc's recommendation, Ray tried chewing tobacco and told me that after three rounds he was under the ring, sick to his stomach.

When I was on my own, back in New York, I had this kid, Johnny Williams. One night Johnny got this big hematoma on his eye, and I was afraid it might bust open. So I asked Teddy Crystal, who was working the corner with me, "Teddy, what would you do if the eye busts open?" And he said, "I'd use pressure and Vaseline." And from that day forward, I learned how to take care of cuts on my own.

Like the time, the next year, when Carmen faced Pierre Langlois. During the fight Carmen's eye was badly lacerated, with the skin of the eyelid split. I used a styptic ointment that became known as "the Dundee ointment," and then I applied thymol iodine and alum and, pressing a solution of chloride 1:1000 into the wound, carefully pushed the loose skin upward until it was immersed into the ointment, stopping the blood. Then I secured it with Vaseline. Carmen made it through the fight without further damage and won the decision.

From then on, I knew I could handle any cuts—especially those sustained by Carmen, who would never have a fight stopped because of them.

Carmen would go on to win the welterweight crown from Tony DeMarco in as two-sided a bout as I've ever seen. And in the picture of the man holding Carmen aloft? Why it's Angelo Dundee with his first champion.

By 1960, to quote a popular song of the day, everything was coming up roses for little Angelo Dundee. I now had a family, my fighters were regulars on TV and rising in the ratings, and I had some new kids to train, many of whom looked as though they had the potential to become champions. I didn't think it could get any better.

But it would. For 1960 was the year that the same youngster who had first knocked on my hotel door in Louisville would once again knock on my door. And this time it opened the door of opportunity for both of us.

FOUR

The "Greatest" Hook-Up of My Life

My fighters were now known worldwide. At least that part of the world in and around Miami Beach. But as their reputations continued to grow, other parts of the boxing world began to know them, too. One such place was Louisville where promoter Bill King booked them for fights—Willie Pastrano, three times; Luis Rodriguez, twice; Ralph Dupas, once; and Joey Maxim, once. And every time I went to Louisville I would run into that same handsome youngster I had first met in the hotel room with Pastrano—the youngster who had introduced himself as Cassius Marcellus Clay.

He was always there with a big, infectious smile, and an even bigger voice, calling out, "Angelo Dundee, Mr. Cutman." For every one of my fights in Louisville, I got passes for him and his family. But young Clay, barely eighteen at the time, was not content to be part of the boxing crowd. No, he desperately wanted to be part of the boxing scene.

Before one of Rodriguez's fights, he befriended Clay. Even though Rodriguez spoke little English, that didn't stop the talkative Clay from yapping with him about boxing. As he came into the arena toting his bag before one of his fights, Luis ran into Cassius standing in the entrance hall. Cassius reached down for the bag saying, "I'll carry that bag for you, Mr. Cuban Champion." To which Luis responded, "That's nice, Mr. Amateur Champion." The next thing I knew the youngster was walking in with Luis, carrying his bag.

The kid always wanted to work with my guys. He was always at the gym waiting for me, sometimes for two hours, hitting the heavy bag, the light bag, working out—just waiting for me. "C'mon," he'd say, "let me work with your guy," meaning Willie Pastrano, whom he now called "Sweet Willie." I'd wave Cassius off, saying something like, "What's the matter with you? I don't like my guys working with amateurs." I've always had this thing that amateurs and professionals don't mix any more than oil and water; that amateurs are for amateurs and professionals are for professionals. But he would persist, continually badgering me. Finally, I gave in and let him spar two rounds with Willie. After just one round I called time, and told Willie, "Oh, man, you're stale . . . no more sparring for you." But Willie, correctly sizing up the sparring session, said, "Jesus, I got the hell kicked out of me." The kid was that fast.

The next time I saw those fast hands was three months later, at the 1960 Rome Olympics when Clay beat the bejabbers out of a Polish fighter with 231 amateur fights and thirteen letters in his name. I was glad Cassius had gone to the Olympics. Before the Pastrano–Alonzo Johnson fight, Cassius had come to me and asked whether he should turn pro or go to the Olympics. I told him, "Don't turn pro now. Go win the gold medal . . . you'll make more money." And then, as an afterthought, added, "Then you can come and see me."

The newspapers were filled with his exploits over in Rome: challenging track star Wilma Rudolph to a race; calling out to Floyd Patterson after winning the gold, "Floyd Patterson, some day I'm going to whup you . . . I am the greatest . . ."; and being interviewed by a Russian reporter who asked him, "How does it feel to win something for a country where you can't eat at the same table with a white man?" Clay answered, "Tell your readers we got qualified people working on that problem. America is the greatest country in the world and as far as places I can't eat goes, I got lots of places I can eat, more places I can than I can't." He was a one-man public relations machine.

Returning to Louisville, still wearing his gold medal around his neck, Cassius was hailed as the conquering hero, toasted and paraded throughout the city. Soon he was being besieged with offers to turn pro. Cus D'Amato, using José Torres as an intermediary, approached him. So, too, did Sugar Ray Robinson, former Olympic heavyweight gold medalist Pete Rademacher, and Archie Moore, who handed Cassius his card that said: "If you want a good, experienced manager, call me, collect."

The first time I saw Cassius after the Olympics was when, as usual, I had a fighter fighting in Louisville. This time, without the big hello, he came over and, with a puzzled look on his face, asked, "How come you never approached me to handle me?" I could only answer, "It's this simple . . . you know my business is boxing. That's all I do. I have a gym in Miami Beach, and if you ever want to become a fighter, come down and see me and I'll work with you." More than somewhat taken back, all he could say was, "You've got to be some sort of nut. Everybody approaches me, offers me all kinds of money and cars. And you, all you can offer me is to come down to Miami Beach?"

"Certainly," I said. "What I'm offering you is what talent I have. I'm sure I can do a good job with you." With that Cassius said, "You've got to be some sort of nut," and turned on his heel and walked away.

Through boxing's most reliable source, the grapevine, I heard that the youngster had signed with a group called the Louisville Sponsoring Group, thus becoming the first athlete-corporation in sports. The group, comprised of eleven men, mostly millionaires associated with, or related to, the Brown families of Brown & Williamson Tobacco and Brown-Forman Distilleries, had given Clay a $10,000 signing bonus, a guarantee of $4,000 for the first two years—or $200 a month—and $6,000 as a draw against future earnings for the following four years.

The kid seemed well set. But then again, nothing in boxing is ever written in stone, as I was to find out one afternoon a couple of months later.

There I was, sitting at my desk in my brother Chris's office the day of a fight (Chris had moved his operations over to Convention Hall when Jackie Gleason took over the Auditorium) trying to make disorder out of chaos when the phone rang for the umpteenth time that afternoon. With Chris down on the Convention Hall arena floor, undoubtedly giving the TV folks assurances he couldn't possibly keep and yours truly the only one in the office giving his best impression of a one-armed paperhanger, I reached over and picked up the phone. "Hello, this is Angelo Dundee," I mechanically answered. An unfamiliar voice came back, "Hi, Angelo . . . this is Bill Faversham. I'm calling from Louisville." The voice went on without a break, "We met in the gym here. . . . Cassius Clay introduced us." Great, another introduction I didn't remember! Lying through my teeth, I said, "Oh, sure, what can I do for you?" fully expecting to have another deadbeat put the arm on me for tickets. The voice, now identified, launched into an explanation of the Louisville Group, how he was acting as its head, and, further, that the Archie Moore–Cassius Clay relationship hadn't taken. "I wanted Clay to learn some tricks from the 'old professor,'" Faversham said. "But it hasn't worked out."

Faversham told me that an old friend of mine, Lester Malitz, who had once produced the Wednesday night fights for New York advertising exec Archie Foster, one of the eleven-man Louisville syndicate, had dropped my name to Foster as a potential trainer. Foster, in turn, had referred Malitz's suggestion to Faversham. Hence the call.

Faversham said he had brought my name up as a possible trainer and the syndicate and Clay both liked the idea. Now he wanted to know if I was interested. "Well, Bill," I said, grateful for the consideration but mindful that I was already up to my nasal passages in commitments, "thanks for thinking of me. But Dick Sadler is a friend of mine, and he's running Moore's training camp, and I don't want to step on his toes. From what I hear, Cassius is in training for his first pro fight. I don't like to come in half-cocked, so let things stay as they are until after that fight. Then we can talk."

During the next few weeks Faversham and I had several telephone conversations. Then he came down to Miami Beach to interview me, asking me questions like what I thought I would do with Clay under my guidance. I told him I'd start him out with six-round fights until he learned and that Miami would be an excellent spot for Clay since we had six two-minute rounds here—something Chris had created for Willie Pastrano and Ralph Dupas. Moreover, I told him the changeover from amateur to professional, while hard, wouldn't be difficult for Clay because of the shorter rounds and the work in the gym with seasoned fighters, some of whom he already knew.

Apparently Faversham liked what he heard because he got back to me with an offer—either so much a week for every week of training and for the week of the fight or a piece of the action. My brother Chris was a charter member of the take-the-money-and-run school. He advised me that "a bird in the hand is worth two in the bush," or something like that, and that I should take the immediate money rather than the prospective money. Now I was taught to respect my elders, and since Chris was my elder, I listened to him. *Marone!* Did I ever miss out on big-time "scratch" by listening to Chris's advice!

Knowing that Cassius had been training under the tutelage of Dick Sadler, in tandem with Archie Moore, I put in a call to Dick to find out what had happened to end what Faversham called their "relationship." "What was the problem?" I asked, already suspecting it had been a case of two star qualities, each set in their own ways, clashing. Stating the obvious, Dick said, "He's some character. . . . He came with Archie and me to Texas. We traveled by train, and at every hick stop, deep in the heart of Texas, he would stick his head out the window and shout, 'I'm the greatest.' I thought we were gonna get lynched." Then Dick, calling the training camp "a salt mine," tried to explain what really happened to cause the breakup. "Cassius would come to Archie every day pleading for a fight," he said, "but Moore would always tell him, 'You're not ready yet.' Then one day Archie gave Cassius a broom and told him to sweep the floor. Clay didn't like that. He said to Archie, 'I don't do that for my Ma, and I ain't gonna do it for you,' and handed the broom back to Archie. And that did it!"

I told Dick that Faversham, head of the Louisville Group, had hired me to train Clay. "If you train that kid," he said, "you deserve a purple heart with seven clusters." A purple heart with seven clusters? Helen loved that.

But I chose not to take over until after Clay's first pro fight. It has always been my policy not to disrupt an ongoing relationship between a fighter and a trainer. And since the Louisville Sponsoring Group already had a temporary trainer, Fred Stoner of Louisville, in place for this bout, I decided not to attend so that it wouldn't look like I was interfering, which would have been unfair to Stoner.

Nevertheless, I heard all about that first fight, a six-rounder in front of Clay's hometown fans against someone named Tunney Hunsaker. Billed as "The Olympic Champion Turning Pro in His First Pro Fight," Clay, wearing his Olympic trunks with U.S.A. on the side, won a decision over Hunsaker. According to my sources, Clay had shown great natural talent, apparently the same talent he had exhibited in his sparring session with Pastrano, and could—and they repeated, *could*—be "the goods." I would see.

In early December 1960 I got another call from Faversham. This time he said, "I'm going to send you the kid." But with Christmas just around the corner, I said, "Not yet, let him spend Christmas home with the family." A few minutes later the phone rang. Again it was Faversham. "Angelo," he said, "the kid wants to fight. He wants to go now. He wants a fight before Christmas."

To the impatient-to-get-on-with-his-career Clay, "now" meant immediately, this instant, and wouldn't you know it, the very next day he arrived by train. At the time no hotel on the beach would accept blacks; even the drugstore below the 5th Street Gym wouldn't allow blacks at their counter. So after I picked him up I took him over to the Charles Hotel in Overtown, Miami's Harlem, where I had rented him a room. Next door was The Famous Chef, a restaurant where I had made arrangements for him to sign for food. The restaurant would send me the tabs, I would pay them, and the Louisville Group would send me the money to cover them. Not wanting him to be alone, I soon found him a roomie, Allan Harmon, who had just come over from Kingston, Jamaica. But because of the size of the room, the two had to sleep together in one bed. After about a month of sharing room and bed, Clay approached me and complained, "You don't like me much, do you? You put me in a stinkin' room with a guy who stinks!" Apparently, Harmon had an island aroma, something Clay had never experienced before, and it bothered him. "Okay," I said, "I'll make different arrangements." It would be the first—and only—time during our long relationship that I ever heard Clay complain.

Each and every morning, after doing his roadwork chasing his shadow, Cassius would run all the way from his hotel in Miami across the MacArthur Causeway to the 5th Street Gym—that's double roadwork, if you're counting. One morning I got a call from the Miami Beach police saying they had a tall, skinny kid (he was only about 183 pounds then) who was running across the causeway and who said he was my fighter. At the time, the City of Miami Beach had a law that "people of color" were not allowed in Miami Beach from sunset to sunrise. The police wanted to know if I would vouch for him. Would I? I said it was just Cassius doing his roadwork.

(Lou Duva had a similar experience with one of his fighters, John John Molina, in Virginia Beach. Seems that Lou had measured the distance from their training headquarters at the Holiday Inn to the first traffic light and told John John to "run to the first red light and back." Well, some two hours later the Virginia Beach police called and told Lou they had someone in custody who claimed to be his fighter and that he was at a different Holiday Inn six or seven miles away looking for him. That someone was John John who later told Lou that he had kept running because "all the lights were green.")

To many fighters, roadwork is like going to the dentist, something they dread. Floyd Patterson called it "nothing but counting beer cans along the side of the road." Some fighters, like Mike DeJohn, merely went out, splashed water on their faces, and came back, claiming they had done their roadwork. Others didn't want to do it at all. Ray Arcel was one trainer who always did roadwork with his fighters—something I must say I never did. He once had a fighter named Joe Baksi who was in London in 1947 to face the British heavyweight king, Bruce Woodcock. Baksi was reluctant to do any roadwork at all, so Arcel would rouse him out of the sack every morning, come sunshine or rain, which was normally the case in "unmerry olde" England at that time of the year. Anyway, according to Arcel, "This one day was the worst of all. It was drizzling and cold. I woke Joe up and he looked at me with hate in his eyes. I knew I had trouble ahead."

Baksi decided to put it to his trainer. Determined to make sure this would be the last time Arcel ever ran with him, he ran with the trainer for the first four or four miles, then, with a half mile left in the five-mile run, he stopped and began jumping up and down and shadowboxing. "Then," said Ray, "he looked at me to see if I was dying." But Arcel was wise to Baksi's ploy and said, "Come on, let's finish this last half mile with a sprint." After that Ray had no more trouble with Baksi or his roadwork. Needless to say, Baksi "ran over" Woodcock.

(In a case of turnaround is fair play, I remember the time I had Carmen Basilio out in Chicago for the second Robinson fight, and Carmen was out doing his roadwork on a cold March morning. Me, I don't do roadwork; I just wait for my fighter to come back. Anyway, there I was standing in front of the hotel, waiting for Carmen to return from his five-mile run, when a patrol car pulls up and the cop in it threatens to run me in for loitering. As I turned to go back into the hotel, who do I see in the back of the car but Carmen, laughing his ass off.)

But Cassius not only loved doing his roadwork, he knew it was the source of his stamina. So he would run until he was tired, sometimes running backward, and then he'd run some more—across causeways, up and down streets, and even over golf courses, cutting his legs on unseen sprinkler heads dotting the fairways; I'd have to treat his bloodied legs all the time. He used to worry the heck out of me. But bloody legs or not, he would run. Then, after finishing his roadwork, he would bound up the stairs of the gym two steps at a time and mischievously holler, "Angelo, line up all your bums for me . . . I'm gonna knock 'em all out!"

Clay was always his own man. A typical dialogue between the two of us would go something like this: Clay: "I'm gonna run five miles." And I'd say, "That's good for your legs." And then, testing me, he'd contradict himself, saying, "No, I'm gonna rest." And I'd say, "Good, you need your rest." No sense in interfering with a boxer who has his own mind. As long as he did his training, who was I to meddle?

They tell of other fighters, like old-time great Young Corbett, whose downfall could be traced to the fact that they were allergic to training, never wanting to put aside the good life or the good things for the rigors of training. But not Cassius. He was a workaholic. He would spend hours in the gym, always the first to arrive and the last to leave, punching the bags, sparring with anyone he could, doing his exercises in front of the gym's floor-to-ceiling mirror—preening and flicking jabs at imaginary opponents. For him, it was like going to a picnic.

Training is the most important part of boxing. It's the laboratory where a fighter's skills and styles are developed. But it's not like a music teacher merely sitting a new pupil down at the piano and instructing that pupil to plunk away at the keys to his or her heart's content. It's more, much more. It's polishing a fighter's assets and filing rough edges, teaching a fighter to develop a style to fit his natural abilities and to correct his faults in the execution. And then to repeat it over and over again, until it becomes instinctive.

Take Gene Tunney, for example. When he returned from France after World War I, Tunney's left elbow was affected by some form of paralysis. He went up to the wilds of Maine, where, day after day, he would chop wood, using only his left hand. Over time the strength returned to his left arm. He then returned to the gym and, with his right hand tied to his side, worked on the fast bag and what was then called the sandbag, only using his left, keeping at it everlastingly until full strength returned to his once-damaged limb. It was that left that tormented Jack Dempsey in Tunney's two fights with the "Manassa Mauler," a left hand that had been developed in training. Dempsey also developed the most devastating left hook in boxing history by having his right hand tied behind his back while training.

It's an old boxing adage that "styles make fights." But styles also make fighters, and perhaps the most important part of training is the development of a fighter's style, one perfected by long hours of training in the gym. Every fighter is different. It's not one-size-fits-all when it comes to styles, rather styles are cut from different cloths, each tailored to a fighter's strengths or weaknesses, less manufactured than sculpted.

All great fighters make it up as they go along, and Cassius was one of the most innovative and imaginative fighters I ever saw. He could imitate the style of any fighter, something very few fighters could do. Sometimes you'd see him imitating the slick moves of Willie Pastrano or Luis Rodriguez, two fighters he watched training at the 5th Street Gym. Other times you'd see him doing his best impression of some of Jersey Joe Walcott's "sand-dancing" moves, or the moves of other fighters whose styles he admired. But the fighter he most imitated was the fighter he most admired, the man he called "the king, the master, my idol," Sugar Ray Robinson. Often when Cassius shadowboxed or sparred, you could hear him acknowledging his debt to Robinson saying, "This is how Ray Robinson used to do it," always accompanying his execution of a Robinson-like move with verbal "bam . . . bam . . . bams." These moves, and some of the others that Clay mimicked, eventually found their way into his soon-to-be unique style.

I remember once, just before the Jerry Quarry comeback fight, Clay wanted to come into the ring as Jack Johnson. "Why Jack Johnson?" I asked. "You're in no way like Jack Johnson. Why do you compare yourself to other boxers? You're not like Sugar Ray Robinson; you're not like Joe Louis. You're new, different. You're yourself, and they can't compare to you." And I believed it!

At this point Cassius's ability and natural stuff were great. I never touched that natural stuff with him. What a fighter has naturally, you can't improve on. You let it alone. You smooth it out, but you never tamper with it. But watching him, I figured he had a couple of things he could use some help on, and I added a few wrinkles. However, training Cassius was not quite the same as training another fighter. Some guys take direction and some don't, and this kid had to be handled with kid gloves. So every now and then I'd subtly suggest some move or other to him, couching it as if it were something he was already doing. I'd say something like, "You're getting that jab down real good. You're bending your knees now and you're putting a lot of snap into it." Now, he had never thrown a jab, but it was a way of letting him think it was his idea, his innovation. Or, "My gosh, you threw a tremendous uppercut. That was beautiful!" Again, he had never thrown an uppercut. It was like going around the mulberry bush. I'd make him think he was the innovator, and after a while Cassius thought it was his own idea.

He always had to be the inventor, the star. It was sort of like the old joke about the magician who invites a volunteer up from the audience to help him perform a trick. Giving the volunteer a baseball bat, the magician instructs him to hit the magician over the head as hard as he can. The volunteer declines, afraid he'll hurt the magician, but the magician urges him on until finally the volunteer swings, smashing the magician's head. Taken off on a stretcher, the magician finally wakes up in a hospital room three weeks later, looks around, and goes, "TA-DA!" It was like that with Cassius. He would make the suggested move and later go "TA-DA!" as if he had done something magical. And every day thereafter he would repeat his newfound move or punch, proud of himself for coming up with the idea. Later he would say to a reporter, "Angelo never trained me," which was technically correct, at least from his perspective.

It did not matter that he was cut from a different cloth. Those parishioners in the 5th Street Gym pews, whose knowledge of boxing styles ended sometime after they read a 1930s edition of *How to Box*, sniffed at his style. To them, he was too *this*, too *that*. "He's off balance when he throws his punches," they sneered. Or, "He holds his hands too low." Or, "He pulls straight back to avoid punches, not side to side." Or, "He never throws punches to the body." (Clay only threw belly jabs. His philosophy was always the reverse of Sam Langford's, that if you kill the head the body will follow.) Or, "If I want dancing, I'll go to Roseland." Or any one of a hundred other things they thought were flaws in his style.

One time, when he was sparring with my boxers, I asked three journalists what they thought about my new kid. The first said that Cassius was too small to face heavyweights. The second complained that he moved around too much and threw too many jabs. And according to the third, Clay didn't have enough power to knock out the big guys.

But no one had ever seen a heavyweight like this before, one who combined grace and power never seen before in a heavyweight. And his speed more than compensated for what others saw as flaws in his style. One writer, upon seeing Cassius, said, "He's a heavyweight who moves like a bantamweight." His style was not, as the ads of the day said, "Your Father's Oldsmobile," it was all new. And this marvelously flawed boxer with the deceptive style would redefine boxing as we knew it.

Clay's second pro fight, and the first under my guidance, came on December 27, 1960, against Herb Siler on the undercard of Chris's promotion of the Willie Pastrano–Jesse Bowdry fight. Siler was KO'd by what the *Miami Herald* described as "a right to the midsection and a left hook to the jaw." Faversham was delighted with the result, and thanked me. "Don't thank me," I said. "I didn't knock out Silas, Clay did." I knew I was only as good as the guy on the stool. And, oh, Clay was pleased too, preening and hollering to the crowd, "I'm gonna be the heavyweight champion of the world." I thought this guy could strut sitting down.

Twenty days later he knocked out Tony Esperti in three. That was followed another twenty days later, in a preliminary to the NBA light-heavyweight title bout between Harold Johnson and Jesse Bowdry, with a two-minute KO of Jim Robinson. Fourteen days after that, he knocked out Donnie Fleeman in the seventh. His style hadn't changed, but I began to notice some of the little modifications he had added, such as a sharper jab. Especially against Fleeman, who had fifty-one fights and forty-five wins and extended Cassius into the seventh, the first time Clay had gone more than six rounds.

I really didn't know how much Cassius had progressed until March 13, 1961. That date doesn't appear on his record, but it does on the records of Floyd Patterson and Ingemar Johansson. For that was the date of their third title match. Before the fight Johansson's trainer, Whitey Bimstein, asked if I had a fighter who would spar with Ingemar in a public workout for the press. I suggested Cassius, who didn't have a problem sparring with Johansson. The only one who had a problem was Ingo, who never laid a glove on the kid. After two rounds of plodding after him and not landing a punch, Bimstein decided enough was enough and called a halt to the sparring session. It was to serve as an omen for the fight itself, Ingemar getting starched in six.

It was now time to step up the competition, to begin adding name fighters to Clay's résumé. For that we selected Lamar Clark, a heavyweight who had forty-six knockouts in fifty fights, forty-five of those in a row—including a *Guinness Book of Records* six in one night. And what better place to take on Clark than Clay's hometown of Louisville?

Before the fight Clay had come up with a new gimmick, predicting that he would knock out Clark in two rounds. And knock him out in two he did, fulfilling his prophecy. Afterward he told newsmen, "I just had the feeling he must fall. I said he would fall in two and he did. . . . From now on they all must fall in the round I call." The newsmen ate it up.

Suddenly Cassius Clay was more than just a boxer, he was an attraction, a celebrity. It was something he worked at becoming, just as hard as he worked at becoming a better boxer and a champion. No stunt was beyond him if it forwarded his name and his fame. I remember the time back in Miami when he went into the pool at the Mary Elizabeth Hotel to pose for Flip Schulke, a photographer who was taking pictures of him throwing punches underwater, even though Clay was afraid of water and couldn't swim. I was scared the damned fool would drown. But it didn't matter to Cassius, who knew a good PR stunt when he saw it.

Cassius was always on the alert for other ways to capture the attention of the media, and he found another shtick after meeting and then watching the wrestler Gorgeous George. Coming away from the wrestling matches, Cassius said in wonderment, "I hear this white fellow say, 'I am the World's Greatest Wrestler. I cannot be defeated. I am the Greatest! I am the King! If that sucker messes up the pretty waves in my hair, I'm gonna kill him. I am the King! If that sucker whups me, I'm gonna get the next jet to Russia. I cannot be defeated. I am the prettiest! I am the Greatest!'" And then, with a twinkling smile, Clay said, "When he was in the ring, everybody boooooooed, boooooooed. Oh, everybody just booed. And I was mad. And I looked around and saw everybody was mad. I saw fifteen thousand people coming to see this man get beat. And his talking did it. And I said, 'This is a g-o-o-o-o-o-o-d idea!'" For Cassius, it was a revelation, a "g-o-o-o-o-o-o-d idea" he would soon embrace, just as he would Gorgeous George's suggestion he wear white shoes instead of black because they made his feet look faster.

Our next fight, Clay's first ten-rounder, was in Las Vegas against a journeyman out of Hawaii named Duke Sabedong, a strong 6'6", 220-pounder with twenty-seven fights. Before the fight when asked by newsmen if he was "nervous," Cassius had answered, "I'm not afraid to fight, I'm afraid of the flight." Afraid of flying, Cassius had wanted to go by train, a three-day trip I hardly relished. (This was long before the then-Ali, on a plane to England, was told by the stewardess to strap on his seatbelt and he told her, "Superman don't need no seatbelt," to which she answered, "Superman can fly.") Without resorting to the same ruse used by Whitey Bimstein, the trainer of Terry Young, who coaxed his scared fighter aboard a plane for their fight in Honolulu by telling him that Honolulu was in New Jersey and that the flight from New York would only take fifteen minutes, I merely overruled Cassius.

Maybe the six-plus-hour flight to Las Vegas affected Clay, who connected with few, if any, clean punches in the fight. But he did come away with a unanimous, if unsatisfying, ten-round decision over Sabedong.

One other thing I remembered about that trip was meeting Joe Louis, then a greeter at Caesars Palace. I reminisced about our first meeting, back in England during the war, and, as a fan, told him how much he had influenced me and my decision to go into boxing. Or something like that; I don't remember the whole conversation. Anyway, a pit boss saw us talking and soon approached me to countersign some of Joe's gambling markers, figuring I was a longtime friend and would stand for him. However, my luck hadn't been much better and, figuring a cosigner was nothing more than a schmuck with a pen, I told him I already had enough of my own markers, but thanks anyway.

I guess that was in keeping with my reputation as a "soft touch." For years I had been in what might be called the money-lending business, giving handouts to any and all who approached me, especially my fighters. The difference between my way of operating and the way other money-lenders operated was that I didn't charge interest. Moreover, I rarely saw my money again. Fighters would go to Chris and try to hit him up for money, sort of an advance on their purses, but Chris would always tell them: "No way! Go and see Angelo, he's the softest touch in boxing." Hell, one of my old fighters used to come to see me and ask me for $20 every time. One time I asked him why he didn't just ask for $100 and he said, "Then I wouldn't see you as much." It's nice to know I was so popular!

The next fight for Clay was back in Louisville, against his first ranked opponent, Alonzo Johnson—the same Alonzo Johnson who fought Willie Pastrano twice. And though the fight went the full ten rounds, this time Clay boxed smartly and won nine out of the ten rounds, connecting time and again with clean punches.

We had two more fights in Louisville against a couple of "worthies" before we could move on to bigger things. The first was against Alex Miteff, a well-worn heavyweight with a name. "He'll go in six," Clay predicted and then delivered on his prediction by banging away at Miteff until the ref, who had had enough even though Miteff hadn't, stopped it in the promised round. Afterward, in his best impression of Gorgeous George, Cassius greeted the assembled press with: "I am the King! I am the Greatest! Nobody can stop me. They'll all fall!"

Next up on his dance card was Willie Besmanoff. And although he was strong, I didn't figure him to be able to get close enough or have the timing to catch Clay. Cassius thought even less of him, saying, "I'm embarrassed to get in the ring with this unrated duck. I'm ready for top contenders." Then gave his prediction: "He must fall in seven." Besmanoff was so irate at Clay's prefight feather-rufflings that he tried to make a fight of it, lunging at the moving Clay. But every time he did, Clay would move out of range and come back to counter him. By Round Five it had become target practice for Clay as he belabored the confused and defenseless Besmanoff. But Clay was more focused on his prediction than on his opponent and merely used his left jab for the next two rounds while I hollered from the corner, "Stop playing around . . . stop playing around . . . finish off the sucker." Finally, in the predicted round, Clay got down to business and hit Besmanoff with several strong jabs and straight right hands, the last putting Besmanoff down and out, delivering on his promise.

Like the steps on the old vaudeville circuit—which were the small time, the medium small time, the big small time, the little big time, the medium big time, and THE BIG TIME—boxing, too, has its stepping-stones. And as Cassius began to look like a champ, at least when he wasn't playing, I felt he was ready for THE BIG TIME, which meant New York.

When we got to the Big Apple, I felt like Dolly from the Louis Armstrong song, "Hello, Dolly!"—I was back where I belonged. Wandering around my old haunts brought back many memories of my start in boxing, although to tell the sad truth, many of the old places were either shuttered or converted into parking lots. But still one magnificent vestige of what once had been remained, right where I'd left it at Fiftieth Street and Eighth Avenue: Madison Square Garden.

The Garden, as it was called by those in the fight mob, was at once a plot of land and a mecca, the place all fighters aspired to. I remember Jackie Cranford saying that he knew he had "made it" when he first saw his name on the marquee overhanging Eighth Avenue.

For Cassius it was a homecoming of sorts, too. Right after winning his Olympic gold, he had paraded around Times Square, Olympic jacket on and gold medal hanging around his neck, to see if anyone recognized the homecoming hero. Few did then, but many did now that he was making his Garden debut.

We were offered the shot through one of those all-too-frequent occur-rences in the world of boxing: a fight between two heavyweight contenders had fallen out the week before their scheduled match and the slot was open. Hustling to fill the open date, Garden matchmaker Teddy Brenner had called and offered us the fight, a match against a hard-hitting fighter out of Detroit named Sonny Banks who had eleven KOs in his fourteen fights. I thought it was right for Cassius. Not only was Cassius unbeaten, untied, and unscored upon in his previous ten fights, but Banks, I thought, was perfect for him—my philosophy in making fights for my fighters always being that I believed on my fighter's "worst" night he could beat the other sucker on his "best" one. And I didn't see Cassius having his "worst" nor Banks his "best" at the Garden that night.

As usual Cassius stood on street corners the week before the fight, almost taking up permanent residence at Forty-ninth and Broadway, wait-ing to see how many people recognized him. One group who did was the sportswriters, who flocked around him to hear the bottomless well of quotes from the fighter they labeled "The Louisville Lip" and "The Mouth That Roared." And Cassius didn't disappoint them, once again chanting, "The man must fall in the round I call." Then, without taking a breath, he added the tag line: "Banks must fall in four."

The only things I told Cassius before the fight were that Banks was a converted southpaw with a helluva left hook and that if Banks went to the ropes not to follow him but to keep him in the center of the ring, figur-ing his bad balance would put him at a disadvantage coping with Cassius's speed.

From the opening bell the scenario played out exactly as it had in my mind, with Banks winging his left hook and Cassius dancing out of reach, smiling and jabbing. However, I noticed something; Cassius was standing too square, giving Banks too much of a target. Then, wouldn't you know it, midway through the round Banks connected with a long left that came out of nowhere, catching Cassius flush on the jaw. Cassius went down, eyes closed. But, when his butt hit the floor, they opened and lit up. Up at the count of two, he took the mandatory eight count, and then went on the defensive, looking more startled than hurt at being floored. Between rounds I told him no more fancy stuff, and, most important, stop standing square against this guy. Looking into his eyes I knew what a great fighter I had, his recuperative powers equal to any I had ever seen in the ring.

By the second he was clear-headed and fighting his own fight. And by the predicted round, the fourth, he had Banks in trouble and down. Once again, his prophecy rang true. And afterward, he shouted to one and all at ringside, "I told you . . . the man fell in four."

Next up on Cassius's hit parade, just two and a half weeks after the Banks fight, was Don Wagner. Clay, again dealing in fistic fortune-telling, predicted, "Wagner must fall in four . . . he should not go longer than Banks." And true to his prediction, Clay felled Wagner in four after playing with him for the last two rounds just so he could take him out in the prescribed number—a pattern he would repeat time and again, allowing his opponent to stay around just so he could fulfill his prophecy.

George Logan, Billy Daniels, and Alejandro Lavorante would also fall in the predicted round, and, by July 1962, Cassius's record was 15–0, with twelve KOs. But we had nobody scheduled after Lavorante. That is, until I spotted Archie Moore in the L.A. Auditorium after the Lavorante fight. I told Cassius to challenge him on the spot, call him out right then and there. Grabbing the microphone from the TV announcer who was trying to conduct his postfight interview, Cassius went around the ring shouting, "Archie Moore . . . I know you're out there." Then, seeing Moore in the audience, he pointed his glove at him and called him out, hollering, "I want you next, old man," and for the first time rhymed his challenge, "Moore will fall in four."

Granted, it wasn't much of a rhyme, hardly Keats or Shelley or even Ogden Nash for that matter, but, hey, it was a start! According to at least one writer, it may have also been the beginning of rap, saying of Clay's rhymes, "Before there was rap . . . there was Ali Rap." Now, as that early day rapper, Clay would go on to concoct those cockamamie rhymes of his, rhymes I helped him with whenever he asked—although my help usually came in the form of lines like, "Have no fear, Angie's here." I still made my contribution, no matter how small. By now the two of us were so much on the same wavelength that we could finish each other's sentences and rhymes, filling in each other's blanks. You might say we were joined at the hip *and* the lip. (There were times, however, when I couldn't help him. Like the time he wanted to know in which direction east was so he could pray before a fight. He asked the wrong guy. I get lost in the little boy's room.)

The Moore fight was made almost before the ranting stopped. Originally scheduled for October 23, 1962, it was pushed back when ticket sales were below expectations. The promoter hoped another three weeks of Cassius promoting the fight would increase sales. "You mean another three weeks of listening to him shoot his mouth off?" Moore groused. "That's good because I'm going to develop the 'lip-buttoner' punch, especially designed for that fresh boy," Moore said, adding to the push-me-pull-you insult preliminary to the main event.

Never one to let a verbal challenge go unanswered, Cassius came back with his own verbal taunt, this one expressed in a poem: "Archie has been living off the fat of the land / I'm here to give his pension plan. / When you come to the fight don't block aisle or door, / 'Cause ya'll going home after Round Four."

As an afterthought, he added, without thought of rhyme or reason: "If I tag him earlier, I'll just have to hold him until the fourth round."

The fight itself was far more one-sided than the verbal jousting, with Cassius moving in and out and throwing fast combinations while Archie continued to move forward at a snail's pace befitting his age. Ol' Archie—there's no other way to express it—was at least forty-five years old; some wiseacres suggested he was fifty-two-going-on-Social-Security with 232 professional fights and twenty-eight years in the ring. He looked every day of it too, his hair gray and his elastic pair of trunks (which looked like they were orthopedic trunks made by Omar the Tentmaker) coming up to his nipples to hide his paunch. It was no fight as Cassius landed almost everything he threw in his pursuer's direction while Archie, for his part, landed but one meaningful punch, a sneaky right that caught Cassius near the end of the first round. By the fourth, with Moore tiring, Cassius began landing his combinations, flooring the "Old Professor" for an eight count. As he arose, obviously the worse for wear, Clay belabored him with another series of combinations and the referee stepped in to save the now-helpless Moore, who had come to the end of the line and his career.

It was yet another win for Cassius. Another promise kept.

FIVE

Young Cassius Punches His Ticket to the Top

B oasting has been part of boxing's historic past since the 1890s when John L. Sullivan would boast, "I can lick any sonuvabitch in the house" and then would lay out anyone foolish enough to take him up on it.

Predictions were something else altogether, usually delivered in a far less boisterous manner, almost with a self-assured, leave-it-to-me confidence. Perhaps the most famous prefight prediction in boxing history was Joe Louis's before his second fight with Billy Conn when, without a boast or a brag, he said, "He can run, but he can't hide" and then proceeded to carry out his prediction by finding the unhidden Conn in the eighth round of their 1940 fight. Louis also predicted his one-round destruction of Max Schmeling in 1938 when writer Jimmy Cannon asked him, "How many rounds do you think it'll go, Joe?" and Louis merely held up his thumb to signify one round, which is all the fight went, two minutes and four seconds of it.

But perhaps the original copyright holder for predicting a fight's result was Sam Langford, who called his rounds. And his shots. Called "The Boston Tar Baby," Langford fought during the first two decades of the twentieth century and often was able to correctly predict how a fight would end.

One time while standing in his corner awaiting the opening bell, Langford looked over at his opponent's corner and noticed one of his adversary's seconds slicing up oranges. "What you doin' with all them oranges?" Langford shouted over to the second. "I'm slicing 'em up for my man to suck on between rounds," came the second's answer. "Man, you ain't gonna need them oranges," promised Sam, and he promptly went out and dispatched his opponent before he had even come close to having his between-rounds pick-me-up.

But Cassius Clay would become the first boxer ever to combine boasting with predictions—and deliver them in rhyme form. He was, as he said unhumbly, "Double 'The Greatest' . . . I not only knock them out, I call the round."

With his knockout win over Archie Moore, Clay thrust himself onto the short list of heavyweight title contenders for the crown won just two months earlier by Sonny Liston. The public was more than somewhat underwhelmed by the prospect of a Liston–Floyd Patterson rematch, what with Liston having taken out Patterson in just two minutes and six seconds of the first round. The only fighter in the title mix who could generate interest in a championship fight was none other than Cassius Clay.

Clay had looked so good in dispatching Moore that Bill Faversham and yours truly believed he was ready for a shot at the title. And so the campaign for his shot at Liston began. Clay began appearing on national TV, talking the talk, and suddenly the press took note and began beating the drums for a Liston-Clay fight, many of them hoping against hope that Liston would button "The Louisville Lip."

Because Liston had signed for a return bout with Patterson in the summer of 1963, we were forced to stay busy to maintain our place in the title picture. Our first post-Moore opponent was Charlie Powell, an ex-NFL lineman, who went, as advertised, in three. Next up was Doug Jones, a light heavyweight now campaigning as a heavy and Number Two in the heavyweight rankings, a "useful" résumé-builder to keep our place in the upper tier of heavyweights.

We arrived in New York for the Jones fight in March 1963 only to find the city in the midst of a 114-day newspaper strike. With the seven city papers quieted, the Garden publicity office was at a loss as to how to publicize the fight. Not so Clay, who made it his personal crusade to go on every TV show, talk on every street corner, and shout to every passing person, "This is unfair to the many boxing fans in New York. Now they won't be able to read about the great Cassius Clay." On and on and on it went, until Cassius, as both a promoter and a self-promoter, had created the Garden's first sellout in thirteen years. Even the pigeons had to move from the rafters to make room for the overflow crowd.

Every time Cassius saw a TV camera or a radio microphone, he would go into his usual pugilistic poetry, saying over and over again:

> Jones likes to mix,
> So I'll let it go six.
> If he talks jive,
> I'll cut it to five.
> And if he talks some more,
> I'll cut it to four.

As Clay circled the ring before the fight, he danced near Jones, close enough to ask, "How tall are you?" Jones responded, "Why do you want to know?" "So I'll know how far to step back when I knock you out in the fourth," said Clay, dancing back to his corner with a smile on his face to await the introductions.

Before the first round was over, Jones had wiped that smile off Clay's face, landing a right cross to Clay's jaw. All of a sudden his legs wobbled and the crowd came alive, cheering Jones's efforts. After a couple of rounds of Jones landing and Cassius more concerned with making him miss than landing his own punches, I decided something was wrong. Here I must tell you that guys were always giving me hell about Clay not keeping his hands up. So I told him to "keep his hands up" before the fight. Well, while he was keeping his "hands up" out there, he was also getting the hell kicked out of him. I had fooled around with his style and was wrong to do so. He came back to me after the third round and I told him the opposite, "Keep your hands *down*." And it worked. (Similarly, Emile Griffith, who trained Bonecrusher Smith, had told him before his fight with Frank Bruno to "be patient and wait until he punches." But after nine rounds of watching a too-patient Bonecrusher, Griffith threw up his hands and said, "Do whatever you have to do." And Bonecrusher reverted to his normal style of boxing for the tenth and final round. Doing it his way, he knocked Bruno out.)

Then, in the fourth, the round predicted by Clay, he began to find his range. But when the bell rang to end the promised round, the 18,732 fans let out a mighty roar. Make that a chorus of boos to express their disappointment that the fighter who had made good on his promises twelve times before had now failed to keep one.

Usually Clay would turn to me in the corner between rounds and ask if he was winning. After the eighth, I had to tell him "it's close" and that he had to "step it up" and close the show to win. And wouldn't you know it, he did, winning a close decision by just one round on two of the judges' scorecards.

For the first time in his career, Clay had to stand in the middle of the ring listening to the boos and dodging the assorted flybys—cups, cigars, programs, and other missiles hurled into the ring.

On the way back to the dressing room I whispered to him, "Well, you told them first that 'Jones likes to mix and you'll let it go six.' Then you said you'd 'cut it to four' . . . so by my count, four and six makes ten, see?" His eyes lit up as the idea registered. And that became Clay's cop-out when the press descended on him to find out, in newspaperese, "Wha' happened?"

Back in 1960 when Cassius first came on the boxing scene, the sport was, at best, on the threshold of being called off on account of lack of interest. There were no Jack Dempseys or Joe Louises or Rocky Marcianos, no charismatic figures to interest press and fans alike. The fighters who ruled the eight traditional weight classes were more a "Who's He?" than a "Who's Who" of boxing—with the notable exceptions of two all-time greats, Sugar Ray Robinson and Archie Moore, both of whom were getting long in the tooth and looking forward to retirement. The others were hardly household names, even in their own households. And the name of heavyweight champion Floyd Patterson inspired even less interest, if that were possible.

And so it was that Cassius stepped into a vacuum, one he filled very nicely, thank you. Not content to stand in the shadows like so many others, including Floyd Patterson and Joe Louis, he knew how to capture the spotlight. And single-handedly he brought the sport back to life with his predictions, poetry, and boasting. To the media he was a godsend. All they had to do was ask, "How ya doin', Cassius?" and he'd take over from there. To the public, this brash youngster was newsworthy, someone who was fresh, new, and filled with the liveliness of a new age. Put them all together and all of a sudden it was the Age of Cassius.

In 1963, it was especially apparent, even with Sonny Liston as the heavyweight champ—an unpopular and surly one at that. Every time the phone rang, the voice at the other end wanted to know more about Cassius. You'd think, what with all the other fighters I handled—like Luis Rodriguez and Sugar Ramos, both now champions, or Willie Pastrano or Ralph Dupas—they'd want to talk about them. But no, all they wanted to talk about was Cassius Clay and his most recent antics.

It was always thus, Cassius *this* and Cassius *that*. And Cassius, who never met a camera or notepad he didn't like, furthered his image with every quote. He was always performing with a presence like a Barrymore or an Elvis, front and center and upstaging everyone around him. One time, before the Jones fight when Cassius had gone to Harlem "to see my people," a boxing fan came over to me and gushed, "You're Angelo Dundee, the trainer, aren't you?" Cassius, overhearing this, couldn't believe someone else was getting attention in his company and demanded to know, "Did you put him up to saying that?"

Everyone now thought Clay was ready for Liston. Despite the closeness of his win over Jones, he had shown an ability to go to the body, something he had never shown before. However, Liston was unavailable, having signed to fight Patterson in a rematch in what the public saw as little more than a watering of last year's crops.

To keep Clay busy and in the public eye, the Louisville Group began fielding offers. There were many, Clay having established his *bona fides*, both as a fighter and as a self-promoter by packing the house at the Garden for the Jones fight despite the newspaper strike. Now everybody wanted in on the gravy train and hoped to book the greatest promoter in boxing, Cassius Clay. The Garden wanted Clay back to fight former heavyweight champion Ingemar Johansson. There were offers for a rematch with Jones. And I received an offer from an old friend of mine, Jack Solomons, the British promoter, for a "go" with British and Empire champion Henry Cooper, which I passed on to Bill Faversham.

Cooper would be the perfect opponent for Clay, or at least so I thought. He had a record of 27–8–1 with eighteen knockouts and reputedly, as one of my British contacts told me, "the best left hook in the business" (called "'Enry's 'Ammer"). But he also had tissue-thin skin as brittle as a fifty-year-old coat of paint that gushed like a geyser under the impact of a punch. Moreover, while Liston was there—and would stay there, as it was almost unthinkable that he would lose to Patterson in their rematch—I thought another bout or two and a little more time was needed for Cassius to reach his physical maturity. Remember, he was only twenty-one years old and still growing, both in size and talent.

And, a trip to London, my old hunting grounds from my time in the service, would be a treat. I had been there a couple of times with Willie Pastrano, and the Brits had loved him, a pure boxer who practiced what the Brits called the "Sweet Science" to perfection. Why not Clay? I asked myself.

Boy, was I wrong! What I hadn't figured on was that the Brits didn't particularly care for boastful athletes. They wanted their heroes humble with stiff upper lips and all that, you know. And Clay was anything but that. In love with his own voice, he told one and all that Cooper, their beloved "Our 'Enry," was almost irrelevant to his potential fight with Liston and that "I'm only here to mark time before I annihilate that big ugly bear."

Everywhere Clay went he created waves. But unfortunately, even as he stirred the promotional pot, making promoter Jack Solomons happy, he was also stirring up the British fans, making them unhappy. Cassius had not only insulted their favorite fighter by calling him "a tramp, a bum, and a cripple, not worth training for," but he had also shown his disrespect for England's most sacred icon, their royalty, by calling Buckingham Palace "a swell pad."

Public opinion turned against him. The press called him "The Clown Prince of Boxing," "ostentatious," and "boisterous" as headlines blared "We Are Not Amused." British TV did impersonations of him, and the British fight fans, oh, they wanted to kill him. They treated him as a royal pain in the butt, booing him at every turn and sighting. It was Gorgeous George done to a "fare-thee-well," as they say over there. Cooper himself best summed up the general feeling for Clay when he said, "Surely by now, Clay knows that everybody in Britain, including me, hates his guts."

Clay continued to add fuel to the fire, telling newsmen he hadn't bothered to train for "this bum." But when newsmen, knowing my reputation for candor, came over to see me I had to tell them the truth—that Cassius had done miles of roadwork in Hyde Park in preparation for the bout and had sparred more than ninety rounds with Jimmy Ellis and his brother Rudy. Reporter Peter Wilson asked me if I thought Clay would ever become champion. Kibitzing, I told him that he'd better, otherwise he would have driven me crazy for nothing.

But Cassius paid no attention to the adverse criticism. He continued being, well, Cassius Clay. The tomfoolery continued, with everyone in the Clay camp joining in. I remember going to the cinema a couple of nights before the fight to see *The Naked Prey* with Cornel Wilde. The story was about a white hunter who was captured by a tribe of African warriors. They kill all the others on the safari but let him live. They free him in the jungle, naked, and then send their best warriors to hunt him down. Well, he knocks off all the warriors. As the action continued with him doing away with the warriors, one by one, I named each of the warriors one of Clay's sparring partners and began hollering, "Oh! Oh! . . . there goes Willie Johnson. . . . Oh Oh! . . . there goes Alonzo Johnson." Cassius loved it. He was always the kid laughing in the back row at commencement. To him, everything was fun.

Always looking for fun, Cassius decided to take a page out of the Gorgeous George handbook and, in his best imitation of the Gorgeous One, told the press, "If Cooper whups me, I'll get down on my hands and knees, crawl across the ring, and kiss his feet. And then I'll take the next jet out of that country, whichever country it happens to be." Now he had another Gorgeous George inspiration. He would play dress-up and have a specially made robe, complete with ermine trim and "Cassius the Greatest" embroidered on the back. He would wear it, along with a crown, into the ring as befitting "The Greatest, The King." It was, he said, a wonderful idea, something only Gorgeous George would do.

But if Cassius thought the idea of wearing a royal-esque robe was wonderful, the British fans thought it was anything but. Now this man they considered overbearing and a "cheeky wanker" (their words, not mine) to begin with was swaggering around the ring in a robe and a crown mocking their queen. They let out a chorus of boos that would have made Gorgeous George proud as Cassius strutted around the ring bathing in the sound just as he remembered Gorgeous George doing. It was pure theater, and for Cassius it was another chance to stand center ring and be the center of attention.

The crowd noise got even louder in Round One as Cooper, normally a slow starter, charged out of his corner and began winging punches. Their hero's every move, every punch, whether it missed or landed, was met with a roar. By round's end Clay returned to his corner with a bloodied nose and Cooper returned to his to be met by a standing ovation. Cassius got his jab going in the second and opened a small cut over Cooper's left eye. By the third, the cut had widened as Cassius began landing his combinations, and by the fourth it had become a full-fledged gash, with blood flowing down Cooper's face. It was obvious Cassius could have stopped Cooper any time he wanted. But there was a problem: he had predicted he would "take him in five," and five it would be, even if it meant playing around with him for another round. It didn't matter that I was hollering from the corner, "Take the sucker out. . . ."

Cassius was alternately taunting Cooper and toying with him, and I figured it was only a matter of time until referee Tommy Little mercifully put an end to this bloodbath.

What I hadn't figured on, however, was what happened next. With but a few seconds left in the fourth, Cooper, frustrated in his attempt to land his left and furious at Cassius for toying with him and humiliating him in front of his countrymen, backed Cassius into the ropes. There he led with a soft left jab, and Cassius instinctively moved away from the right cross that was sure to follow. Instead, Cooper uncorked "'Enry's 'Ammer," his big left, catching Cassius flush on the jaw with a punch Cassius later said "made me feel as if I had gone back and visited all my ancestors in Africa."

Cassius fell heavily on the seat of his trunks, his arm entangled in the second rope, his eyes glazed. Referee Little started tolling the count over him, "One . . . two . . . three . . . four . . . ." As the count reached four the bell rang ending the round. Somehow Cassius managed to get to his feet and began staggering around the ring. I rushed into the ring at the bell, grabbed his arm, and led him back to the corner.

As to what happened next—well, it's sort of like that old tale of the three blind men who tried to describe the anatomy of an elephant. I've heard what happened described several times, no two times alike and none accurate. But, hey, I was there, so let me tell you what *really* happened.

As Freddie Brown used to say, "You see what you see." Before the fight, as I was loosening up and stretching out Clay's arms to get the blood flowing through his tightened muscles, I had seen a small split along the seam of one of Cassius's gloves, the leather sticking up. Now who knows when some little thing like that will come in handy? So between Rounds One and Two I told Cassius to keep his glove down so that the ref wouldn't notice. Come the rest period between the fourth and fifth rounds, as Cassius slumped on his stool like a sack of potatoes, looking as if he was out of it, I decided it was time to use that small split to our advantage. Call it gamesmanship, if you will, but whatever you call it, call it timely and time-consuming, for now I stuck my finger in the split, helping it along until it was a bigger split. I then yelled at the ref, the secretary of the British Boxing Board of Control, the president of the group, anybody I could find to yell at, to come over and examine the glove. I wanted a new pair. Meanwhile, as I was trying to buy time, Chickie Ferrara, who was working the corner with me, was dropping ice cubes down Cassius's trunks, breaking vials of smelling salts under his nose, massaging his legs, doing everything he could to bring the dazed Cassius back to life.

The authorities quickly told me that there was no second pair of gloves to be found anywhere—an oversight that would soon be remedied by a new rule at all boxing bouts, something I like to call "Angie's Second Pair of Gloves Rule." Write-ups later had the officials running back to the dressing room to get another pair, an event that most said took anywhere between half a minute to six minutes. The time, in actuality, was but a few seconds. But even those few seconds were vital, as, given the benefit of time, Chickie's handiwork had brought Cassius back to life while I fiddled with the glove and stalled. And when the referee came over to me and said, "Mr. Dundee, there are no other gloves," I told him, "Don't worry, we'll use these." Never took them off. But the ruse worked.

You try to help your fighter any way you can—even by unconventional means, if necessary. There was the time I was in Puerto Rico working the corner of Wilfredo Gomez in his bid to win the junior lightweight championship from Rocky Lockridge. By the tenth round Gomez was completely gassed, his condition described as "deplorable" by my old friend Mario Rivera. It was so bad that I even thought about stopping the fight. But the stamina-challenged Gomez pleaded with me to let him continue, and with Lockridge now dancing around the ring, I thought maybe, just maybe, we had a chance. Especially if I could somehow buy him more time to gain his second—or third or fourth—wind. There had to be something I could do in this crisis. So, to gain time, I untied his shoelaces between rounds, every round, and each time I would call it to the ref's attention and he would give me a couple of extra seconds each time to retie the laces I had untied only a few seconds before. Naturally, being fumble-fingered, I took as much time as possible to retie them, even double-knotting them, to give Wilfredo a couple of seconds of extra rest every time. And wouldn't you know it, double-knotted or not, those shoelaces would come undone at the end of every round. And, out of necessity, I would have to retie them again. With those few seconds of precious rest between rounds, Gomez was able to suck it up and pull out a close fifteen-round decision—without a tie.

The echo of the bell signaling the start of the fifth had barely died down before a rejuvenated Cassius was out in the center of the ring jabbing the bloodied Cooper, determined to end it then and there rather than tempt the fates again by playing around. Besides, this was the predicted round. Cooper's cut, which had spouted blood for the last two rounds, were now a ghastly red smear over his entire face. And the fans, who had implored referee Little to stop the fight earlier, were now on their feet shouting "Stop it! Stop it!" They further emphasized their shouts by throwing missiles into the ring. Finally, a minute or so into the fifth, Little did the only thing he could: he stopped the bloodbath. Cooper didn't complain, only turning to Little and saying, "We didn't do too bad for a 'bum and cripple,' did we?"

Almost immediately after the bout was stopped, Cassius's brother Rudy jumped into the ring carrying Cassius's crown, wanting to put it on his head. Looking at some of the trash already in the ring and dodging more flying by, I pushed him away, hollering, "Get out of here. You're going to get me killed."

In the dressing room Cassius would take back his "bum" reference to Cooper, saying, "Cooper is a real fighter. He hit me harder than I've ever been hit." Then, seeing Jack Nilon, Sonny Liston's advisor, in the dressing room crowd, he launched into his favorite topic. "I'll demolish Sonny in eight rounds . . . and he'll be in a worse fix if I predict six." Then he added, "I'll fight Liston—if the price is right." Nilon answered back, "You can have the fight, kid, the price will be right!"

Challenges go back as far as the sport of boxing itself. In the very old bareknuckle days it was not uncommon for the claimant of the championship to stand in the middle of the ring and demand of those in attendance, "Who fights?" Hence the name "challengers" for those who took him up on his dare.

After defeating Jake Kilrain in the last major bareknuckle fight in boxing history, John L. Sullivan would hurl his challenge by making the haughty pronouncement: "I hereby challenge any and all bluffers to fight me for a purse of $25,000 and a bet of $10,000. The winner of the fight to take the entire purse. I am ready to put up the first $10,000 now. First come, first served." Unfortunately for Sullivan, his challenge was accepted by one of the three "bluffers" he specifically mentioned, James J. Corbett, who took his title in twenty-one rounds back in 1892.

Sometime during the next twenty years the equation changed with the challengers issuing the challenge, as Jack Johnson did when he invited heavyweight champion Tommy Burns to step into the ring with him. For two years Johnson dogged Burns, backing up his challenge by taking on every potential contender between himself and Burns, mowing his way toward the champion. He made offer after offer, including every type of inducement, but Burns continued to cup a deaf ear. Finally, after following Burns around the world, Johnson tracked him down in Australia and, after making every conceivable concession, got him into the ring where he soundly trounced him and won the heavyweight crown. (Ironically, Sam Langford would follow the same game plan and tour map to track down and challenge Johnson. But all Langford got for his efforts was a turndown with Johnson telling him, "Sam, nobody wants to see two black men fight for the heavyweight championship.")

Through the years others have issued challenges to champions to put their titles on the line, offering money, inducements, and just plain old blandishments. Among those have been light-heavyweight champion Archie Moore, who challenged heavyweight champion Rocky Marciano through the press, authoring a piece for *The Ring* magazine in which he called on Marciano to meet him as the "only legitimate challenger."

Another who invoked the power of the press was 1960s middleweight Joey Archer. Archer, an excellent boxer who held wins over the likes of Denny Moyer, Holley Mims, Sugar Ray Robinson, and even Dick Tiger, now wanted a return bout with Tiger, who was then the middleweight champ. But Tiger showed less than no interest in facing Archer, preferring instead to fight welterweight champ Emile Griffith in defense of his championship. Feeling left out in the cold, Archer turned to one of Madison Avenue's most creative admen, George Lois, who wrote a small space ad for Archer that read: "Dear Dick Tiger: The Middleweight Champion should meet the best middleweight (not a welterweight). I'm a middleweight, and

I licked every man I ever fought, including you. Respectfully, Joey Archer. P.S. How about a fight, Dick? I'm going broke on these ads." The ads created what in adspeak could be called a "furor," and Archer began turning up on talk shows and even on the front page of the *New York Daily News*, challenging a snarling tiger at the Bronx Zoo. As things turned out, Archer did get his bid for the middleweight title, but against Griffith, not Tiger, inasmuch as Griffith had beaten Tiger for the title. Archer would lose to Griffith in his title shot, not exactly the happy ending he had hoped for.

Cassius Clay didn't have to bother buying ads or writing articles in magazines to land his title shot with Liston. Instead he issued his challenge verbally, taunting the champion into the fight.

He began his campaign by pushing his way through the mob scene in the ring at Comiskey Park in Chicago after the first Liston-Patterson fight and into Liston's corner where he loudly delivered his first challenge. The shocked Liston could only say in return, "You're crazy, man."

The campaign continued in Las Vegas, where Cassius approached Liston in a casino. Warned that Clay was heading his way, Liston pulled out a gun and shot it in Clay's direction. Clay quickly scooted under a nearby craps table, visibly shaken. Only later did Willie Reddish, Liston's trainer, let on that the gun was a cap pistol loaded with blanks. But the first round had gone to Liston.

Later, Clay would come back, this time to find Liston at a craps table where he was losing heavily. According to eyewitnesses, Clay shouted, "Look at that big, ugly bear. He can't even shoot craps." Liston merely glared at him, picked up the dice, and rolled again. Another losing roll. Again Clay hollered at Liston, but in a voice loud enough for half the casino, if not half of Las Vegas, to hear him, "Look at the big ugly, bear . . . he can't do nothin' right." This time an enraged Liston dropped the dice and walked over to Clay. Standing face-to-face and eyeball-to-eyeball, he menacingly said, "Listen, you nigger faggot, if you don't get out of here in ten seconds, I'm gonna pull that big tongue of yours out of your mouth and stick it up your ass." With that Clay turned and lickety-split it out the casino door, having gotten the Bear's goat if not the Bear himself.

This went on and on and on. Another time Clay taunted Liston with a blackjack table between them, "You're so ugly that I don't know how you can get any uglier." And Liston, who viewed Clay more as a small annoyance than a big threat, growled back, "Why don't you come over here and sit on my knee and I'll feed you your orange juice." To which Clay, a lit-

tle hurt by being one-upped, shot back, "Don't insult me or you'll be sorry
. . . 'cause you're just one ugly, slow bear."

The campaign to get Liston into the ring took a lot of doing and didn't
happen overnight. People don't understand that we worked on it for almost
two years. We did anything and everything we could think of. It was a
combined operation of planning and scheming, and all of us took part in
the number we did on Liston. How many gimmicks could we use? There
was the honey we got for the Bear. The chains with leather thongs to hold
the guy down—you know, "Come here, Bear . . . come here." We even
went "Bear hunting," in bear-hunting costumes, with bib overalls and big
boots to stalk the Bear. Believe you me, it was all done in fun, but we were
out to get the Bear, to land him for a shot at his title.

Then there was the bus trip. Cassius had just purchased a brand-new bus,
"Big Red," and had it adorned with signs that looked like they came right
off the set of *The Harder They Fall*—signs reading "The World's Most Col-
orful Fighter" and "Liston Must Go in 8." The original plan had been for
Cassius and his entourage to go from Los Angeles to New York. But someone—I don't remember who—decided they should go "Bear huntin' " and
make a stopover in Denver to visit Sonny in his new house. So Denver it
was. With Cassius at the wheel driving like a Formula One hopeful, the bus
pulled up to Sonny's house at 3:00 A.M., lights flashing and everyone hollering, "Oink, Oink" and "Where's the Bear?" It wasn't long before they
found out as Liston emerged, accompanied by his dogs, screaming, "What
do you want, you crazy bastard?" As Cassius flickered the lights on Sonny,
spotlighting him in his pajamas holding a poker in his hand making ready
to smash the bus's windows, the police arrived and warned Cassius and crew
that they'd better leave or face a charge of disturbing the peace. For Cassius,
it was a promotional triumph. After all, as he said, "You know how them
white people felt about that black man who had just moved in. We didn't
help it much."

A few months later Cassius was in the ring for the prefight introductions
before the second Liston-Patterson fight. Turning to Patterson, he bowed
with a flourish; turning to face Liston, he dropped his jaw, threw up his
hands in a make-believe surrender sign, and beat a hasty retreat from the
ring. Everyone laughed. Everyone, that is, except Liston.

After the fight—which took just four seconds longer than the first go-
round for Liston to mop up the floor with Patterson—TV commentator
Howard Cosell, mike in hand, tried to conduct a postfight interview with

Liston. It was really a three-way interview, with Clay, just behind them, constantly interrupting. Cosell asked Liston, "Sonny, a workmanlike performance . . . who's next? Are you going to fight the noisome one, Cassius Clay?" In a supercharged voice Cassius shouted, "The fight was a disgrace!" Liston tried to answer Cosell, saying, "Well, I'm gonna take them as they list them . . . and if they list Clay, it'll be Clay." And again, Cassius could be heard hollering, "Liston's a tramp . . . I'm the champ." Losing control of the situation, Cosell quickly cut short the interview, saying, "All right, Sonny Boy. Go back to the dressing room, we'll see you there. That's the story from the ring." But it wasn't the end of the story as the voice belonging to Cassius still could be heard in the background shouting, "Don't make me wait, I'll whup him in eight."

Liston, who had heard all the shouting, now went over to Cassius, and in a less menacing voice than normal said, "Clay, don't get hurt now, little boy, we're gonna make a lot of money." Then he added, "I'm gonna beat you like I'm your daddy," before turning away and heading for the dressing room.

Cassius's campaign had apparently worked. At least he had lured Liston into accepting him as his next opponent. Now all that stood in the way of a Liston-Clay fight was the "lot of money" Liston had mentioned.

Knowing there were megabucks to be made, Cassius now began staking his claim. "I've talked up the greatest fight in history," said the greatest self-promoter in boxing history. "Man, I don't need Liston . . . he needs ME!" And he was right. Cassius was the one with the drawing power, the one the fans wanted to see. And the one making the fight.

Liston acknowledged the potential of a fight against Clay only by saying, "If they ever make this fight, I'll be locked up for murder." Finally, after listening to those around him telling him this would be an "easy fight" and that he would make "lots of money," he relented.

The fight was on, Cassius's challenge had produced the desired results.

SIX

Baiting and Beating "The Bear"

Few observers gave Cassius Clay a snowball's chance in hell against the supposedly invincible Sonny Liston. Others gave him even less.

The heavyweight division had never before seen another quite like this chocolate-covered version of the man Jack found at the top of the beanstalk. A physically intimidating giant compressed into a 6′1″ frame, Sonny Liston was too strong, too tough, too everything. His fists were 15 inches in circumference, larger than Primo Camera's or Jess Willard's. He had an 84-inch reach, 16 inches longer than Rocky Marciano's. He strengthened the muscles in his 17½-inch neck by standing on his head a couple of hours a day. His left jab, a battering ram, could make a guy's teeth go soft. His left hook was a lethal weapon, comparable to Jack Dempsey's. He could go to the body with all the ferocity of some of the great body punchers of the past, such as Tony Zale and Billy Petrolle. His uppercut was as powerful as any seen in the history of the division. It was almost as if some geneticist had bred him for the sole purpose of beating up others.

I saw Liston destroy Cleveland Williams. *Destroy him.* He hit Williams with a shot and flattened him in two rounds. And when he flattened, he covered the whole ring. It was awesome.

But for all his raw power, Liston's biggest asset was more psychological than physical. He made a science out of inspiring fear in the hearts and minds of his opponents. I know a lot of guys who completely collapsed when they saw the guy. In the ring he'd wear a big hood on his head and stuff towels under his robe to appear even bigger than he was. And in training he would awe the press by knocking the heavy bag off the hook and having trainer Willie Reddish throw medicine balls into his middle to the tune of "Night Train." (Although I don't know what that mattered, my guy Cassius never threw to the body anyway.) In short, he was the meanest "Mutha" on the boxing block and wanted everyone to know it.

The Liston who signed to fight Clay admitted to being thirty-three years of age, but his public record said thirty-six, and his friends placed it closer to forty. (When one writer doubted his age, Liston roared at the cowering questioner: "My mammy says I'm thirty-three . . . are you calling my mammy a fuckin' liar?" Interview over.) The only way to tell his real age, I figured, was to pull the bark back and count the rings. Dating back to his close twelve-round decision over Eddie Machen in September 1960, Liston had engaged in just four fights lasting a total of six rounds. The fine edge he had honed in his climb to the top of the heavyweight mountain had been dulled. And despite the one-sided nature of both his one-round KOs of Patterson and his twenty-one knockouts in thirty-two wins, he had been ten rounds only three times and twelve rounds once. Even at his peak, when he was fighting regularly, he had never demonstrated great stamina.

After signing for the fight, Cassius and I watched several films of Liston's previous fights. Certain people beat certain people. Certain styles trump others. I knew Cassius would kick the hell out of Liston. So together we identified several flaws in his style, the most notable of which was that boxers adept at slipping punches and using the whole ring frustrated him. Eddie Machen, a quick scientific boxer, had gone twelve full rounds against him and come within a couple of points of beating him. And the one loss on his record had been inflicted by a little-known journeyman named Marty Marshall, a defensive-minded fighter who employed lateral movement. Not only had Marshall beaten Liston, but he had lasted ten full rounds in their return bout. I thought that Cassius was the master of lateral movement, and if he could keep away until Liston depleted what had to be a limited supply of energy, we could beat him.

In order to do this I came up with a strategy only a Cassius Clay with his exceptional speed and extraordinary reflexes could carry out, something I called "surround the jab." By this I meant Cassius should continually go to his left, away from Liston's wall-breaking jab, making him reach, frustrating him, and, as a consequence, tiring him. You know, a frustrated fighter loses the snap out of his punches.

Everything Liston did came off that jab. It was a timing thing. If he hit you with that sucker, everything went in sequence. Boom! He'd nail you with it, and if you were in front of it, you'd be destroyed. So take it away from him, "surround" it, circle to your left, away from it. He can't hurt what he can't reach.

I didn't have to tell Cassius much. I just kept reminding him, "You're quicker, you're smarter, you're not gonna take his shots. Don't trade with him, don't try to fight him in close . . . outside, in, and out . . . nail him!"

This went on for months and months before the fight. We were prepared for Liston.

You would have thought by now, with the fight signed, sealed, and about to be delivered, that the taunting was through. I mean, here we were in the final stages of training and Cassius had taunted Liston into the fight, why continue the campaign? But no, there were still more taunts up Cassius's ample sleeve.

When Liston arrived at the Miami airport, Cassius, having found out when the plane would arrive, met Liston and chased him around with a cane shouting, "Come here, Bear, I'll get ya. Bear, come here." Everybody in the group was running around like thieves and chasing everybody they could find. I didn't because my legs would get tired.

Then we had a couple of to-dos at the 5th Street Gym, where Sonny was training. Cassius would taunt him, hollering, "Hey, Sonny, how ya doin', Baby?" and the enraged Sonny would try to get at him. Cassius would tell me, "Angie, hold me back." And there I'd be, holding him back with my frightened pinkie. It was all a put-on and good theater.

Cassius also taunted Liston in words, telling reporters, "I'm not afraid of Liston. He's an old man. I'll give him talking lessons and boxing lessons. What he needs most is falling down lessons." Then he would stroke his face, telling one and all, "I'm pretty. Look, not a mark on my face." To which Liston could only glower and say, "He won't be when I get finished with him."

But perhaps Clay's best—and I say "best" because I helped him just a little with the rhyme—jab at Sonny came in a prediction delivered in one of his patented poems:

Clay comes out to meet Liston, and Liston starts to retreat.
If Liston goes back any further, he'll end up in a ringside seat.
Clay swings with a left, Clay swings with a right,
Look at young Cassius carry the fight.

Liston keeps backing, but there's not enough room.
It's a matter of time, and there! Clay lowers the boom.
Now Clay swings with a right, what a beautiful swing.
And the punch rises the Bear clear out of the ring.

Liston is still rising, and the ref wears a frown
for he can't start counting till Sonny comes down.
Now Liston disappears from view, the crowd's getting frantic,
but our radar station's picked him up over the Atlantic.

Who would have thought when they came to the fight
that they'd witness the launching of a human satellite?
The crowd didn't realize when they put down their money,
that they'd see a total eclipse of the Sonny.

As the fight date neared, Cassius continued his psychological campaign needling Liston every chance he got. But, as Jimmy Durante used to say, "You ain't seen nothin' yet!" And what no one had ever seen before came at the weigh-in the day of the fight.

Most weigh-ins are humdrum affairs. The fighters get on the scales, get weighed, have their weights announced, have their pictures taken, and go back to their hotel rooms to rest. Sometimes there's even an exchange of words along the lines of "good luck." But that's it, period.

But when one of the fighters has difficulty making weight, the weigh-in becomes anything but humdrum, with fights won and lost on the scales. Titles, too. Benny Lynch, a flyweight, Charley Phil Rosenberg, a bantamweight, and Diego Corrales, a lightweight, all lost their titles when they were unable to make their division's weight limit at the weigh-in.

Some fighters, failing to make weight, merely pay a penalty. Jackie Paterson, a former flyweight champ, failed to make weight for his fight against Fernando Rosa, instead opting to hand the Italian a forfeit of fifty pounds rather than take off fifteen ounces. He then proceeded to knock Rosa out. José Luis Castillo paid a heftier penalty to Diego Corrales in their second fight because he couldn't take it off before getting it on. Then he KO'd Corrales. In both cases it paid to come in overweight.

Then there were fights that were cancelled because one of the fighters couldn't make the contracted weight, like the recent third Diego Corrales–

José Luis Castillo fight and the Eddie Mustafa Muhammad–Michael Spinks light-heavyweight title bout back in the early 1980s. (One impish writer, watching the Spinks–Mustafa Muhammad weigh-in, doubted the accuracy of the ancient Fairbanks scale used to weigh the two fighters. He went out and bought a ten-pound bag of flour that, when put on the scale, weighed two pounds more than the advertised weight—the same amount Mustafa Muhammad had scaled over the 175-pound limit!)

Lest you think coming in *under* a given weight is the only problem a fighter faces, consider the case of Buster Douglas. He proved that while no man is an island he could come close, scaling 246 pounds, some 20 pounds more for his first heavyweight title defense against Evander Holyfield than he weighed when he won the heavyweight championship in his previous bout against Mike Tyson. (Lou Duva, Holyfield's trainer, crowed, "It was all those pizzas I sent him in the steam room.") Douglas performed down to his bloated form, fighting sluggishly and getting KO'd in three.

Despite the months of long effort to make weight, trainers and even fighters will pull an end run at the weigh-in to ensure they "make" weight. There was Tony Galento, better known as "Two-Ton," who, when the official reading the weight was occupied by reaching over for his glasses, took his left hand and leaned against the metal siding, taking a good twenty pounds off his registered weight. The official, now bespectacled, looked back at the scales and could only sigh and say, "Damn, it sure looks like it ought to read 249, but it's only 220." Others have tried to tip the scale in their favor as well, including one trainer for José Luis Castillo who was caught with his foot under the scale during Castillo's attempt to make weight for the Corrales fight.

Sometimes other things happen at weigh-ins that are out of the ordinary, such as the time when fighter Allen Thomas took one look at his opponent, Jimmy Remson, on the scales and decided then and there that he didn't want to go through with the fight, taking off without even a "goodbye." Or the time when, before his title bout with Primo Camera, Max Baer went over to Camera as he stood on the scales and began plucking the hairs off his chest, chanting, "She loves me . . . she loves me not."

There have been putdowns, staredowns, and even some shovedowns at weigh-ins. But perhaps the most heated—and, ultimately, tragic—incident ever to occur at a weigh-in happened at the weigh-in for the third Emile Griffith–Benny "Kid" Paret fight. Griffith had been taunted by Paret for as long as he could take it and, at the weigh-in, had confided to his trainer, Gil Clancy, "If Paret says anything to me before the fight, I'll knock him out here." Now, as Griffith took his place on the scales, Paret came up from behind, thrusting his pelvis forward in an obscene manner and grabbing Griffith's ass. In a soft, low voice, he cooed: "Měricon, I'm going to get you and your husband." Unfortunately for Paret, Griffith would make him pay dearly for his insult, battering him senseless and leaving him for dead in their fight that night.

But, even if you put all these incidents together, they wouldn't add up to what happened at the Liston-Clay weigh-in.

What was to become known as "the weigh-in to end all weigh-ins" began around 10:00 A.M. February 25, 1964, when Clay's entourage began gathering at the site of the fight, Miami's Convention Hall. There, in concert assembled, were Sugar Ray Robinson; Cassius's brother, Rudy; yours truly; cotrainer Chickie Ferrara; a couple of sparring partners, including Jimmy Ellis; Luis Sarria, chief masseur; and a new addition to Cassius's growing fistic family, Drew "Bundini" Brown.

Bundini, pronounced "BOO-dini" by Cassius (who sometimes shortened it to just "BOO"), had descended upon the 5th Street Gym right before the Liston fight. As I learned later, he had introduced himself to Cassius as having been part of Sugar Ray Robinson's entourage. But I had worked against Robinson twice with Carmen Basilio and gotten to know everyone in Robinson's camp from his manager, George Gainford, on down. And, for the life of me, I couldn't place him. Nevertheless, whatever his credentials were, he had ingratiated himself to Cassius, who, finding a kindred spirit, adopted him as someone who "makes me laugh."

I remember one day Cassius coming up to me in the gym and saying, "Ang, I'm bringing Drew Brown down from New York." Now I had heard about him from my sources in New York who said he was "some sort of nut," always talking in outerworldly tongues about such things as the sun, the moon, and black satellites as if he were possessed by some alien spirits. So I said to Cassius, "For God's sake, don't do that. He'll drive me nuts and run everyone, especially the newspapermen, out of the room." "Don't worry," Cassius said, "I'll take care of him." And although his arrival had the effect of a lit match thrown into a powder keg, Cassius took care to keep him away from me and prevented him from bothering me or anyone else in the camp. Brown turned out to be a positive addition, working toward the same end as we all were: winning. And he proved to be a great plus for Cassius, who believed Bundini "charged my batteries."

Unable to find "charging batteries" on any boxing job spec sheet, nobody ever quite figured out exactly what it was that Bundini did. He billed himself as an assistant trainer. But you sure could have fooled me. He couldn't even perform the simple task of putting on a pair of gloves. One time he came to me after Cassius had slapped him for screwing up even that basic job. "Angie," he cried, "I can't put gloves on." So I showed him how.

Another time he called himself a "witch doctor . . . a good witch doctor." If I were to describe what he really did, it might be somewhat along the lines of being a mascot, several boxers having had mascots—Bob Fitzsimmons had a lion and Sugar Ray Robinson and Sonny Liston, midgets. But, thinking about it, his function might be more accurately described as being the camp's court jester or cheerleader. No matter what you called him, he sure added a touch of Barnum & Bailey to our traveling circus.

It was in his role as a cheerleader that Bundini excelled. In his own words, he believed, "You can't cook if the stove isn't hot, and Bundini puts the right things in the soup." Bundini continued to put his "things" in the pot, steaming Ali up. Now he steamed him up with his line "Float like a butterfly, sting like a bee"—although I always thought butterflies flitted, not floated. It was a line that would earn him a spot in Boxing's Bartlett, alongside such memorable quotes as Bob Fitzsimmons's "The bigger they are, the harder they fall," Joe Gans's "Bringing home the bacon," Joe Louis's "He can run, but he can't hide," and Kid McCoy's "I'm the real McCoy." That line was Bundini's and nobody else's, but it would become Cassius's, as he practiced saying it time after time, committing it to memory.

Both Bundini's cheerleading and his soon-to-be-famous line would come into play at the weigh-in. Cassius's band of merrymakers had gotten to Convention Hall early and come down the hallway to the Cypress Room where the weigh-in was to be held, chanting and whoopin' it up. Some of us were wearing denim jackets with the words "Bear Hunting" on the back and others wore cowboy hats, though I still don't know why. Anyhow, the first to get to the Cypress Room door were Cassius and Bundini. Flinging it open, they began chorusing at full volume: "Float like a butterfly, sting like a bee. . . . Rumble, young man, rumble!" Then the two, now screaming in each other's face, ended with the sound of two men choking to death, a long echoing "aaaaaargh!" Cassius then banged the floor with his cane, the same cane he had chased Sonny around with at the airport, and shouted, "I'm the champ! Tell Sonny I'm here. Bring on that big ugly bear." And with that they were gone, leaving those in the room to wonder just what the hell they had witnessed.

About three-quarters of an hour later, the same madcap group made their way back to the Cypress Room. This time Cassius, now clad in a terrycloth robe, hit the door and immediately scanned the room for his adversary, hollering, "Tell Sonny I'm here with Sugar Ray Robinson." Not spotting him, he went on, "Liston is flat-footed, but me and Sugar Ray are the prettiest dancers around." Then he added, "Round Eight to prove I'm great." Turning to Bundini, the two amped up their earlier shout in unison: "Float like a butterfly, sting like a bee . . . rumble, young man, rumble."

Cynical boxing writers, used to almost anything, could only stare in amazement at the mind-boggling scene taking place in front of them. They had expected something out of the ordinary from the kid they thought, in boxingese, was "daffy as a southpaw," but this? Watching boxing's equivalent of the Marx Brothers' stateroom scene playing out before them, they could only believe that instead of his usual self-display of verbal pyrotechnics, Clay had finally gone over the edge. He was frightened, scared. What else was there to think?

A few minutes later Liston and his entourage walked into the madhouse to a round of applause. What puzzled me was how Liston, the man who had gone to jail for crushing men's skulls like eggs as an enforcer for the mob, could suddenly go from being an antihero to a hero. I mean, this was a man who had been treated like a leper with a slight case of Bright's disease thrown in for good measure only a few months before when he had beaten the popular Floyd Patterson, and now he was being applauded? There was something wrong with this picture.

One person not applauding was Cassius, who now, in what appeared to be a fit of hysteria, made as if he was going to charge the champion, who was just stepping on the scales. Thrashing about, he screamed, "I'm ready to rumble now. I can beat you anytime, champ. You're scared, chump. I'm gonna eat you alive." As he shouted and squirmed, seemingly about to make his move to the platform, he whispered to me, "Hold me back,

Angie!" wink-wink, which I did with all of two fingers and one thumb. Even Bill Faversham and Sugar Ray Robinson got into the act, both trying to "hold" him as Cassius gave out a couple of more winks in their direction. It was bedlam, but Cassius played it to the hilt and as realistically as any Hollywood star ever played a role.

As Liston stepped off the scales—weighing in at 218, three pounds more than what most had expected him to scale—and began to put on his silk robe, Cassius yelled, "Hey, sucker . . . you're a chump. You've been tricked, chump." Not quite sure how to handle the hullabaloo swirling around him, Liston's only retort was, "Don't let anybody know. Don't tell the world!" It was almost drowned out by the next bombast from Cassius, who screamed back, almost in a shrill, "You are too ugly. You are a bear. I'm going to whup you so baaaaad. You're a chump, a chump, a chump." More bedlam.

Next up on the scales was Cassius. As he began to make his way to the platform holding the scales, he beckoned to Sugar Ray and Bundini to join him, hollering, "I got Sugar Ray in my corner. . . . Sugar Ray was a dancer . . . just like me." However, the special police surrounding the platform stopped them. More screaming from Cassius. "Let them up. . . . This is my show . . . my show," he hollered until the police waved all three up. Taking off his robe, he stepped on the scales. "Clay, 210 and ½ pounds," the Miami Beach Boxing Commissioner shouted for the benefit of the newspapermen.

The weights, however, were only part of the story. For Ed Lassman, the commissioner, who earlier had warned Cassius, "I will tolerate no ranting or raving," followed his first announcement with a second: "Cassius Clay is fined $2,500 for his behavior on the platform and the money will be withheld from Clay's purse."

The weigh-in portion of the weigh-in over, the two fighters now stepped off the platform for their physicals. As Clay sat in front of Dr. Alex Robbins, he held up eight fingers, indicating eight rounds. For his part, which up to now had been one of total bemusement during the brouhaha taking place around him, Liston sat in a nearby chair holding up two fingers for photographers, as in two rounds. Dr. Robbins busied himself taking Cassius's blood pressure, which registered an alarmingly high reading of 200/100, and shook his head, saying, "That's more than twice your normal rate." Syndicated columnist Jimmy Cannon was hovering nearby, pen poised, and asked, "Does that mean he's frightened, Doc?" To which Dr. Robbins nodded, replying, "He's in mortal fear or he's emotional. We'll have to call the fight off if his pressure doesn't come down before he goes into the ring."

That did it! When Cannon, in a game of "Telephone," told the other writers what he had been told, the reporters, most of whom were probably thinking the kid was goofy to begin with, began to use words like *hysterical, frightened*, and *terrified* to describe his bizarre behavior. Words like these eventually found their way into their prefight stories, under screaming headlines that read: "Hysterical Outburst at Weigh-In" and "Clay Left Fighting at Weigh-In," followed by reports that the fight was in danger of being called off.

Up to this point I had contained myself, answering a few questions from reporters. One, Jack Fried of the *Philadelphia Bulletin* asked, "What will Clay do when he gets knocked down?" to which I answered, "If he gets knocked down, he'll get up. But I don't think he will because he'll beat Liston." Another, I'm not sure who, asked, "What effect will Clay's being scared have on him?" Believing that the "scared" one was Liston, who was so shook up he couldn't talk and didn't know what to do with the kid, I said, "With that kind of fear, I'd face a cage of lions. Cassius will win."

When it came to boxing, my fighters were fearless. But when it came to their health almost everything terrified them. Like the hypochondriac's tombstone that read "Now do you believe me?" they would have me believe that every headache was a brain tumor, every upset stomach an ulcer, and every cold a case of pneumonia. In order to ease their minds and get them back on boxing, I had them visit Dr. Ferdie Pacheco, a super fight fan I had gotten to know through Chris's Tuesday night fights. Ferdie would furnish each of the so-called "sufferers" with aspirins and other harmless medication, telling them they were now "fine" and, as a favor to me, never charged them for his services. I'm not sure I did Ferdie any great favors by referring my boxers to him since they soon began showing up with their wives, kids, and entire families, always expecting to be treated the same way, which meant for free. (I borrowed Ferdie's method of treatment by feeding my fighters aspirins before fights, always telling them they were "pep pills" and that when the pills kicked in, the fighter would be able to knock down walls. Then I would keep coming back and asking, "Do you feel it yet?" Most did!)

Now I had something far more important for Ferdie to do than merely treat hypochondriacs. Concerned that the commission was not going to allow the fight to go on in the wake of Dr. Robbins's remark that Clay was "in mortal fear," I asked Ferdie to come with me—quickly. We raced off to Cassius's house, where, to our amazement, we found the supposedly hysterical Cassius sitting on the front steps playing with a bunch of kids from the neighborhood. Ferdie examined him right then and there, taking his pulse and temperature, and found him "normal" and in perfect condition to fight. Using my contacts with the press, I went inside and made calls to Jack Cuddy at the Associated Press and to Ed Pope at the *Miami Herald* to tell them Clay was fine, his blood pressure now fifty over forty. Better than fine, he was in "good shape" for the fight that night.

Clay, who former light-heavyweight champion José Torres said was "the only fighter I know who can bullshit himself," had now successfully bull-shitted the writers, the commission, and the commission doctor. But not Liston, who knew the look of fear on a fighter's face, having induced fear in so many opponents. And this wasn't it. Madness, craziness perhaps, but not fear.

But even though Cassius had been examined and found "fine," he was any-thing but to the oddsmakers, who made him a 7–1 underdog. (Cassius's take on the odds was: "If you'd like to lose your money, be a fool and bet on Sonny." Sonny's view was: "The odds should be ten to nothing that he don't last for the first round.") He was an even bigger underdog to the comedians, Jackie Gleason predicting, "Clay should last about eighteen seconds and that includes the three seconds he brings in the ring with him." And Joe E. Lewis quipped, "I'm betting on Clay . . . to live."

Cassius was more than just fine. He was so composed that one hour before the fight he was in the audience watching brother Rudy getting the bejabbers beaten out of him in a prelim bout, discussing what Rudy was doing wrong and not doing at all.

An hour later he stood midring, face-to-face with a scowling Liston, awaiting referee Barney Felix's prefight instructions. Liston looked his men-acing self; his bathrobe stuffed with six towels, giving him a wall-to-wall terrycloth look, his death-ray eyes fixed on Cassius. But instead of cower-ing like the rest of Liston's opponents, a confident, almost cocksure Cas-sius met his gaze squarely. And with Cassius following my instructions to "stand tall and look down at him, he's shorter," Liston now realized, for the first time, that he was facing a taller opponent, the only time in his career that he had. But even more devastating was what happened next. As referee Barney Felix droned on with his instructions, Cassius hissed, in one final "gotcha" that must have hit Liston harder than any punch he had ever taken, "Chump! Now I gotcha, chump!"

(Not every psyche job tried during the prefight instructions works, however. When Carmen Basilio met Sugar Ray Robinson the first time, as referee Al Berl was going through the usual "the fighter scoring the knockdown must go to a neutral corner" stuff, Robinson leaned forward in the direction of Basilio and, teeth bared, snarled at him. Carmen's reaction? He came back to the corner roaring with laughter. He couldn't have cared less what Ray did before or during the fight. He was going to beat him. And did.)

Before the bell sounded for the start of the first round, Liston stood in his corner shuffling his feet like a bull seeing a red cape, the way he always did, and giving Cassius the evil eye. As Cassius would say later, "Man, he meant to kill me."

At the opening bell, Liston lurched out of his corner, an energized Frankenstein coming to life, running at Cassius and throwing the first punch of the fight, a long left jab. As soon as he started his jab, Cassius slid gracefully to his left, away from the punch, which missed by a foot or more. At times Cassius almost seemed to be running as he circled around the champion, moving backward and from side to side. Liston jabbed and jabbed again, missing him by wide margins—nobody there, as Cassius was gone by the time the jabs arrived. Pressing forward with bad intentions, Liston loaded up on his ponderous right hand, trying to maneuver his challenger into a corner to decapitate him. Cassius, who had been told that "Liston's eyes tip you when he is about to throw a heavy punch," kept moving and moving some more, not bothering to throw a punch in anger until the round was almost over. Then out came a left jab, almost like a switchblade, flicking into the champion's face. Liston seemed frozen. By the time he recovered and surged forward, Clay was gone again.

The bell ending the round sounded, and Liston stomped back to his corner, not even bothering to sit down. Clay had already won an important psychological victory by lasting the round. I knew then and there that we "had" Liston. Now, as Clay looked over at Liston, he told me later he could only remember thinking, "Man, you're gonna wish you had rested all you could when we pass this next round."

Remembering what his trainer, Willie Reddish, had told him, that if he didn't take Clay out early he would have to slow him down by clubbing him to the body, Liston came out for Round Two intent on inflicting bodily damage. But even though he cornered Cassius and landed some brutal blows to Cassius's liver and kidneys, Cassius wiggled out to center ring and moved away, almost galloping to his own left as Liston came straight at him with his left extended. Now Cassius was picking his openings with the care of a scalpel-wielder, his jab rarely missing and his fast combinations landing with increasing frequency, freezing Liston every time he was hit. Bang-bang, in and out. He was kicking the hell out of Liston.

A tiny cut, barely perceptible, had opened on the champion's left cheekbone, under his eye. It was the first time in his thirty-four professional fights that Liston had been cut. Liston retaliated with his first meaningful blow of the fight, a long left like a two-by-four coming out of a basement window, catching Cassius. But even though Cassius was momentarily rocked, Liston didn't follow up, either not realizing how hard he had hit his challenger or already too tired to capitalize on it.

In Round Three Liston continued to lumber forward, almost as if treading in quicksand, hacking away at where Cassius had been, not where he was as the challenger continued to move in and out, out and in. Midway through the round, Cassius inflicted the first real damage of the fight. Feinting with his left, he drove home a right hand, busting Liston's cheekbone. Suddenly the tiny wound gushed open. At the end of the third, Liston walked back to his corner, a weary and wounded warrior, and for the first time, sat on his stool.

During training we had heard the usual rumors, that Liston had sustained a minor injury to his left arm or his left shoulder, nobody was sure which. Now, between Rounds Three and Four, Liston's handlers were busy working to close the deep cut under his left eye and massaging his left shoulder with liniment. The fourth round was the most uneventful of the fight. Cassius, who had gone ten rounds only three times, was pacing himself to go the full fifteen. But, as he walked back to the corner after Round Four, he was squinting and blinking, and came to the corner saying, "I can't see, Angelo. My eyes are burning!" Nobody in the corner was sure why. Maybe, we thought, he had been blinded by some foreign substance, something called Monsel solution, a caustic substance that had been used on Liston's cut. Cassius sweats profusely, and he may have touched it with his forehead and whatever it was had run down into his eyes because both eyes were affected. Or it might have been the liniment used on Liston's shoulders and Cassius had somehow gotten it into his eyes by leaning on Liston during a clinch. Whatever it was, my fighter was blinded.

Something like this had happened in the first Rocky Marciano–Jersey Joe Walcott fight back in 1952. Marciano had come back to his corner after the fifth round half blind. He told his cotrainer Freddie Brown, "I can't see," probably because some of the solution used to close Walcott's head cut had leaked into his eyes. So Freddie grabbed the water bucket and washed out Marciano's eyes. Two rounds later he was alright, and eight rounds later he knocked out Walcott to win the heavyweight title.

I didn't know what the problem was nor what the solution was. I put my pinkie in his eyes and then mine. It burned like hell. Like Freddie Brown had done with Marciano, I tried to clean his eyes out, first with a sponge and then a towel. I threw both away, not wanting whatever that stuff was to get back in his eyes. But that didn't help, he just kept blinking. For the first time there was a hint of something resembling fear in Cassius. For no man, however brave, would be willing to take on a wounded beast like Liston without full sight. And now he had none. As the blinking continued, he stood up and, thrusting out his gloves, screamed, "Cut them off . . . I can't see . . . I want the world to know there's dirty work afoot." I told him, "You can't fight without gloves. Sit down!" and sent Bundini over to tell the referee that there was something on Liston's gloves—he never made it, getting halfway across the ring before getting flustered and coming back to the corner without having told the ref anything. But referee Felix, sensing something resembling confusion in our corner, began to make his way over. Catching sight of Felix coming halfway across the ring, I shouted to Cassius to get up and half-lifted him off the stool to show that he was all right.

Seeing my guy get up, Felix stopped and went back to position in a neutral corner. At the sound of the bell for Round Five, I put my hand in Cassius's back, propelled him out into the ring, and shouted, "This is for the big one, son, the world championship. Now get the hell out there . . . AND RUN!!!" Who knows? Maybe the what-if history of boxing was written right then and there.

Nobody knew what it was that had caused Cassius's temporary blindness. A group of brothers sitting in the first row began cursing me, saying something or other about it being a "conspiracy" and that I was "trying to blind" Cassius. So, as I came down the steps after shoving Cassius out into the ring for the fifth round, I wiped my own eyes with the discarded sponge to show them there was nothing in it.

Later, much later, I was to hear that two of Liston's previous opponents, Zora Folley and Eddie Machen, had both complained of a burning sensation in their eyes during their fights with Liston. And Liston's behind-the-scenes manager, Blinky Palermo, was later to confide to my brother Chris that indeed Liston had "put something on his gloves." But I didn't know, or even suspect, it at the time. All I knew was that my kid was blind in there.

The between-rounds activity in our corner had not gone unnoticed in the other. In fact, during the rest period, which was anything but, one of Liston's handlers had been hollering, trying to get referee Felix to go over to ours, hoping against hope that the activity was a prelude to our stopping the fight. Maybe he knew something, maybe not.

Liston came out of his corner for the fifth round, as Ferdie Pacheco put it, "like a little kid looks at a new bike on Christmas." As Cassius tottered out with unsteady legs and unseeing eyes, Liston, swinging those huge meat cleaver–like fists of his, scored several times with agonizing wallops to the midsection and a few left hooks to the head. Cassius began moving blindly along the ring on radar-like instinct alone, sometimes keeping Liston off by holding his left hand out like a blind man his cane. I guided him from the corner hollering, "Keep off the ropes," as Liston continued to try mightily to tear his head off. About halfway through the round, Cassius's eyes finally cleared and he took control again. As the round drew to a close, Cassius was lashing out again with needle-sharp jabs, raising red welts under both of Liston's eyes.

Referee Felix had the ring doctor come over to the corner and take a precautionary look at Clay's eyes between Rounds Five and Six. On the other side of the ring, Liston's corner was a somber one. The champion was clearly tired, having gone just one round less than he had in the preceding three years, and now sat slumped on his stool, looking almost one hundred in boxing years. Slowly he got off his stool for the sixth round.

Now clear-sighted, Cassius quickly went on the attack, missing with a left hook but scoring with a wicked right-left combination to the head. When Liston failed to return the fire, Cassius machine-gunned him with six consecutive unanswered punches—three lefts, followed by three rights. Liston jabbed back, almost out of habit, and Cassius ripped home a pair of lefts into the soon-to-be ex-champion's now welty puss. Cassius then moved out to long range where he circled and continued to pump his snake-like left jab into Liston's face—a jab Bundini said "could hit you before God gets the news." The punches made a loud, almost painful thud as they whacked home. There was a purple lump under Liston's right eye and a four-inch gash under his left. Now Cassius threw a big right hand that drew a roar from the crowd and followed up with his left, driving it into Liston's unprotected face four times in succession. Liston responded with a short right, but Cassius made him pay for it with two more razor-sharp lefts at the bell.

As Cassius came back to the corner, he shouted at the press section, only three of whom had picked him to win, "I'm gonna upset the world!"

The opposite corner was hardly as upbeat as Liston's handlers worked feverishly, massaging his shoulder and tending to his cuts and bruises. Meanwhile, over in our corner we were going through our usual sixty-second routine beginning with holding Cassius's trunks open so he could take a deep breath, then taking out his mouthpiece and washing it right away, and wiping his face preparatory to putting his mouthpiece back in at the buzzer for the next round, Round Seven. However, just as we were about to put his mouthpiece in, Cassius suddenly was on his feet, hands held high over his head in a victory celebration. Me being so short and Cassius so big, sort of the small and tall of it all, it was easy for Cassius to look over my shoulder. Now he was staring over my shoulder to see what he could see in Liston's corner. And what he saw was Liston slumped on his stool, spitting out his mouthpiece. The fight was over!

Cassius, jumping around like his feet were on fire, leapt around the ring, doing everything but cartwheels, shouting, "I am King . . . I am the Greatest . . . I am the King" over and over again, only interrupting his victory dance to lean over the ropes and holler at the press, "I shook up the world."

And then picking out those in the press who had doubted him, he shouted, "I told you . . . and you . . . and you. . . . I'm king of the world. . . . All of you must bow down to me."

Afterward, announcer Steve Ellis began his postfight interview with, "You told me in Los Angeles that you could do it in eight . . ." but never finished his question as Cassius interrupted him with, "I had him going in eight. I was getting ready to take him in eight, as you can see. But the man stopped it just to keep me from looking so great." "All right," said Ellis, finally able to get in a word. "Give us the poetry for number seven." And with that Cassius unveiled a whole new poem: "He wanted to go to heaven so I took him in seven." And then added a loud, "I AM THE KING OF THE WORLD!"

Back in the dressing room Cassius was holding court—after all, they didn't call him "The Louisville Lip" and "The Mouth That Roared" for nothing. Red Smith, the noted New York sportswriter, cornered me. "Congratulations, Angie," he said. "I didn't think Clay could do it. I was beginning to think that Liston was unbeatable."

"Come on, Red," I responded to my old friend, "I told about forty newspaper guys six days ago how this fight would go. Who did Liston ever knock out? Albert Westphal and Cleveland Williams, that's all. Willie Besmanoff was stopped on cuts. Forget about Patterson . . . he was psyched out. Liston was the toughest guy in the world, so he couldn't believe what happened to him. This kid's slapping him around. He thought he was going to have a picnic with this kid, but what he didn't realize was that the kid had become a man. And it demoralized him. Boxing beat Liston. Boxing and Cassius Clay!"

Out in the parking lot a strange scene was taking place. Lou Duva, who had brought both Rocky Marciano and Joe Louis to the fight, was standing next to his car watching Marciano sprint across the lot. "What the hell ya doin', Rocky?" shouted Duva, puzzled at the sudden activity of the ex-champion. "Didn't ya hear that?" shouted back Marciano as he continued to run. "Clay's going to get one million for his next fight. I'm comin' back." And with that, Louis said, "Stand back, Lou, I'm gonna run, too."

SEVEN

Boxing Becomes Cassius Clay
Who Becomes Muhammad Ali

The next day, Wednesday, February 26, 1964, all hell broke loose. For that was the day of the day-after-winning-the-championship press conference, when the new champion usually tells the newspapermen how happy he is to be the champion, how it feels, when he thinks he had the fight won, who his next opponent will be, and so on and so on.

Only this time it was different. Instead of answering questions from the press, Cassius took the microphone and launched into: "Everything with common sense wants to be with his own. Bluebirds with bluebirds, redbirds with redbirds, pigeons with pigeons, eagles with eagles, tigers with tigers, monkeys with monkeys. As small as an ant's brain is, red ants want to be with red ants, black ants with black ants.

"I believe in the religion of Islam, which means I believe there is no God but Allah, and Elijah Muhammad is His Apostle. This is the same religion that is believed in by over seven hundred million dark-skinned peoples throughout Africa and Asia.

"I don't have to be what you want me to be. I am free to be who I want." Then he added that he had renounced his "slave name" Cassius Marcellus Clay and would henceforth be known as "Cassius X"—four weeks later he would change his name again, this time to Muhammad Ali, *Muhammad* meaning "worthy of all praise" and *Ali* meaning "most high."

The reaction to the conversion from Cassius Clay to Muhammad Ali was swift, and I thought unfair. Headlines like "Black Muslims Take Over" were in all the papers, with many of the writers, like Jimmy Cannon, overreacting. Cannon, in his overheated style, wrote that "Black Muslimism" was "a more pernicious hate symbol than Schmeling and Nazism."

Sportswriters who never had any trouble calling other fighters by their chosen names—like Henry Jackson as Henry Armstrong, or Joseph Louis Barrow as Joe Louis, or Arnold Cream as Jersey Joe Walcott, or Walker Smith as Sugar Ray Robinson—found they couldn't and wouldn't call him Muhammad Ali, instead continuing to call him Cassius Clay.

But the most troubling stories were those that referred to the fact that I was the only white guy in Ali's entourage as if there were a black-white thing between Ali and me. We had this special thing, a unique blend, a chemistry. I never heard anything resembling a racist comment leave his mouth. He accepted me for what I was, his trainer and friend. Between the two of us, we never had anything but a wonderful time. There was never a black-white divide. And, hey, I was working for Muhammad Ali, not the Muslims, and he was "fine" with me.

So when writers asked me if I had any problems with Cassius changing his name to Muhammad Ali, I didn't have to think twice about it. No, I'd tell them. Hey, my original name wasn't Angelo Dundee, so why should I care about him changing his name?

I did, however, have one very small problem. You see, I had become fairly adept at rhyming Cassius Clay for Cassius's poems. How in the name of the poetry muse (I think her name's Erato) was I going to find a rhyme for Muhammad Ali? I mean, what rhymes with Ali? Other than that I had no trouble with Muhammad's religion or name change. As I said, my name was originally Mirena, so why not Muhammad Ali if he wanted? I had always stayed out of my fighters' private lives, and there was nothing more private than a fighter's choice of religion. I refused to be a micromanager. My fighters' private lives were their own business. Period, end of paragraph. And that was how Muhammad and I got along from that day forth.

I had more important things to do than worry about his name change or his religion. We had another fight coming up with Sonny Liston, a return bout as called for in the contract.

In the meantime, in between the time of the two Liston fights the acting head of the Louisville syndicate, Bill Faversham, had had a heart attack and a syndicate lawyer had taken over. Now he, too, was ill. The syndicate decided that I would take over as manager. That meant I would be doing virtually the same things I already had been doing, but that I would get an increase in salary.

Here I must tell you that I like money as much as the next guy, but money wasn't the main reason I enjoyed working with "Cassius-hyphen-Muhammad." I liked Muhammad, I enjoyed working with him, and I was proud of the job I had done. And it was for these reasons I had taken over the job of training him, without a contract and with only a handshake, which I guess they knew was as good as the most binding contract in the world. To show their appreciation, the syndicate decided to rectify the mistake I had made in taking a straight salary (as my brother Chris had suggested) instead of a percentage by giving me, with Muhammad's approval, a $20,000 bonus for my work. It was good to know such nice people.

As the return bout with Liston neared, I had my work cut out to get Muhammad in shape. You see, after the first fight Ali had taken a victory lap. He went to Africa, where he had been given a tremendous reception as the first Muslim to win a world championship with crowds chanting "Ali . . . Ali . . . Ali" everywhere he went. The problem was he returned from his African tour bloated, looking like a latter-day Fatty Arbuckle. Ali was a sweet freak, loving anything sweet, including chocolate and pies—especially pumpkin and banana pies. And now, *Marone!* he looked like he had eaten half of Africa. To lose weight he adopted an idea from Archie Moore, putting on a plastic suit to sweat it off even though I told him he shouldn't. And wouldn't you know it? He became so weak that in one sparring session a sparring partner, named Johnson, I think, knocked him down and then stood over him saying, "I didn't knock you down . . . I didn't knock you down."

There was, however, one small change. Muhammad had chosen Herbert Muhammad, the son of Elijah Muhammad, the spiritual leader of the Islamic movement, as his new manager. I could understand Ali's desire to have the guidance of his religious leader. And even though I was no longer the "manager," I had no problems with the change. In fact, Herbert told me he knew what kind of job I was doing and that I would be Ali's trainer forever. The transition was smooth. I could live with the fact that there had been a change just as I could live with the change in Cassius Clay's name.

After all, the world is in constant change, why shouldn't I be? Besides, you can't eat ego.

Oh sure, maybe every now and then one or two of the guys in the ever-increasing circle of "helpers" who surrounded Ali didn't feel too happy about having a "honky" close to the champion. But I never heard anything said. Heck, I was working for Muhammad, not them, and Muhammad stood up for me, stood by me, and stood with me.

Some fans thought that Liston had thrown the first fight in order to get a big payday in the return bout—that he would now show his power and stop Ali. There were more speculations and more half-baked theories than there were after President John F. Kennedy's assassination the previous year. But any fan who thought that didn't understand what it meant to be a champion. No champion would ever willingly throw away his title—especially the heavyweight title; that's where the money is. Now it would be harder for Liston to win it back because Ali was not about to give it away. In fact, I thought the return bout would be a lot easier for Ali, having already destroyed Liston's confidence and torn away his cloak of invincibility.

The fight was originally scheduled to be in Boston on November 16, 1964. Two nights before the scheduled bout I had left Muhammad in his hotel room watching the movie *Prince Valiant* on TV and gone with John Crittenden, a writer for the *Miami News*, to watch a closed-circuit telecast of my adopted football team, the University of Miami, playing Boston College. Sometime during halftime, the commentator announced that Muhammad Ali had been taken to a hospital. I shot up in my seat, saying something to the effect of "What the hell!" I had left him only an hour or so before and he had been perfectly OK, just lying in bed watching television. What could have happened to him in that short period of time? I was later to find out that he suddenly suffered some pain and had called the hotel doctor who had immediately checked him into a hospital. By the time I reached the hospital he was in the operating room, being operated on for a strained hernia.

When word reached Liston's camp, Sonny could only say, "Shit . . . I worked hard for this fight." Then, thinking about it, he added, "But it could have been worse. It could have been me."

The fight, of course, was postponed. Now the promoters were having trouble rescheduling the fight in Boston because veterans' groups and superpatriots of all stripes were jumping out of the woodwork to protest Muhammad's draft deferment. In addition, the Massachusetts Athletic Commission found that Liston had what they called "mob connections" and that Liston and his advisor, Jack Nilon, were the promoters of the fight. Citing a rule about conflict of interest, they withdrew their approval. The fight was now a fight without a site. With Muhammad convalescing, his Louisville syndicate continued its search for possible alternatives to Boston. At this point an offer came in from the little town of Lewiston, Maine, to host the fight. The syndicate wasted no time in accepting the offer. The Liston rematch was on again, rescheduled for May 25, 1965, in Lewiston, Maine—the smallest town to host a heavyweight championship since Shelby, Montana, hosted the Jack Dempsey–Tommy Gibbons fight back in 1923.

Lewiston, Maine, was exactly what you thought it would be—a small town. How small was it? One writer joked that the town's "Welcome" sign was also the "Come Back Again" sign. Because of its proximity to French-speaking Quebec, a good number of the inhabitants spoke French, but there was no French restaurant in sight. Luckily for me, there was an Italian restaurant. And a good one, too.

There was little to do in Lewiston except find the Italian restaurant and talk about the fight. However, there was one thing that wasn't talked about, even mentioned, and in fact was kept from the press. Just two days before the fight, in Muhammad's last sparring session, Jimmy Ellis had bruised Muhammad's rib cage. When he told me, all I could think of saying was, "That's good, now you'll know to stay out of clinches." But maybe, just maybe, knowing he couldn't take a chance of having Liston pound on his bruised rib cage was enough to inspire Muhammad to take action—and quickly. I don't know, but I think that may have had as much to do with the quick ending as anything else.

While news of Ali's bruised rib was kept out of the papers, other so-called "news" circulated, most of it in the form of rumors with no great attachment to fact. These were not the ordinary fight rumors, mind you— you know, so-and-so can't make weight—but dark and frightening rumors, rumors of possible assassination attempts, which gained currency because of the recent assassination of Malcolm X. And each rumor fed others. I didn't pay them much mind. But when the sheriff of Chicopee, Massachusetts, where our training camp was, told us that "people were headed our way in a pink Cadillac to do harm to Ali," we sure as the dickens pulled up our stakes in Chicopee and moved to Lewiston quickly. In a pink Cadillac, I might add.

I have always believed those rumors were the handiwork of the great publicist Harold Conrad, who was doing what other publicists had done before him, merely ballyhooing the fight. It has long been believed by those around in those days that Francis Albertani, the publicist for promoter Mike Jacobs, fanned the flames of publicity before the second Louis-Schmeling fight by letting writers in on the "scoop" that anti-Nazi pickets would be outside Yankee Stadium the night of the fight carrying placards protesting the fight. What he did not tell them was that Jacobs himself had not only approved of their actions but had, in fact, underwritten their efforts. Albertani's efforts had made front-page headlines around the country. Now Conrad's did, too, especially after he took writer Jimmy Cannon into his confidence and Cannon rushed into print with his alarmist Chicken Little "scoop," further inflaming the situation. And not incidentally, generating more press for the fight.

I usually don't pay much attention to the prefight chitchat. But one particular bit of information did get my attention. A couple of days before the fight, Dave Anderson of the *New York Times* caught me in the lobby of the Poland Springs Hotel and told me to "go look at the ring." It was, he said, a wrestling ring. Now I normally inspect the ring right after the weigh-in, but this time I raced over to the arena on Dave's say-so to look at the ring. And was I glad I did. For sure enough, it was a wrestling ring, one with loose ropes and a mat like a trampoline. I found whoever was in charge and told them to quickly import a boxing ring, my guy doesn't do trampoline tricks, although at times it might look like he did.

The night of the fight was a night to end all nights. It began with those attempting to gain entry into St. Dominick's, a high school hockey arena done over into a boxing arena by putting floorboards down over the ice, being searched for weapons at the door. And ended with the weapon used by Muhammad going largely unnoticed.

The fight was scheduled to start at 10:30 P.M. By 10:00 a less-than-capacity crowd of 2,344 had taken their seats in the made-over bandbox of a high school ice hockey arena, most sniffling and wiping their noses, the cold weather outside and the melting ice underneath the wooden flooring inside making it extremely cold. In the press section most of the writers were looking under their desks for a place to hide when, as Jimmy

Cannon put it, "the trouble starts." But what happened wasn't the trouble Cannon expected, but the biggest controversy since the Dempsey-Tunney "long count" some thirty-eight years before.

As the fighters entered the ring, Liston looked anything but confident. This time, as referee Jersey Joe Walcott gave the prefight call to arms there was no stare-down, just a cold, unblinking look at Muhammad. Then the bell, and Liston came shambling out of his corner, intent on impaling Muhammad on the end of his outstretched left. Before the fight I had told Muhammad: "Show him you're the governor, show him you're the boss." And wouldn't you know it? Boom! Nailed him one-two with his first two punches. Liston kept coming forward as he always did, sticking out that lethal left jab of his. But Muhammad just skirted away. Again Liston tried, again the same result. You could see that Liston was trying to cut off the ring, get Muhammad into a corner, but Muhammad was almost free-floating away from him. Now Muhammad was taunting Liston, something I'm not too fond of, but you could see it was affecting Liston, psychologically getting to him as he tried harder to get to Ali. He seemed hesitant. When Ali stopped, he'd stop. He was just following Ali around the ring now almost as a course of nature. Suddenly, as he seemed to momentarily get Muhammad on the ropes, he stepped forward, reaching, almost lunging with his left and sticking out a slow jab. At that exact moment my guy took a step back and then, moving his head ever so slightly to avoid the jab, came over with a swift straight right hand that caught Liston squarely on the sweet spot, his temple.

Oh yes, the punch did make contact. Ali hit Liston so quick the cameras couldn't take it. He hit him with a shot Liston didn't see. They're the ones that knock you out. You see, for Liston that one punch brought back memories of the beating he took in the first fight, it demoralized him. So no, it wasn't a fix. People can say what they think. If they think the punch didn't land, I tell them they shouldn't have looked away when he landed it. They shouldn't have gone out for a hot dog. And despite Jimmy Cannon's comment that "I saw it, it couldn't have crushed a grape," if you look at the punch in stop-action, you can see Liston's head snap back, his leg come up from the force of the blow and then see him go down. It was that hard.

Liston toppled over, flat on his back. Muhammad now stood over the fallen Liston, screaming, "Get up and fight, sucker. . . . Get up and fight, you bum. . . . You're supposed to be so bad. . . . Nobody will believe this," daring him to get up as referee Walcott tugged at him, trying to maneuver him to a neutral corner. By the time Walcott had succeeded, a hurt Liston had staggered back to his feet and was trying to protect himself as Ali swarmed all over him, throwing punches from every angle.

As Muhammad and Liston continued to do battle on one side of the ring, two little men stood up on the other side waving their arms and hollering, "It's over . . . it's over." I looked over at the two standing near me and thought they were twins, both munchkin-like and bald-headed. At first I mistook Nat Fleischer to be the timekeeper. Then I realized it was the publisher and editor of *The Ring* magazine, and the second little man was, I would find out later, the timekeeper, Francis McDonough. But nobody could hear them in the chaos following the knockdown. So I helped them out by screaming to Walcott in my high-pitched voice, "Joe . . . Joe . . . it's over. Go talk to Nat." Joe finally heard me and, sticking his head through the ropes, talked to Nat Fleischer while the action, such as it was, continued. Then, having been told by Fleischer that Liston had been down for more than ten seconds, Walcott walked back, broke up the two fighters, and held Ali's hand aloft.

Sometimes shouting at the ref works. I remember one story that was told of the time when Jack Dempsey fought Jack Sharkey and, after taking a pasting for seven rounds, Dempsey hooked his left to Sharkey's body and Sharkey turned to the ref to complain that the blow was low. That was all Dempsey needed. When Sharkey's head was turned to the referee, Dempsey brought a left hook up to Sharkey's chin and Sharkey crashed to the floor with a thud. The next sound came from Dempsey's corner as his second, Bill Duffy, shouted, "Count that man out." And referee Jack O'Sullivan did, even while shouts of "Foul" filled the stadium.

Ali had won even though there never had been a referee's count, not even a "one . . . two . . . ." And the time, when announced as having been one minute, was off by almost a minute, the actual time having been 1:52. But what did I care? Count or no count, one minute or two, my guy had won and kept his title.

Afterward, turmoil not only reigned; it poured. The fans, especially those who hadn't seen the punch, were screaming, "FIX . . . FIX . . ." in unison. Come on, a two-minute "fix"? If it was rigged, it had to look better than *that*. Newspapermen, trying to make sense and a story out of what they had just seen or not seen, were writing that it was a "Phantom Punch" that felled Liston. Liston, still in a fog, was telling anyone who would listen that he didn't get up immediately because "crazy" Ali was standing over him and he was afraid he would have been hit again if he tried. And there was Muhammad, over on the other side of the ring screaming to the press, "I am the Greatest" and attributing his knockout to something he called an "Anchor Punch," taught to him by the old actor Stepin Fetchit, who said it was taught to him by none other than Jack Johnson. Ali even gave an explanation of sorts as to why the punch hadn't been seen: "It was faster than the blink of an eye and everyone at ringside missed it because they all blinked at the same time."

You would have thought that as holder of the greatest title boxing can bestow, Muhammad Ali would have been appreciated for what he had done in the ring. But those keepers of the journals of record, the newspapermen, along with fans and politicians alike, tended to discount his talents at less than face value, concentrating instead on his conversion to Islam—and his name change.

Former heavyweight champion Floyd Patterson went so far as to send Muhammad a written challenge, reminiscent of challenges of old. "Cassius, I have admiration for you as a boxer and feel that you should be a symbol that all Americans should look up to," Patterson wrote. "However, I don't honestly believe what the Black Muslims portray. I am proud to be an American and proud of my people, and no one group of people could make me change my views. Therefore, I challenge you not only for myself, but for all people who think and feel as I do."

In response to Patterson's challenge, Muhammad issued one of his own: "I'll fight Patterson in a winner-take-all bout. I would give my purse to the Black Muslims, and Patterson could give the purse to the Catholic Church if he is the victor."

The two now engaged in a public debate with Floyd reiterating his challenge and responding to Muhammad's with an "I am willing to fight for nothing if necessary just so I can bring the championship back to America." Muhammad answered in an interview published in *Playboy*, "The only reason Patterson's decided to come out of his shell is to try to make himself a big hero to the white man by saving the heavyweight title from being held by a Muslim." In another interview, Muhammad said, "I'll play with him for ten rounds. He has been talking about my religion. I will just pow him. Then, after I beat him, I'll convert him."

The fight, scheduled to take place November 22, 1964, in Las Vegas, had all the makings of a boxing Holy War, a crusade.

Muhammad was up to his usual prefight shenanigans, visiting Patterson at his training camp carrying a handful of carrots for the man he called "The Rabbit." When a reporter asked Patterson if he "got mad with these things," Floyd answered, "Well, I'm happy that the heavyweight champ, Mister Clay, took time to . . ." Here he was interrupted by Muhammad, who shouted, "That ain't my name. You know my name. C'mon Rabbit, what's my name?" Floyd started again, "As I was saying . . . I was happy to see Ali . . ." "The full name," demanded Muhammad. "I didn't hear you callin' me by my full name." "Well," answered Floyd, "Cassius Clay is the name his mother calls him."

I knew firsthand how important Ali's Muslim name was. It was not a topic for taunts or jokes. One time when Rudy, Muhammad's young brother, announced that he too had converted to Muslimism and had changed his name to Rahaman Muhammad, I jokingly said that I would call him "Rocky" Muhammad. But Rudy, seeing no humor in my joke, said, "Oh, no, Elijah Muhammad gave me my name. I would never change it." From that day on I made sure to always call him Rahaman.

It was the same with Muhammad. You called him Muhammad Ali or you lost a friend. Muhammad even had some heavy words with his idol Sugar Ray Robinson because Ray was reluctant to call him Muhammad Ali. And if Muhammad had trouble with Sugar Ray, you knew he was not going to take anything less from Floyd. (Five years later, while in exile, Muhammad attended the Joe Frazier–Jimmy Ellis fight at Madison Square Garden. As the ring announcer called off the names of former champions in the audience to come into the ring, the crowd began to call for Muhammad to be introduced. But when Garden Vice President Harry Markson wanted to introduce him as Cassius Clay rather than Muhammad Ali, he walked out rather than answer to his former name.)

The Patterson fight was no fight. As a trainer I do not like "hate" fights. Boxers are professionals and should not let personal feelings get in the way of their execution. They've got to control their emotions, not get mad. Was it the Greeks who said, "Those whom the gods wish to destroy they first make angry"? But it sometimes happens, and there isn't much you can do about it. And on that night in Las Vegas, Muhammad Ali not only outboxed Floyd, but, I'm sorry to say, humiliated him.

For the first few rounds Muhammad taunted Floyd with a barrage of "What's my name?" sneers, throwing more taunts at Patterson than punches. He just moved, bent and pulled back, hands down, daring Floyd to land. By the third Floyd's back was up for adoption, thrown out of whack after Ali hammered on him in the clinches. Every round thereafter his trainer, Al Silvani, had to carry his game warrior back to his corner, trying at the same time to yank his sacroiliac back into place. Every time Floyd tried to throw a punch his face contorted with pain, and by the sixth round the fans at ringside were yelling for referee Harry Krause to stop the fight. But even though Muhammad had floored Floyd in the sixth, he couldn't finish the job. With both hands hurt he was content to continue pounding on him and accompanying each punch with a verbal "Bop! Bop! Bop!" and a "What's my name?" Referee Krause finally called a merciful halt to this sadistic humiliation of the popular ex-champion in the twelfth. It was an ugly fight to watch, and one that did little to help Muhammad's popularity.

There is a postscript to this story, one told to me by Gene Kilroy, a friend of both. According to Gene, Ali was never mad at Floyd, although for years Patterson continued to call him "Clay." The "situation," as Gene called it, was patched up years later when Gene was having lunch with Floyd and his wife at the Las Vegas Hilton and Ali came over. Ali greeted his former opponent, calling out, "Floyd Patterson!" and Floyd called him "Clay." Gene discreetly suggested that Ali "preferred" to be called "Muhammad," and Floyd again addressed him, this time as "Muhammad," saying, "Thanks, Muhammad for the good payday in the ring." Ali smiled and said, "Floyd, you earned it." And that was that.

But Muhammad's popularity—or, realistically speaking, his unpopularity—would suffer a much greater hit on the afternoon of February 17, 1966, three months after his fight with Patterson, when he uttered nine little words: "I ain't got no quarrels with them Viet Cong."

Let me backtrack a little here. In an attempt to piece together the incidents leading up to those nine words as best I can through the bits of information I gleaned from others and Muhammad himself, it all began in

January 1964, just days after his twenty-second birthday and a month before his first bout with Liston.

On that day Number 15-47-42-127 sat in a room at an Army Induction Center in Coral Gables, Florida, studying questions like: "A vendor was selling apples for $10 a basket. How much would you pay for a dozen baskets if one-third of the apples have been removed from each of the baskets?" As the then-Clay would tell me, "When I looked at a lot of the questions they had on them army tests, I just didn't know the answers. I didn't even know how to start after finding the answers."

He missed enough of those questions to score 16 percent on the Armed Forces Qualifying Test, and since a passing mark was 30 percent, he was classified 1-Y. The Army gave him another test two months later in Louisville. Same result. ("I said I was the Greatest, not the smartest," he said as a partial rationalization.)

During the years he was classified as 1-Y and busy defending his championship, his local Louisville draft board received a torrent of outraged letters condemning the draft board. Most of them were racially charged, looking for Muhammad to be drafted and shipped overseas, hoping that he would return home in a body bag.

Two years later he was relaxing on the lawn of his rented house in Miami when Bob Lipsyte of the *New York Times* dropped by to see him. One of Muhammad's friends came out of the house and told him he was wanted on the telephone by one of the wire services. The wire service reporter told him that the military had expanded its draft call and the passing percentile had been dropped to 15, making him eligible. Muhammad had been reclassified 1-A by his local Louisville draft board and would be called up for service duty shortly.

"How can they do this without another test to see if I'm wiser or worser than the last time?" he asked Lipsyte, half in disbelief and half in anger. "Why are they gunning for me?" Then he blurted out the words that made him cannon fodder for politicians and editorials across the country: "I ain't got no quarrels with them Viet Cong."

In normal times such a comment wouldn't have caused a furor. But these were not normal times. The very same day as Muhammad's comment, General Maxwell Taylor had answered Senator Wayne Morse's attack on the war by stating that Hanoi would be only too pleased with such dissension in the United States. And Muhammad's comment was viewed as just that—dissension.

The reaction was immediate. Overnight Muhammad became a national subject, newspaper headlines blaring out "A Tool of Hanoi" and every politician worthy of his soapbox denouncing him. Congressman L. Mendel Rivers of South Carolina even threatened to conduct an investigation of the entire Selective Service System, Louisville's in particular.

But Ali's troubles had only just begun.

Ali's next fight was tentatively scheduled to be for the unification of the world heavyweight championship. See, the World Boxing Association (WBA), citing something about a return bout being against their rules—although it seemed to me to be a case of selective application since they had sanctioned an earlier return bout between Liston and Patterson—had stripped Muhammad of his crown for fighting a return bout against Liston. They then staged a "championship" bout between Eddie Machen and Ernie Terrell for *their* title early in 1965, with Terrell winning a fifteen-round decision.

However, there was a suspicion that the WBA had taken Muhammad's title away because of his conversion to Islam. Especially since almost immediately after Muhammad's announcement of his conversion, WBA president Ed Lassman had said, "Clay is a detriment to the boxing world. Clay's general conduct is provoking worldwide criticism and is setting a very poor example for the youth of the world. The conduct of the champion before and after winning the title has caused my office to be deluged with letters of torrid criticism from all over the world."

Whatever the reason, whether because of the WBA rules or merely because of boxing politics at work, there were now two heavyweight champions and a desire to once again unify the crown.

And so the Ali-Terrell fight for the reunification of the title was made, to be held in New York. However, the New York State Athletic Commission found that Terrell had been seen in what they called "undesirable company" (read: the mob) and for "reasons detrimental to boxing" banned the fight from being held in New York. With that the fight was quickly moved to Chicago. But Muhammad's "Viet Cong" remarks were the stuff of which political capital is made, and now it was the turn of sanctimonious politicians to make such capital. First it was Illinois Governor Otto Kerner who, feigning moral outrage, labeled his comments "disgusting." Then Richard J. Daley, mayor of Chicago, got into the act saying, "I hope it won't be held in Chicago, and I am confident the commission will take the proper action." With that the Illinois Commission banned the fight on the grounds of "moral turpitude or action detrimental to boxing on the part of fighters," pending a hearing.

But even before a hearing, Ali fanned the flames, saying, "If they'd just let me fight, I would pay for two modern fighter planes in two fights or I could pay the salaries of 100,000 men."

The hearing was called merely to hear Ali "apologize" for his "unpatriotic" statements. Not surprisingly, Ali refused, saying, "I'm not apologizing for nothing like that because I don't have to." Then, claiming the commissioners were taunting him by calling him "Mr. Clay," he walked out of the meeting. And out of Chicago as well.

The fight was now shopped around with Louisville, Pittsburgh, Bangor, and even Huron, South Dakota, all taking a pass, refusing to host it. Finally, the promoters took it north of the border, first to Montreal, then to Edmonton, and finally to Toronto, where it came to rest.

However, a funny thing happened to the fight on its way to Toronto: Ernie Terrell pulled out, claiming a "contract dispute." With a site and a date, March 29, 1966, Muhammad needed an opponent, and who better than the Canadian heavyweight champion and Toronto native George Chuvalo?

Chuvalo was one tough customer. Called "The Washerwoman" by Ali— I guess because in his fight with Mike DeJohn he had KO'd him with a series of punches that looked as if he were scrubbing clothes. Sportscaster Larry Merchant said his best punch was "a left jaw to the right glove," and it may have been, along with a left to the right jaw. But whatever it was that Muhammad hit him with that night he kept coming back and back and back. Ali never came close to flooring the granite-chinned contender who had never been knocked down in his previous forty-eight fights and was, in Muhammad's words, "one of the toughest men I ever faced." Still, Muhammad won at least thirteen of the fifteen rounds on all three scorecards. And the fight as well.

With a political draft call-up hanging over his head and his Viet Cong remarks having made him a political lightning rod in the United States, Muhammad's promoters decided to take him abroad and mapped out a grand European tour for him. First stop: Great Britain and a return bout with Henry Cooper.

The Cooper rematch, to be held in London's Arsenal Soccer Stadium, was Britain's first heavyweight championship fight since 1907 when Tommy

Burns knocked out another British battler, Gunner Moir, who had assumed the legendary position realized by so many English heavyweights throughout history—horizontal. After fifty-nine years, a heavyweight championship bout was being fought again in the cradle of boxing, England, and was being called "The Fight of the Century" by promoter Jack Solomons.

Solomons looked to Ali to provide the wattage for the fight and Muhammad didn't disappoint. Unlike the first time he had come over to England to fight Cooper when he had received an underwhelming reception, this time he was treated like a "bloomin'" rock star, adoring fans besieging him everywhere he went. I remember being at the Towers on Brewer Street where the fans punctured the tires of his limo just to make sure they would be able to see him. We had to run back into the hotel rather than face the hordes of British fans turned stargazers in the streets outside the hotel.

Television, too, got into the act with ABC filming Muhammad strolling down London boulevards sporting a formal cutaway, bowler hat, and cane, doing his best impersonation of Fred Astaire. All this was scored to Roger Miller's then-popular number, "England Swings Like a Pendulum Do," and scheduled to run thirty minutes leading up to the fight itself.

However, another one of my fighters, Jimmy Ellis, obviously had not been in the ABC production meeting and in the semifinal had taken out a boxer from Fiji named Lewine Waga in one round. With the sudden ending of the final prelim, officials of the British Boxing Board of Control made their way to our dressing room to notify us that, according to the rules of the commission, we were to go on in two minutes.

It was at this moment that the man Ali called "HOW-WARD CO-SELL"—ABC's Howard Cosell—sprang into action. Making his way to Ali's dressing room, he implored Ali to save the beginning thirty minutes of the ABC show, pleading, "Muhammad, remember that great footage we had of you walking around London? Well, they're not going to be able to see it in the United States if you go out there now." That was all Ali had to hear. He stood in the dressing room for eighteen minutes while the crowd, which had been there since a little after six in the evening, now fidgeted in their seats after four hours of preliminaries. Ali never missed a chance like this. Cooper and the crowd could wait while fame called.

The Brits have always had this thing with heroic failures, and Cooper's "almost" win in the first fight was one of those, along with the Charge of the Light Brigade and Dunkirk. This time they turned out in droves, hoping against hope that their 'Enry could land his 'ammer and erase that "almost." But it was not to be as, just as in their first fight, Cooper's brittle eye split open in the sixth round and the fight was stopped.

The scene after the fight was not a pretty one. There were what Muhammad described as "a few little title fights outside the ring," but they were worse than that, spilling over into the ring. Immediately after the fight was halted by referee George Smith, several groups of Teddy Boys jumped over benches and stormed the ring, screaming racial slurs. Ali just looked at the rowdy mob, one of whom cuffed him, saying later, "I thought it was just someone offering me congratulations."

Two-and-a-half months later Muhammad fought in England again, this time against the hapless British heavyweight Brian London.

This time ABC put together a pre-package to the tune of "A Foggy Day in London Town," which included insert shots of Muhammad doing roadwork with Jimmy Ellis to the line, "I met the morning with such alarm," and a musing shot of Ali to "How long I wondered could this thing last. . . ."

But the supposed piéce de rèsistance was to be a shot of Brian London over the line "for suddenly I saw you there." For that Howard Cosell flew up to London's training camp in Blackpool. Sitting London down on a bench next to Cosell, the interview began with Cosell saying, "Brian, they say you're a patsy, a dirty fighter, that you have no class, that you're just in there for the ride and a fast payday. And that you have no chance against Ali. What do you say to that?" London, who knew neither Cosell nor his technique of always attempting to provoke his subject, screamed, "Go fuck yourself!" "No, no, no," shouted the producer of the segment. "Those really weren't Howard's descriptions of you, they were the opinions of others." "Oh, I see," said the more-than-slightly-confused London, who really didn't. So when the same question-statement was repeated, he flared back, "Whoever said that can go fuck themselves." Scrub that portion of the pre-fight program.

As for the fight itself, the man whom Ingemar Johansson claimed "couldn't beat my sister" and whose manager boasted "He might be a bum, but he's a good bum," went down under Ali's barrage of punches in the third round. TV producer Chet Forte, who had planned an entire "Wide World of Sports" show around the fight, hollered over the production line from New York to ringside, "Does he look like he's going to get up?" Joe

Asceti, the production assistant, took one look at the inert form lying just above him and hollered back, "Well, his tongue's hanging out of his mouth, and he's drooling, and his eyes are white . . . but other than that, he's all right."

There was one more fight left on Muhammad's European itinerary, this one in Frankfurt, Germany, against the European heavyweight champion Karl Mildenberger, pronounced "Milton-berger" by Ali. However, it was not only Mildenberger's name Ali had trouble with; he also had trouble with his style. For Mildenberger was a southpaw, the first Ali had ever faced, and the first left-hander ever to fight for the heavyweight title. From the moment Ali walked to the center of the ring and was met by a *right* jab he had difficulty coping with Mildenberger. It wasn't until the middle rounds that Ali finally solved Mildenberger's style, going to his left instead of his right to evade his opponent's right-hand jabs. Pressing his attack rather than moving, Ali finally overcame Mildenberger and his style, knocking him out in the twelfth.

With no more worlds to conquer in Europe, having single-handedly decimated the ranks of European heavyweights, Ali headed home to face Cleveland "Big Cat" Williams. A big, powerful fighter, Williams possessed an impressive record, having won sixty-five of his seventy-one fights, fifty-one of those by knockout. And his punching power was reputed to be the equal of any heavyweight, past or present.

Besides his record and reputation, Williams also carried something else: a .357 magnum slug lodged in his body, compliments of a Texas State trooper who had taken exception to something Williams had said. That trooper was now one of the 35,460 at the Houston Astrodome, a new indoor record for a fight, cheering their local hero on.

However, it wasn't Williams's punching power that was on display, instead it was Ali's. After moving away from the pursuing Williams in the first minute of the fight, Ali threw a flurry of punches, shooting a left to the body, followed with three lefts to the head. As Williams, both hypnotized by the speed of the punches and paralyzed by their accuracy, stood there resembling Lot's wife, Ali rattled off eight bull's-eyes to Williams's head, bringing a trickle of blood. Ali proceeded to smear the flow of blood across the whole of Williams's face with a straight right, a hook, and another right, all thrown asfastasyoucanreadthis at the bell.

The second round began as the first had ended, with Ali connecting with a left and then a right reminiscent of the one he had caught Liston with at Lewiston, all accompanied by a five-step in-place tango maneuver he later called "The Ali Shuffle." Williams momentarily hung in midair and then fell to the canvas. Up at eight, Williams was met with a dizzying barrage of lefts and rights that sent him spiraling to the canvas. This time he was up at the count of five. Coming forward, the only gear he had, Williams was met with a left and right and fell in as broad a fall as any Hollywood stuntman had ever managed. As referee Harry Kessler counted over the spread-eagled form on the canvas, the bell rang to end the round—and save the Big Cat. At least, momentarily.

In the third Ali kept up his attack, nailing Williams with another left-right combination and sending the challenger to the canvas yet again. And again, incredibly, he arose. But as Williams stood exactly where he had arisen, making no attempt to defend himself, referee Kessler did the only thing he could, he stopped the fight. It was over at 1:08 of the third round. It hadn't been a great fight, but it had been one of Muhammad Ali's greatest performances.

There was one piece of unfinished business to attend to: Ernie Terrell, the "other" heavyweight champion. Terrell's advisors, who had abruptly pulled him out of their scheduled match earlier, now decided that if Mildenberger's unorthodox style had given Ali difficulty, then Terrell's equally unorthodox style would also give Ali some trouble. That and the fact that they believed Terrell possessed an equal or better jab than Ali led them to now make the match for the unified title.

However, we looked at Terrell a little differently, feeling that Terrell's style could be summed up in just two words: left jab. Ali even took it one step further, calling Terrell "The Octopus" for his jab-and-clutch methods.

But what Ali focused on most was that Terrell continued to call him "Cassius Clay." And that made me more than a little apprehensive about the fight. I had no fear of Muhammad losing under normal conditions. But personal feelings can get the best of a fighter and affect his judgment, and I always say you can never tell what will happen in a boxing match. However, I shouldn't have been so anxious about Ali. From the very start of the match, when Terrell came out and threw his first jab and missed, Ali was laughing at and taunting Terrell, almost in a cruel repeat of his performance against Patterson, only worse. By the fifth round it was clear that Terrell, who kept missing with his jab and throwing a sloppy right behind it, was in over his head. For the next ten rounds Ali, who had promised to "torture him . . . a clean knockout is too good for him" contented himself with throwing lightning-quick punches and "What's my name?" poison darts, more interested in protecting his name than his title. Between rounds I hollered, "He knows your name! Now, dammit, go out there and fight!" It was a painful fight to watch, made all the more painful by Ali, in a post-fight interview, wringing maximum humiliation out of the situation by gratuitously calling Terrell "a dog." Hardly a Hallmark sentiment. Still, it was a win, even if a painful one.

With a date set for Ali to report for induction in April, a hurry-up fight, just one month after his systematic destruction of Terrell, was made for Ali to defend against the WBA's number one contender, Zora Folley, in March 1967 in Madison Square Garden—the Garden's first heavyweight title bout since Ezzard Charles KO'd Lee Oma back in 1951.

Folley had been around forever, or so it seemed, so long in fact that nearly a decade before he had accused then heavyweight champion Floyd Patterson of ducking him. Now, with a record of seventy-one victories against seven losses and the number two ranking, he would get his shot.

The buildup to the fight was strangely subdued, the best Ali could come up with was "Folley's such a nice man with eight children, I'm glad he's getting a payday."

Ali also looked somewhat subdued in the fight as well, doing little in the first round but moving away from the advancing Folley on legs that seemed to have wings on them. By the second he was jabbing and in the fourth he dropped Folley with an overhand right. By the sixth, Folley looked as if he were searching for a place to fall as Ali stepped up his attack. Then, in the seventh, as the outclassed Folley tried mightily to hit Ali with a left, Ali planted a right to Folley's jaw and Folley went down in a heap. And out.

When he knocked out Folley, Muhammad looked like a million dollars because he was maturing. In other words, he was special in there. He had negated him, and Zora Folley was one heckuva fighter. He was a great counterpuncher, but he couldn't counter my kid.

Muhammad had had nine successful title defenses, more than Liston, Patterson, and Johansson put together, and a number of defenses surpassed only by Joe Louis and Tommy Burns. He was twenty-five years old and just reaching his prime. But because he had refused to play his hero's role the way the public demanded, the boxing establishment, unable to see him beaten in the ring, decided to beat him out of the ring by taking his title away from him. We never saw the best days of Muhammad Ali.

Ali arrived at the U.S. Armed Forces Examining and Entrance Station on Friday morning, April 28, 1967, along with twenty-five other young men, all summoned to face induction. After filling out the necessary paperwork and undergoing physicals, these men formed a line in front of a young lieutenant for one last ritual, the calling of their names and their stepping forward as a sign they had accepted induction. The officer called each potential recruit's name and told him to take the symbolic step forward. Finally came the call "Cassius Clay! Army!" No movement. Again came the call, this time, "Ali." Again, no movement. At this point another induction officer came into the room and led Ali to a private room on the third floor where he advised him of the penalty for refusing to volunteer for the draft: five years' imprisonment and a fine. Asked if he understood, Ali said he did. To give him another chance to respond to his name and step forward, Ali was escorted back into the first room where the other twenty-five men still stood. Again, in answer to his name, he stood stock-still.

One of the officers now told Ali to write out his reasons for refusing. Ali wrote: "I refuse to be inducted into the Armed Forces of the United States because I claim to be exempt as a minister of the religion of Islam."

You would have thought Muhammad Ali was a descendant of Jack the Ripper the way boxing commissions fell all over themselves in a rush to strip him of his title even before news of his refusal to step forward had been set in type for morning delivery. It was almost a patriotic chest-thumping contest to see who could strip him of his title the fastest. So much for that old phrase "innocent until proven guilty."

Even though politicians had made him their "red meat," newspapers had tarred and feathered him, and boxing's powers-that-be had stripped him of his most prized possession, Ali remained true to his convictions, standing up, if not stepping forward, for what he believed.

He responded to the storm swirling around his unbowed head in an interview in *Playboy*, saying, "Why should they ask me to put on a uniform, go ten thousand miles from home, and drop bombs and bullets on brown people in Vietnam while so-called Negro people in Louisville are treated like dogs? If I thought going to war would bring freedom and equality to twenty-two million of my people, they wouldn't have to draft me, I'd join tomorrow. But I either have to obey the laws of the land or the laws of Allah. I have nothing to lose by standing up and following my beliefs. We've been in jail for four hundred years."

His resistance to authority, which had seemingly started out as racial, soon widened its scope as more and more antiwar youngsters took his side and supported his stance.

When I was asked what I thought about Ali's refusal to step forward, I could only answer that, like millions of other Americans, I didn't understand the whole Vietnam situation. All I knew was that American boys were getting killed over there and we weren't even certain it was our fight. Now, don't get me wrong, I am as proud as anyone of being an American. And I would have accepted my own draft, as I had once before in World War II. But I can't honestly say how I would have felt if my own son, Jimmy, had been drafted. I thanked God he was too young and prayed he would never have to go to war.

As for Muhammad Ali, I respected him and I respected his religious beliefs. I couldn't help but feel that if the media hadn't hyped up the Nation of Islam angle, the authorities might have treated the whole affair differently. Muslims were not too common in America at the time, and maybe it was a case of being scared of the unknown.

I had heard of some well-known actors who, for one reason or another, had escaped the draft. And of others who had gotten deferments. And still others who went to Canada. So I'm still not sure what the obsession with Ali was all about. It seemed more than a little overblown to me, almost as if they were out to get him for more than just failing to step forward.

I tried to isolate the problem in the back of my mind and carry on the best way I could with my life, which meant working with my other fighters. But that did not mean I could block it out entirely.

I would miss Ali. For seven years we had a special something. Every day was an all-you-can-eat buffet, with him playing jokes on me. Like the time at a Los Angeles hotel where we both were staying in connecting rooms. He had this long cord, which went through our adjoining bathroom, and he would shake it to shake my blinds. All night long I heard this strange noise and was scared to death. What the hell was going on, I thought. We were on the twelfth floor and I'd look down, nothing there. All around, nothing. It was just Muhammad playing games on me. Another time he put a burning towel under my door. I called the hotel manager, telling him I smelled smoke and that he'd better get up here, pronto. He checked the whole floor and finally came back to me and said, "I'm sorry, Mr. Dundee, we can't find anything." Again, it was Muhammad playing his little games.

There would be many a night when I'd come back from a press conference or just being out with the guys and the irrepressible Ali, full of playfulness, would jump out of a closet with a white sheet over his head and scare the bejesus out of me, his eerie moans quickly giving way to belly laughs. Always there would be Muhammad, laughing at his own jokes. And I would take part in some of his shenanigans, like the time he asked me to put tape on his mouth for a photo opportunity. Nobody could put his finger in a pot and stir it with as much mischievous charm and enthusiasm as Ali.

I would also miss the way he stood up for me. Many times someone in Muhammad's ever-increasing circle of newfound friends would complain to him about having a "honky" like me so close to the champion. And he would defend me, saying it was all right. I even remember, once, when members of the Fruit of Islam, appointed to be his bodyguards, clustered too close around him at a press conference guarding him like the queen's jewels, and I suggested to him that it "didn't look right," that the reporters felt intimidated, and he agreed with me and asked them to leave. Muhammad always stood up for me, by me, and with me. I never heard a bad word from him.

No matter how well I had done with my other fighters, I was known and perhaps would always be known as Muhammad's trainer. He was the spotlight that shone on whatever other talent I had. Sure, Willie Pastrano, Carmen Basilio, Luis Rodriguez, and Ultiminio Ramos were the stars, but Ali was the moon. Know what I mean?

EIGHT

Ali's Exile—and Things to Do in the Meantime, in Between Time

Although my life had been dominated by the charismatic Muhammad Ali, I still had other fighters who were important to me, every one an individual.

There was Willie Pastrano. Or, more accurately, there once was Willie Pastrano. For Willie had retired back in 1965 after losing the light heavyweight championship to José Torres. Toward the end of his career, Willie had been messing around with some bad dudes. Willie attracted bad guys like honey attracts bees. I would see these weird guys hanging around the gym and I didn't like it. I barred them from going into his dressing room. They'd come crying to Willie, calling me a "square bear." Willie knew I was no "square," but I didn't go for those weirdos. I told him how I felt about his so-called friends, but he just laughed it off, saying the guys were okay and that they were just a little "way out." Later he would find they were no laughing matter.

After his retirement I began to hear stories that he was taking drugs. I called him, and although he was always flip when we spoke, he knew that I was concerned and that I'd be there if he ever needed me. And he did, calling me at all hours of the night, sometimes when he was hallucinating. Once he called me in the wee hours of the morning because he said there were "things" in his garden. Other times, it was other "things." Willie had a choice: carry on and sink deeper into the ugly and destructive pit or give up booze and drugs and rehabilitate himself. Sometimes he did and other times he just couldn't. But whatever he did, until the very end, he remained a friend, and nothing will ever replace the affection I held for him.

Another of my fighters was "Sugar" Ramos. Ramos had won the feather-weight title back on that tragic night in Los Angeles in 1963 when he knocked out Davey Moore, and then he lost it to Vicente Saldivar the following year. But even then he was having trouble making the feather-weight 126-pound limit, time putting pounds on his small, hard-muscled body. We decided that Ramos should campaign as a 135-pound light-weight where he met with immediate success, winning four straight fights and rising to the top of the division. Unfortunately, the champion atop the lightweight division was all-time great Carlos Ortiz, who beat Ramos twice—once in 1965 and again in July 1967, both times by KO. Ramos did a "Goodyear," boxingese for "retire," after the second Ortiz fight, but made a moderately successful comeback two years later before retiring again.

I also trained the great Luis Rodriguez, who had fought Emile Griffith three times for the welterweight title, winning one—although I thought the score should have been two wins for Rodriguez to one for Griffith. Luis had fought once more for the welterweight title, losing to Curtis Cokes in 1966, before taking his slick moves and outstanding skills upstairs to the middleweight division where, in 1969, he challenged Nino Benevenuti for the title. For ten rounds Luis moved, jabbed, and boxed his way to a sizeable lead. Benevenuti was one tough cat and, although tired, had strength enough to throw one desperation Hail Mary shot to the jaw of an equally tired Rodriguez in the eleventh and that was it. Luis fought on for another three years. But he was never the same Luis Rodriguez and retired in 1972 with 107 wins in 121 bouts and only thirteen losses—one, against Griffith, still disputed in my mind.

But if those fighters were so far beyond their primes they couldn't find them in their rearview mirrors, I still had one whose career was in front of him: Jimmy Ellis.

Jimmy, who had split two decisions with then–Cassius Clay in the amateurs, had served his apprenticeship as Muhammad's sparring partner. Now I abhor the words "sparring partner." I hate them because my kids work with each other, help each other. They are not sparring partners, per se, but really assistants.

And Muhammad Ali was the worst gym fighter I ever handled. He never looked to win a decision in the gym. In fact, if truth be known, he was the one who looked like the "sparring partner," if I may use the phrase in its accepted meaning. But believe you me, Jimmy Ellis was no sparring partner in the traditional sense.

From the beginning, when John L. Sullivan first introduced sparring partners into the world of boxing (with a fighter named Jack Ashton with whom he gave sparring exhibitions) most sparring partners' names were lost to the ages—or, when remembered at all, then only as having served as sparring partners for so-and-so.

The primary responsibility of sparring partners is to prepare "their" fighter for his upcoming bout. For instance, Jack Dempsey always had George Godfrey as his chief sparmate; Joe Louis, George Nicholson; Rocky Marciano, Keene Simmons; Sonny Liston, Amos "Big Train" Lincoln; George Foreman, Eddie "Bossman" Jones; and so on and so on. And sometimes a fighter might have more than one, each with a specific function, just as Jack Dempsey had six-foot-six-inch Bill Tate for strength, Jamaica Kid for brawling, and Panama Joe Gans for speed. Sparring partners may come and go, depending on how much punishment they can take or how useful they are in preparing their fighter for his fights. Not only are they in there for their employer's benefit—plus the good pay and food, as well as sharing in the reflected glory of their fighter—but many are in there to learn, as well, and maybe make a name for themselves.

Some sparring partners have used their experience as sparmates as a curtain raiser on their own careers. For instance, James J. Jeffries was Jim Corbett's chief sparmate. Ditto Jack Johnson, who served as a sparring partner for welterweight champ Joe Walcott. Likewise, Jersey Joe Walcott served as Joe Louis's. And, of course, Larry Holmes served as a sparring partner for Muhammad as well as for Joe Frazier, Jimmy Young, and Earnie Shavers.

Throughout history several sparmates have gone further than the men they were hired to help train. The most famous case was James J. Braddock, aka "The Cinderella Man." According to the story, Joe Gould had a prospect named Harry Galfund and an attractive offer from another manager to buy Galfund's contract. So Gould took the prospective purchaser to a gymnasium to show off Galfund's wares. Not finding anyone to spar with

Galfund, Gould picked an awkward unknown to go a few rounds with Galfund and the novice, who happened to be the young Braddock, displayed enough raw punching power to cost Gould the sale. Losing his chance to sell the contract of Galfund, Gould did the next best thing: he took over the managerial reins of the unknown novice and guided him to the heavyweight championship.

Another who learned about his prospective opponent was James J. Corbett, who, after sparring with the then-champion, John L. Sullivan, said, "I can beat this man. He's a sucker for a feint."

Perhaps the best example of a sparring partner learning at the knee of the man who had hired him was that of "Kid" McCoy, who was hired as a sparring partner by then–welterweight champion Tommy Ryan for his fight against Mysterious Billy Smith. Ryan not only taught McCoy some of the finer points of the game, he also taught him some of the more sadistic, trying out his kidney punch and other maneuvers on McCoy in preparation for his 1896 bout with Smith. Leaving Ryan's nest, McCoy was determined to get revenge on his tutor tormentor. He did, later that year, employing his newfound "corkscrew punch" to knock down Ryan no less than twelve times before KO'ing him in the fifteenth round.

"I got so I knew Ryan's every move," the man known as "The Real McCoy" would say. "He had a sound style, was an excellent athlete and a strong man. But there was nothing tricky about his stuff. He was a sound fighting man and born for the game, but I found out what he had in the training camp and knew what to do about it when I got Tommy in the ring."

Another who learned from his sparring sessions with Muhammad was Jimmy Ellis, who was to prove that old boxing adage: "Yesterday's sparring partner is tomorrow's potential champion."

The first time I laid eyes on Jimmy there wasn't much to look at. A skinny kid who weighed close to 150 pounds, he was beset by medical problems, not the least of which were painful carbuncles and chronic tonsil infections. I had a job nursing him back to health before I could even train him. Doing everything I could, I finally got him into shape and got him on the undercards of several Cassius Clay–hyphen–Muhammad Ali fights, ten times in all—including his one-round knockout of Johnny Persol on the semi to the Ali-Folley fight—gradually bringing him along. I thought his victory over Persol, a ranking light-heavyweight who had beaten Harold

Johnson and Bobo Olson, was an indication that he might make one hell-uva light-heavyweight. The best place, I thought, for him.

But Jimmy had other ideas. Still growing, he was now a heavyweight, even if at 190, soaking wet—that's just "90" in boxing lingo—he was a small heavy amongst the division's tall timber. He wanted to fight at heavy for the same reason Willie Sutton robbed banks: "'cause that's where the money was."

Then the World Boxing Association (WBA), which had fallen all over itself to strip Ali of his crown, announced an eight-man heavyweight box-off to determine the champion for their newly vacated title. Those selected to participate were: Floyd Patterson, Ernie Terrell, Oscar Bonavena, Jerry Quarry, Thad Spencer, Karl Mildenberger, Joe Frazier, and Jimmy. And when Frazier's manager, Yank Durham, decided to take a pass on the tourney, the WBA added Leotis Martin.

In his first bout as a full-fledged heavyweight, Jimmy knocked out Leo-tis Martin and then followed that up four months later with a decision win over Oscar Bonavena. In the finals of the tournament, he defeated Jerry Quarry. Three fights as a heavyweight, three wins, and one "world" championship—at least that part of the world overseen by the WBA. Not bad for a heavyweight newcomer!

After watching the WBA tourney, Teddy Brenner, the Garden match-maker, came away saying, "The elimination tournament was a real success . . . it eliminated everybody." Well, not quite everybody. There was still Jimmy Ellis. And Joe Frazier.

Six weeks before Ellis had captured the WBA's version of their "vacant" heavyweight title, Joe Frazier had won the New York State version of the same—New York having stripped Ali quicker than the WBA, if that were possible. New York's clueless commissioner, Ed Dooley, in announcing the participants of its fight to fill the vacancy had gotten caught up in his mental underwear and identified them as Joe Frazier and "Buddy" Mathis. Be it "Buddy" or Buster (his real name), it made no difference to Frazier as he knocked out his Olympic rival in eleven rounds.

Now, with two "world" champions and public opinion running in favor of one, Ellis and Frazier were signed to fight for the whole enchilada, the unified heavyweight championship of the world.

The bout was scheduled for Madison Square Garden in February 1970. And two weeks before the bout was to take place, Muhammad Ali announced his retirement, and promised to give his *Ring* magazine championship belt to the winner.

While most of those professional pundits and guess-your-weight peddlers who traffic in predictions made Frazier an overwhelming favorite, I thought that Jimmy's style was perfect for Frazier. Joe was made for Jimmy. But, then again, I remember once thinking that the *Titanic* was faster than the iceberg. For two rounds it looked like I was the one who might have had the crystal ball as Jimmy outboxed, outmoved, and outmaneuvered Joe. Then, in the third, Joe unloaded that left hook of his and Jimmy staggered backward, halfway across the ring and into the ropes. He momentarily recovered, but the fight was over right then and there. Late in the fourth, Joe cornered Ellis and nailed him with several trip-hammer lefts, flooring Jimmy. Jimmy got up, but was in no condition to defend himself. Trying to keep Frazier off him, he succeeded momentarily. Then, just before the bell, Frazier unloaded with one of his patented howitzers, a left hook flush on Jimmy's jaw and Jimmy went down in sections, his foot grotesquely wedged under his body.

How he got up I'll never know, but get up he did and made his dazed way back to the corner, the round over. I asked him how he was and he responded, "Fine," which all fighters do regardless of whether they are or not. Chuck Wepner, upon once being asked by a referee, "How many fingers do I have up?" answered, "How many guesses do I get?" The ref, believing he was fine, allowed the fight to go on. However, I didn't think Jimmy was "fine," although he told me in the corner "Geez, Angie, I was a little dazed, but I'm fine. I was only put down once." That did it! Hell, if the kid didn't know how many times he had been knocked down, why should I break the news to him? So I told him, "Jimmy, you were down twice, but you only remember once. That's why I'm stopping the fight."

Frazier was now the recognized world heavyweight champion. But there was still an elephant in the room—or division, if you will—the man Budd Schulberg called "The Once and Future Champ": Muhammad Ali. Now his name was being mentioned as the only logical opponent for Joe Frazier.

In the prime of his life and at the peak of his career, with his title stripped, his passport revoked, and banned from boxing, Muhammad Ali was suddenly without a way to earn a living. His legal bills appealing his conviction, which had come down two months after his refusal to step forward for induction—a $10,000 fine and a five-year prison sentence—were bleeding him dry. Left with little more than rent money and hope, he refused to carry a beggar's cup, continuing to look for ways to keep afloat and cope with his uneasy existence, one away from the spotlight he craved and away from the millions he had once earned.

Here entered Gene Kilroy, a class act if there ever was one. I had first met Gene after Ali's fight with Zora Folley at the Garden. Well, to be truthful, I didn't so much meet him as shoo him out of the dressing room after the fight with a "no . . . no . . . no," thinking he was just another of the horde of well-wishers trying to crowd into the dressing room. Little did I know that he had befriended Ali, then Clay, at the Rome Olympics. Nor that he would play an important role in Ali's being able to make it through his three-and-a-half-year exile.

Gene had been an executive with the Philadelphia Eagles and was now with MGM. Through his many contacts, Gene was able to bring Ali to the attention of Richard Fulton, who handled college lecture tours. Fulton booked Ali for speaking engagements at colleges all over the country, including Yale, Harvard, and Howard. The usual fee for Ali, now a hot property because of the growing "unrest" of the 1960s, was between $2,000 and $3,000 an appearance. And, said Gene, calling him "a good, decent human being," after each appearance Ali would hurry down to the Western Union office to wire home the money to his mom and dad. (Back in 1962 the famous William Morris Talent Agency had Cassius Clay under contract but let him go thinking he had no future. And now, six years later, a poll found that only Senators Edmund Muskie and Edward Kennedy were more sought-after speakers on the college circuit than Ali. How ironic!)

Ali's college appearances gave him a platform and widened his audience, his one-time racial politics becoming the social politics of the late 1960s as more and more young men and women were becoming disillusioned with America's involvement in Vietnam. With the counterculture revolution going on, they held Ali up, not so much as a spokesman but as a symbol for standing up to the system. And stand up he did, never with a touch of self-pity, but with a strength of character vowing to "stick to my religious beliefs 1,000 percent regardless of what happens."

His college tour continued to keep Ali's name in the news and got him several offers for appearances, one of which was the lead in the short-lived

Broadway show, *Buck White*. Another offer that came his way was to star in the movie *Heaven Can Wait*, a remake of the 1940s movie with Robert Cummings starring as a boxer who dies in an accident and comes back to life to win the championship. But the Nation of Islam turned the role down, and although the movie was ultimately remade, it was Warren Beatty starring as a football quarterback instead of Ali as a boxer.

Another "appearance" made by Ali was on the cover of *Esquire*, posing as the martyr Saint Sebastian, complete with arrows piercing his body to signify his martyrdom. But this presented a problem not dissimilar to the one in the *Heaven Can Wait* offer. Before the photo shoot, Ali, studying a museum postcard of the painting that hung in the Metropolitan, blurted out, "This cat's a Christian!" George Lois, who was then in the process of setting up the photo shoot, could only answer with a "Holy Moses, you're right, Champ." And before Lois could affix any arrows to his body, Ali made a beeline to the phone to call his religious advisor, Herbert Muhammad. After explaining the pose, Ali expressed his concerns about using a Christian saint to represent his martyrdom. After a long discussion about its propriety, Ali hung up and said it was okay. A resounding success, the cover was ultimately reproduced and sold as a protest poster.

The only "fight" Muhammad was able to get during his exile was a computerized one against Rocky Marciano. The fight had come about because of a computerized elimination tournament conceived by Miami businessman Murray Worner that matched sixteen heavyweight champions of different eras against one another. But when Muhammad lost in the very first round to old-timer Jim Jeffries, he sued Worner, saying, "I've never been defeated, and they won't let me fight to earn a living anymore. My name is all I've got. Now somebody is trying to ruin that, too."

Faced with Muhammad's suit, Worner came up with another idea: instead of the tournament being staged (good word, that!) on radio, why not film it and show it on television? Better yet, why not in theaters on closed-circuit? And so he put together a "reel" fight called *The Superfight* between Muhammad and former heavyweight champion Rocky Marciano—sort of a "Rocky Marciano–Muhammad Ali Fight of the Century." The "fight" was 70 one-minute rounds, head shots pulled, but body shots fair game, with seven different endings played out against a blank background in a Miami studio with my brother Chris as the referee (in patent leather shoes!). And, just like old times, yours truly was in Muhammad's corner with an announcer dubbing in the blow-by-blow "action" afterward. And although Rocky was to say, "It's all bullshit," overflow crowds in 850 closed-circuit locales bought it lock, stock, and ending—which, in the United States, had Rocky winning by a knockout and, in England, Muhammad stopping Rocky on cuts. For all this Muhammad was paid the generous amount of $999.99!

Throughout it all there were rumors of a potential Joe Frazier–Muhammad Ali fight. I had heard rumors of Kilroy, Herbert Muhammad, and even Harold Conrad and Mike Malitz of Main Bouts crisscrossing the country in search of a place where Muhammad could fight a real fight, where he could get a license to fight Joe Frazier—or anyone for that matter.

Getting a license, however, was no guarantee of a fight. It was almost as if Muhammad had become radioactive—every time a license was granted he suddenly became untouchable. In Mississippi, one of the few states not belonging to the WBA, Governor John B. Williams had issued a license to Muhammad to fight in Jackson with plans to donate the live gate to the Salvation Army. But later Williams would deny he had issued a license, even though Muhammad had it in his possession. In Charleston, where Muhammad was supposed to fight an exhibition for charity, the local City Council called it off. In Seattle, threats of a boycott by the local chapter of the American Legion, which claimed that "even if that unpatriotic slacker is given a license, no one would show up," forced the cancellation of a scheduled fight. It was like that all over the country as the American Legion, the Veterans of Foreign Wars, and White Citizen Councils lined up to proclaim that they would boycott any fight of Muhammad Ali's and would shut down any arena that dared to stage such a fight. In all, it was estimated that the efforts of those seeking to stage a fight for Muhammad had been turned down more than seventy times, even after a license had been issued. As Harold Conrad said, "Every time we were finished with the preliminaries, word would leak out and we were dead."

Suddenly there was a breakthrough and in the heart of the south—Atlanta, Georgia, of all places. There the head of a spice-processing firm, whom Ali described as having "the right complexion and right connections," called upon a friend of his, Senator Leroy Johnson, who, not incidentally, was of the black persuasion. Johnson, who had become the first black politician to be elected to office in Atlanta in ninety-two years and helped put the current white mayor of Atlanta in office, went to the mayor and got the "okay" to hold an Ali-Frazier fight in Atlanta. There was no Georgia State Boxing Commission, and Atlanta didn't have one to speak of. Or to. A sponsoring group called "House of Sports" was formed, Muhammad Ali was issued a license to fight in Atlanta, and a date was set for October 26, 1970.

Only then was Frazier's camp contacted. Frazier's manager, Yank Durham, first complained that "nobody ever talked to us about money." Then, skeptical of Ali's chances against his fighter after a three-and-a-half-year layoff, he said, "Prove you're ready for us, then we'll fight you." Durham's turndown, plus the fact that Frazier had already committed to a title fight against light-heavyweight champion Bob Foster, meant that an alternative had to be found. And quickly. As luck would have it, they found one in "Irish" Jerry Quarry, the number one–rated contender to Frazier's title.

Harold Conrad, somehow finding the silver lining in lining up Quarry instead of Frazier as Ali's comeback opponent, said, "Why Quarry is even better than Frazier. Whitey's got to have someone to pull for, and Quarry, let's face it, is paler than Joe." And Ali, showing he was in his old verbal, if not fighting, form added: "Great! You got it! Nigger and draft dodger against the Great White Hope. That'll sell a lot of tickets."

For Ali, it was his return to the ring, his coming out of exile, his "Second Coming"—a triumphal march led everywhere by Bundini Brown who, in that amped-up voice of his, led the parade screaming, "PRETENDERS, GET OFF THE GODDAMN THRONE! THE LAMB'S COME TO CLAIM HIS OWN!" For Ali's fans it was a coming-out party, a rite of passage as black America entered the mainstream. Everyone who was anyone was there, lending a festive Mardi Gras air to the fight. They had come to Atlanta to cheer their idol on. To them he was forever twenty-five years old, and they had come to see him recycle those electric-quick skills that had made him "The Greatest" forty-three months before.

All during the week of the fight Ali had mingled with his well-wishers, dealing out autographs and handshakes. One policeman assigned to "protect" our group came over to us and said, "Champ, if you don't mind, we're going to double the guards around you." But I had seen some of those guarding Ali shove some of those wanting autographs away, almost starting a fight, and told him, "There's no fence around Ali. There's no barrier. He takes to the people and the people take to him." Ali and the people were one that week.

Ali tirelessly glad-handed his fans, handing out autographs and greeting one and all. Forty minutes before the fight, when he should have been over at the arena preparing for Quarry, he was standing in front of the Regency Hyatt Hotel giving out passes to people without tickets and helping to load them onto the buses.

Unable to renew his unrenewable youth, Ali's skills had declined during his enforced layoff. You could see it from the opening bell. Little things, but things that nonetheless told me he was a little bit rusty and no longer the Ali of old. His timing was off, his jabs and uppercuts weren't there, he had openings he saw but couldn't capitalize on, he couldn't quite pull the trigger, and, by the end of the third, he was bordering on exhaustion. Still, two right hands had inflicted a deep gash over Quarry's left eye, a gash that went right down to the bone, causing the fight to be stopped at the end of the third. Despite reporters at ringside falling all over themselves writing that Ali was "back," I knew he would need a lot more work before he faced Joe Frazier. As famed writer Budd Schulberg said, "He may have gone back a step . . . but he was good!" But just being "good" wasn't good enough for Frazier.

After the Quarry fight, Ali quickly became licensed in states that had previously denied him one. One of those was New York where Ali challenged the New York State Athletic Commission's denial by arguing that their decision was a violation of his Fourteenth Amendment rights and that the commission had licensed an assorted group of felons, from murderers to military deserters. The judge hearing the case found the commission's refusal to grant Ali a license "astonishing" and ruled in Ali's favor.

Having his license reinstated, the way was now clear for Ali to fight in New York, at the Garden, against the ponderous and awkward Argentine bull Oscar Bonavena—nicknamed "Ringo" because Garden publicity head John F. X. Condon had heard him singing "I Want to Hold Your Hand." Bonavena was one tough customer, a rough barrel-chested do-anything-you-can-to-win fighter who had twice gone the limit with Joe Frazier, even knocking Joe down twice in their first fight.

The fight was scheduled for Madison Square Garden for December 7, a date which didn't sink in initially. We would soon realize that not only was it the "day that would live in infamy," but it was also a day that would be as controversial as Muhammad Ali himself. Letters poured in, all carrying messages like, "You're making a mockery of the day you helped disgrace" and "They should put you in jail on December 7, not in the ring."

A New York State legislator went on record denouncing the fight and calling for the mayor of New York to stop what he called "a disgrace to the people of New York to allow a draft dodger to perform on the anniversary of the Japanese attack on Pearl Harbor." And one newspaper's editorial even called for "War veterans to finish the job of destroying the Garden," saying that "any place which harbors such an insult to those who died at Pearl Harbor isn't worth keeping."

Harry Markson, the Garden's director of boxing, was concerned that "they" as he put it, whoever "they" were, "threaten to boycott us unless we kill the fight." Nevertheless, two weeks before the fight every seat in the house was sold out. It was to be the biggest gate ever for the Garden, threatened boycott or no.

The night of the fight, with the largest force of security guards in Garden history patrolling the streets surrounding the world's most famous arena—and even inside where every seat was searched after bomb threats were received—we decided to stay in our hotel until it was time to go over. There Ali received several fans and made drawings of his prediction—a KO in nine rounds.

As we made our way over to the Garden, wouldn't you know it, Ali decided to get out of the cab and take a subway the rest of the way. And when he finally arrived at the fighters' entrance, he turned to the crowd that had followed him and personally escorted each and every one in through the door as his personal guest while thousands were being turned away at the front entrance.

In the dressing room we went over last-minute details. All I did was make Muhammad aware of what to look for, like reminding him of what Yank Durham had warned us about Bonavena, namely that he would throw elbows, butt heads, hit below the belt, behind the head, and do anything he could not just to win but to "muss" him up. But Muhammad would handle it on his own. I never programmed him.

As Bundini put on Ali's robe, Ali turned and said, "Bundini, don't shout so loud out there," which may have been a futile request since Bundini, who took a B_{12} shot before every fight to calm his nerves, was incapable of calming himself once the bell rang.

As we made our way down the aisle to the roar of the crowd, something odd struck me. Maybe I was wrong, but I could swear I hadn't heard the playing of "The Star-Spangled Banner." I found out later they hadn't played it, probably fearful that because of the commotion over the fight being held on December 7 it might set off the crowd.

Once the bell sounded, Bonavena came rushing out of his corner. With virtually no balance and little style, he threw punches from everywhere except his ass. And, at times, it seemed as if he was throwing them from there, too. Ali danced away, but Bonavena kept coming, again with that unorthodox style of his, which was really no style at all, just bullying his way inside. Awkward and rugged, it seemed as if Ali had underestimated him and his strength. Ali's timing was off as he missed punches he usually connected with. He was fighting the wrong fight. Then, in the predicted round, the ninth, Ali went all out. But it was Bonavena who hurt Ali in that round, shaking him up with a desperation left that gave Muhammad a "buzz" he hadn't felt since the first Cooper fight. The fifteenth and final round came, and Bonavena's corner, sensing he was behind, sent him out to score a knockout. Instead, as he kept his head up in harm's way, an Ali left hook caught him solidly—one Ali told me later even jarred him—and Bonavena went down. Now Bundini was screaming, "Take him out! Take him out! Take the wrinkles out of his face!" And Ali, almost standing over the fallen Bonavena, floored him twice more to end it all. It was the first time in his career of fifty-four fights that Bonavena had been knocked out.

Now only Joe Frazier stood between Ali and *his* crown.

NINE

"The Fight": March 8, 1971

Ali-Frazier! But was Ali ready, *really* ready for Frazier? After viewing him against Jerry Quarry and Oscar Bonavena, one writer thought that, at least for one minute each round, he was the Ali of old—the 1967 model. Another thought he was great, but not the man Budd Schulberg had called "a genius fighter" before his forty-three-month exile. Looking at the two fights I thought he could once again be the Clay-Ali of old, the super-talented boxer who had defied description, the one with the specialized intelligence and radar-like moves no heavyweight ever had. But, I wondered if the hinted-at March date, just three months after his bruising fight against Bonavena, would give us enough time to rejuvenate those once-great talents diminished in part by time and inactivity, talents he would need to beat Frazier.

I would have liked more time to hone those skills and, if possible, make the new Ali as close as possible to the old Ali. But the wheels had already started turning with both Herbert Muhammad and Yank Durham shopping the fight around. One of those who answered was talent agent Jerry Perenchio. Realizing the value of the fight, Perenchio decided that since the two participants wanted $6 million, $3 million apiece (and by his figures he thought they were worth $4 million), he would offer $5 million for "the outright purchase of all rights to the fight—down to the trunks and gloves."

Perenchio's offer was not only listened to but also encouraged by the managements of both fighters. With the backing of financier Jack Kent Cooke and the inclusion of Madison Square Garden, the deal was signed, sealed, and to be delivered at a press conference at Toots Shor's.

And so there I was, twenty-two years after I had first visited Toots Shor's, back in the old watering hole again at the press conference for what Madison Square Garden Vice President Alvin Cooperman had already called "The Fight." As I looked around the room, I could identify many of the same newspapermen I had once shared tables, drinks, and stories with—Shirley Povich, Jack Cuddy, Bob Waters, Al Buck, and others. Only now, associated with Muhammad Ali, I was no longer their "go-to" guy for stories. Instead, I was their second banana, a mere footnote. In ten years I got one interview. After the kid got through with them they were dead, there was no paper left in their notepads after he rope-a-doped them with his quotes, so I never got a word in edgewise.

After giving me a quick "How-ya-doin', Angie," they clustered around the table at the front of the room trying to get close enough to hear the nonstop quote machine drop a few their way. They needn't have worried 'cause you could hear him across the room, for no cover charge, mouthing pet phrases like, "Now we'll see who the real champ is" and "Look at me, I'm pretty, not a mark on me," and "If he whups me, I'll crawl across the ring and kiss his feet." If I had a dollar for every time I had heard those lines, I'd have been a millionaire. At least Ali's mouth was in shape.

Now, as New York State Boxing Commissioner Ed Dooley took his place at the head table between Ali and Frazier, trying at first to keep the two apart and then to ignore them as if he were missing the festivities still going on at the bar in the next room, a well-dressed gentleman entered the room, unnoticed by all: Jerry Perenchio.

As Perenchio attempted to address the reporters, photographers, and assembled hangers-on, he was constantly interrupted by Ali's chatter. Turning to Ali, he said with a firm voice, "For $5 million, Ali, I think I have the right to talk," pause, "uninterrupted." For a second Ali was quiet.

That silence lasted only until Perenchio began to present the bottom-line figures, rattling off numbers, all with the sound of the *ka-ching* of a cash register, as he vowed to "cut up and sell every part of the carcass, just like whaling." When he announced that the net would be somewhere in the neighborhood of $40 million, Ali broke his silence to shout over to Frazier, "Joe, we've been had!"

Muhammad's jawing had just begun. He called Frazier everything from an "Uncle Tom" to a "chump" and because, as he said, Frazier "talks about he's hot, he always talks about he's gonna come out smokin'," he came up with a poem:

Joe's gonna come out smokin'.
And I ain't gonna be jokin'.
I'll be pecking and a pokin'
Pouring water on his smokin'.
This might shock and amaze ya,
But I'm gonna retire Joe Fraz-yah.

Frazier didn't get caught up in the war of words, saying only, "He calls me an 'Uncle Tom' and I call him a phony." Later, during one phone call between the two filmed by the hair tonic Vitalis as part of the prefight hoopla, the two came as close as they ever would to exchanging words. And insults. Their conversation went something like this:

Ali: "Hey Joe, will you be smokin' that night?"

Joe: "I'll be smokin' right on you."

Ali: "Well, you gonna be smokin' and I ain't gonna be jokin', I'll be a-peckin' and a-pokin' pouring water on your smokin'."

Joe: "The rest of those fighters, you jived them. You can't jive me. And you can't scare me. Hey, Clay . . . hey, Clay. . . ."

Ali: "What'd you call me?"

Joe: "Clay!"

Ali: "Why do you call me Clay?"

Joe: " 'Cause that's your name."

Ali: "You gettin' yourself in trouble with the brothers. You shouldn't call me that name. Even white people call me Muhammad now."

Joe: "You ain't nothin' but a big phony."

Ali: "Well, I'm just sick and tired of it. I'm through with you. I'll see you fight night, boy! Listen, boy! I got somethin' for you and I want you to come out smokin'. You hear me. Listen to me. I'm gonna hold you to it."

Joe: "Yeah, yeah, yeah, chump. Go ahead, chump."

And with a last "shit" to punctuate his words, Frazier hung up. Click! But Ali wasn't finished. Besides, I don't think he wanted anyone to know Frazier had hung up on him. Clearly stung, Ali kept right on going. "I'm gonna talk to you when I whup you," he said. "Now you know I'm crazy. I'll see you fight night. Bye." Click!

Ali walked away from the telephone, barely managing to mask his rage. Visibly wincing at the disrespect Joe had shown him by calling him "Clay," he sputtered angrily to anyone who would listen, "It's getting serious now. If he keeps calling me 'Clay,' I'm gonna have to make him say my name! It's getting serious."

Trying to psyche out your opponent, or, as it used to be called, "getting their goat," is a sometimes thing. Sometimes it works; sometimes it doesn't.

Go all the way back, as some of the old-timers used to tell it, of how James J. Corbett got John L. Sullivan's goat before their heavyweight championship battle. Sullivan, as was his habit as well as his right, demanded to come into the ring last when he took on Corbett. But Corbett had other ideas, and as he came down the aisle and climbed the stairs to the ring, he put one foot through the ropes as if to enter the ring. Sullivan, upon seeing this, gave him a second or so and then entered the ring, only to find that Corbett had suckered him into entering first, not last, by pulling his foot back out of the ring in sort of a do-si-do fashion. Corbett had faked John L. out of his habit and his shorts. And Sullivan, so irate at the actions of Corbett, spent most of the fight just trying to take Corbett's head off with his huge right hand rather than boxing. In the process, Sullivan came out second even if he had entered first, being carried out, feet first, after twenty-one rounds.

But such baiting is not confined to the ring nor to the heat of battle. It can happen anytime. Like when the then-champion Primo Carnera and contender Max Baer appeared in the movie *The Prize Fighter and the Lady*. In the two boxers' first meeting, Madcap Maxie jumped to his feet to greet Carnera, hollering, "Hello, you big gigolo!" at the same time mussing the champ's hair with a none-too-gentle rub. Not used to being treated like that, Carnera never got over the snub, one he wore in the ring when the two finally battled for the title, which Baer won, doing more than merely mussing up Da Preem's hair.

Not all such goat-getting works, however. Like the time Tony Canzoneri fought Jimmy McLarnin in the Garden. "Canzi," as was his habit, always wanted to occupy his "lucky" corner—the corner on the Fiftieth Street side of Madison Square Garden—believing it to be his good luck charm. But McLarnin's manager, Pop Foster, insisted that he, too, wanted the Fiftieth Street corner, so a coin was flipped by a deputy commission for the right to have the right corner. Canzoneri won the toss and the corner as well as the fight that night with a brilliant effort. Afterward Canzoneri said, "McLarnin didn't care what corner he sat in. He just wanted to get my goat." Apparently, he lost that battle, too.

Fight writer José Torres once wrote that Ali begins "throwing psychological punches long before throwing a physical one." (Future generations of sociologists may very well identify those "psychological punches" as the beginning of trash talking.) Many opponents had fallen under the weight of those "psychological punches." But not Frazier. By hanging up, Frazier had acted as no one ever had before in the face of Ali's psyche job. It was almost as if he had not lived up to his part of the bargain of serving as a punching bag for Ali's verbal abuse, instead giving out some of his own. To Ali it was unthinkable.

In the weeks leading up to the fight, Ali continued his one-note assault on Frazier, saying things like: "The only people rooting for Joe Frazier are white people in suits, Alabama sheriffs, and members of the Ku Klux Klan. I'm fighting for the little man in the ghetto. . . . Joe Frazier is too ugly to be champ. Joe Frazier is too dumb to be champ. The heavyweight champion should be smart and pretty like me. . . . Anybody black who thinks Frazier can whup me is an Uncle Tom." He continued to salt his barbs with words like *ignorant, dumb, ugly,* and, worst of all, *Uncle Tom* when referring to Frazier.

To Ali they were only words, his "psyche" job to gain a mental edge. But to Frazier they were more than a head game, they were personal, and even though hurt by what I thought were some of Ali's below-the-belt comments, Joe wouldn't take the bait. His only response was to call Ali "a phony" and "a clown." Instead of returning Ali's "jive" he turned his intense hurt inward, taking it out on the heavy bag and on his sparring partners and vowing to do the same to Ali between what he called "the four squares" come March 8.

Meanwhile, the fight had captured the imagination not just of fight fans worldwide but even those peripheral fans who saw this as an event, one being fought on a world stage. Possessing all the elements of a great matchup, including two undefeated heavyweight champions, one a puncher, the other a boxer, fighting for the most money ever earned by an athlete, $2.5 million apiece, fought in the midst of a turbulent debate over the Vietnam conflict with one of the participants adopted by those in support of the war, the other the representative of those opposed to it, and held in the mecca of boxing, Madison Square Garden, the fight needed little ballyhoo.

Nevertheless Perenchio, saying, "What we have here is the *Mona Lisa*. You expect us to sell it like chopped liver?" pulled out all the stops. True to his background as a Hollywood agent, he marketed the fight like a blockbuster movie, something "colossal," "stupendous," and "bigger-than-life," hiring superstar Burt Lancaster as a closed-circuit broadcaster, filling the airwaves with news and interviews, and getting the two participants on the cover of every major news magazine. And, not surprisingly, using Ali as his primary pitchman.

In one of the most improbable promotional schemes ever hatched to hype a fight, John F. X. Condon, who had been hired by Perenchio to handle the publicity for closed-circuit, came up with a lulu. Believing that the fight was a generational war and that Ali was "a young guy" and that "in a couple of years the young people are going to have a bigger voice in this country than they ever had before, the country needed a new leader and that new leader should be Ali," he approached Ali with an idea. Finding Ali at the 5th Street Gym after he had just returned from his roadwork, he began to lay out his idea in a train-of-thought manner. "Look," Condon said, "I'm going to tell you something. Don't talk until I get done. When I get done, we'll have a chat, but don't say a word till then." On a roll, Condon then laid out his scheme: "At twelve o'clock today, you're going to go into the lobby of the Playboy Hotel here in Miami Beach and you're going to make a formal announcement that in 1976 you're going to run for President of the United States."

With that Ali jumped up, slapped his thighs, and yelled, "Man, oh man, that's just what I need . . . that's just what I need!" Then, as an afterthought, he said, "But you've got to do one thing, you've got to check it out with Herbert Muhammad."

Condon hollered "fine" over his shoulder as he raced out the door of Ali's private little gym room in search of a telephone. First he called Perenchio and, after repeating his warning not to interrupt, went through the idea again. "Hello, hello . . . are you there?" A long pause and finally Perenchio came back on the wire. "Yeah, I'm here," he said softly. "Jesus Christ, John, if you can pull this off it's the greatest goddamn thing that could happen to us!"

Next Condon called Herbert Muhammad. Unable to get through, he reached John Ali at Nation of Islam headquarters in Chicago. After hearing Condon out, John Ali merely said, "He can't do it, John. No Muslim is allowed to run for public office." And even though Condon argued it was merely a "publicity stunt," the verdict stood. Still, in exchange for having his stunt vetoed, Condon was able to extract a promise that Ali would present one of his drawings of what he called "Predictions Before a Fight" on the closed-circuit telecast just before the bout.

But even though that promotional scheme hadn't, as they say on Madison Avenue, "flown," obviously several had as on-site tickets at the Garden—ranging up to $150 ringside, and soon to be scalped anywhere from $750 to $1,000 apiece—sold out in little more than a day. And closed-circuit ticket sales were bringing SRO signs at almost all theater box offices.

For me, the promotional goings-on were somebody else's business. My job, pure and simply, was to get Muhammad ready for "The Fight," which was no easy task. For Muhammad was taking it easy, not training, convinced that his stoppage of Bonavena—something Frazier had failed to do in their two meetings—was a sure "sign" he was fated to win. Ali also read into the fact that most writers, just as they had before the first Sonny Liston fight, had picked his opponent to win as yet another "sign" he would "whup" Frazier just as he had Liston.

Knowing that fights are won and lost in the gym, not in "signs," I finally got him back in the gym. From what I had seen in his two comeback fights, he was not the Ali of old; he was a little rusty around the edges. His frame had been thickened by age and his brilliant moves diminished by his three-and-a-half-year layoff. Now, instead of evading punches by merely moving away from them, he blocked them with his arms and gloves. He no longer danced on his toes but was more flat-footed. And his stamina was in question. He had become, in the words of one writer, "less an artist than a fighter," one who had gone from "superhuman to extraordinary."

Even with a natural ten-pound pull in weight and a 4-inch advantage in height and reach, Ali was going to be facing a fighter who would be willing to take everything Ali had to offer just to be able to land that thunderous left hook he possessed, probably one of the best in the history of boxing. And it was my job to prepare him, both mentally and physically, to take on the fighter who was described as fighting like "a wild beast caught in a thicket."

But by now Ali had become the darling of the press. And every training session was attended by—or should I say, interrupted by—both a horde of members of the press as well as a roundup of celebrities, all coming to talk to him. Never one to miss an opportunity to get his name in the papers or his face on TV, Ali took valuable time off from training to accommodate their every question and comment, making it more difficult to fully prepare him for "The Fight."

Still, as we broke training camp in Miami Beach and headed to New York I thought we were ready. Or at least as ready as we were ever going to be.

In New York we faced another problem. Somehow during his exile Muhammad had became more than just a boxing celebrity. He now had an aura, call it a mystique. And even though we were housed at a hotel across the street from the Garden, we couldn't go anywhere without crowds following him, wanting to see him, touch him, just walk in his footsteps. Everyone, or so it seemed, from the casual celebrity spotter just wanting to catch a glimpse of him to the most devoted fan wanting to get near him, fell in lockstep behind him, almost as if he were a Pied Piper heading up his own parade with a band of admirers in his wake as he walked the streets of Manhattan. Not only couldn't we walk the streets for our daily constitutional, it became difficult to do roadwork in Central Park. All of which gave us a feeling of claustrophobia, what with hordes of fans following us everywhere, even into restaurants interrupting our daily meals.

That became a major problem the night of the fight. Right after the weigh-in, the powers-that-be at the Garden asked us to stay inside rather than return to our hotel so that the crowd, which by now had blocked off the streets surrounding the Garden, wouldn't become a major traffic problem—the city's police already straining to maintain order. Ordinarily I get the commission's okay to bring Ali to the arena an hour before the fight rather than the normal three. See, some guys can relax in their dressing room before a fight, like Joe Louis, who always took a wake-me-if-there's-a-fire catnap before his fights. But Ali had so much nervous energy he would have worn himself out. Now we were stuck in the Garden the entire afternoon before the fight. And what do you think Ali did to pass the time? He counted the seats in the Garden, one by one!

The fight was as much an event as it was a fight. Bored to tears by having to stay in the Garden, I would occasionally go outside to look at what was going on. It had the look of Mardi Gras. Hours before the doors officially

opened at 7:30 P.M., thousands, with or without tickets, milled around outside, there to be seen if they were celebrities, or unseen if not. Among the
crowd you could see scalpers offering $150 tickets for up to $1,000 a pop.
What was going on was pure excitement. There were limos backed up from
in front of the Garden all the way uptown—some said as far away as 110th
Street.

When the doors finally opened many went through hell just to get
inside. Even those with tickets had to wait an hour as the crowd surged
toward the doors, many of those dressed to the nines in full-length white
mink coats—and those were the men; the women were in tight-fitting
extreme clothes with hot pants and low-cut blouses. One woman in tears
had just held up her ticket for the ticket taker when a hand emerged out
of nowhere to snatch it from her. The doorman, a witness to what had happened, was powerless to help.

As the twenty-thousand-plus slowly began to fill the arena, you could
see the celebrities of the day, all creating a stir as they were recognized by
the fans. All the while we were back in the dressing room, going over our
last-minute preparations: the strategy, the taping of the hands, the placing
of the red robe over the shoulders of Ali as we stood ready and anxious for
that knock on the door telling us, "You're on!"

Finally the knock came, and we made our entry into the main arena.
The house lights had dimmed, and the people were on their feet screaming, "Al-li! Al-li," as they caught a glimpse of Ali, dressed in white with red
stripes and a mini-robe, his shoes red tasseled with red bow-like laces. He
threw punches in the air and waved to the people he recognized. Climbing through the ropes, Ali extended his arms into the air and did his "Ali
Shuffle" as the crowd roared in appreciation and picked up the volume of
their "Al-li! Ali-li!" chorus.

The arena momentarily quieted. Then there was another roar as the
familiar form of Joe Frazier emerged from the shadows, clad in velvet-
brocaded green and gold trunks with matching robe. Contrasted with Ali, Joe
was throwing punches, looking down, not seeing the crowd, all business.

The crowd, which only seconds before had been on their feet cheering
the two fighters, quieted just enough to hear the two fighters announced,
bursting into wild applause with each name. During the introductions I
looked down at ringside and saw Frank Sinatra on one side of the ring,

camera in hand, taking pictures; on the other side, Burt Lancaster was at a microphone. Other too-numerous-to-mentions were seated ringside. It was exciting, even to me.

Referee Arthur Mercante then brought the two fighters to the center of the ring for their last-minute instructions, and as I escorted Muhammad back to the corner before the opening bell, I gave him some final "words of wisdom" and Bundini Brown supplied some final exhortations. Then the fight was on!

Frazier immediately walked right in on Muhammad while Muhammad came out in a circle, both meeting in the center of the ring. Ali feinted with a jab, and Frazier threw one of his own, missing. As advertised, Frazier kept coming straight in at Muhammad, his head bobbing, his hands moving, his chin buried in his chest. But Ali, true to his word, was "a-peckin' and a-pokin'," throwing quick jabs at the approaching Frazier and then moving away, out of trouble. For two rounds the same pattern continued with Ali circling, feinting, and then throwing his jab at the ever-pursuing Frazier who was following my guy but unable to cut off the ring. And when Frazier came close enough for Muhammad to grab, he did, smiling and nodding at the crowd, even talking to Frazier.

At the bell ending the second, Ali stood in the corner, mouthpiece still in place, listening as I gave him instructions and told him to quit his "grandstanding," while Bundini, who had spent the entire round screaming at Ali, uncharacteristically remained quiet while I talked.

Round Three was different. Instead of circling, Muhammad met Frazier in his corner and then retreated into the ropes where Frazier began to work him over, connecting with a right to the body and launching long left hooks that missed their mark as Ali, as in times of old, pulled his head back at the last second. Ali tried to move, but Frazier, having pinned him on the ropes, wouldn't let him. A left hook by Frazier landed to Ali's face, but Ali had seen it coming and rolled with the punch. Ali came off the ropes with Frazier pursuing, throwing vicious punches. But Ali shook his head no, as if to tell the crowd he wasn't hurt. The crowd laughed and applauded, but to me it was no laughing matter. He even took time to talk to Frazier, one time telling Frazier, "God wants you to lose tonight." To which Frazier snorted, "Tell your God He's in the wrong house tonight."

The momentum of the bout had changed; Frazier was making the fight and Ali was throwing mostly pitty-pat punches. Now Frazier was the one smiling, and his fans smiled and laughed with him. The round ended where it began: with Ali on the ropes.

The fourth and fifth rounds were more of the same with Frazier moving Ali to the ropes and banging away with what they call "mean intentions," his murderous punches landing. Afterward, Ali sat on his stool for the first time, his breathing heavy and labored.

In the sixth, Ali got up on his toes, moving more and throwing jabs. But Frazier was still there, cutting off the real estate and coming in flat-footed to get near Ali. Ali began to throw uppercuts to meet the advancing Frazier and moved back to throw jabs. The momentum had swung again, this time back in my guy's favor, and continued throughout the seventh.

By the tenth, both men seemed tired. Ali again went to the ropes where Frazier teed off, almost all his punches missing their mark. Ali dropped his hands, daring Joe to hit him, and Joe dropped his in response. Ali accommodated him, throwing a one-two that caught Frazier flush. Now it was Frazier who laughed, pushing forward and trapping Ali on the ropes where he lashed out again, forcing Ali to hold on. During one of the many clinches, as referee Arthur Mercante separated the two, he accidentally poked Joe in the eye. But Joe didn't even seem to notice, wading back into Ali with more of the same, body punches and lefts to the jaw.

Ali came back to his corner after the round, and I gave him a what-for, telling him to "quit fooling around"—and fooling himself as well. He couldn't see that every time he invited Frazier to come in and punch, Frazier did just that, and Ali wasn't doing much to respond. "For cryin' out loud," I shouted. "Stop playing. Do you want to blow this fight? Do you want to blow everything? You're giving away rounds and letting him build not only a lead but also his confidence."

Ali responded in Round Nine, dancing beautifully, floating like Bundini's butterfly, almost as if he had found what they call a "second wind." All the while, he snapped jabs in Frazier's face. It was now Ali's fight.

But in Round Ten Ali reverted to the form he had shown in Rounds Three, Four, and Five, as he retreated to the ropes while Joe went to work again. A wicked left hook landed to Ali's body, a right to his forehead. Ali just rested while Joe worked. Then, with twenty seconds left in the round, Ali suddenly came alive again, throwing one . . . two . . . three jabs, all direct hits, and then a left-right combination. The fight was two-thirds over, and Ali was seemingly in command once more, with the so-called "championship rounds"—Rounds Eleven through Fifteen, to go.

Everything changed in Round Eleven. Ali once again retreated to the ropes, and Frazier was on him, throwing a left hook from hell that caught Ali on the button. For a second Ali's knees went rubbery and his shoulders sagged. Frazier was back on the attack, raking my guy's body with vicious punches. A second left hook and Ali's legs buckled like a drunk's, his eyes glassy. Ali began to play games, wiggling his hips, pretending he was hurt worse than he really was, momentarily halting Frazier's attack as Joe stopped to consider whether his opponent was playing possum or not. Then it was back to the attack, just as the bell sounded.

As Ali walked slowly back to the corner, Bundini was up on the ring apron spritzing him, along with those in the nearby ringside seats, with water. Ali plopped down on the stool. This time there was no split glove to save him, only advice. I tried, shouting into his ear to "get back on your toes," to "get off the ropes," to "use your jab," to do anything to turn the tide of battle, all the while massaging his legs to bring them back to life.

Slowly Ali rose from his stool for Round Twelve and, trying on unresponsive legs to recover from the beating he had absorbed the previous round, moved away from Frazier, all the while holding his right hand close to his cheek to avoid Frazier's savage left hooks. Another Frazier round in the bank.

Round Thirteen began the same as Round Twelve had ended, with Frazier backing Ali up, beating on him, dealing out more punishment. For the full three minutes he showed no signs of stopping as long as his energy held out as he pounded away at Ali, who spent most of the round with his back to the ropes, almost as if some strange magnetic force kept him pinned to them.

Ali managed to change the course of the fight one more time in the fourteenth, connecting with a vicious left hook to Frazier's head and then a right. Pushing Frazier back, he hit him with a one-two combination and then exploded with several more punches to Frazier's head. Finally off the ropes, Ali was a moving target, one the slower Frazier couldn't catch.

Last round! As the fighters came center ring and touched gloves the crowd rose to their feet. The outcome still seemed in doubt, with no one sure who was winning—especially after Ali's offensive outburst the previous round. Ali moved deliberately, with Joe almost on top of him, trying to reach him. Then, as Ali went to move straight back, he moved his left foot as if he was getting ready to throw a punch, and Joe started a left hook of his own. Only Joe pulled it back, reloaded again, and then almost leapt off the floor to launch it, getting every ounce of his 205½ pounds behind it. The left hook exploded to Muhammad's jaw, sending his legs skyward with the red tassels on his shoes shooting upward and accentuating his fall as his eyes rolled back and went white. For only the third time in his career Muhammad Ali crashed to the canvas.

Joe Louis once landed a similar crushing blow just eighteen seconds into his fight with Eddie Simms, and Simms, although able to get back to his feet, turned to the referee and asked to go for a "walk on the roof." When Tommy Loughran was coldcocked with a single punch by Jack Sharkey, he asked the referee for "a place to sit down." But Ali's eyes somehow refocused the second his butt hit the ground, and he made it back to his feet by the count of "three." He then took the mandatory eight-count, the right side of his face ballooning up to the size of a misshapen pumpkin where Frazier's bomb had exploded. (Afterward Bundini would say, "That's the blow that did it . . . that blew out the candles.") Trying to survive the remainder of the round, Ali desperately held on to Frazier, hoping to avert a knockout. The final bell rang, and Frazier playfully cuffed Ali across his head. But Ali's head was hung low as if to acknowledge what the crowd already knew.

The reading of the judges' scorecards was a mere formality—eleven rounds to four, nine rounds to six, and eight rounds to six, one even, all Frazier.

The scene in the dressing room after the fight was different than that of any of Muhammad's previous ones. The usual backslapping and boisterous hollering was replaced by an almost wake-like quiet as the few well-wishers who were allowed in commiserated with Ali. One, Diana Ross, was crumpled on the floor in front of Ali, crying. But Ali was uncharacteristically humble—even once, when Bundini started in, calling him "Champ," he quickly quieted him down with, "Don't call me Champ . . . Joe's the Champ now." And then, through swollen jaw, he said, "I'm not crying; my friends should not cry."

Superstitions and boxing go hand in glove. Willie Pastrano always tied his wedding ring on his shoes. José Napoles would burn candles and pray before every fight—one time gutting his room in Los Angeles. Sugar Ramos had a trainer named Kid Rapidez, an expert in Santeria (Cuban witchcraft), who would perform rituals for Ramos before every fight. Kid Chocolate always tied his shoelaces behind his shoes. Joe Louis always put on his left glove first. Jake LaMotta wouldn't enter the ring without his leopard robe. Et cetera, et cetera, et cetera—the et ceteras could go on for at least six more pages.

For me it was always a trip to the hair stylist the day before a fight. When my hair began to thin on top, I'd have the stylist spray goo on top to make it look like I had a full head of hair. Well, one time the heat from the overhead lights melted the goo, making it run down my face. That scared the hell out of my fighter so I stopped having my hair sprayed and decided to go *au natural* from that point on.

That wasn't the only thing I gave up. After the Frazier fight I "lost" my sweater with Muhammad's name emblazoned on the back. Well, I didn't really "lose" it, I knew where it was, but it would stay there. See, it was only the second time in my entire career that I had worn a sweater with the name of my fighter on the back. The first time had been Luis Rodriguez's return bout against Emile Griffith in Madison Square Garden, and he had lost that one, too. So, in a bit of reverse superstition, from that day on and forevermore, I would never wear a sweater with a fighter's name on it. It was bad luck!

Taken to the hospital for x-rays of his swollen jaw after the fight, a proud Ali refused to stay overnight, saying, "It makes me look like Joe Frazier put me in the hospital . . . that's not true!"

He asked to be taken back to the hotel, and Dr. Ferdie Pacheco and I helped him down the hall and into the elevator. As the doors closed, he said softly, "The Greatest is gone."

TEN

The Path from "People's Champion" to World Champion (Again)

The ability to take the bitter with the sweet, defeat with victory, or basically how they react to adversity is an essential element in the psychological makeup of fighters. Many fighters have been ruined by one setback. They become so accustomed to winning that when they meet defeat they don't know how to accept it. Instead of trying to learn from it, they lose confidence in themselves.

I remember, back in 1949, just after I'd come to New York, there was a kid from Omaha, or someplace in the Midwest, named Vince Foster. He couldn't miss. He was a rough, tough, good-looking kid with great credentials. I think he had thirty wins. Anyway, they brought him to the Garden for his New York debut and he got knocked out in one round by Charlie Fusari. It broke Foster's heart, and he never got over it. He took to drinking, and two months later, while driving drunk, he was killed in an auto accident.

Not so Muhammad Ali. By the very next day he was not only coming to grips with his defeat, he was acknowledging his mistakes. "When you get as big as I got in this game," he said, "you get intoxicated with so-called greatness. You don't think you just have to run three miles a day. That's all I did for this fight. And I didn't properly rest, didn't train as hard as I used to. You convince yourself you'll get by on talent alone, that it will all just explode in there. But it don't."

And then, almost without switching gears, he was back to the Ali of old, his voice rising a decibel, his face parting in a half-smile through his swollen jaw as he said, "Get me Frazier. No man ever beat me twice. I'll straighten this out. . . . Joe, you hear me?" Now, with the volume turned up to a full-throated shout, "Joe, if you beat me this time, you'll *really* be the greatest."

Muhammad Ali was hardly going quietly into the good night. Nor was he saying, "Good Night." He would be back.

In the hearts of his millions of fans, Ali had never gone. He was still a champion, if not *the* champion. You could see it in their faces when they spotted him. You could hear it in their voices when they called out his name, "Al-li!" And you could read it—as in the graffiti that adorned the wall on the subway station underneath the Garden the night of the fight, "Ali Lives!" To them he was, as he now called himself, "The People's Champion."

Being the "People's Champion" was one thing. Owning a piece of the heavyweight title another. And although the Supreme Court had upheld Muhammad's contention that he was a conscientious objector and over-turned his 1967 draft conviction, they couldn't restore his title. Seeking a title, *any* title, Ali now looked to win the vacant North American Boxing Federation (NABF) heavyweight title against his former sparmate, Jimmy Ellis.

A matchup between Ali and Ellis gave me problems—or, as they say in New York, *tsouris*. With Muhammad I was the trainer, only part of the team. With Jimmy, I was *the* team. Jimmy paid me one-third of his purse for my services, and he was entitled to them.

So I went to Muhammad and explained my dilemma. Muhammad understood and respected my decision to work Jimmy's corner that night. Some of the newspapers took literally Muhammad's remarks about this being the end of our relationship and that he had found someone far bet-ter than yours truly to work with. He also told the press that he would take me back if I didn't talk too much. Imagine that! You've got to know Muhammad and understand his offbeat sense of humor to appreciate that, as well as his ability to hype a fight by now directing his remarks at me.

For only the second time in his career—the first being his debut—I was not in Muhammad's corner. Instead, I was in his opponent's. Nevertheless, I was 100 percent behind Jimmy. I didn't let my personal feelings for Muhammad interfere one little bit working Jimmy's corner.

Know what? It really didn't matter. Ali was too good, too strong, and too much for Jimmy. With only fifteen seconds left in the fight, the referee stepped in and stopped it, awarding the fight and the NABF belt to Muhammad.

After the fight, the two boyhood friends from Louisville were reunited. As for me, I was back in Muhammad's corner for his next fight—and every fight thereafter throughout his career.

The only way back to the top is to fight your way back, and for Ali that meant taking on all the top heavyweights. After defeating Ellis, Ali made an exhibition tour of South America. Then, beginning in November 1971, he embarked on an almost-every-month campaign, fighting ten times in twenty-three months in five countries, meeting and beating Buster Mathis, Mac Foster, Joe Bugner, Bob Foster, and Al "Blue" Lewis as well as repeating his earlier wins over Jerry Quarry, Floyd Patterson, and George Chuvalo.

Measured against the yardstick of his performances before his exile, there were some flashes of the Muhammad Ali of old, some pockets of the old brilliance, but more often than not he looked like he was going through the motions without the emotions, as if on autopilot, content merely to win. He seemed to be missing that old piss and vinegar, that certain "something" that gave him his psychological edge. The only time he looked motivated was when he predicted how a fight would end, as he did against Mac Foster, coming down the aisle of the Tokyo arena to the ring carrying the round card for Round Five, his predicted round. However, when the fifth round ended without the promised result, the Japanese fans began to yell "*Taoshite Kure*," which, I was told, roughly translated into something like, "Come on, sucker, knock him out." But Ali was less interested in knocking Foster out than in going on his merry, carrying the action and winning twelve of the fifteen rounds in a workmanlike manner, but hardly the Ali of old.

What Ali needed was something to psyche himself up, another Joe Frazier fight. What he got instead was one against Ken Norton, a little "home television show" before going for "Smokin' Joe." (There I go again with my rhymes.)

Ali had sparred with Norton a couple of times. But when Muhammad had wanted to spar with Kenny another time, Norton's trainer, Eddie Futch, said that the only way Kenny would fight Muhammad again was in the ring, for real.

I knew, just knew, that Norton would be a tough opponent for Muhammad, that it would be no walk in the park, so to speak. The winner of twenty-nine of his thirty fights, with twenty-three of those coming by way of knockout, Kenny was a finely tuned, finely sculpted fighter. Stealing a page from Muhammad's book, I labeled him "Hopalong Cassidy" because, with that lurching, herky-jerky splay-footed movement of his, you just couldn't time him. He promised to give Muhammad as much trouble, style-wise, as Joe Frazier had given my guy trouble, physical-wise. But Muhammad, with his usual unshakable self-assurance, thought he could handle Norton and didn't put his all into training. It would prove to be a mistake that would cost Muhammad.

From the opening bell Norton was all over Ali, coming in behind that strange swaying style of his with his arms crossed in front of his face in what Archie Moore called an "armadillo defense." Midway through the first round, Norton pinned Muhammad on the ropes and let fly with a devastating punch, one that Ali felt and would tell us between rounds had cracked his jaw. But despite his broken jaw, Ali was in the fight the whole way, courageously coming back time and again, only to lose a close split decision, more to Norton's finishing kick in the twelfth and final round than to the broken jaw.

When I took him to the hospital to have his jaw wired, I was almost in tears. But Muhammad consoled me, telling me, "Don't worry. We'll be back."

With his jaw wired and his voice somewhat stilled—though he could still mumble a couple of Ali catchphrases every now and then through clenched teeth—Ali repaired, if that's the right word, to his new training camp in Deer Lake, Pennsylvania, to convalesce.

Deer Lake had come about because of one man, Gene Kilroy, the same Gene Kilroy who had helped Ali get college speaking engagements and a few commercials during the difficult days of his exile. Gene had been instrumental in making order out of Ali's chaotic financial mess, teaching him how to balance his expenses against his income, how to pay his bills, and how to file his taxes by taking him to an accounting firm. But perhaps Gene's biggest contribution came the day he visited Ali, sometime before the Mac Foster fight, at the 5th Street Gym. Looking around the gym and making a crack about the place being in such sad shape the termites would call it junk food, Gene said, "This is crazy. You should have your own place . . . a training camp." Besides, he added, "It would be a tax write-off."

Muhammad sparked to the idea and told Kilroy to go look for just such a place. Well, Gene originally came from Mahanoy City, Pennsylvania, a little town near Pottsville. I had never been to that part of Pennsylvania, having never left South Philly. But Gene knew it well, well enough as it turned out to also know several of its inhabitants, one of whom, a fight fan named Bernard Pollock, happened to have some land for sale in nearby Deer Lake. So he bought five acres for $5,000 for what would turn out to be Ali's training camp.

The first time I saw the camp I fell in love with it. High on a ridge of the Pocono Mountains overlooking a valley with pine forests, rolling fields, and rich farmland, it was beautiful. And Ali would soon turn it into what he called "Fighter's Heaven."

Remembering that Archie Moore had decorated his camp with boulders bearing fighters' names, Ali visited a nearby excavation site and saw several huge rocks, some of which were mammoth chunks of anthracite coal. Kilroy had them trucked back to the camp, and there Ali had his dad paint the names of former champions on them, fifteen in all. These included a huge boulder painted with the name Joe Louis; a big, flat one, Rocky Marciano; a twenty-ton chunk of coal, Jack Johnson; a rugged boulder, Jersey Joe Walcott; boulders labeled Gene Tunney, Archie Moore, Sugar Ray Robinson, and Kid Gavilan; and even a smaller one with my name on it.

For some reason Ali loved log cabins and decided to build a compound of log cabins. He helped put together the logs for a cabin for himself, two bunkhouses for his crew, a gymnasium, a stable and corral for horses, two guest houses for visitors, and the kitchen, the hub of the camp run by his Aunt Coretta and adorned with an "Old Rules" kitchen plaque painted in red letters and signed by his father, "Cassius M. Clay Sr."

Of all the cabins the kitchen was the most popular. As big as the gymnasium, it not only served great food, prepared by Aunt Coretta and later by Lana Shabazz, but also was the place where Ali was the most comfortable, holding court and conducting rap sessions. But the guest houses also did a thriving business, with a continual stream of celebrities coming to visit Muhammad on the mountain.

Ali always had a fascination with celebrities. After the first Henry Cooper fight, out of the thousands in attendance, the then-Clay was most impressed by the fact that "Cleopatra was at ringside," referring to Elizabeth Taylor, who had just finished filming the epic movie. And celebrities were equally fascinated by him. I remember the Beatles, who were huge fight fans, coming to visit Ali down at the 5th Street Gym. We even set up a scene where he flattened all four of them. I didn't know what all the fuss was about, but hell, it was good publicity. We used to set up scenes like that—it was good for the media.

Now the celebrities came to Deer Lake in droves. Boy, did they come. There was Elvis, who fell asleep in one of the guest houses and never left the building, nobody knowing where he was. And Tom Jones and Kris Kristofferson and Mike Douglas and Richard Harris and Pierre Salinger, who came to get a pair of gloves signed for President John F. Kennedy, and Howard Cosell and many, many more. It was an endless parade.

I vividly recall the visit of the great Irish actor Richard Harris. Upon being introduced to Harris, Ali, noticing his accent, asked him, "Where you from?" Harris replied, "Ireland." To which Ali said, "My grandfather came from Ireland . . . Grady." Stunned, Harris looked at him for a few seconds and could only say, "You're kidding!" "No, truth," said Ali, whose grandfather on his mother's side really had. Harris stood dumbfounded for a second, then said, "I just thought everyone wanted to be Irish."

The only thing I didn't like about the camp was the fact that Muhammad was a captive there. People would come at 6:00 in the morning and stay all day. Muhammad was such a great host he'd want to entertain people and it would take him away from his training. That's the part I didn't like.

I needn't have worried about all that stuff. When Ali wasn't entertaining, he was training—hiking up hills, chopping wood, and sparring with his sparmates, which included Larry Holmes, Jimmy Ellis, Alonzo Johnson, Gene Wells, and, the best of all, his brother Rahaman, who wouldn't back off, saying, "Shit, opponent's not going to back off, I won't." And as usual, Ali took it easy on them, didn't try to beat them, working mainly on his defense.

You'd have thought Ali would be bored, way up in the hills of Pennsylvania, away from his adoring fans. After all, he had always had a traveling circus surrounding him. Depending upon the city, the number varied from thirty to one hundred—although I never quite understood what each and every one did, he was happy with them around him. Now he was out in the boonies, but it only took him a few days to become accustomed to the solitude of Deer Lake and the fellowship of his smaller fistic family, all of whom were fiercely devoted to him.

To that group known as Ali's "family"—which included myself, Gene Kilroy, Pat Patterson, Luis Sarria, Bundini, Rahaman, Aunt Coretta, Lana Shabazz, the sparring partners, and his wife, Belinda, as well as the kids— now came yet another member, Wally Youngblood, or just plain ol' "Blood." I never quite knew what he did or where he came from, though he was a friend of Bundini's so I guess Bundini had just brought him aboard, but nevertheless Ali welcomed him into his camp. In order to give him something to do, I made him the "official" timekeeper. He would stand there, watch in hand, and scream "TIME!" at the three-minute mark during Ali's workouts. That was it! Not much, but enough for him to qualify as another member of Ali's ever-growing "family."

Deer Lake was so restful, Ali even became accustomed to the crickets serenading him to sleep at night. But if there was anything even hinting at boredom, the irrepressible Muhammad, his hyperactive imagination a perpetual fountain of ideas, would quickly remedy it. It was almost as if he had reinvented the whoopie cushion and the squirting lapel flower (used in boxing camps of old to break up the monotony) as he created his own excitement to the comic approval of his adoring entourage. One day he'd be showing off card tricks taught to him by master magician Jimmy Grippo. Another, he'd steam up "fights," like the one he made between Gene Kilroy and Pat Patterson, Ali's bodyguard, after Patterson had mouthed off, calling Kilroy a "white boss." Gene accommodated him, putting on the gloves and, with Muhammad the ref, stopped Patterson, who ran out of gas. He even tried to get me into a fight with Rahaman, telling his brother to "beware" of me or I'd "beat up on him." *Marone!* That was all I needed. I told him, "Muhammad, you're trying to get me killed!"

Ever the mischief-maker, Ali impishly had Kilroy, who could do a perfect imitation of Howard Cosell, call Bundini over at the kitchen from the training quarters. Pretending to be Cosell, Kilroy asked Bundini, "What does Drew 'Bundini' Brown do?" Bundini answered "Cosell" with his stock, "There are good witch doctors and bad witch doctors." "And which are you?" the Cosellean voice asked. "I'm the good witch doctor." The voice went on, "And what does Angelo Dundee do?" "He comes in a couple of days before the fight, but I handle all the training," boasted Bundini. "Thank you," said Cosell-Kilroy, and hung up. Within seconds Bundini ran into the gym to tell Ali and the others, all hiding behind their smiles, that Howard Cosell had just called and that he had told him that "Angelo was here all the time and that he was a good guy." It was always like that, a picnic every day with Ali. No, make that a never-ending banquet.

For the first time since Frazier, Muhammad was committed. In fact, he was more than committed, he was psyched. Deer Lake had been a tonic for him. He was now well rested and ready to redeem himself against the man who had bested him six months earlier. There was no way he was going to lose his rematch with Norton.

It all paid off as Ali won a close split decision win, as he carried—some said "stole"—the last round and the fight. Carried or stole, it made no difference, we won. Now he could turn his attention to recapturing what he thought was his due: *his* heavyweight title.

A boxer's hands are the tools of his trade. Their importance cannot be overemphasized. Several fighters, like former middleweight champ Al Hostak, lost fights because of brittle hands. Now, after twenty years of wear and tear, of hitting bags, sparring partners, and opponents, Muhammad Ali's hands, like rock pulverized by constant pounding, had become fragile. He had developed calcium deposits on his hands, and they were hurting him more than any opponent's punches.

One month after the Norton rematch, Ali was back in the ring, this time against Dutch heavyweight Rudi Lubbers. But Ali couldn't give Lubbers enough thought to cause a headache. Instead his hands caused his headache. I remember listening to the tape of the Lubbers fight and hearing Howard Cosell say, "Ali hasn't used his right hand six times throughout the fight. Is something wrong with it?" Yes, Howard, there was. Training for the fight, Ali began to experience what he called "almost unbearable pain" every time he landed his right hand. It even pained him when he blocked his sparring partners' punches. Against Lubbers he changed his style, holding up on his follow-through punches to avoid the agonizing pain that came with the punch. He still won the fight, hands down.

Having beaten Lubbers and evened the score with Norton, Ali now looked for more worlds to conquer. At the time the heavyweight division was arguably the best in its long history, with *Ring* magazine including among its top ten such worthies as Ron Lyle, Earnie Shavers, Jerry Quarry, Oscar Bonavena, Jimmy Ellis, Joe Bugner, and Chuck Wepner—all of whom Ali had either faced and beaten already, or would eventually. And the top four in the division—Ali, Frazier, Norton, and George Foreman—were in play, so to speak.

It had always been Ali's plan—no, make that hunger—to get Joe Frazier back into the ring to avenge his defeat and win back *his* heavyweight title. However, Frazier's bitterness at the many slights he had endured from Ali erupted and he turned down a return bout. Using the excuse that he would never fight Ali again "for even money," a tormented Frazier cried out, "I'll never fight that bastard again. I'd rather die and go to hell." And so, rather than give Ali a return shot, Frazier turned down $4 million and instead signed to fight challenger George Foreman for $800,000.

Frazier's short-money gamble turned out to be a large miscalculation as Foreman administered what Muhammad would call an "ass whuppin'" to Joe. Foreman bounced him off the floor a half dozen times like a rubber ball—one time lifting him from the canvas as if Frazier were a tree stump being uprooted. Foreman managed to lift the heavyweight crown off Frazier's head as well, doing so in just four minutes and thirty-five seconds of fungo practice.

Foreman now stood atop the heavyweight mountain, and both Frazier and Ali needed to face each other again to determine the number one heavyweight contender in order to force a fight with Foreman. The bout was set for January 1974, back where their first classic was fought, Madison Square Garden

While training for the Frazier rematch, Ali began to experience more problems with his hands. Now it was not just his right hand, it was both hands. Every time he hit a bag or a sparring partner the pain brought tears to his eyes. It was even worse when he blocked his sparring partners' punches. Something, anything had to be done. But what? I remember Ray Arcel telling me about his fighter Jack "Kid" Berg who suffered from tender hands and before fights had them shot up with Novocain to deaden the pain. Unfortunately, before one fight he visited a doctor who viewed the practice as unethical and instead of Novocain injected Berg's hands with water.

We looked into going to a doctor, but after a hand specialist at Massachusetts General Hospital recommended a long and complex treatment, one that included an operation, I rejected it, remembering something I had heard about Bob Baker. Baker, a ranking heavyweight back in the '50s, had broken both of his hands in a fight against Sid Peaks and had them operated on. The operation was a success, but Baker was affected psychologically and never punched hard again, always thinking that if he did his hands would break. So I wouldn't let them operate on Muhammad's hands, preferring to treat them back at Deer Lake. Turning to Gene Kilroy, who had NFL connections, Ali had him bring in a hot wax applicator that he used every day. And I had him hit the light bag barehanded as therapy, which he did, over and over again, until he scraped the skin off his knuckles. Then, he'd tear the dead skin off his knuckles and, after resting his hands for a week to let them heal, he'd go back at it again, toughening up his hands.

Still, Ali suffered. But while he suffered the excruciating pain in silence, it was evident that something was wrong. Watching him in the ring with his sparring partners, Bundini was so moved by Ali's reluctance to block his sparring partners' punches he cried out, "Champ, if there's something wrong, let's leave boxing." Reporters covering his training also saw that something was wrong with Ali and reported their suspicions to the muck-a-mucks at the Garden. The Garden considered calling the fight off, even directing Muhammad to have his hands x-rayed as a precaution. But when the x-rays were taken, perhaps the quickest x-rays in the history of x-ray-dom, Ali, puzzled by the almost nonchalant way they were taken, asked publicist Harold Conrad what that was all about. And Conrad told him: "The Garden's sold out. You can't beg, borrow, or steal a ticket. Nobody's gonna find anything wrong with the fighters at this late date. Two legs missing might help. Otherwise, good luck."

But if Ali's hands pained him, Joe Frazier suffered his own hurt. One that played out on ABC's "Wide World of Sports" five days before the fight. The two were seated side-by-side in the ABC studio for the stated purpose of analyzing their first fight. But, in reality, they were there to hype their second. As the tape rolled and commentator Howard Cosell led them through a blow-by-blow analysis of what was on the screen, Frazier, in an offhanded remark, said that Ali had gone to the hospital after the fight. Stung by Frazier's comment, Ali retorted, "I went to the hospital for ten minutes, you went for a month." Trying to parry Ali's thrust, Frazier came back with, "I was resting." That opened the door for Ali to rub some salt in an old wound. "That shows how dumb you are," Ali said, reiterating his putdowns before their first fight. Then he piled on with, "People don't go to the hospital to rest. See how ignorant you are?"

That did it! After suffering all of Ali's barbs about his intelligence in silence for so long, Joe's temper now boiled over. Suddenly Joe rose out of his chair and, in a them's-fighting-words stance, stood over Ali. "I'm not ignorant," he shouted at the still-seated Ali. Then he challenged Ali with a "Stand up, man!" Regarding the figure hovering over him with the mild dismay of a man annoyed by a pesky fly, Ali tried to shoo Joe away. "Sit down, Joe," he said. When it became apparent that Joe wasn't going to "sit down," Muhammad, half-rising, put his arm around Joe's head and pulled him down toward him. Joe bulled his way into Ali and the two were soon rolling around on the floor as Cosell told the viewing audience, "Well, we're having a scene. It's hard to tell if it's clowning or if it's real."

Unfortunately, the fight itself was not as exciting as their TV skirmish. In fact, you could almost say it bordered on the dull side, lacking all the excitement and brilliance of their first match. The only real action came in the opening rounds as Ali strafed the ever-advancing Frazier in the first, hurting his hands several times on the top of Joe's head as Frazier came in under his patented bob-and-weave attack, and then, in the second, nailing Joe with a right hand that left him wobbling. But Ali felt the impact of the punch through his glove, and although he tried to finish Frazier off, he couldn't put all his power behind his now tender right hand. Still, who knows what might have happened had not referee Tony Perez, in the mistaken belief he had heard the bell ending the second round, prematurely halted the action on his own with about twenty seconds left in the round. Ali would go on to win a twelve-round decision, bad hands and all, by doing what he hadn't done in the first Frazier fight: pop, pop, popping Joe and keeping him off-balance so he wasn't solid on his feet and couldn't put the pressure on.

He had avenged his loss to "Smokin' Joe," just as he had with Norton. But more important, Ali now was in a position to reclaim, as he called it, "the championship that was taken away from me for refusing to register for the draft."

ELEVEN

"The Rumble in the Jungle": October 30, 1974

The George Foreman–Muhammad Ali fight was penciled in for the fall of 1974. But, as it turned out, the pencil used must have been a very light one because the fight was almost a "no-go" before it was a "go."

Ali was in place. He had already signed a contract calling for $5 million, plus $400,000 in training expenses and $100,000 as a good-faith advance. But there were problems with Foreman's end, as well as with the money to underwrite the fight.

To go back, within a year of becoming the new heavyweight champion Foreman had defended his title twice—once in Tokyo against a nobody named Joe "King" Roman, annihilating him in a single round, and the second time in Caracas against Ken Norton, coldcocking him in two. After Foreman had finished stepping over the prone body of Norton, he headed for the Caracas airport. From what I heard, the Venezuelan authorities reneged on their promises to the promoters, Video Techniques, and the two fighters to grant them tax-free status. To enforce their demands, the government refused to let anyone leave the country until they had paid an 18 percent tax. And to ensure they would receive their extorted amount, both Foreman and Norton were put under what amounted to house arrest and all of Video Techniques' equipment was impounded. And although Video Techniques posted $250,000 to "ransom" him, Foreman held Video Techniques responsible for his being held captive. Foreman was furious and vowed to have nothing to do with Video Techniques even though they now held an option on a Foreman-Ali fight.

While negotiations with Foreman had come to a standstill, other plans were afoot, including Ali considering Jerry Quarry, who was loudly proclaiming that black fighters were "boycotting" him. But even though promoter Bob Arum made an offer for a third Ali-Quarry fight, Herbert Muhammad turned him down. Then others made a run at a potential Foreman-Ali fight, including the promoter of the first Ali-Frazier fight, Jerry Perenchio.

But, in the end, it was Video Techniques' vice president, Don King, who pulled their chestnuts out of the fire and the fight together by getting Foreman to agree to a contract. Putting what he called "my well-known talking machinery to work," King chased down Foreman, finally cornering him in a parking lot, and challenged him to sign a contract by telling him that "until you beat Ali, the world will never recognize you as the champion. As long as he's fighting and you don't show the world who's the best, they'll look at Ali as the master." That sealed the deal and Foreman signed.

Still, there was a problem with money. Or, more correctly, no money. To underwrite a bout of this magnitude, Video Techniques had to find someone to put up somewhere in the neighborhood of $11.5 million dollars, $5 million for each fighter and another $1.5 million for up-front money. Video Techniques was already out the $150,000 it had paid in good-faith money and the meter was running on their options. Trying everyone on their Rolodex, from A to Z, all they got were turndowns and "we'll get back to yous" when the A's to Z's in question heard the amount of money needed to float the fight. Finally, after exhausting almost every avenue, street, and alley, Hemdale Leisure Corporation came to the rescue, putting up irrevocable letters of credit. Then, with Herbert Muhammad granting another thirty days to Video Techniques to "put the deal together," Hemdale and King sweet-talked President Mobuto Sese Seko of Zaire to underwrite all costs in the name of international public relations.

The high stakes game of finance was over, and the fight was on. Finally.

Negotiations are usually conducted with tact and subtlety. But not where Ali was concerned. Sometime during the negotiations for the fight, Ali and Foreman had a telephone conversation to discuss the deal that was on the table. In his characteristic manner, Ali opened the conversation with a challenge: "George, you think you got the nerve to get in the ring with me?" George growled back, "Anytime, anywhere, for the money." "Money?" said Ali. "They're talking about $10 million dollars. Let's make history." Then, with more taunt than tact, he threw in a towel-snapping, "Let's get it on . . . that is, if you're not scared!" To which George, in his best imitation of Sonny Liston, snarled back, "Scared of you? I only pray that I don't kill you." Ali came away from the conversation convinced that George "sounded shaky."

And although he would continue to believe that George was, in his words, "shaky," and that it was eating Foreman up to be World Champion and still have people calling Ali "The People's Champion," Ali knew Foreman was a formidable opponent, one who had practiced outpatient surgery on the two men who had beaten him, Frazier and Norton, reducing each into smaller, neater pieces with his sledgehammer punches without breaking a sweat.

Moreover, in one of those long-ago-but-it-seems-like-only-yesterday flashbacks, Foreman reminded Ali of Sonny Liston, which was only fair since Liston was Foreman's idol and model—Foreman having roomed and sparred with Liston as a member of his camp. He even had to read to him, Liston being semiliterate at best. Now Muhammad would have to face this younger clone of Liston, ten years after fighting the original—with Ali at thirty-two, the same age Liston was when they had met in Miami Beach so many rounds ago.

Much of the media, including several who had been his avid supporters and fans during his exile and post-exile days, like Howard Cosell, were fearful of Ali's well-being. One, Scottish sportswriter Hugh McIlvanney, wrote that the only way to beat Foreman "involves shelling him for three days and then sending in the artillery." And the *Chicago Tribune* headlined its fight story: "Ali Needs a Miracle to Survive." To all such comments Ali merely said, "Black men scare white men more than black men scare black men."

And yet the comments fed the perception that Foreman was unbeatable, even "invincible." Off his record he looked damn near "invincible," with thirty-seven knockouts in forty wins. Going back to his very first fight, a three-round KO of Don Waldheim—after which Foreman said, "I can knock anybody out. Lord, I'm tough"—this Bunyonesque figure had chopped down nearly everyone who dared stand in front of him. Twenty of whom, in wham-bam-thank-you-ma'am fashion, he had KO'd in the first two rounds, including Frazier and Norton. Indeed, he looked invincible. But I knew there was always somebody who could beat somebody and to me, when it came to Foreman, that somebody was Ali.

Ali continued to be his usual brash self, at least on the surface—calling Foreman "The Mummy" and imitating his slow tree-chopping punches while shuffling forward and throwing in more than his share of verbal digs, like "I got all the rednecks and Uncle Toms pullin' for me to lose." But you damn well knew he was taking this fight seriously.

George Kalinsky, the official Garden photographer, clued me in as to just how seriously years later. According to George, about a month or two before the fight Ali, who was then in New York, called John F. X. Condon, publicist for the Garden, and asked if he could come over to talk. The Garden being "dark" that day, John invited Ali to come over and invited George to sit in. Suspecting that something was bothering Ali, Condon asked him what was the matter, and Ali admitted he was concerned about Foreman, saying he was "too big" and "too strong." Remembering a photo he had taken of Ali sparring at the 5th Street Gym where he was leaning back over the ropes, far away from his sparring partner, George said, "Why don't you try something like that? Sort of a dope on the ropes, letting Foreman swing away but, like in the picture, hit nothing but air." By the end of the meeting, George remembered, Condon had somehow changed "dope on the ropes" to "rope-a-dope."

Whether you believe the story in its entirety or not, it might give you a clue to what Ali's mind-set was like before a fight. It was something he gave voice to by saying, "I always go in there hopin' I can do it—not really doubtin', but I'm not sure. I wouldn't use the word *doubt*, but I'm not really that sure and this is a good sign. When you get too sure, when you're not nervous, most likely you're gonna get beat. The first Frazier fight I wasn't too nervous. I was confident, too confident. So when I'm a little nervous, when I get that doubtful feeling, then I'm a little frightened and nervous. And that's a good sign."

And so, with what he called "that doubtful feeling," Muhammad trained as he had never trained before, running up and down the mountain trails surrounding his Deer Lake camp, putting in extra time working the bags, skipping rope, sparring, and thinking of little else than Foreman, Foreman, and more Foreman, morning, noon, and night, 24/7.

For Ali's entire career I had selected sparring partners who could best prepare him for his upcoming opponents. They needed to be able to duplicate his opponent's movement and style and enable Ali to gauge his own offensive and defensive effectiveness. For instance, to prepare him for George Chuvalo, I got Cody Jones, a short slugger; for Floyd, Jimmy Ellis, a crafty boxer-puncher; for Karl Mildenberger, a left hander; for the second fight against Henry Cooper, a fighter with a hard left hook; and so forth and so on. Now, for Foreman, I had selected three: Roy Williams, a rugged banger with heavy hands who was an inch or so taller than Ali; Larry Holmes, another tall heavyweight who could also bang but had great boxing skills as well; and Bossman Jones, who had been Foreman's sparring partner.

When Bossman first came to Deer Lake, we all crowded around him to hear what he had to say about Foreman—his work habits, his strengths, his weaknesses, everything. Bossman filled us in. Foreman, he said, had been training harder for Ali than he had for any opponent, running up and down mountains, fighting four-minute rounds to increase his stamina, and practicing alternating his punching with boxing. Then Bossman said, "George is the first person I have been in the ring with I know can kill you." Bossman told us that Foreman had what he described as an "anywhere" punch, a punch Foreman "ain't aiming anywhere," but anywhere it lands "it breaks something inside you . . . a muscle, a bone, a finger, a shoulder, a rib." Furthermore, he told us, "It's a punch that starts out being a hook, but ends up a slider."

'Nuff said. As soon as Bossman told us what George was doing in training and how he was preparing, we went back to watch Foreman's previous fights, to dissect his past performances frame-by-frame, including those in the Olympics and against Frazier and Norton. I was convinced that the sum of all his parts was less than the whole. So, knowing he had not gone more than four rounds in over three years and had fought only five total rounds over the last twenty-two months, we paid particular attention to the three fights in which he had gone the distance for telltale signs about his stamina. And what did we see? In George's first fight with Gregorio Peralta, his trainer-manager Dick Sadler had told him that the ninth round was the "last" round. When George came back to his corner after the bell ending the ninth and held out his gloves to have them cut off, Sadler then told him that there was one more round to go. To hear George tell it later, he nearly fainted. We knew then that if we could take George past the third round, "his parachute wouldn't open," as Ali put it.

And so, after two full months of preparations, of watching and re-watching films, training hard, and thinking of nothing but Foreman, morning, noon, and night, we were as ready as we were ever going to be. Now it was time to go to Zaire to acclimate Ali to the local food, the temperature, and the people—to make him as comfortable in Zaire as he had been at Deer Lake.

Alighting from the plane in Zaire, Ali turned to Gene Kilroy and asked, "Who don't they like over here?" "Belgians" was Kilroy's answer. Putting his finger to his lips, Ali said, "Then tell 'em George is a Belgian."

Ali's campaign to make Zaire his home turf and make George the outsider had begun—which, as Ferdie Pacheco pointed out, was not too difficult, there being "a lot more people in Kinshasa with the name Muhammad or Ali than George or Foreman."

On the way into the capital city of Kinshasa from the airport all we could see were signs along the road reading, "The Foreman-Ali Fight Is Not a War Between Two Enemies, But a Sport Between Two Brothers," and "A Fight Between Two Blacks in a Black Nation Organized by Blacks and Seen by the Whole World—This Is the Victory of Mobutism," referring to the president of Zaire. Watching the signs go by, I thought to myself that before we left Zaire there might well be another sign erected reading, "This Is Ali Country," as Ali laid out his plans to make himself the country's hero and George the antihero.

Never fully understanding that Ali was, in effect, hijacking the fight, George, in his innocence and arrogance, played into Ali's hands. From the very first moment he arrived, leading a huge German police dog down the steps from the plane—the very same breed the Belgians had used to control the crowds during the occupation of their former colony and which the newly independent Congolese fell upon and ate after their departure—George hardly endeared himself to the local populace. While Ali was out on the street mingling with the locals, winning their attention and affection, there were so few sightings of George he might as well have been in the witness protection program. For the next few weeks George became a one-man alienation machine as Ali worked his charm.

I wasn't overly fond of his dog either. At one of our joint press confer-ences, the dog, named Diego, was spooked by something or someone and took off for parts unknown. Seeing his dog run off, George said, "They're going to eat the dog." He then barked to one of his trainers, Doc Broadus, "Go find the dog." Now he was hollering, "Diego . . . Diego . . ." I couldn't quite make out what George was hollering so I asked Kilroy what Foreman had said. "Dago," said Kilroy with a smile on his face. "He's calling you a Dago." Now I'm Italian and I'm used to being called a Dago or a Wop by my friends. It's part of my heritage. But you'd better be careful how you use those words, whether in a friendly way or with malicious intent. And thinking that George was trying to get at Ali through me, I interpreted his comment as being anything but friendly. So all I could think to say in response was, "Kiss my ass, you big son of a bitch." A little harsh, I admit, but I was upset. Both at George and his dog.

Almost from the moment we set up our headquarters some forty-five minutes outside Kinshasa Ali went to work converting the people of Zaire into Ali fans. He would mingle with the crowds of onlookers, run with them, and lead choruses of "Ali, *bomaye,*" which loosely translated, I found out, is Swahili for "Ali, kill him!" Ali was like a church choir-master leading his throng of worshippers as they continually shouted his name and chorused their chant of "Ali, *bomaye!*" On the other hand, George, when not training, stayed squirreled away in his suite at the Inter-continental Hotel surrounded by bodyguards and his faithful companion Diego. It was indeed Ali country, and he was playing the underdog card brilliantly.

But Ali didn't spend all his time courting the people. There was work to be done, hard work, in the gym and out there on the road, running. Believing, as he said, that "the fight is won or lost far away from witnesses, behind the lines, out there on the road, long before I dance under those lights," Ali ran to exhaustion, sometimes at 4:00 A.M. to approximate the time of the fight, knowing that his defense depended on his legs and that the only times he had lost were because his legs had given out.

The gym, where we worked out daily, was a large, two-mile outdoor facility shared by the two fighters, with Ali at one end and George at the other, separated by the press and TV mob. Ali would work out first, then Foreman. Our daily ritual was to first work the bags, then skip rope, and, finally, spar with our three sparring partners. But because we didn't want to show anybody anything, Ali did most of his work in the back room away from prying eyes, like those of George's trainers, Dick Sadler and Archie Moore, who were always in attendance. Moore took notes on Ali's every move and stowed them away in what he called his "cabinet," a large picnic basket that he carried with him.

Me, I didn't need no stinking picnic basket to spy on George. My reconnaissance was simple. All I had to do, after Ali had finished his workout and turned the gym over to George, was to go to the dressing room window, which overlooked the gym, pull back the drapes and, using a telescopic lens borrowed from Ali's official photographer, Howard Bingham, sneak a peek to see what I could see. And what I saw was George, back turned as if he knew someone was watching, banging away on the heavy bag with thunderous punches, leaving huge dents in the lower portion of the bag. After punching the bejabbers out of the bag, he sparred with his sparring partners—six of them compared to our three, most of whom had sparred with Ali at one time or another—fighting four-minute rounds instead of three with only a half-minute's rest in between. Obviously, as Bundini Brown said, "They ain't planning for him to get tired."

But, from what I'd heard, George was almost contemptuous of Ali. Convinced that Ali was scared, George hadn't watched any films of Ali in action and thought he didn't need much roadwork or sparring. After all, knocking out Ali would be a mere formality.

We hardly shared the same view. Conventional wisdom had it that George was a bullying, intimidating, terrorizing fighter who was, to use that word again, *invincible*. But as someone once said, conventional wisdom is always an underdog at the betting window. To us, George was beatable—especially by Ali who had all the tools to make George *vincible*: hand speed, footwork, and, most important, what we called "ring smarts." Even his hands felt fine. I was so sure Ali would win, I began telling anybody who would listen, "My guy could win in a phone booth."

With a little over a week to go Ali was at his peak, feeling the fatigue he'd feel in the fight by going nineteen rounds each day—three rounds on the speed bag, four skipping rope, three on the heavy bag, and nine three-minute rounds of boxing with his three sparring partners. All was going according to plan. My guy was as ready as he would ever be.

But what we hadn't planned for happened eight days before the fight. As one newspaperman who had been present at one of George's sparring sessions told us, George was sparring with a college kid named Bill McMurray, and as George was whaling away at him with McMurray covering up, McMurray had raised an elbow to protect himself and caught Foreman above the right eye, cutting him. The cut was a quarter of an inch deep and Foreman was bleeding all over the place. The fight was off

Everything, all those months of planning, all the hard work, everything, was now out the window. Chaos would have been a step up for what followed. George, distrusting the local doctors, had trainer Dick Sadler temporarily tend to the cut, closing it with a "butterfly" bandage before planning to take off for Paris to get what he considered proper medical treatment. Writers, convinced the bout was not just postponed but canceled, began making plans to take the next flight out. And the promoters, trying to make chicken salad out of the chicken droppings they were suddenly left with, were seen scurrying around in an attempt to salvage the promotion.

Amidst all the hullabaloo there was one logical voice to be heard, that of Muhammad Ali. Make that semi-logical. After considering the situation, and convinced that if George left the country he would never come back, Ali sent a message, via the press, to President Mobuto, saying: "I appeal to the President not to let anybody connected with the fight out of the country." Shifting into high gear he went on: "Be careful. George might sneak out at night. Watch the airports. Watch the train stations. Watch the elephant trails. Send boats to patrol the rivers. Check all the luggage big enough for a big man to crawl into. Do whatever you have to do, Mr. President, but don't let George leave the country. He'll never come back if you let him out." Then he added a word from the sponsor: "Because he knows I can't lose!"

I don't know if it was Ali's warning or not, but almost immediately after Ali had pointed out that George might not come back once he had left Zaire, George and his entourage suddenly decided against going to Paris, or wherever it was he was going, and agreed to stay.

"The Rumble in the Jungle"—which came by its name because Ali had said upon signing for the fight that "we're gonna rumble in the jungle"—was now rescheduled instead of canceled. This time for October 30.

With the fight back on, everything returned to normal. Writers, who swore they would leave, now didn't. President Mobutu, who was afraid his country would lose its fight, now wasn't. And the promoters, who had nothing to do, now did.

The thirty-six-day delay now gave us the feeling that the pendulum had swung in Ali's favor. For while we were able to go back to the gym to fine-tune Ali and work on his final strategy for the fight, George was unable to resume training, his doctors having advised him that because of his cut eye he couldn't work up a sweat for at least ten days lest the sweating delay the healing process. This meant he couldn't spar or do any roadwork—not that George felt he needed to do either anyway. And so, while George sat in his room under guard growling and grumbling that he couldn't win for losing, Ali continued to prepare for the fight. The only time there was any communication between the two came when Ali's old instructor, Archie Moore, delivered a poem parodying Ali's style to our headquarters reading:

> Your poetry is nothing but rhyme,
> Fifteen rounds is a long time.
> Frazier couldn't even make two,
> Ken Norton was the victim of George's Coup.
> Foreman's left will make you dance,
> Dance Turkey in the Straw.
> When his right connects with your lower mandible,
> Goodbye jaw.

Ali's retort to Archie's poem came the next day in the gym. While shadowboxing against a backdrop of press and onlookers, he spotted Archie in the audience and, calling him out, said, "Folks, there's Archie Moore, one of the greatest of all time. Go back and tell George I'm gonna throw on him some of the stuff you taught me in your camp. You remember? The cut eye gives George a chance to get in shape, but it won't change nuthin'. He's never met a dancing master before."

Ali would continue to bait George with his biting comments. And continue to work his "home-court" advantage, leading the locals in cries of "Ali, *bomaye!*" as he did his daily roadwork through the streets of Kinshasa.

My problem was not with Ali, it was how to fill my time between training sessions. I once read somewhere that "Africa marches patiently through time." Good for them; bad for me. My time was creeping along at a snail's pace. Every day seemed like Groundhog Day: up at dawn, to the gym, and then back again to our encampment. That was it. Boredom was beginning to border on comatose.

Our encampment was a government complex, with slightly less than four-star accommodations. I had a nice villa I shared with Luis Sarria, Ali's masseur. But while most such places have amenities like mints, spas, and extra towels, ours was supplied with an overabundance of lizards and bugs—some so big that if you swatted them, they swatted back. I was so bored I joked that I was teaching the lizards to do push-ups just to break the monotony.

Having heard about the potential of civil unrest in Zaire, I had left Helen at home. That left me on my own to find something to do. I could have gone into Kinshasa and watched the rowdy militia roaming the streets, carrying guns like toy soldiers and drinking beer like college kids on Easter break. That didn't sound like such a good idea. Or I could have just sat around the encampment, twiddling my thumbs and practicing for the Olympic solitaire competition. Great!

I came up with a few ideas, although I must admit they hardly raised the noble pastime of wasting time to an art form. I introduced a game of cards to the camp, one played for matchsticks. Then I expanded it to include anyone and everyone I could find to come out to the compound to play, a group of hail-fellows-well-met that included the likes of writer Budd Schulberg, Don King's matchmaker Bobby Goodman, and any similarly bored writer or hanger-on I could persuade to come and play or just kibitz. Other so-called "activities" included spending time outdoors between monsoon rains trying to catch some sun and eventually getting a suntan that became the envy of all the brothers (one even telling me I looked like a *schwartza*) and reading anything I could get my hands on, up to and including the Kinshasa phone book.

So imagine my excitement when one day I noticed a couple of strange faces in the crowd at the gym watching Ali during his daily workout who, by their looks and their language, I immediately identified as *paisanos*. Seems that they were over in Zaire on some form of lend-lease from Italy to build steel mills for the government and lived in their own Italian city somewhere in the jungle. They not only invited me to come over to visit them and enjoy Italian food direct from Italy at an Italian restaurant, but also asked me to bring along as many as I wanted, which I did, in Mercedes buses provided by the government. It was heaven! Or, at least, a little bit of Italian heaven in hellish Zaire.

Most evenings we'd be on the phone, calling back home or wherever. Since the time difference between Zaire and America was six hours or more, we called early in the evening, right after supper, so as not to disturb anyone in the early morning hours. Getting the phone was almost as difficult as getting through, but, fortunately, I was able to reach Helen almost every night just to hear her voice and tell her all was okay.

Another who made great use of the telephone was Gene Kilroy. One time, talking to his mother back in the States, he was told that Howard Cosell on "Monday Night Football" had announced that Muhammad Ali had reached out to call him from Zaire. Hanging up, Kilroy turned to Ali and asked if he had called Cosell. "No," said Ali, puzzled by the question, "I didn't talk to How-ward Cosell," pronouncing the commentator's name in that distinctive style of his. It would remain a puzzlement, at least until the next year. That was when Kilroy, in Cleveland for Ali's fight with Chuck Wepner, chanced to meet a young man from Canada who, inspired by the man whose voice had launched a thousand imitators, admitted he had imitated Ali's voice to call Cosell during the Monday night game. And had the phone bill to prove it!

As the days dwindled down to, as they say, a precious few, the bore-snore of the weeks before the fight gave way to excitement. We were ready; we were there. I could feel it. This would be Ali's defining fight, the fight that would forever cement his claim to being "The Greatest."

Fight day finally arrived. Well, not exactly fight day, really fight night since the fight was scheduled for the ungodly hour of 4:00 A.M. to accommodate closed-circuit showings back in the United States where the Eastern portion was six hours earlier. But fight day or fight night, it made no difference as the camp was in its usual prefight uproar. At one end of the camp was Ali as he consulted with Dr. Ferdie Pacheco over whether to have both hands or just his left deadened to ease the pain, eventually deciding to forgo treatment entirely. At the other was Bundini, packing the robes, which he usually had specially made for Ali before every fight—and kept afterward. And everywhere else was filled with the usual commotion an entourage of about thirty people can make.

My job was to go to the stadium early to inspect the ring. I especially wanted to look at the canvas. Heat like we'd been experiencing in Zaire (between monsoons) can really screw up a canvas, softening the padding underneath and making it more difficult to backpeddle, which Ali planned to do. Then I wanted to inspect the ring itself, remembering the "mux-ip" in Lewiston when the ring was a wrestling ring, not a boxing ring. I recalled one story of Sugar Ray Robinson who threatened to call off a fight when the ring hadn't met his approval. As the story went, before the fourth Robinson–Gene Fullmer fight in Las Vegas, Robinson went out to the arena to check the ring. Finding that the ring was a 20-foot ring rather than the 24-foot ring called for in the contract, he refused to go on with the fight. Publicist Murray Goodman was equal to the task, producing from somewhere a fabric tape measure that, when extended, showed the ring to be 24 feet, thus saving the fight. Only later did Goodman admit that he had 4 feet cut out of the tape and then had the tape restitched so that the ring measured 24 feet when it was, in fact, exactly what Robinson had thought it to be, a 20-foot ring.

To inspect the ring, matchmaker Bobby Goodman and I took the forty-minute bus ride from the camp in N'Sele into Kinshasa, arriving at the stadium early in the afternoon just as the crowds were assembling outside, mannerly and orderly, maybe made all the more so by the presence of armed guards everywhere. The stadium, a relic built back in the teens by King Leopold of Belgium, had been refurbished by President Mobutu, who had gussied it up with a new coat of paint and renovations to make it a showcase for his big night and fight, even clearing out the prisoners kept there. He had also renamed it the 20th of May Stadium to commemorate the day of Zaire's independence. (I thought, why not? After all, he had renamed the country, the cities, and the river, why shouldn't he have the naming rights to the stadium as well?)

There in the center of the stadium was the ring. Or something that looked like a ring. It was even worse than the Lewiston wrestling ring, so slanted it looked like a miniature ski slope with droopy ropes that hung from the ring posts like wet wash, which was almost what they were, having sagged from the brutal humidity. Bobby and I tried to capture the attention of some of the workmen in the vicinity, but they paid us no attention, not sure what our problem was. But then again how could they? They had never seen a boxing ring before.

For more than a quarter of a century I've been constantly accused of loosening the ring ropes. Nothing could be further from the truth. In fact, I tightened them, not loosened them. Seeing the sagging ropes, I knew I had to fix them, to make them tight so that Ali wouldn't be driven over them into our laps by one of George's "anywhere" punches. But how? Nobody had a knife, the government probably forbidding anyone to carry one. Finally, I found someone who had a razor and used their double-edged Gillette Blue Blade to work on the ropes, cutting and refitting them so that they were taunt and could bear the brunt of two fighters' weight.

The next order of business was making the ring level so that Ali could dance his dance. Not uphill, thank you! Bobby and I managed to corral a couple of workmen who had been standing around watching us in amazement as we worked on the ropes and asked them to go find some strong wooden blocks so we could straighten the tilted ring. And although they didn't seem to be too happy about it, they brought back something that passed for blocks and we were able to right the ring.

Exhausted after hours of working on the ring and making it as battle-ready as it would ever be and soaked through by a torrential downpour, I finally made it back to the encampment. What I needed was a hot shower and about ten hours' sleep. What I got instead was a lukewarm shower and two cups of black coffee. There was still much work to be done and, like Santa Claus, I had my list and was checking it twice. First I checked my little black bag to make sure everything was in readiness, even my solutions for working on a cut, just in case—although Ali had only been cut once in his career, that by Bob Foster whose corkscrew-like left had broken his skin. And if those in charge couldn't construct a ring properly, I would leave nothing to chance, making sure little things like the water bucket and water bottles were taken. I had Bundini and Wally "Blood" Youngblood wrap up two water bottles, one containing honey, orange juice, and water—an old recipe used by Sugar Ray Robinson—wrapping them in white tape and making them look like mummies. I even remembered to take a spare pair of gloves for Foreman, just in case. I was as ready as I was ever going to be.

Time to go. Everybody boarded the buses for the forty-minute ride to the stadium. The mood on the buses was upbeat, as compared to the weather outside, which was menacing. Still, everyone was confident. As we approached the outdoor arena, we became even more confident as the crowds, recognizing our convoy, greeted it with cheers of "Ali, *bomaye!*" That brought a smile to Ali's face.

Then it was inside to the dressing room, one of the nicest I had ever been in. The carpets were restfully blue, the walls were freshly painted, and the—what's the word I'm looking for here?—*ambience* was the best I'd ever seen. Soon I was taping up Ali's hands with gauze and trainer's tape while an emissary from Foreman's group, Doc Broadus, oversaw the taping. It's sort of an old ritual in boxing that someone from the other camp be on hand to see that nothing fishy is going on, no horseshoes or whatever are wrapped into the hand wraps, and that not too much tape is used to give the fighter an extra "oomph" in his punches.

All the while Dr. Broadus was sitting there, watching, Ali kept talking to him, telling him what he was going to do to George. Meanwhile, the representative we sent to Foreman's dressing room, Ferdie Pacheco, was barred, and Dr. Broadus eventually had to escort him in. Another of George's mind games.

Ali rose from the rubdown table and flexed his taped fists a couple of times to test his level of pain, saying to himself, "I'll hit him until the pain tears my hands off at the wrist if necessary." He then went over to the full-length mirror and began shadowboxing, almost hugging the mirror as if it reflected not only his image but his future as well, all the time dancing lightly so as not to work up too much of a sweat.

The countdown was on! A last-minute visit from Herbert Muhammad, some words of wisdom and a short prayer, and Ali was ready. A government official came to the door of the dressing room and gave us a time check, "Twenty minutes to go." Ten minutes later he was back with "ten minutes to go." Then he came to the door once more, saying, "George wants you out first . . . he's the champion." Great! I thought. The prima donna just wants to make Ali wait in the ring.

I knew George and how his mind worked. He thought the extra wait would "ice" Ali, make him nervous and edgy. But like everything George had touched, this, too, would work to his disadvantage. As Ali entered the ring to cheers, he began dancing around, testing the ropes and the overhead lights, as well as getting the feel of the canvas. Then he leaned over the ropes to greet some familiar faces at ringside, Jim Brown and Lloyd Price among them, and nodded at those he knew in the press section. Moving about the ring, from side to side, Ali began leading the crowd in cheers, exhorting them with a wave of the glove. In the ten minutes or so that George made him wait, Ali had entertained and enchanted the crowd, making every one of them a fan. And they expressed it, excitedly cheering and chanting, "Ali, *bomaye!*"

Now I heard another cheer, this one more muted, almost polite, "Foreman . . . Foreman . . ." I almost wrenched my neck swiveling it around to see George running down the aisle to the ring leaving the rest of his entourage trotting behind him like little ducklings chasing their mother. The way he was running it looked like he was in a hurry to get this thing over with. He entered the ring and promptly plopped down on his stool. No testing of the ropes, no feeling of the canvas, no nothing. He just sat there waiting for referee Zack Clayton to call him to the center of the ring for the prefight instructions.

As the two came to the center of the ring, Bundini, towel around his neck, turned to me and said, "That's some mean-looking man." I answered, "I don't know, the ref looks OK to me." Bundini smiled for the first time, but I knew what he meant. For the closer we got to George, the bigger he looked. He had NFL-thick arms and legs and even his muscles had muscles. I thought the only thing he was missing was a necklace around his neck strung with his opponents' teeth.

As the two stood mid-ring, Ali hissed at Foreman, "Chump, you're gonna get yourself beat in front of all these Africans." "Quiet, Ali, no talking," referee Clayton barked. "Listen to the instructions. No hitting below the belt . . . no punches to the kidneys." Ali again: "Never mind that stuff, I'm gonna hit you everywhere but under the bottoms of your big funky feet, chump." Clayton tried to quiet Ali, but Ali continued, "Ref, this sucker's in trouble." A furious Clayton turned to Ali and said, "Ali, I'll disqualify you." Then he tried to finish with the usual, "I want a good, clean fight . . . or I'll call a halt to it." Still Ali managed to get in the last words, "That's the only way you gonna save this sucker . . . he's doomed." "All right . . . all right," a resigned Clayton said. "Go to your corners and come out fighting . . . and may the best man win."

And with that Ali turned quickly, leaving George to glare at his back, and returned to his corner. Then, as announcer Don Dunphy used to say, "There's the bell."

CLANG! The bell sounded, and I gave Ali's rump a light go-get-'em good-luck tap as I sent him out to do battle with the man-giant Foreman. Ali immediately moved out to the middle of the ring and hit George with two quick shots, BING! BANG! Two "take-that-get-acquainted" punches. Ali began to dance, moving away from George and catching him with that lightning-fast jab, which came asfastasyoucanreadthis. Ali may have lost a little something through forty-six fights and 367 rounds, but it sure as hell wasn't his jab. George had no answer for it, almost as if he couldn't see it. Now Ali began talking "smack" to George, "Come on, chump . . . show me what you got." But George could show him nothing, plodding after him in that one-two step of his, unable to catch up with Ali who was performing as advertised. The round ended as it began, with Ali snapping his left jab on and off like an electric light switch. And, despite the naysayers, still there.

Round Two began as Round One had ended, with Ali dancing and throwing jabs and an occasional right-hand lead. But now George was cutting the ring off on him, better than we thought he would, forcing Ali to move six steps to his one-two. George was placing his left lead foot between Ali's feet, forcing Ali to stand either in front of him and trade or move backward, which is what Ali did, moving to the ropes above our corner where George began to pound away at him with heavy-handed clubbing blows. I hollered, "MOVE, ALI! MOVE!" But he just looked down at me and went back to covering up. Down in the press section writer George Plimpton, watching Ali retreat to the ropes, let out with an "Oh, Christ . . . it's a fix!"

But those concerned with his well-being needn't have worried. For between Rounds Two and Three, Ali told us, "I know what I'm doing." He knew that George's cutting the ring off and making him move those extra steps would tire him out in the later rounds and had decided to change his strategy. Now I've always been of the mind that the trainer is supposed to be the boss, that his directions are to be followed to the letter. Going back through the history of boxing there have been many times when the boxer thought be was the boss and it had cost him. Take Buster Douglas, who had everyone in his camp, trainers included, scared to death of him and would take directions from no one, something that cost him dearly in his fight with Evander Holyfield. But Muhammad Ali was different. He always had a mind of his own, a ring intelligence second to none. And now he decided to change the rules of engagement, change the equation, and make his defense his offense. In the process making George work, and work some more, with the aim of making George wear himself out. It went against all common sense, but it was working.

Paying no heed to my instructions, Ali came out for Round Three and immediately went back to the ropes, using his now legendary "rope-a-dope" strategy—though I thought it was just the "dope." I didn't have anything to do with it. It was all Ali's idea. There he stood in a "come-into-my-web" pose, leaving George to hew away at him as a lumberjack would a tree, most of his punches looking as if they were launched from somewhere in the third row. George was throwing everything he had, but Ali was blocking them with his arms or evading them completely by leaning back over the ropes out of harm's, and George's, way. George Plimpton, sitting ringside, thought at times that Ali "looked like he was leaning out a window to see if there was something on the roof." Bundini was beside himself, screaming, "DANCE! CHAMP! DANCE!" But there was no dancing, just Ali standing in front of George, making him miss, and miss again. Continuing to throw his cluster bombs, George finally landed one of his "anywhere" punches, a wicked right that hit Ali just under the heart. But Ali just looked at George with one of those "is-that-all-you've-got" looks, causing George to momentarily stop, not knowing what to do. Every now and then, as George took target practice on the covering-up Ali, Ali would grab George and tie him up, leaning on him and pressing his elbows into George's back. The bell ending Round Three sounded, and Ali was still there as George slowly walked back to his corner, beginning to show signs of wearing down.

I couldn't believe what I was seeing. By the end of the third it was evident that not only wouldn't George's parachute open, but that it was beginning to close. What I couldn't understand for the life of me was why George's corner kept telling him to "Go out and mash him" after every round instead of telling him to pace himself, to change his tactics instead of just continuing on the attack, round after round, wearing himself out. I told Ali, "George is tiring . . . go get him." But Ali had other plans. Taking his "rope-a-dope" further, Ali punctuated his punches with taunts, saying, "Come on, sucker, show me something. I can't feel it. You ain't nothing but a chump. You done run out of gas; now I'm gonna kick your ass." And then he'd pop George a couple of times between his verbal punches.

After watching Ali lean back over the ropes for most of the past two-plus rounds, making George miss and air-condition the entire arena with wild punches in the process, Ali's change of strategy was obvious. At least to me. However, Bundini didn't see it that way. Believing that the ropes, now limp from the tropical heat, should be tightened to enable Ali to, as he had been hollering, "Get off the ropes," Bundini jumped up on the apron and made as if ready to do so. But I grabbed him before he could leave the corner, shouting, "No . . . no, for Christ's sake . . . don't!!! Leave them alone!" I figured if it ain't broke, don't fix it. And Ali's strategy of staying on the ropes was working fine, thank you. And no thank you, Bundini!

What was surprising was that every time Ali landed a punch it was met with loud cheers while every time George exploded one of his bombs to Ali's head, ribs, kidneys, wherever, it was met with almost complete silence. And make no mistake about it, had the bombs landed, the effect of those punches would be like someone getting hit with a railroad tie. One of those punches did explode in the fourth, George catching Ali with a thunderous right to the back of his neck. But Ali, in an I'm-not-going-to-let-you-hurt-me ruse, grabbed George and said into his ear, "Is that the best you got? Is that the hardest you can hit, chump? Show me sumthing, George. That don't hurt, that's a sissy punch!" And then, head cleared, Ali closed out the round with a stinging combination or two.

As Ali sat down on his stool at the end of the fourth he said, "He's mine . . . he's got nothing left. I can knock him out now." "So DO IT," I shouted. "Not yet," said Ali. "He had his turn, now I'm gonna play with him." That said, he got off the stool and led the fans in the familiar "Ali, *bomaye!*" chants.

For the next three rounds that's exactly what Ali did. He played with Big George, lulling him into a false sense of invulnerability as he continued to whale away. It was a little like a lab test I had seen conducted during one of my high school science courses where the teacher had put a toad in a pan of water and turned up the heat little by little until the toad, unaware of the temperature change, was a goner, toasted alive. Now it was George who was being toasted, little by little. Ali first established homesteading rights to the ropes in the early part of the rounds picking off George's punches, now as weak as day-old ginger ale, and then came to life toward the end of each round with bursts of his own, turning up the heat.

By now Ali was so confident he was not only playing with George, he was hollering at Archie Moore in Foreman's corner who was trying to instruct his fighter. "Be quiet, old man, it's all over," he taunted, leading the cheers of the crowd with his free hand. I didn't like what I was seeing. He was playing, grandstanding, and paying no attention to George. I screamed, "Don't play with that sucker. Don't play!" Having heard me, Ali quit his talking and moved away from George, back to the ropes. I hesitate to think what could have happened if he hadn't, no matter how tired George was. For although he looked like a flaccid water hose whose pressure had been turned off, George Foreman still had the power to throw one of his Hail Mary punches and catch Ali when his guard was down and his mouth open.

As the bell for the eighth sounded I shouted, "HE'S OUT OF GAS! TAKE HIM OUT OF THERE . . . HE'S READY TO GO!" And George looked it, rising unsteadily from his stool. Lumbering to the middle of the ring he began winging punches, but now they were coming with all the speed of a responsive reading and taking longer to reach Ali, who greeted each of his missed-by-a-mile swings with a "Sucker, you look bad" or "Chump, you missed me again." Toward the end of the round, with Ali back on the ropes, George began pummeling him again, one of his shots moving Ali slightly to Ali's right. Trying to follow up, George momentarily lost his balance and fell into the ropes. That was enough for Ali, who shot over a right, then a left-right combination, the effects of which were magnified by George's leaning into him as he tried to regain his footing. Quick to take advantage of George's imbalance, Ali threw another combination, with more snap, more power, and finally let loose with a bodacious right that caught George flush on the jaw. With that final right, George lost his struggle with gravity's pull and submitted to it, as he began a slow, lazy pirouette to the canvas.

As George slowly reeled to the floor, Bundini let out, "Oh, Lawdy . . . he's on queer street!" For there he was, down for the first time in his career, and referee Zack Clayton was leaning over him tolling the count, "One . . . two . . . three . . ." as George stirred. "Four . . . five . . . six . . . seven . . . eight . . ." George got to his knees and made as if ready to rise. Then "nine . . . ten . . ." or was it "nine-ten . . ."? Or maybe just "nine . . . and out"?

I never heard the fatal "ten." I still don't think that "ten" was ever tolled—maybe as part of "nine-ten" but not "ten." But whatever, George didn't protest. He merely got up and walked disheartedly back to his corner knowing he had been beaten—mentally and physically.

Ali had won! Or more correctly, he had *"BOMAYE'd"* Foreman. All of a sudden the ring was overrun with an uncountable number of people, all jumping up and down with the joy prisoners feel at the announcement of their release. Over on one side of the ring George was silently leaving the ring as more and more fans brushed by him, trying to become part of the most riotous scene since the French Revolution. Me? I had detached myself from the scene to hang over the ropes and talk to the press in one of my I-told-you-so moments.

Later, in the dressing room, as Ali, tongue firmly implanted in cheek, was telling the press, to roars of laughter, "That couldn't have been me out there, 'cause I can't punch," I ran into sportswriter Skip Myslenski. "You sure called that right, Angie," Skip said, "except you said it would be Round Ten." "Yeah I did, didn't I?" I said with a wide grin on my puss. "Sorry about the round. Muhammad thought it was gonna rain so he decided to finish it." And wouldn't you know it, almost as soon as the fight had ended the heavens opened up and a storm the likes of which you've rarely seen came down in proverbial buckets, leaving three feet of rain in our dressing room. Not only had I called the fight, I was also now practicing to be a weatherman!

If the Sonny Liston fight was the formative one of Ali's career, then the Foreman fight was his most satisfying. To what extent was witnessed by sportswriter Jerry Izenberg, who had been with Ali in the early morning hours after his victory. The two had been down on the banks of the Zaire River where Ali had stood, looking out over the water for the longest period of time as if he were somewhere else. Finally, Ali turned away from the water's edge and said to Izenberg, "You'll never know how long I've waited for this. You'll never know what this means to me."

There was one other footnote to the fight. Some six months after the fight a squib tucked away under the shipping news completed the financial arrangements for "The Rumble in the Jungle." The story told of how Zaire, in a *Mouse That Roared* scenario, had requested and been granted a loan of $5 million from the United States for defense assistance—the exact amount it had cost them to stage the fight!

TWELVE

"The Thrilla in Manila" and Joe Frazier

Having beaten George Foreman to become only the second ever two-time heavyweight champion, Muhammad Ali's fame now bordered on the mythic. He could easily have walked off the stage after his dramatic accomplishment, like Ted Williams retiring after hitting a home run in his last at-bat, assured of his legendary place in boxing history. But even though he hinted at retirement—and would again and again, announcing his retirement and then coming back more times than Frank Sinatra and Barbra Streisand combined—nothing short of a grappling hook could have gotten him off. His ego wouldn't let him. He delighted in the spotlight and the attention his win had earned him, telling Madison Square Garden photographer George Kalinsky, "I can't get off the stage now . . . if I do, nobody will remember me." Rather than taking his newly won heavyweight belt and tucking it under his arm, he embarked upon a campaign to defend it every two to three months.

Making all the world his stage, Ali began what would be a manic every-other-month title tour beginning with a defense in Cleveland against Chuck Wepner. Hardly a marquee name, the hulking 6'6" Wepner was better known for his nickname, "The Bayonne Bleeder" than for his fistic feats. His thirty wins defined him less than his losses to the likes of Jerry Judge and Randy Neumann. Two of his nine losses had come at the hands and gloves of George Foreman and Sonny Liston—Liston being asked after his KO of Wepner, "Was he the bravest man you ever fought?" To which Liston replied, "No, but his manager was."

With prefight predictions ranging anywhere from a walkover to Wepner beginning to bleed somewhere between "O say" and "can you see," Wepner gave it what you would call in boxing "a good try," hitting Ali on the back of the neck, on the back of the back, anywhere he could. He would have hit Ali on the bottoms of his feet if he had had his chance. In the process, he managed to shock the boxing world by knocking Ali down in the ninth round and staying just nineteen seconds short of the scheduled fifteen rounds.

Besides his gallant effort, which became the inspiration for Sylvester Stallone's *Rocky*, Wepner and his manager, Al Braverman, made the fight all the more memorable with their unforgettable lines. Before the fight, after being warned by the Ohio Commission that he couldn't use any "foreign substances" to stem the expected flow of his fighter's blood, Braverman added a quote to boxing's quote book by telling the commission, "These ain't no foreign substances. I bought them right here in the United States." And after the ninth-round knockdown, Wepner returned to his corner crowing, "Get in the car . . . we're going to the bank . . . we're rich." Braverman, who had seen Ali get up with an if-you-ever-dream-of-beating-me-you'd-better-wake-up-and-apologize look in his eyes, told his warrior, "You'd better turn around 'cause he just got up and is he pissed!" But perhaps the funniest of all the lines came from Wepner himself when he told of how he had bought his wife a nightie and told her that she "would be sleeping with the champion tonight." To hear Chuck tell it, when he returned to his hotel room after the fight he was greeted by his wife, sitting on the edge of the bed clad in the nightie, with, "Is Ali coming to our room or am I going to his?"

Next stop on the Ali tour was Las Vegas just two months later, against Ron Lyle, the third-ranked heavyweight in the world. The sinister-looking Lyle had been, by his own admission, "to hell and back," having spent seven-and-a-half years for second-degree murder at the Colorado State Penitentiary where, after a prison brawl, the seriously injured Lyle had been declared "clinically dead." His life in the ring had also been one of survival, his career a series of comebacks. He had lost to Jerry Quarry but had come back to beat Oscar Bonavena and Jimmy Ellis. Now he brought a record of thirty-one wins and twenty-one knockouts into the ring against Ali.

You'd have thought that facing a challenger with a capital "C" would psyche up Ali. But the pursuit of the championship seemed to be more exciting to Ali than his possession of it. And it showed as Lyle outworked and outscored him, leading on all three cards after ten rounds. However, in the eleventh Ali suddenly reawakened the echoes and, resembling the Ali of old, threw an avalanche of punches that forced referee Ferd Hernandez to call a halt to the proceedings—a halt Lyle's trainer, my old mentor, Chickie Ferrara, indignantly screamed, ". . . wasn't kosher. It wasn't a four-round fight, it was a championship fight." As Chickie said, "It was a championship fight," and another successful title defense for Ali, his second in his second reign and his tenth overall, second only to Joe Louis.

Now the Ali title tour traveled many of the same roads Hollywood legends Bob Hope and Bing Crosby had taken three decades earlier in their famous *Road* movies, first going to Kuala Lumpur, Malaysia, where Ali defended his title against Joe Bugner, the European heavyweight champion. The two had met two years before, Ali defeating Bugner in a twelve-round decision in Las Vegas. This time, going through the motions without any emotions in a forgettable fight, the result was the same, only the site and number of rounds were different, with Ali ultimately winning a fifteen-round decision.

Before the fight Ali had announced his retirement for the umpteenth time. But retirements don't mean much in boxing, which has seen more retirements than the Social Security office. And after the fight, Ali, lying on his bed back at the hotel watching films of his second fight with Joe Frazier, suddenly jumped up and hollered, "Get me Joe Frazier." His brief retirement was over. Now it was on to Manila.

There have been twosomes in almost every imaginable field that are as inseparable as salt and pepper—biblically, Cain and Abel; musically, Gilbert and Sullivan; comedically, Abbott and Costello; and on and on. But if you're a boxing fan, there has never been a more famous pairing than Muhammad Ali and Joe Frazier. It's almost as if they were linked together in boxing history, always to be connected by a hyphen, the average fan unable to say the name of one without the other. Together these two greats had had two fights and twenty-seven rounds filled with almost nonstop action and great thrills. Now they were to fight a third time. A rubber match for bookkeeping superiority in a fight that would give the fans one of the greatest matches of all time and give boxing a new word, *trilogy*.

Convinced that Frazier was all but through, a mere facsimile of what he once was, Ali wanted a third match with Frazier to prove to the world that by beating him two out of three he was indeed "The Greatest."

Almost before the ink was dry on the contract for their third matchup, Ali, his juices flowing once again, reverted to his old psychological tricks and *shticks*. First he added Frazier's name to his rogue's gallery of opponents, a list that included "Bear" for Sonny Liston, "Rabbit" for Patterson, "Washerwoman" for George Chuvalo, and "Mummy" for George Foreman. To these, Ali added "Gorilla" for Frazier. Then he incorporated it into a poem: "It'll be a killa, a chilla, a thrilla, when I get the Gorilla in Manila"—hence the name of the fight: "The Thrilla in Manila."

Continuing the beat, Ali once again brought up the "H" word, as in *hospital*, the word that had so angered Frazier in the ABC-TV studios that he had challenged Ali to a fight right then and there. Now Ali said, "I've got two punches for Frazier, the balloon punch and the needle punch. My left jab is the balloon and my right is the needle. I promise Joe Frazier will be in the hospital again!"

My opposite number this time would be Eddie Futch, who had taken over Frazier's corner from Yank Durham, Joe's original manager-trainer, who had died the year before. A master of psychology, Eddie was alert, shrewd, and instantly responsive to any situation. His concern now was Joe becoming overly emotional. "Joe was a little too emotional in the second fight," Futch said, assessing Joe's performance. "But he's not seething anymore . . . he's got quiet resolve."

However, Eddie's assurances about Joe "not seething anymore" apparently hadn't reached Joe, whose resentment of Ali and his mocking remarks, especially being called a "gorilla," reached the boiling point, with Frazier retorting, "It's real hatred. I want to hurt him. I don't want to knock him out in Manila, I want to take his heart out."

I have always tried to blend with my fighters, have a personal touch with them. But there was one place I could not and would not go and that was their personal lives. I just could not get involved. For a trainer, it was a no-no. It was that way with Willie Pastrano, with Doug Vaillant, and with all my other fighters, including Muhammad. However, there was one time I almost got caught in the undertow of a personal problem that came bubbling to the surface.

I don't think it is any secret to tell you that the world contains very few saints and even though Muhammad had posed as one for the cover of *Esquire* magazine, there were times he wasn't up for sainthood. Despite all the myth-making, he was a human being, flaws and all. He also was a dashing, overly masculine man with matinee idol good looks who just happened to be one of the most famous people in the world. As such he never had any trouble attracting women. In fact, you might say he was catnip to women.

While we were in Manila preparing for the Frazier fight, Ali was seen about town in the company of a beautiful young woman named Veronica Porsche—so much so they became an "item," fodder for the press. In response to the attention being paid the twosome, Ali, without any shame or sense of embarrassment, said almost matter-of-factly, "I know celebrities don't have any privacy. The only person I answer to is my wife, Belinda Ali. And I don't worry about her." Maybe he should have.

You could have posted storm warnings when Belinda heard about her husband's high-wire marital act. Hopping mad, she hopped aboard a flight to Manila and after a twenty-two-hour flight went directly to Ali's suite at the Manila Hilton to confront him. I just happened to be there watching him tape an interview when she blew in. Hitting the door with tornado force, she bellowed in a voice turned up to Volume 11, "We've got to talk!" And with that she almost dragged Muhammad into an adjoining room. When "the fit hit the shan," so to speak, I was talking to Dick Schaap, the editor of *Sport* magazine. Dick knew something about Ali's marital excesses having heard Ali, in response to a question about his out-of-the-ring conquests, say, "Nobody knows where the nose goes when the door close." But he had never seen a scene like this before. The two of us looked at each other, realizing that we were intruding on something that was meant to be private. As we stood there silently debating whether to put on our sweaters in the suddenly frigid room or beat a hasty retreat, I finally grabbed him by the arm and said, "Let's get the hell out of here," and made straight for the door. But not before we heard Belinda hurling curses and chairs with the sound of exploding grenades from the next room. And you ask me why I never get involved in my fighters' personal lives!

Belinda wasn't the only problem. After Zaire Ali hadn't wanted to pay the price, hadn't wanted to put in the effort, going through his training motions without any accompanying passion, merely scratching the surface. Now he found excuses not to, considering Frazier unworthy of being a challenger for his title. He thought Frazier was washed up, a mere shadow of his former self, continually asking, "What kind of man can take all those punches to the head?" He was equally contemptuous of Frazier the man, calling him "stupid" and "ugly" (as in "Frazier is so ugly he should donate his face to the U.S. Bureau of Wild Life").

Ali was so disdainful of Frazier that before the fight, looking down from the ring and spotting Herbert Muhammad with a bottle of mineral water, he shouted, "Whatcha got there, Herbert? Gin? You won't need any of that. Just another day's work. I'm gonna put a whuppin' on that nigger's head."

Ali couldn't have been more mistaken.

You might have gotten a clue of just how deep Frazier's raging undercurrent of resentment at Muhammad's slights of words was when, after a largely uneventful weigh-in, he leaned over to Ali and whispered, "I'm gonna whup your half-breed ass." But while Joe may have been burning with resentment, it was Ali who came out smokin'. Believing that Frazier was but one punch away from annihilation, at the bell he came out to mid-ring and stood flat-footed in front of Joe and, with distanced precision, began pot-shotting Frazier with cluster bombs, raking the unprotected head of his challenger with jabs, one-twos, and left hooks, jarring him once, twice, thrice in the opening minutes of the round.

It was the same in the second round as Ali continued his assault on Frazier, peppering him time and again as Frazier continued to press forward into the line of fire, head up, trying his mightiest to get within striking distance. The one-sidedness of the bombardment prompted Bundini Brown to scream out, "He won't call you Clay no more." Before the third, encouraged by the ease with which he had been able to land on the inviting target in front of him, Ali threw kisses to the crowd of twenty-eight thousand packed into the Philippine Coliseum, most in the direction of President Ferdinand Marcos.

In the third Ali caught Frazier with two lead lefts, jerking Frazier's head back. But Frazier, an Energizer Bunny in boxing trunks, kept coming forward, forcing Ali into the ropes where Ali grabbed his shorter foe, pushing his head down. Referee Carlos Padilla would have none of that, batting Ali's hands off the back of Joe's neck. (I never understood that, freeing up one man's hands in a clinch does the fighter a favor, giving him a hand he can now use.) Separated, Joe finally got through with a left to Ali's chin, but Ali went into one of his little charades, giving Joe and the crowd the impression it was only a glancing blow.

That one blow signaled a subtle shift in the fortunes of the two combatants, sort of a balancing of the ledgers as the human fireplug named Frazier began to close the real estate. He got closer and closer to his tormentor and started to land his patented left hook, almost as if he were testing Ali's temperature for fighting.

Although my bride, Helen, was always worried I'd make myself permanently hoarse by constantly screaming at ringside, I couldn't help myself now as I continued to scream to Ali, "Get off the ropes! Get off the ropes!" But screaming couldn't help Ali. Frazier had almost lashed him to the ropes with his left hook, snorting as he ripped it home, time and again. All of a sudden the man Muhammad had thoroughly discounted was now so alive his breath could cloud a mirror, and Ali couldn't believe it. At the bell ending the fourth, all he could do was sniff at Joe, "You dumb chump, you!"

The fifth was Frazier, Frazier, and more Frazier. Now a whirlwind of pure short-fused energy, he trapped my guy in his own corner and raked his body with thunderous-sounding shots. My screams became shriller and more insistent: "Get off the goddamn ropes. Get out of the goddamn corner. Stop playing!"

By the sixth any and all thoughts of an easy victory for Ali had vanished as Frazier attached himself to Muhammad's chest and let fly with several left hooks from hell, catching Ali with two that caused the crowd to gasp, President Marcos to wince, and Imelda Marcos to stare down at her shoes. All of a sudden Muhammad's legs acted like strangers to each other as he momentarily staggered, showing the effects of Frazier's blows.

For the first time in the fight, Muhammad sat on his stool as I searched for the right words to tell him "We blew those rounds. You don't rest on the ropes against Joe Frazier . . . you take a licking."

Coming out for the seventh Muhammad, knowing he was now in a fight, grabbed Frazier and whispered in his ear, "Old Joe Frazier, they told me you were washed up." Frazier merely snorted back, "They lied, pretty boy," and punctuated his answer with a bone-rattling left.

Having tasted Frazier's power, Ali got back on his toes, snapping out his jab. Muhammad would land and then tie Frazier up whenever he could, feeling Frazier's heat and relentlessness. He now knew how wrong his pre-fight assessment of his old foe had been.

For the next couple of rounds Joe continued his assault, taking the measure of Muhammad, testing the depths of his ability and his will to survive. An army of acupuncturists couldn't have applied more pressure than Joe as he hammered away, doubling up on hooks to Muhammad's kidneys and head. Muhammad was neither floating nor stinging, merely covering up on the ropes. At the end of the tenth, his once-delicate legs leaden, his head bowed in agony, his eyes clouded with exhaustion, Muhammad slumped on his stool. "Force yourself, Champ!" Bundini screamed into his ear. "Go down to the well once more! The world needs ya, Champ!"

Bundini's exhortation seemed to have little effect on the pattern of the fight as Frazier continued his attack on Ali, catching him in the corner and raining blow after blow to Ali's head. The brutal beating continued throughout the eleventh and brought a cry of "Lawd, have mercy!" from Bundini, but nothing in the way of retaliation from Muhammad.

Somehow, someway, somewhere with both gladiators running on empty, Muhammad found that something extra in his gas tank in the twelfth after I had exhorted him to "got get him." Using his long right, he reversed the by now all-too-evident flow of the fight by getting back on his toes and pummeling Frazier's face, turning it into a mass of lumps, bringing a trickle of blood from his mouth and closing his left eye. It was unbelievable! Here was Muhammad, who in the eleventh round looked like he could have tossed it in, sucking it up and dominating Frazier.

Now we were up to the thirteenth, the beginning of the championship rounds, three more rounds in a fight that had had more plot turns than a Russian novel and a chance for my guy to close the show and prove both to himself and to the world that he was the better fighter of the two. Sensing that Frazier's punches had lost their power, I screamed at Muhammad, "Look at him . . . he ain't got no power left. Go get him!"

And "go get him" he did. In the intensity of the battle in that heated auditorium, Ali picked up where he had left off, landing a solid left that froze Joe and following with a right that staggered him, sending his mouthpiece flying out into the farthest reaches of the press row. Joe did a little three-step retreat to keep from falling and came back in again in the only gear he knew, forward, only to be caught with another combination. Then another and another. With hands held low and head held high, sucking air like a fish out of water, Frazier kept coming in through frightful punishment, unable to defend himself.

Incredibly, Frazier was still there at the bell. Barely. His face now had the look of an apple that had been halved and pieced back together off-center. He was in need of a tin cup, his left eye closed and his right eye, as he later admitted, impaired. His legs were barely keeping their promise of keeping him upright. But anyone who knew Joe Frazier knew that this gallant man would only go out on his shield. Still, I thought now was the time and as the bell rang for the fourteenth, I shoved Muhammad out of the corner shouting, "He's all yours. Go get him!"

Muhammad did just that, connecting with nine straight rights against his unseeing opponent, slashing him with combinations that dug deeper and deeper into Frazier's flesh and ripping him with everything he threw. At the bell ending the fourteenth, referee Padilla had to guide the all-but-blind Frazier back to his corner.

"Sit down, son," Frazier's trainer, Futch, said as he slowly lowered him onto his stool. Then "Joe, I'm going to stop it." Frazier, who would walk through a minefield to get at Ali, started to plead, "I want him, boss. . . ." But Futch was adamant. "You couldn't see in the last two rounds, what makes you think you're gonna see him in the fifteenth?" Joe began to rise, ready to go back into action again. But now Futch, putting his hand on Joe's shoulder, said, "Sit down, son . . . it's all over. Nobody will ever forget what you did here today." And with that the greatest two-sided fight in boxing history came to a close.

Over in our corner, Kilroy saw Futch waving his hand in surrender to referee Padilla and hollered, "It's over . . . it's over. . . ." And as we tried to raise a bone-weary Ali off his stool to accept the plaudits of the crowd, he collapsed, his legs giving way to fatigue, his body to pain, totally drained. It was a question whether *he* could have gone another round. Bundini lifted him up off the canvas and I cradled his legs as we plopped him back on his stool, where he sat slumped, too exhausted to move.

Afterward, the two gallant warriors, who had just gone through what Ali called "the next thing to death," threw bouquets rather than punches at each other, Frazier saying, "Lawdy, Lawdy, he's a great champion." Then, turning to Ali, he said, "You one bad nigger. We both bad niggers. We don't do no crawlin'." Muhammad returned the compliment, "I'll tell the world right now that's one helluva man and God bless him." And then stated the obvious: "I have nothing bad to say about Joe Frazier. Without him I wouldn't be who I am and without me he couldn't be who he is. We've been a pretty good team for four, five years." The two had forever cemented their names together as a boxing hyphenate.

The next morning, still nursing his pains and barely able to move, Ali said, "You may have seen the last of Ali. I want to get out of it. I'm tired and on top."

You would have thought that Ali, having had fifty-one fights and a career that spanned sixteen years—about the same career average as the twenty-two heavyweight champions who preceded him—would, as he said, "Get out of it." He had made a convincing argument for being "The Greatest" with his hat trick over Liston, Foreman, and Frazier. He had beaten every fighter he ever faced—including the two who had beaten him, Frazier and Norton, in rematches. After all, he was no longer the dancing master of years past. He was showing signs of wear and tear, slowing down and, when compared to the Clay-Ali of old, looking merely mortal. And, most important, there was no telling how much the third Frazier fight had taken out of him, how much of the mortgage on his body he had paid by absorbing the many brutal body shots from Frazier.

There's one clear message that applies across the board: when you're fighting, you think you're going to be fighting forever. There's no eye on the inevitable end. And here Muhammad Ali was no different from any other fighter.

Having given supporting documentation for his claim that he was "The Greatest," Ali had no plans to retire, to step away from the spotlight. It was not merely a case of him not knowing how to fill his leftover life once retired. It was more that he understood that accomplishments begin to fade over time and that his idol, Sugar Ray Robinson, had become irrelevant once he had retired, his name and feats unknown to many of the younger fans. Knowing that he was the most famous name and face in the world, Ali wanted to remain in the spotlight as long as he could, continuing to be the center of attention. He wanted to stay relevant.

THIRTEEN

Boxing's "Greatest" Leaves the Stage

There was another reason over and above Muhammad Ali's need for attention and relevancy for him to continue fighting. With his win over Joe Frazier, Ali had established a going price for his appearances: $1 million, no matter whom he fought.

With this in mind, we scraped the bottom of the heavyweight barrel and came up with one of those "no matter who's," Jean Pierre Coopman, for Ali's next title defense. Called "The Lion of Flanders" for no apparent reason, Coopman proved to be one of life's losing stuntmen, a pussycat instead of a lion. He was so small that to make him look like a heavyweight we had to put high heels on him for the weigh-in. In the ring he was even worse than we had anticipated. After the first round, Ali made his opinion of Coopman's limited abilities known by leaning over the ropes and shouting at Tommy Brookshier and Pat Summerall who were broadcasting the fight for CBS-TV, "You guys are in trouble . . . this cat's got nothin'. . . . Ain't no way you gonna get all your commercials in." Four rounds later, after toying with Coopman to eat up TV time and just slapping him around because of his sore hands, Muhammad took him out. It was embarrassing.

Next up was Jimmy Young, a fighter who could do the most with the least. A steady technician, Young was a real cutie, a member of the jab-and-grab club who would do anything to keep from being hit. He would bend his body, stick his head out between the ropes, and, on occasion, even turn his tush toward his opponent. But even then you couldn't hit him in the backside with a handful of buckshot. It was almost as if he wore an invisible cloak. Ali tried to get him, oh how he tried, but, no matter how hard he tried, there was no there there to be gotten. For fifteen rounds Ali chased the slick Young, never quite catching up with him, but he still won the controversial fifteen-round decision, one that was hardly pleasing to the eyes or the fans.

In dizzyingly quick order, the month after Young Ali defended his title against Richard Dunn, the British and Commonwealth heavyweight champion. The lantern-jawed Dunn went "down as he must" as Red Smith once wrote about all such "British heavyweights" in five rounds.

Ali's next "fight" was not a fight in the traditional sense. Nor was it one that shows up on his record. It was a novelty fight, a mixed bout against Anonio Inoki, a Japanese wrestling champ. The so-called "fight," which I considered just one step removed from taking on a dancing bear, appealed to Ali's ego, one that gave him a chance to prove he was not only the best boxer in the world but also the best *fighter*.

This was not the first time Ali had entertained such a cockamamie idea. Back in 1971 he had come thisclose to taking on Wilt "The Stilt" Chamberlain in the Houston Astrodome. But the fight never came off. Some say it was because at the last minute Wilt had demanded $500,000, tax free. Ali said it was because the 7'1" Chamberlain had heard his claim that he only needed two words to predict the outcome: "Tim" and "Ber."

Jack Dempsey and Jersey Joe Walcott had taken on wrestlers for ring superiority, so it was nothing new. But it was to Ali, who didn't know what to do. You see, before we left for Japan we had agreed on the rules, only now nobody seemed to remember what they were or what was allowed. Early in the first round, after trying to grab Ali and drag him to the canvas where he could practice that voodoo he did so well—and being caught with several stinging jabs as a result—Inoki decided to drop to the canvas and, from a safe position, kick at Ali. Getting the hell kicked out of him, Ali, in turn, jumped up on the ropes to escape Inoki's kicks. This went on for ten rounds, Inoki on the canvas kicking up at Ali and Ali on the ropes flailing down at Inoki. Halfway through Ali wanted to forget the whole deal and go home. I reminded him that he was the world champion and talked him into finishing the farce to the very end. Ten rounds of this crap and the bore-snore was finally over. Now it was the referee's turn to render a decision of who did what and to whom. As he was trying to make up his mind, I went over and said, "Hey, pal, let's call it a draw." And that's what it was, a draw.

Nobody lost "face," as they say over in Japan, but Ali's legs were severely bruised by Inoki's kicks and soon there were dangerous blood clots. I wanted to get him back to the States to get checked out, but he had already promised to go on an exhibition tour of the Orient and foolishly went through with it. I don't know how he got through it because he could hardly walk, but he did. When he returned, still complaining about the bruises, I had him admitted to a hospital in Santa Monica to get checked out and recuperate. If those clots had traveled to his upper body, the Ali era might have ended right then and there.

With Ken Norton already scheduled for September, which was just a couple of months away, there was not much time for Ali to recuperate. Ali wanted to make it two out of three against Norton, just as he had against Frazier. He also didn't want to miss out on a paycheck worth $6 million.

Like Mark Twain who, in response to hearing he had died, said, "Rumors of my death are greatly exaggerated," so, too, were the exaggerated rumors coming out of St. John's Riverside Hospital in Santa Monica. Reports had it that Ali was near death, that he had suffered hemorrhaging from ruptured blood vessels, and so on. It seemed the only thing the rumors didn't mention was a fatal case of ingrown toenails.

One man who chased the rumors down and found them to be untrue was "Unswerving" Irving Rudd, who was doing the publicity for the upcoming Ali-Norton fight. Not only did he visit Ali, he brought along Ken Norton to see the convalescing Ali—Norton saying, "I don't care what Ali is like in the ring. Sure, I'm gonna try and beat his brains out, but as far as I'm concerned, he's a helluva man and I wanna go pay my respects to him while he's sick."

Ali set out the ground rules for the visitation by Norton and Rudd, telling Irving, "Bring the sucker up here tomorrow. But I don't want no press around when you do. No press. Ya hear?" So what happened? Knowing full well that the press was downstairs, he grabbed Norton and, getting into his wheelchair, said, "Come on, let's go down and see the press. How 'bout we show those muthas we're alive." With that, Ali wheeled off toward the elevators before any of the attending doctors could stop him. Arriving downstairs where the press was waiting for word on the meeting between the two, Ali, looking bravely upbeat, got out of his wheelchair and hobbled toward Norton, throwing a punch in his direction for the cameras. Calling Norton "Mandingo"—a reference to the movie Norton starred in as "Drum" the slave—Ali told the press how he was going to "whup" Norton when they met at Yankee Stadium, how he was "gonna knock him on his ass." There was no doubt in my mind that Ali was "whuppin" himself into shape mentally for the bout.

The next thing I knew, Ali had checked out of the hospital and gone to . . . who the hell knew? Nobody had a clue. That is until I got a call from Ali telling me, "We're opening a training camp in Miami. That's right, Miami, *Arizona.*" Where the hell's Miami, Arizona? I asked myself, my grasp of geography so bad that if I had been on the Lewis and Clark Expedition I wouldn't have been able to find Pittsburgh.

But wait, it got worse. It's not Miami, Arizona, it's some place called Show Low, Arizona. That's right, Show Low. Sounds like East Overshoe. Even Rand and McNally wouldn't have been able to find that on their maps, somewhere between Fughagawee and Nowheresville. Helen and I got out the atlas and began looking for anything sounding like Show Low and finally found it, a small town of 1,625 or so residents and one dog on the Main Street licking itself, about a hundred miles east of Phoenix. Great! There'll be no Italian restaurants there!

Who knew why Ali picked this remote spot to set up his training camp. Maybe it was because he had come across it a year before on a tour with Dick Gregory or maybe it was another of Ali's flights of fancy. But whatever it was, I was soon headed west to join Ali, kit bag and all. And believe me, getting there was no flight of fancy, flying a crop duster that barely made it off the ground. I think the pilot's name was Eddie Rickenbacher.

Almost before I had taken my jacket off, John F. X. Condon, the Madison Square Garden publicist, was on the phone. Figuring that the press would have as hard a time finding Show Low as I did and wanting as much ink for the fight as we could get, he wanted Ali & Co. back East where the press could see him, interview him, and write about him. So it was back East for us, back to the Concord Hotel, up in the Catskills Borscht Belt, where Ali applied himself, training as hard as he ever had, straining himself to get back into fighting shape and running up and down the mountainous terrain to get his legs back into dancing shape.

It was the Ali of old as he alternated his training with vocal exercises, throwing one-liners and sound bites to the press and sneering remarks at Norton. However, those cynics in cynics' clothing, the press, still had questions about Ali's readiness: How much had the "Thrilla in Manila" taken out of him? What about his legs, could they go the scheduled fifteen rounds? And so on and so forth.

Yankee Stadium was a sight for sore eyes and sticky fingers the night of the Norton fight. The New York City police were on strike, and the few who were there stood idly by, supposedly guarding the stadium. At least the stadium wasn't stolen, but most everything else was as hordes rampaged through the stadium, splintering the seats and knocking down barriers. Roaming pickpockets couldn't help helping themselves to everything else—including Herbert Muhammad's wallet.

Many in the crowd also thought the judges had picked Norton's pocket as well by giving Ali the decision. Norton, as in their two previous fights, had come constantly forward in that strange hippity-hop style of his, hands across his face in a defensive posture, while Ali circled the ring countering his charges. This tense dance had gone on for fourteen rounds with all three judges reflecting the closeness of the battle by scoring it even going into the fifteenth and final round. However, it was not the judges, but Norton's corner that cost him the fight. Knowing how close the fight was, I exhorted Ali, "You've got three more minutes. Fight like hell. . . . We need this round." But over in Norton's corner, believing they had the fight in the bag (or as Red Smith wrote, "in the burlap"), his manager, Bob Biron, told his fighter to "stay away." This strategy of staying away had cost others before and after—like Jersey Joe Walcott in his first fight with Joe Louis and Oscar De La Hoya against Felix Trinidad. Now it was to cost Norton as he became strangely inactive while Ali closed the show, winning the round decisively. That one round proved to be the difference. Although Ali felt he had lost the fight, it was that last round won by Ali that had picked Norton's pocket, not the judges.

After Norton, Ali took a little R&R, which meant a series of exhibition bouts—including six on the same night in Boston against such "worthies" as Peter Fuller, the son of the former governor of Massachusetts and owner of a car distributorship who had been a fair amateur boxer in his day.

Finally, eight months after the Norton fight, Ali defended his title again, this time against Alfredo Evangelista, the eighth-ranked heavyweight in the world and one of the most famous unknown heavyweights in history. How he was ranked eighth in anything in the world I could never figure out. He had had just sixteen fights, winning fourteen of them, twelve by KO, but they all seemed to have been against fighters who weren't even household names in their own households. In fact, ABC-TV issued a disclaimer about his ranking before the fight went on the air. To say that Ali took Evangelista seriously would be like saying Joan of Arc was Noah's wife. He didn't and it showed, looking as if he had telephoned the fight in, holding his hands down, taunting Evangelista to throw punches—to throw anything—while he danced through fifteen rounds for an instantly forgettable win.

Five months later Ali was back in New York again, this time at the Garden to face Earnie Shavers. Unlike Evangelista, this was to be no easy fight and we all knew it. To say that Earnie was a hard hitter would be an understatement. He could knock down tall buildings with a single punch, as attested to by his fifty-three KOs in sixty-one fights—a slugging average (.869) to rival Rocky Marciano, who had forty-three KOs in forty-nine fights for an .878 average. But we also knew that bodacious punch or not, Shavers had a problem with his stamina, forty of his fifty-three knockouts coming in the first three rounds. If we took him into the middle rounds he had a tendency to wilt.

Meeting Shavers before the fight, Ali trotted out some of his old chestnuts: "Your bald head makes you look like an acorn. That's going to be your nickname, 'Acorn,'" adding to his rogue's gallery of names. Then he threw in: "I might shine your head for you, Earnie." Still not satisfied with trying to psyche out the mild-mannered Shavers, Ali added one of his insulting barbs: "And then I'll teach you to talk. You gotta learn to talk, Shavers."

But Shavers, while a quiet gentleman outside the ring, was anything but inside, where he let his hands do his talking for him. In the second round he almost had the final word, catching Ali with an overhand right from hell. Ali's senses suddenly played hide-and-seek as he wobbled from the force of Shavers's blow. Shavers, unsure whether Ali was hurt or merely playing possum to draw him into a trap, failed to follow up. For the better part of the next ten rounds Ali covered up, staying away from Shavers's right-handed might and bing-bing-binging him with his jab, piling up points in the process.

For the fight television had come up with a new gimmick. After each round NBC announced the judges' scores—not to the Madison Square Garden audience, just to the home television viewers. I had prepared for this in advance by putting my pal, Baltimore matchmaker Eddie Hrica, back in the dressing room where we installed a television set. After each round Eddie would run from the dressing room to the ramp where we had entered the arena and flash me a signal: a thumbs-up if we won the round, a thumbs-down if we lost, and a wave of the hand, palm down, if it was even. Well, with three rounds to go, by virtue of more thumbs-up than down, I knew that Ali had the fight in the bag, so to speak, four rounds up on the judge's scorecards. So I told Ali to "be careful," and that the fight was his if he didn't get knocked out. Maybe he was too careful, going into a defensive cocoon and letting Shavers beat the bejabbers out of him with sledgehammer shots, some the hardest he'd ever been hit with, blows that could have felled trees, but not Ali. Almost from memory Ali hung on, surviving the battering in Rounds Thirteen and Fourteen only to come back and win the fifteenth big, and the decision. But I had the feeling that some victories are harder than defeats and that Ali was, to cop a line from someone or other, a victor by victory undone.

Coming off the Shavers fight there was genuine concern for Ali. It was obvious to all, especially those close to him, that the floating butterfly whose feet had barely touched the ground in his prime was now a stationary sitting duck, absorbing punishment he never would have in his prime from the likes of an Earnie Shavers.

Ferdie Pacheco had left the corner, no longer able to watch Ali take punches he shouldn't have had to. Gene Kilroy told Ali, "You can beat everybody, but you can't beat Father Time." And Garden matchmaker Teddy Brenner, never one to pull his punches, told Ali the morning after the Shavers fight, "Sooner or later some kid that couldn't carry your jock is going to beat you. You're going to get hit, you're gonna get hurt. You've proven everything that a great champion can possibly prove. You don't need this. Get out!"

Ali heard out each and every entreaty to retire with a polite indifference, responding only with a "Wha' for?" having already decided to carry on. As he had in the past, he looked for an "easy" opponent to take on after his hard fight with Shavers. Having single-handedly decimated the division of available challengers, he finally narrowed the short list down to one name: Leon Spinks.

In Spinks, Ali had found that "kid that couldn't carry your jock" that Teddy Brenner had warned him about. Winner of the 1976 Olympic light-heavyweight gold medal—the same title Ali had won sixteen years before in Rome—Spinks had had only had seven pro fights. Ali asked of no one in particular, "How can someone with seven nothin' pro fights beat me?" He fairly salivated at the prospect of fighting a youngster he considered to be a green novice who was little more than a puffed-up light-heavyweight, so raw Ali fully expected Spinks to come into the ring still clutching his Olympic medal.

But I knew how tough Spinks was. I had had a kid named Lee Canalito fighting in St. Louis on the same card as Leon in Leon's hometown debut. Getting up at five in the morning of the fight to make sure Lee was doing his final roadwork I chanced to look out the hotel window and caught Leon getting out of a cab, kissing his lady friend of the evening, or morning, or whenever goodbye, and then taking a swig out of a bottle—no glass, mind you, that would have wasted a step, just straight out of the bottle. That night he went into the ring and coldcocked his opponent, Pedro Agosto, in one round. Now, that's tough!

I knew this was going to be a tough fight. Small guys always gave Muhammad trouble. But I couldn't convince him, try as I might. He was so contemptuous of Spinks, whom he called "Dracula" because of his missing front teeth, that he walked through training. He had none of the fire he had shown in preparing for Sonny Liston, George Foreman, Joe Frazier, or Ken Norton. This time Ali trained as if he was doing it from memory, thinking it unnecessary to do anything more than punch the clock for someone with just seven fights.

By the time I arrived at what laughingly could be called his training camp, Ali was shockingly unprepared, having sparred only about twenty rounds or so. His weight, which had been as high as 242, was still a problem. You could see it. His face was soft, lacking the usual fighter's tautness, and his stomach was encased in rolls of flab. Writers, noting his condition, used descriptions like "out of shape," "soft," and "paunchy" to describe him. Bill Gallo of the *New York Daily News* drew a cartoon of Ali lugging his belly around in a wheelbarrow. I tried to get Ali back on a rigorous regimen, but he successfully avoided doing anything more than what could best be described as walk-through exercises.

The fight itself was an embarrassment. I knew, just knew, from the moment Muhammad came out in an oh-hell-let's-go-fishing posture, hands down, taunting Spinks, that we were in trouble. Hell, this guy would walk through ten scotches to get at anything. You knew that if he was so unconcerned about a fight that he could come in at five in the morning swigging liquor straight out of a bottle and then go out that night and KO his opponent in one round he wasn't going to be bothered by Ali's grandstanding. He just kept coming, coming, coming, barrel-chesting his way inside and countering Ali's punches, what few there were, throwing my guy off guard. As the fight wore on, Ali's jab became more and more a pawing motion, his speed and reflexes AWOL, and Spinks, looking anything but a 10–1 underdog, stayed right on top of him, throwing those bad-intentioned ponderous punches of his. Come the so-called "championship rounds," the thirteenth, fourteenth, and fifteenth, I expected Muhammad to pick it up, to mount one of those "close the show" rallies he had almost patented. But despite the fact I kept trying to tell him he was losing and now was the time to "close the show," he kept telling me, "I know what I'm doing." What he was doing was losing the fight—a close split decision—and his title.

Back in the dressing room, some of the faithful were hollering about Ali being "robbed." His face puffed out, his lip cut, his kidneys bruised, an exhausted Ali slowly looked up and said, "Look, we ain't gonna have any sore losers in here tonight. The boy whupped me and whupped me fair. That's it, hear? I don't wanna hear any more talk about how they 'robbed me.'" Then he shouted to his brother, the leader of the "we wuz robbed" clan, "Look, make up your mind . . . first, you got me robbed, then you got me in no shape." There were no alibis, no couldas, wouldas, or shouldas as he told the press at the Las Vegas Hilton after the fight, "I'm sorry men, I messed up. I was lousy. But I don't want to take anything away from Spinks. He fought a good fight and never quit. He made fools of everybody, even me." A pause, then, "I'll win it for the third time. I'll get in better shape."

Saying, "What keeps me going is goals," his goal was now to win back the title he had "lent" to Spinks and become world heavyweight champion for an unprecedented third time. Knowing he had not been in shape the last time, he undertook a tough and dedicated conditioning program, one that started with slowly resting and getting back his energy and then methodically building himself up into top physical condition for the rematch in New Orleans.

However, the rematch wouldn't be for the *world* heavyweight title. For the World Boxing Council (WBC) had decided in their infinite nonwisdom that inasmuch as Spinks was not defending his newly won title against their number one contender, Ken Norton, they would strip Leon of his belt and anoint Norton as their champion even though he had never won a title bout. (Did I see the heavy hand of promoter Don King behind this?) Nevertheless, that other alphabet-soup group, the WBA, or World Boxing Association, continued to recognize Leon as their champion. And since the championship that Leon held traced its lineage back to John L. Sullivan, we would be fighting for the *real* world heavyweight championship title no matter what those clowns in clowns' clothing, the WBC, said.

In a case of turnabout is fair play, this time it was Ali who did the hard training. The soft flab was gone, the hard edge back. He had even done 8,014 sit-ups, approximately 8,013 more than he had before the first fight. "This is the hardest I've ever trained for any fight in my career," he told newsmen who were covering the fight like the Creation of the World, Part II. "I've never suffered in my life like I have for this one. I'm sacrificing all the things I love, the pie, the ice cream, everything. I'm sacrificing so much because I can't afford to lose. This is my last chance. If I lose, it will plague me the rest of my life." Meanwhile, Leon was running around like a truant on a romp, chasing every which way in pursuit of life, liberty, and happiness. So much so that only a couple of days before the fight he was MIA, with no forwarding address.

This time the fight was a one-man exhibition, the Ali of old, a dancing master again, constantly befuddling Spinks. Quick-stepping and quick-jabbing, Ali always seemed to be two steps in front of Leon, who looked as if he was only interested in catching the first train going home. No rope-a-dopes or lying on the ropes this time. Ali was perpetual motion, in and out, around, and everywhere but where Leon was. It got so that by the fifth round I couldn't help myself as I hollered, "Where did he go, Leon? Where did he go?" Spinks had no idea where Ali went or how to get to him. When

Spinks did get close enough, Ali would grab him in a bear hug, pulling him off balance. By the middle rounds Ali was catching Leon with three-punch combinations, bang-bang-bang, and I hollered up at Spinks, "Goodbye, Leon." But Leon had gone "goodbye" long before and knew it, responding to my shouts with only a gap-toothed smile.

At the end of the seventh Muhammad performed a little Ali shuffle on his way back to the corner, a tiny celebration to be sure, but one I wouldn't put up with, and I told him to knock it off. He didn't need any of that, we were beating Spinks with plain ol' boxing. No frills, thank you. The hapless Spinks returned to his corner in search of something, anything, that might help. But, truth to tell, his corner was in worse shape than Leon, if that were possible. I looked over and saw what looked like organized madness with everyone in Spinks's dysfunctional corner shouting instructions at once and I thought to myself, their crazies could certainly match our crazies.

As I was to find out later, Sam Solomon, Spinks's principal trainer, was joined in the corner by Georgie Benton, the architect of Spinks's win in the first fight. Solomon's plan for instructing Spinks called for Solomon and Benton, along with anyone else in Spinks's corner, to speak to Leon only after every third or fourth round. If they had something to communicate to Spinks and it wasn't their turn, they had to tell whoever's turn it was to relay it to Leon. That is, if they chose to. It was almost as if they needed a scorecard to keep track of who was telling who what. It reminded me of that old limerick about two people arguing all night over who had the right to do what and to whom. Over on our side of the ring we could hear people in Leon's Tower of Babel corner screaming "wiggle" or "move" or "don't get hurt" or other such nonsense. One of the saddest sights I've ever seen was a disgusted Georgie Benton, having given up with all that craziness, walking up the aisle, away from the ring, eyes on the ground, while Leon came out for another round still not knowing what to do.

It wouldn't have mattered much what anyone told Leon; he was lost. So, too, was the fight, as every round began to mirror the previous one with Muhammad still dancing as if he had discovered his own personal wayback machine, and Leon chasing him but never quite catching up. The huge Superdome crowd, now sensing they were part of boxing history, began cheering loudly with every punch Ali landed. They cheered even more loudly when Ali began leading their cheers. But their loudest roar came when the decision was announced—a unanimous one, 10–4–1, 10–4–1, and 11–4, all for Ali.

Ali had done it! He had become heavyweight champion a third time. Is there anything grander than a grand comeback?

The second Spinks fight was hardly "Fight of the Century" stuff. Far from it. From a "sweet science" standpoint, it was sloppy. But it was beautifully sloppy, wonderfully sloppy, gorgeously sloppy. No showboating, no rope-a-dopes, no taunting, just Muhammad getting in there and doing his number. It was vintage Ali.

Muhammad always had a sense of history. He had wanted to become the first and only heavyweight champion to win the world title for a third time. And he had. Now he wanted to, as he said, "be the first black champion to get out on top." And to listen to him, he intended to, retiring the morning after the Spinks fight.

Oh, I know he had retired before. So many times he was probably listed in the *Guinness Book of Records* under "Most Times Retired." But when Ali said, "I don't want to fight no more. I've been doing it for twenty-five years, and you can only do so much wear to the body. I can see it, I can feel it," I thought this time he really meant it. This time he was finally prepared to call it a day and venture out to discover life after boxing.

"The Ali Years," as my bride Helen called them, had finally come to an end. We had traveled many roads together on Ali's magic carpet, faraway places like Zaire, Manila, Kuala Lumpur, Las Vegas, Tokyo, Munich, San Juan, New York, and New Orleans. I was always in his corner, sometimes cajoling, sometimes suggesting, and sometimes demanding things from him in both hard and easy fights. And it had always been a gas just being around him. These were some of the best days of my life, exciting times that would provide memories I would cherish forever. But now it was time for me to close the book on the Ali chapter and get on with my life.

Or so I thought. Jump-skip almost two years later and there I was up in Montreal with my fighter Sugar Ray Leonard preparing for his fight with Roberto Duran, and here comes Muhammad hardly looking like that handsome bright-eyed, beaming-faced youngster of yesterday who used to say, "Look at me, I'm so pretty . . . not a mark on my face." His once magnificent shape had gone to pot over a disappearing belt line, his once powerful voice was muffled, his hair was graying. He bore all the vestiges of middle age. During those intervening months he had toured the world doing star turns, cashing in on his brand name by appearing here, there, and everywhere. Still, that old fire burned within. Believing he had one more good fight left in him and one more chance to stand there basking in the glow and hearing his fans chant "AL-LEE" one last time—and no doubt also seduced by the chance to make history by winning the heavyweight title a fourth time along with an $8 million guarantee for such a fistic first—he now wanted to fight current heavyweight champ Larry Holmes. And he wanted me in his corner again.

When I joined Muhammad at Deer Lake for the final stages of his training for the Holmes fight I barely recognized him. He had lost more than thirty pounds, his voice was back in full throttle, and his hair was now black (courtesy, he said, of "a little black hair rinse"). He looked terrific. He told me that when he saw me up in Montreal "my thyroid glands were acting up." But, he said, "I took two pills a day for a month and it's all cleared up now." Those "two pills a day" he referred to were a thyroid medicine, Thyrolar, prescribed by Herbert Muhammad's personal physician.

His great looking physical condition was like something that looked good in a store window, but when you got it home it was nothing like what you thought it to be. He had nothing, no reserves, no strength, no fatty tissue to burn up. And you knew it was more than just Father Time taking a toll on his thirty-eight-year-old body, it was those damned pills, which help you lose weight but take your strength away. Their effect, in the words of Dr. Ferdie Pacheco was "like burning the tires off a race car and telling the driver to race without wheels."

On October 2, 1980, after an absence of two years and seventeen days, Muhammad Ali climbed back into the ring again looking for five or six minutes like the Ali of old. Unfortunately, those five or six minutes came before the opening bell. There was Ali playacting, leading the Caesars Palace crowd in cheers for himself and boos for Holmes, hollering, "I want you, Holmes, I want you," at the WBC champ, and lunging first at Holmes's championship belt, then at Holmes himself, forcing Bundini Brown and yours truly to "restraint" him—and almost causing me to sprain my little finger "holding" him back.

As for the fight itself, Ali had nothing, zip, zilch, nada. It was a futile left jab that never jabbed, a cocked right that never uncocked, and a battle plan that never went into battle. Almost from the first punch thrown, a stiff jab by Holmes, it was obvious this was the ghost of Ali past. By the fourth he was a rag doll, the only thing holding him up was his pride. By the ninth he was all but defenseless.

After the ninth referee Richard Greene came over to our corner to ask whether Ali wanted to continue. Not wanting to suffer the humiliation of being stopped on his stool, the bone-weary Ali, who had given the boxing world 539 rounds, decided on yet another one, nodding his head "yes" to my question of "Do you want to do it?" I told him, "If you don't start throwing punches in this round, I'm gonna stop this fight."

But Round Ten was no different from any other round as Holmes drove Ali to the ropes, battering his already sore body, raking his puffed eyes with battering-ram jabs and prolonging the misery by holding back his right-hand shots to the totally unprotected body of Ali, all the while pleading with referee Greene to come to the aid of the man he idolized. It was three more minutes of pure agony for Ali and his faithful. And then the bell.

Once again referee Greene hurried over to the corner, concerned about Ali's inability to defend himself. I knew that Ali was looking for someone to save him since he couldn't do it himself, and I wigwagged my hands to say it was "over." All of a sudden I felt someone tugging at my sweater. It was Bundini, refusing to believe the fight was over, pushing and pulling at me, pleading for "one more round." I couldn't help myself, but I had to scream at Bundini, who was in tears, "Take your goddamn hands off me. He can't take any more. He's defenseless. Get the hell away from me. . . . I'm boss here. *It's over.*" I knew I was right and so, too, did Muhammad who, through swollen lips, muttered, "Thank you."

It broke my heart to stop the Holmes fight. It was the worst beating Muhammad ever took. He not only hadn't won a round, he hadn't won one second of any round. If you believe there is any truth in advertising you would have believed that his fight against Holmes, billed as "The Last Hurrah," was exactly that, Ali's last hurrah, his last fight. But then again this was boxing, so what do you expect?

And so, fourteen months after his sad performance against Holmes, Ali decided to take one more fight, sort of a "Son of the Last Hurrah," this time against Trevor Berbick. Offering up the excuse that his poor effort against Holmes was due to those debilitating thyroid pills, Ali wanted one

more fight, one fight strictly for himself. He was two months shy of his for-
tieth birthday and still thought there might be a chance to close out his
career with a "W," not the ugly "L" that marked the result of his fight with
Holmes.

The less said about the fight the better. The wheels had come off the
once beautiful fighting machine known as Muhammad Ali, and there was
nothing there that night in the Bahamas when he lost to the tag team of
Trevor Berbick and Father Time. Afterward Ali said, "I couldn't show and
now I know . . . Father Time got me."

The final bell, a cowbell substituted for the missing ring bell, not only
signaled the end of his ten-round fight with Berbick, it also tolled the end
of his great sixty-one-fight career, one of the greatest in the history of the
sport. With a résumé that included every leading heavyweight from Floyd
Patterson to George Foreman—whose careers spanned forty-five years, from
Patterson's first fight in 1952 to Foreman's last in 1997—this embodiment
of athletic intelligence who flaired to be different had become an international hero, one whose face had become the most recognized in the world.

But over and above those hard-edged facts and figures that can be found
in any old *Ring Record Book*, there were those many outside-the-ring
moments that went unrecorded that tell the story of Muhammad Ali better than his ring record. Those moments when he gave of himself, like the
time he was being led into a Super Bowl Party for VIPs and detoured into
the kitchen "to see my people," the kitchen help. Or the time, just hours
after beating George Foreman, when he went into the nearby village and
spent time showing the kids magic tricks. Or when he left the ring after
beating Brian London to comfort London's son, telling the young London
that his father was "not hurt" and "was a good man." Or when, in the company of Gene Kilroy, he visited a nursing home and one ancient gentleman
looked up and said, "Joe Louis?" His whole life this man had wanted to
meet Joe Louis, so Ali signed an autograph for him as "Joe Louis," saying,
"We all look alike to him so let him think he met Joe."

That clanking cowbell that ended the Berbick fight also marked the end
of my close boxing relationship with Ali, one that had begun, fittingly
enough, twenty-two years before with the ringing of the phone in my
Louisville hotel room. During the two decades we were together I came to
enjoy his wonderful love for life. Let me tell you, the big key was laugh-

ter. That was the whole key with this kid. He always had fun. No matter how tough the situation was, we had fun. He always found a way to laugh and make others around him laugh.

I can't do better than quote the great poet Maya Angelou who wrote of Ali: "His impact recognizes no continent, no language, no color, no ocean. . . . Muhammad Ali belongs to all of us." And for almost twenty-two years I was fortunate that he belonged not to me as much as *with* me. Great men and great monuments don't relinquish their hold on anyone. And Muhammad Ali was both. Especially to me.

The English wanted to know what magical potions I had in my kit to stop
bleeding, along with everything else I kept in store to work a fight, both
before and after—so I showed them.

Helen and me on our wedding day.

Helen and me on the couch with our daughter, Terri, our son, Jim, and our dog, Wong.

Willie Pastrano and me in Bologna, Italy, for his fight with Franco Cavicchi. He won, by the way.

At the 5th Street Gym (from left to right) me with Johnny Holman (heavyweight), Willie Pastrano (light-heavyweight), Jimmy Beecham (middleweight), and Andy Arel (lightweight)

Dressed up with friends (from the left) Johnny DeJohn, Carmen Basilio, and "Big Julie" Isaacson.

Angelo Dundee

(Left to right) Luis Rodriguez, Ingemar Johansson, me, and Florentino Fernandez.

At the 5th Street Gym. Top row (left to right): Ernesto Corrales, Hignio Ruiz, the great Cuban trainer Luis Sarria, and my friend Ciro Garcia. Middle row: Guillermo Dutschmann, featherweight champ José Legra, Willie Pastrano, and Allan Harmon. Floor: Douglas Vaillant, Florentino Fernandez, me, Luis Rodriguez, and Muhammad Ali.

This is me showing Muhammad how I wrap hands, taken at the restaurant below the 5th Street Gym.

Ali, me, and Drew "Bundini" Brown.

Bundini (on the right),
Muhammad, and me.

This was taken in 1950, at the dinner for the NY Boxing Manager's Guild, at the Hotel Edison.

#1 (Table 26, left to right around the table): Cus D'Amato, Billy Stevens, Jack Monaghan, Vince Monaghan, George Kobb, unknown, unknown, Duke Stefano

#2 (Table 24 from left to right): Jimmy Doyle, Bob Melnick, Nick Baffo, Lefty Remini, unknown, unknown, Dick Vick, Eddie Brown, Tony Marenghi, unknown, unknown

#3 (Table 20 from left to right): Johnny Dundee (a junior lightweight and featherweight champion, but no relation), unknown, unknown, Dewey Fragetta, unknown, Gaspipe Voccala

#4 (Back of room): Blinky Palermo. In front of Palermo is Moe Fleischer, the matchmaker for Ridgewood Grove in Brooklyn.

#5 (Table 22, along the fold): Freddie Brown, Eddie Cocoa, unknown, Whitey Bimstein, unknown, Fats Gary, Billy Graham (the great New York fighter), unknown, unknown, Irving Cohen (Rocky Graziano's manager)

#6   (Table 29, from left to right): Joe Woodman, unknown, Charley Rose, Willie Gilzenberg, unknown, unknown, unknown, me, my brother Chris, John Abood

#7   (Table 28, from left to right): Billy Brown (matchmaker for the New York Garden), Jimmy DeAngelo (Roland LaStarza's manager)

#8   (right side of picture): Rocky Castellani, and to the left of him is Tommy Ryan

#9   (Table #15, below the second light fixture): Charlie Goldman (Rocky Marciano's trainer)

#10 Al Weill

#11 (back wall from left to right) Chick Wergeles, Charley Johnson (Archie Moore's Manager), Jesse Abramson, Al Buck (writer for the New York Post), unknown, Dr. Vincent Nardiello, Jack Dempsey

#12 (back wall from left to right) Jimmy Braddock, Doc Kearns.

All trainers, taken at the Boxing Hall of Fame. Top row (left to right): Emanuel Steward, me, Lou Duva. Bottom row: Georgie Benton, Eddie Futch, and Gil Clancy.

My rock at Deer Lake Training Camp

My office, shared with brother Chris, at the Miami Beach Convention Hall.
P.S. I had to reimburse Chris for the phone calls.

Taken in Sweden, this postfight interview with Howard Cosell and Jimmy Ellis took place after Ellis defended his title against Floyd Patterson. From left to right: Cossell, Ferdie Pacheco, Ellis, and me.

Me, Howard, and Ray Leonard.

April 26, 1997. George Foreman standing between rounds, with me in his corner, during his fight against Lou Savarese. *Courtesy of Marty Rosengarten.*

From left to right: Muhammad Ali, Harold Conrad, me, and Jack Palance.

Pat Patterson, Sylvester Stallone, Gene Kilroy, Muhammad Ali, and me.

Me and Jerry Lewis at the Touchdown Club in Washington, D.C.

Me and *The Cinderella Man*, aka Russell Crowe, at the International Boxing Hall of Fame. Crowe is pointing to Willie Pastrano's picture.

My grandson Ryan, me, and my son, Jim.

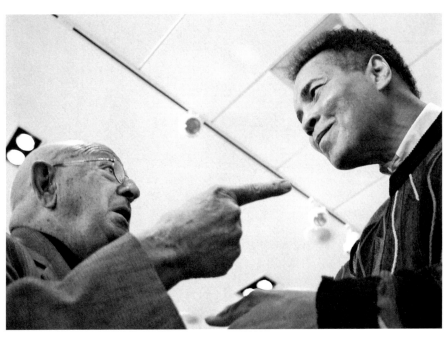

Having kicks with Muhammad at the Muhammad Ali Center in Louisville. We always had fun! *Photo by Jeff Julian, March 2007.*

FOURTEEN

Filling Ali's Size-50 Shoes with Sugar Ray Leonard

By nature, boxing is an orderly sport with one champion following another in a systematic progression. That continuity also occurs when one boxing legend passes the torch to another, whether in the ring or in the public's mind.

And although Muhammad Ali would say, "After I retire, boxing will die," there was already someone waiting in the wings to take his place even though Muhammad hadn't quite deeded it over. Not yet anyway.

By 1976 Muhammad Ali was in the twilight of his career, his glory days behind him. It looked like the sport of boxing's glory days were behind it as well. But at that magic moment, boxing was about to reenter the spotlight again, this time courtesy of amateur boxing.

Now what I knew about amateur boxing could be written on the head of a pin with more than enough room left over for the Lord's Prayer. I really didn't know one amateur boxer from another. However, the 1976 Olympics would change all of that, not only for me but for millions of Americans as well, as ABC-TV showcased the American boxing team during prime time. Never before had so much attention been devoted to amateur boxing. On the American boxing team were Leo Randolph (flyweight), Howard Davis Jr. (lightweight), Ray Leonard (light-welterweight), Michael Spinks (middleweight), and brother Leon Spinks (light-heavyweight). During the previous Olympics, the American boxing team had won just one gold medal. This 1976 team would come away with a record *five* gold medals.

Behind the microphone, ABC announcer Howard Cosell shared in their glory, focusing on each with his own special brand of "tell-it-like-it-is" enthusiasm. The man who had been attacked by many after he had championed Muhammad's cause was now lauded by the very same people who had once questioned his patriotism. The favorable mail came flooding into the ABC offices. One came from the Commandant of the Marine Corps who thanked Cosell "on behalf of the Marines" for "taking time to include mention of the fact that Corporal (Leon) Spinks is a United States Marine." The Commandant's letter went on to add, "Your own characteristically professional performance added greatly to the enjoyment of the evening."

Spinks was hardly the only object of Cosell's attention. He spread his multisyllabic words around to paint a verbal picture of each American Olympian. But none received more attention than the light-welterweight gold medalist, the fighter he called "Sugar" Ray Leonard. Cosell focused on Leonard's boy-next-door looks and, more than occasionally, mentioned that Leonard carried a picture of his girlfriend and two-year-old son in his sock. But what was obvious to anyone watching the telecast—even the man he was named for, singer Ray Charles—was Leonard's incredibly fast hands and exceptional movement. The kid had so much talent that it should have been ruled illegal. "Sugar" Ray Leonard was Americana, he was home cooking, and he was the symbol of a new era in boxing. And guess who first brought Ray to America's attention? Howard Cosell, that's who.

The next time I saw Ray was in person. Madison Square Garden had thrown a gala to honor the Olympic champions the week before the third Muhammad Ali–Ken Norton fight, and my friend Gene Kilroy brought Ray over to sit next to Muhammad Ali. As Ray sat there like a starstruck twelve-year-old with saucer-cup eyes looking at his idol, Muhammad turned to him and said, "You're good, you're fast, and you're going to be like me." Then he added, "And if you ever go pro, you need pros around you." It was at that moment that Kilroy introduced me to Leonard with a " . . . and here's the guy who made Muhammad Ali, Angelo Dundee." Ali, never far from a conversation, chimed in with, "Yeah, Angelo Dundee, and if you ever go pro, he's the guy for you. He's a good guy, loyal, dedicated, and honest." And that was that. At least for the moment.

After his Olympic triumph Ray retired—the first of his many retirements— wanting instead "to go to school and work with kids." However, his father needed medical attention and as the breadwinner of the family, Ray needed money to cover the necessary expenses. So, he changed his mind, telling his longtime friend Janks Morton, "I'm going to fight as a pro."

Now that he had decided to carry on with his career, Ray became a hot property with several offers made to handle him. One of the first came from Abe Pollin, the owner of the Washington basketball and hockey franchises and of Capital Centre in Landover, Maryland. Pollin proposed lending Ray $50,000 to start his training. Ray would then "pay me back from his purses," Pollin cutting himself in for 60 percent. That offer met with a "Thanks, but no thanks."

Another who made a pass at Ray was promoter Don King who, between rounds of the Ali-Norton fight at Yankee Stadium, invited Ray and Janks to the men's room where he pushed a contract under their noses. Janks took one look at the numbers and told Ray to "flush it down the stool" and with that Ray washed his hands of it.

It now became apparent to Ray that he needed help preparing himself for his pro career. And so it was that Janks took him to see the manager of his softball team, Mike Trainer, who just happened to be a lawyer. Trainer, from what I gathered, told Ray something along the lines of, "If you're really thinking about doing it and if you really think you can box professionally, why do you want to sell part of yourself? Why don't you just set it up as a business where you own 100 percent of yourself? You go to the bank and borrow some money; then pay off your loan and everything's fine."

But banks weren't in the habit of lending money to boxers, especially black amateur boxers. So, following the business model set by Joe Frazier's original Cloverlay group, Trainer went to a group of friends and clients to grubstake Ray, telling them, "Don't lend him any more than you can afford to lose. This is a fun thing. If you lose the money, it's like going to the racetrack." Twenty-one of them kicked in $1,000 each to form Ray Leonard Inc. Four months later they all got their money back—plus interest of $40, which one of them neglected to report as income, prompting the Internal Revenue Service to audit his tax return.

This was also about the time Trainer decided Ray needed a public relations man and recommended Charlie Brotman, who was known around the Washington, D.C., area as "Mr. Sports." It's also the point in the story when Ray Leonard and I became an "item."

Following Trainer's suggestion, Janks and Ray, along with Ray's father, visited Brotman at his office. After telling Brotman, "I'm ready to do what I've got to do," Ray asked *what* to do. Charlie, who had handled the PR for the local Golden Gloves and Amateur Athletic Union (AAU) tournaments—and had publicized Ray as the drawing card to sell tickets for the events—told them that Ray "needed a manager, a trainer, and a cutman." "But who?" they asked. Again Charlie came up with an answer, sort of a three-part answer: Eddie Futch, Gil Clancy, or yours truly. The threesome then told Charlie to go ahead and contact the three names and see which one he would recommend. With that, Brotman drew up a questionnaire and called all three of the potential managers/trainers. His call to me went something like this: "Sugar Ray Leonard is considering going professional . . ." and then he rattled off a series of questions like, "Where would he train?" "Where would his home base be?" "What opponent should he fight first?" "Could you help publicize Ray?" I must have given the right answers for somehow, someway, Brotman's recommendation as to who, as he put it, "could do the most good for Sugar Ray, both in and out of the ring," was, TA-DA, Angelo Dundee.

The next thing I knew, there was someone named Mike Trainer on the phone. I didn't know Mike Trainer from Adam—never heard of him, never met him, never talked to him. But there he was explaining to me that he was Leonard's lawyer and that he had formed a corporation to look after Leonard's potential earnings and was looking for a manager for Sugar Ray. I wasn't sure if he was asking me if I wanted to handle Leonard or not, so I let him go on without asking. Trainer finally got around to asking me if I was interested. Sure, I was interested. I knew the kid and liked him; he had won me over with his first hello. Besides, the kid, from what I had seen in the Olympics, was lavishly talented. What was not to like? We discussed my involvement, and Trainer sent me a copy of a proposed six-year contract to review to act as Ray's personal representative, boxing advisor, and manager. I was to receive 15 percent of Leonard's boxing earnings.

Satisfied with the terms, I flew to Washington to sign the contract. Trainer personally picked me up at the airport and took me immediately to a press conference to announce my signing on as Sugar Ray's manager. There was little doubt that my association with Muhammad Ali and my list of champions gave Sugar Ray instant credibility. My addition to the team was what one of my writer friends told me looked like "the bread they had cast upon the waters would come back bread pudding covered with cream." And Ray called me "the missing piece of the puzzle."

Having signed on as manager, my first job was to get a close look at my fighter. To get to know Ray better and evaluate his skills, I asked that Ray come down to the 5th Street Gym in Miami with Janks Morton and Dave Jacobs, his trainer from his amateur days.

How do I evaluate a boxer's skills in a gym situation? I watch him spar and then take notes, normally on the back of any handy old envelope or piece of paper available, breaking down a fighter's style the way an English teacher would a sentence. My notes usually include observations on the boxer's hand movement, ability to slide, balance, jab, and so on. With Ray there were very few such notes. From what I saw, he had an awful lot to offer—great balance, lightning reflexes, and a big punch.

But he needed to be nursed along. After all, like all amateur fighters he had never fought more than three rounds. So my first job was to build up his stamina. After stamina-building exercises, Ray underwent long sessions of sparring and shadowboxing. I hardly touched his style, it was near perfect. What I did was tweak it a little, teaching him to get down on his punches a little more so that he punched rather than slapped, as well as showing him angles and other subtleties that would allow him to translate those skills into professional success.

My next job was to make matches for Ray that would provide him with on-the-job training. Matchmaking is not like spinning the wheel on "Wheel of Fortune" and coming up with a match/opponent. Nor was it spoon-feeding him fighters with toe tags from the local cemetery, as many managers do to build up their fighters' early careers. No, you've got to make the right matches, matching your fighter with guys he can learn from, not only to increase your fighter's experience but also so you can gauge what your fighter's got. By constantly raising the bar on your fighter's training wheels, you increase the odds of his success and his chances of moving up in competition. Raising the bar also gives you an opportunity to see how high his ceiling is. You've got to be very careful you don't overstep your kid's talent. Don't try before he's ready. This happens to a lot of fighters—kids are called upon to show their talent before they're ready for the big time, and they can't handle it. You've got to put your fighter in the best possible matchups for him, ones he'll learn from. And, needless to say, the less risky, the better.

Take Gene Tunney, for example, a self-taught boxer who learned as he went along. He improved by applying what he picked up from past opponents. Another who learned on the job was Tony Canzoneri who waded through a grueling schedule with few milk-fed opponents and by the time he won the lightweight title at the unripe age of twenty-two, he was a well-seasoned veteran of eighty-three pro battles.

You can also learn as much from failures as from small triumphs. Floyd Patterson's fight with Joey Maxim is an example. Floyd was undefeated in his first thirteen fights. Thinking Floyd was ready for better opponents, manager Cus D'Amato put him in with former light-heavyweight champ Joey Maxim, then in his 105th fight. Maxim, one of those cuties who could box your ears off, took Floyd to school, winning an eight-round decision. But D'Amato thought it was a good loss, one he called a great learning experience. "That's why I matched him with Maxim," D'Amato said.

On the other hand, matchmaking is also the quasi-science of avoiding those fights that serve no purpose or are counterproductive. One bout that served absolutely no purpose was Rocky Marciano's fight with Lee Savold. In his thirty-ninth fight, coming right after his destruction of Joe Louis, Marciano was so busy trying to get his thirty-fourth knockout he didn't learn a thing. He simply looked like a wild young man throwing leather to the winds. And although he came away with the win, one writer was moved to write, "You can't teach a fellow to fight if he isn't forced to learn in the ring."

There was also another problem in finding the right matches for Ray. Ray's reputation was so awesome that managers of other preliminary fighters nearly fell all over themselves running away from any suggestion they match their fighters against him. Others tried to overmatch him with far more seasoned fighters.

Nevertheless, offers came in. Sometimes directly to me, sometimes to Trainer—especially those fights around the Washington, D.C., area. I checked out every potential opponent. Those I hadn't seen personally, I checked out with others who knew the style and quality of the fighters whose names were submitted. We had to find the right opponent for his debut, one who was not so bad, not so good; one who could put up a good fight—not *too* good, mind you—and still give Ray a chance to learn how to pace himself through six rounds and be comfortable in front of a large crowd. You see, you learn from doing. You learn from the fights. All the training in the world is not like being in a fight—the actual combat, the crowd, learning how to deal with people, everything.

I finally found what looked like the perfect opponent for Ray's first fight: Luis "The Bull" Vega, a welterweight out of Allentown, Pennsylvania. I say "looked like" because, although I had never seen him, his record was perfect for Ray, fourteen total bouts with seven wins, five losses, and two draws. He had three knockouts and had never been KO'd. But when I finally saw him on the day of the fight, I was embarrassed. He was so small that it was almost a guarantee he would never hear the words "Jump Ball" in his lifetime. So I made him wear a sombrero at the weigh-in and stand on the scale on his tiptoes. Meanwhile Ray crouched over so the two wouldn't look like a replica of the 1939 World's Fair symbol.

The long and short of it was that Ray won his debut in convincing fashion in front of a sellout crowd at the Baltimore Civic Center and a national TV audience. We were off and running.

When I first entered boxing way back when, television was no big deal. Back then fighters got $4,000 or so for fighting on TV. Then the TV camera changed our entire business, making faces as recognizable as those seen in the mirror every morning. A boxer's earning power has become greater because the public knows the face. Just ask Muhammad. He captured the TV cameras and captivated the TV audience. And in so doing reaped the benefits, earning millions.

The same thing happened to Sugar Ray Leonard. Everyone knew Ray Leonard, thanks to ABC and Howard Cosell. The question was now: how best to exploit it?

Ray was one of the two Olympic gold medal winners ABC had embraced with their cameras, the other being Howard Davis Jr., the lightweight medalist and winner of the Val Barker Award as the outstanding boxer in the Montreal Games. Now CBS-TV, looking to get the jump on ABC and beat them at their own game, sought to sign both to long-term contracts. Unable to decide which to sign first, they turned to their in-house boxing consultant, Gil Clancy, to find out which of the two he preferred. Clancy reportedly said, "I like Davis. He's the better fighter, and Leonard's got bad hands." Nevertheless, CBS signed both. Davis was signed to fight six times over the next year and eight months, receiving $40,000 for a six-rounder, $50,000 for an eight-rounder, and $200,000 for a ten-rounder if Davis supplied the opponent. (He would earn $165,000 for a ten-rounder if CBS had to dig up a suitable victim.) Ray received $40,000 for his first bout, his six-rounder with Vega.

The Vega bout, however, was a one-time thing with CBS as ABC stepped in to sign Ray just as Ray was on the threshold of signing a long-term contract with CBS. Charlie Brotman, who was in on the negotiations, told me how that happened. According to Charlie, CBS had contracted Ray to do the color on a fight they televised from Puerto Rico, but the contract also gave them a right of first refusal for his first pro fight. After Mike Trainer had negotiated that first-fight contract, Charlie asked Trainer if he had checked with anybody else to see what the going price was. Told no by Trainer, Charlie, thinking it was in Ray's best interest to check, called Howard Cosell. Cosell, like everyone else in the industry, said he "was under the impression Ray was committed to CBS." When told by Charlie it was only for his first fight, Cosell said he'd talk with Jim Spence in the sports department and get back to Charlie.

Charlie and Trainer had scheduled a meeting with CBS to sign a long-term contract at noon, but Spence called at the behest of Cosell and told them to come up to ABC before going over to the one-eyed network to "see if we can talk." So the two members of Leonard's brain trust flew up to meet with Spence and Cosell. Spence's first question was, "What will it take?" Charlie threw out a number saying, "Oh, $100,000," and Spence quickly agreed. At that point, again according to Brotman, Trainer and Brotman asked to be excused and went to the men's room where, in Charlie's words, "It was like the popping of champagne bottles, both of us laughing hysterically." They then went back and signed, figuring they had driven a good deal. After all, they reasoned, CBS had offered less than one-half of that for Leonard's fight with Vega. Later, when they called Barry Frank over at CBS to tell them what they had done, Frank was livid and said, "Do you know what you've done? We would have gone higher than $100,000."

Ray was never meant to be a bit player. His 100,000-watt smile and enormous likeability coupled with his extraordinary boxing skills tabbed him as boxing's coming superstar. Moreover, he wore the name of one of boxing's all-time greats: Sugar Ray Robinson. That name had been given to Robinson by a sportswriter who, watching him, said, "He's sweet." And his manager had filled in the blank, saying, "as sweet as sugar." And Robinson protected the name in the face of other "Sugars," as if he had a copyright on it. One time, so the story goes, when Robinson faced another of the pretenders to the "Sugar" crown, George "Sugar" Costner, he reputedly told Costner during the prefight instructions, "Now I'll show you who's the *real* Sugar." Robinson proved his point by laying out Costner in one round. Afterward Robinson chided the artificial "Sugar" with, "Now go out and earn yourself the name."

But now Robinson accepted his new namesake, Ray Leonard, saying, "I'm gratified he's using my name. I think it's great when kids think enough of you to use your name."

And so the fighter first named after Ray Charles was now named after Ray Robinson. In an ironic twist, it just so happened that Ray Charles's real name was Ray Charles Robinson. He had dropped his surname because he was being confused in the public's mind with the fighter.

By February 1978 Sugar Ray had graduated to eight-round bouts, beating Rocky Ramon in his sixth fight. I was pleased with how quickly Ray was coming along and knew that within a couple of months he would be ready to make the big jump into ten-round contests. Still, I was in no hurry. I thought it better to let Ray take a year longer to reach his goal than move him up into longer bouts and tougher opposition too quickly. After all, it had taken Muhammad four years before he won the title. It's always been my belief that it's not who you are, but what you can become that counts. And now I honestly thought that Ray would someday become champion. But in time.

When you're in the glass slipper business, hoping against hope your next Cinderella fulfills his promise, there's one word you avoid like the plague, the word *great*. It's a word too easily tossed around and not often enough earned. But with each passing fight Ray began leaving his calling card for future greatness. His laser-like punches had clinical precision. His balance was such he could franchise it, his center of gravity as near perfect as any fighter I'd ever seen. And he could feint any opponent out of his jockstrap. Even Sugar Ray Robinson sat up and took notice of his namesake, saying, "He's learning every time he fights. He's putting it altogether well. He's not great yet. But I know one thing . . . he wins."

It was now time to up the level of competition, to match Ray against some of the first-tier fighters in the welterweight division in ten-rounders. Not just schedule-fillers, mind you, but higher and higher stepping-stones to see just how far his skills would take him. When you have a young talent, the idea is to bring him along gradually to make him learn his profession without getting destroyed. A lot of guys take the wrong kind of opponents. You're not picking stiffs, you're picking guys to teach your fighter. You're teaching him how to handle a tall guy, how to handle a short guy, how to handle a quick guy, how to handle a tough guy. To be a champion, you've got to be able to handle all sizes and shapes.

Now matchmaking is always a risk-benefit process. Some matchmakers overestimate the risk; others underestimate it and take the risk. Throughout my long career I've been able to calculate the risk. By Ray's eleventh fight, I had decided to match Ray with more than the usual suspects, instead matching him against the likes of Rafael Rodriguez, Dick Ecklund, Floyd Mayweather Sr., Randy Shields, Johnny Gant, Fernand Marcotte, and Adolfo Viruet, each a rung on Sugar Ray's ladder to the top. All tough fighters, they had a cumulative record of 171 wins in 208 fights for a winning percentage of .822, and each presented some sort of risk for Ray. But Ray, continuing to grow both professionally and personally with every fight, came through this welterweight baptismal of firepower with flying colors, winning all seven, four by knockout.

As Ray's number of wins continued to grow, so too did his fame, as evidenced by his drawing power. Everywhere he fought he drew record numbers. In his pro debut against Vega, 10,170 jammed into Baltimore's Civic Center even though the fight was on TV. His third fight against Vinnie DeBarros drew the largest fight crowd in the history of Hartford. And a record crowd of 19,243 jammed into Landover Capital Centre in Maryland to see him fight Johnny Gant in his eighteenth fight, breaking the record set in Ali's defense against Jimmy Young two years before. Ray's star was continuing to rise, and we needed to keep it going with more star turns against other worthy opponents.

Finding worthy opponents is not exactly like ordering salami. You can't order it by the pound, in this case 147 pounds, you have to search it out. After Ray had run through most of the top-notch welterweights, I had to find someone Ray could fight so that he would continue to develop his talents *and* continue his march to the welterweight title.

There was talk of Sugar Ray meeting Tommy Hearns, who was on a parallel path with Ray. Up to this point, through his first twenty fights, I had scheduled each of Ray's fights by design, each when he was ready and the time was right. But I didn't think the timing was right for a fight with

Tommy. Not now, anyway. Talking with Emanuel Steward, Hearns's manager, I told him, "It's too early, wait till the time is right . . . wait till it builds up. Why now for a little bit of money, when later *mucho dinero*?" But I knew that somewhere down the line it would happen.

With Ray having fought almost on a once-a-month basis, I wanted to fill in his boxing card so that he stayed busy on his way to a bout with World Boxing Council (WBC) titlist Wilfred Benitez. But we were fast running out of eligible candidates. Shopping around, I finally came up with someone I thought was right for Ray: Marcos Geraldo.

From what I had heard Geraldo was one tough sucker, a middleweight in welterweight clothing who was the Mexican and California middleweight champion and possessed an imposing record of forty-one wins and twenty-three knockouts. However, according to my sources, he had a suspect chin—what we call in the business a "china chin"—having been knocked out eight times, five times in the first round. Studying his record and his style like a scientist would a specimen and overcoming the protests of others in Leonard's camp, I thought it was time to raise the bar even higher and see how Ray would do against a bigger, stronger opponent.

I was acutely aware of the peril of putting Ray in against a more physically imposing opponent. But it's always been my belief that easy victories can do as much harm as good. You don't learn. So we had to take the calculated risk of stepping up Ray's level of competition. Ray acquitted himself beautifully, winning a very physical fight with Geraldo and proving he was tough enough to tangle with natural middleweights.

Ray had answered my questions. He had matured physically, adding some weight so that he was now a solid 146 pounds. And mentally he had matured even faster, absorbing everything I tried to teach him—a little bit of Carmen Basilio, a touch of Ali, a shade of Willie Pastrano, and something of Ralph Dupas. And yet he was an original. He had his own style, a great change of pace, and tremendous speed. Jimmy Jacobs, who owned boxing's film library, said, "When you watch Leonard's fight films, you see a fighter who can throw combinations of four, five punches, missing you with the first two and knocking you out with the third."

And yet, even though veteran fight observer Cus D'Amato called Ray "the best finisher since Joe Louis," many in the fight racket were calling him "punchless." Punchless? The kid had twelve KOs in his twenty-one wins and he was called "punchless"? Come on! But these professional naysayers, many of whom could walk into a room filled with flowers and begin looking for the casket, had to find something wrong with every fighter. And for Sugar Ray, they wrote that while he was fast, "his speed took away from his punching power."

Maybe the reason the press downplayed Ray's skills and accomplishments had something to do with the fact that he had been anointed by Howard Cosell as the second coming of Muhammad Ali. And if Howard had said it, then it could be discounted at less than face value. One boxing writer, former light-heavyweight champion José Torres, said, "If there is a soul in our midst who thinks that Howard Cosell is a knowledgeable man of the sport of pugilism then it must be Howard Cosell." (Cosell was so disliked by sportswriters that when, in a voice sounding like a public prosecutor trying to nail a defendant for jaywalking to a life term, he bombastically proclaimed, "There are fewer great sports announcers than you think there are," one writer within earshot came back in an "Oh, please!" manner with, "Howard, there's one fewer than you think there is.") But Howard knew a superstar when he saw one, and he knew that Ray had the makings of one. "Forget it!" responded the pack of boxing writers who viewed Ray as just a made-for-TV phenomenon, unable to bring themselves to acknowledge that Leonard was as good as he was because that other medium, TV, had found him first.

But when Ray took out Tony Chiaverini in four and followed that with a knockout of North American Boxing Federation (NABF) champion Pete Ranzany in the same number of rounds and then put a exclamation point on his ability to punch with a one-round starching of Andy Price, the hardboiled press finally came around, giving him his due. And, for lack of a more descriptive word, *respect*.

For Ray it had been like going to school. First he had to get through the elementary grades before graduating to the school of higher learning. Having passed through that with flying colors, he was now ready, only three years out of the amateurs, for his advanced schooling at the University of Fisticuffs against one of the professors of the "Sweet Science," the fighter who called himself "The Bible of Boxing"—Wilfred Benitez. The prize was the welterweight title.

A funny thing—not funny ha-ha, but funny absurd—happened to me on the way to the Benitez fight for the welterweight championship. I almost didn't make it to Ray's corner.

Just before Ray fought Floyd Mayweather Sr. in August 1978, I received what was tantamount to a "Dear John" letter from Ray's attorney, Mike Trainer, which read, in part: "I am concerned by the lack of time and effort you've put into Sugar Ray. As the second highest paid person in the organization we all expected more. To date your involvement has consisted of arriving approximately two days before a fight, meeting with the press, and working Ray's corner at fight time. More was expected of you. We must adjust your compensation so that it is more in line with your duties." I particularly liked the "sincerely" at the bottom.

It all read like an elaborate practical joke. I couldn't even begin to understand the depth of such idiotic remarks. How the hell did he know what went into the training of a fighter? He was a lawyer, one who admitted he "didn't know that much about boxing," and now he was accusing me of everything but overstaying my coffee break. Didn't he know that I had handpicked each and every one of Ray's opponents? Taken a fight apart like a watchmaker a clock, putting the pieces back together again and devising a strategy that would enable Ray to win? Improvised last-minute strategic changes? And advised him in the corner between rounds on how to carry out my instructions? Obviously Trainer had no understanding whatsoever of what trainers did or how valuable they were.

And what would he know about the little things a trainer does? It takes a lot of effort to make things look so effortless. Like going to the arena the day before a fight and looking at the location of the dressing room to see how far it is to the ring. And if there is no john in the dressing room, seeing how far it is to the closest available one. Little things like that, but important all the same because you want to get rid of the strangeness before a fight and make everything run smoothly. As a trainer, you have to think of everything or you don't think at all.

Mike Trainer had no clue. Nor did he care. This was the kind of man who would fake a sneeze when the collection plate came around. His only measuring stick was the amount of time spent and the dollar value of that time. That struck me as somewhat like the lawyer who, when asked by his client his opinion on a legal matter, went out of the room and came back in five minutes with the answer and a bill for $500.25. Asked by the client what the quarter was for, the lawyer answered that it was for looking up the answer to the question and the $500 was for knowing *where* to look it up. The same thing with a trainer. It's not just doing your day-to-day job, being yoked to the gym, it's the knowledge, the experience, and the expertise that a trainer acquires over years of practicing his craft and how he applies it.

Trainer further trivialized both me and my craft by treating me like some nine-to-fiver who punches a time clock like a lawyer fills in a timesheet. He wanted me to be with Ray every minute of every day. Only my wife gets that. What was I supposed to do? Open up the gym every morning and count the towels? Make sure the bags were hung up properly? Dave Anderson of the *New York Times* had once called me "the Michelangelo of boxing." Had Mike Trainer been around while Michelangelo was painting the Sistine Chapel, he probably would have had the great painter take his scaffolding home with him every night after he had finished that day's work and reconstruct the scaffolding the next morning before he started in again.

Oh, I knew all the things Trainer told the press to justify his desire to break the contract—things like: "Angelo was pushing himself to the front a little too much." And, "He was letting other people give him too much credit for matchmaking and career guidance that he knew he wasn't responsible for." All of which rang as phony as a sitcom laugh. When someone starts talking about the principle of the thing, it's all about the money. And that's what this was all about: the money, now that Ray had become an ATM machine.

When I had signed the contract Trainer had drawn up I agreed to receive 15 percent. At that time that was 15 percent of nothing. I took a flyer on how things would turn out. Who knew? One punch could end his career. And with his fragile hands, who could be sure that after only one, two, or three fights Ray's hands, or some other injury, wouldn't end his career? I had gambled on Ray's formidable talent and on my abilities. That had been okay when Ray was making $40,000 a fight and my take had been $6,000. But now, with visions of big-money fights dancing in their heads and the possibility of making money that hadn't even been printed yet, I was thought to be expensive and Trainer & Co. wanted to void the contract. How do you like them apples? They were shaking the tree for surplus money, and I was the one they were shaking out.

Now my mother had taught me to be "nice." She always had a pot of coffee on the stove in case visitors dropped by and was always the first to take food to shut-ins. "It doesn't cost anything to be nice" was her motto. It was something I tried to carry with me all my life. Gene Kilroy once said of me, "If you told Angelo that Charles Manson was a bad guy, Angie would say, 'Well there's one or two things about him that aren't so bad.'" So it was that it took me a month to reply to Trainer's insulting letter, nicely pointing out to him that I believed I was doing a great job with Ray and that my value was not to be dictated by other people's opinions but by the fact that Ray was unbeaten and coming along, growing with every fight. Furthermore, I expected to be paid what had been promised in the contract.

Trainer's reply was laughable, his letter stating, "Unfortunately, Ray Leonard's win-loss record is not the only measure of your performance." Can you believe that? What would have happened if he had been beaten? Trainer would probably have had me tried for a hanging offense.

For the next year-plus the contract dispute continued to simmer as Trainer continued to prod me—not gentle prods, mind you, but elbow-poking ones. With more important things to do, like focusing on the things that could win Ray's fights, I hired a lawyer to communicate with Trainer. But Trainer wouldn't answer my lawyer's calls or letters, only calling me to snarl, "Quit badgering me . . . get him off me." It was less a communications divide than no communications at all. So much for trying to resolve the matter amicably.

And so it dragged on. Needless to say, the dispute hardly created a harmonious relationship with the Leonard camp or with Trainer. In fact, whenever I was around Trainer I would suddenly develop a fierce desire to be lonesome and avoid him. The one time we talked about the contract, he told me that Ray Leonard Inc. would agree to pay me 15 percent of the fight proceeds as long as Sugar Ray "chose to let me appear in the corner." What was that? If Ray wanted me in his corner, why not leave well enough alone? And if he didn't, why not come right out and say it? I couldn't believe that Ray was behind all this. It had to be Trainer.

The whole thing finally came to a head before one of Ray's fights, I think it was the Johnny Gant fight. I was in the dressing room with Ray, Janks Morton, Ollie Dunlop, Dave Jacobs, J. D. Brown, and the entire Leonard team, minus Mike Trainer. Then Trainer walked in, sucking all of the air out of the room. Holding a yellow piece of paper, he came up to me and said, "Ray doesn't want any long-term contracts." I looked at him, looked at the paper, and said nothing. He almost crammed the piece of paper down my throat, bullying me where persuasion would not work, and told me, "Just sign this . . . it's okay . . . sign it or you're out of here!"

While I had hoped to avoid such a scene, he had obviously chosen the dressing room for a showdown, stage-managing the whole thing so that he could pressure me with his "or else" ultimatum while everyone was there to witness it. Their staring-at-ceiling-tiles silence gave tacit approval to his breaking the contract. He had me at a disadvantage and was pushing me to sign that piece of yellow paper releasing Ray and Ray Leonard Inc. from any long-term obligation to me, substituting a fight-to-fight contract and a cap on my earnings. And so while everyone stood around shuffling their feet and clearing their throats, under compulsion I did the only thing I could, I signed the damned paper.

Almost immediately after I signed the piece of yellow paper, Ray came over and said, "It'll be alright." Then he gave me a "You're the greatest" hug, one he held so long I was afraid rumors about the two of us would start. I could feel a circle of sadness in his hug as if he knew he could have stood up for me and didn't, instead passively acquiescing to Trainer's chicanery. I have always wondered why he didn't step forward and say something, just as Muhammad Ali had to promoter Don King when he told King to "leave Angie alone." Instead, Ray chose to second Trainer's actions.

Everyone in the boxing community said I should sue Trainer and Ray Leonard Inc. for forcing me to sign under duress. But I didn't want to make a fuss. After all, I hadn't built Ray up only to tear him down. And a nasty legal battle, letting the public in on our private affairs, would have done that. It would have hurt Ray, and I couldn't do that.

As for Mike Trainer, his very name still gives me a problem! It's always been my policy that if I don't have anything nice to say about someone I don't say anything at all. So instead of saying anything derogatory about Trainer, I'll let the words of my old friend, publicist Irving Rudd, speak for me. Rudd once said, "How can you work for that *putz*? He's the worst son-of-a-bitch alive."

Well, maybe not the worst, but I'd put him in the competition and bet on him. It's a guarantee we won't be exchanging cards at Christmas time.

But as I look back, I wish Ray had said something, anything, and stood up for me. I have always liked him and always will, but that I'll never understand.

A few months after my confrontation with Trainer the situation lightened up. I had an all-new two-year contract, albeit one with a cap on my future earnings, and Ray, as a way of reaching out to me, came down to Miami to visit Helen and me. When he returned home he sent me the following note:

> Hello Buddies,
> Just a few lines to say things are going well, and I am very happy to say that not only have I found the world's greatest manager and wife but two dynamite friends.
> Love Ya!
> The Next World Champ, Sugar Ray

How could you not like a kid like that? It restored my faith in Ray. We were once again a team, the same team that had come this far together and now had a chance to fulfill his promise to become "The Next World Champ," although Mike Trainer had broken the trust between us somewhat. The only thing that stood in the way was the current welterweight champ: Wilfred Benitez.

Wilfred Benitez was a slick, sleek fighter, well-nigh impossible to hit. A turnaround right-hander who fought with his feet spread wide apart, Benitez was a throwback to fighters of old who, with great head and body movement, could offer up their heads as bait and then, bending and bobbing to evade their opponents' punches, almost as if by radar, make you miss and counter with catlike springiness. An ambidextrous counterpuncher, Benitez was most effective with what Carlos Palomino called a "sneaky" right hand.

Benitez had become boxing's youngest-ever champion when, at the tender age of seventeen, his face still a stranger to the razor, he had beaten the legendary junior welterweight champ Antonio "Kid Pambele" Cervantes. After three successful defenses, Benitez had vacated the junior welterweight title to campaign as a full-fledged welterweight, winning the world welterweight title in January 1979.

But despite Benitez's 37–0–1 record, the fight mob had installed Sugar Ray as a 3–1 favorite. There was no way they should have made Sugar Ray the favorite. And not a 3–1 favorite. You had to respect Benitez's experience and skill. The only reason I could think of was that almost from the night he had turned pro, Sugar Ray had been acclaimed by the TV networks and accepted by the boxing public as the greatest thing since "The

Greatest" himself, Muhammad Ali. Hey, Ray had been on TV more than Archie Bunker and was someone with charisma, what I call "IT." He was not just another of boxing's flavor of the month, but boxing's new poster boy.

Dave Condon of the *Chicago Tribune* had another reason for the odds favoring Sugar Ray, writing, "The oddsmakers may feel that Sugar Ray has the edge because Angelo Dundee is in his corner. The boxing and betting fraternities, which sometimes have a working agreement, do not forget that Ali became heavyweight champion because Dundee shoved him out of the corner back into that 1964 fracas with Sonny Liston." I was flattered that someone suggested that Sugar Ray had an edge because I was working with him. But as I've said time and time again, it isn't me but the guy in the ring who wins. Hey, I'm only as good as the guy who answers the bell.

No matter what the odds were, I still thought that this fight was a coin toss. Sugar Ray was in against another potential all-time great, in many ways a mirror image of Ray—and, yes, using another of boxing's overused phrases, "the best man" would win.

The fight itself was almost a finishing school for boxing, an instructional lesson in how to box. From the moment both climbed into the ring, you knew it was going to be less a war than a chess match between two grandmasters, each intent upon leaving his own indelible stamp of greatness on the outcome. There was Benitez drinking in the cheers of the crowd, bowing to each of the four corners while Ray was holding his arms aloft in his familiar victory pose. Then they squared off in a staredown worthy of the word, Benitez shamelessly posturing with an air of self-absorption bordering on arrogance while Ray, standing nose-to-nose with Benitez, stared back with unblinking eyes affecting his own "I can" attitude. As Ray would later say, "He won that round."

The two fought with the same confidence, Leonard continually pumping his left jab in Benitez's face while remaining wary of Benitez's "sneaky" right. For two rounds, while I continued to holler, "Use the left, Ray, the left," Leonard peppered Benitez with that schoolbook jab of his, bringing tears to the eyes of Benitez and tears of joy to mine. Toward the end of the third round, Ray knocked the squared-up and off-balance Benitez down with a cross between a left jab and a left hook. Benitez arose, more embarrassed than hurt, smiling to himself as much as to the crowd.

But if Ray was going to school, constantly learning, so, too, was Benitez who sometimes made lighting-quick moves, making Ray look foolish by slipping under his big right-hand bombs and countering on the inside. By the sixth round—a round in which the two collided with freight-train force, leaving Leonard dazed and Benitez's forehead bloodied—Benitez began to lose his eight months of ring rust and started landing right-hand leads to Leonard's head. Despite Benitez's twenty-three knockouts, he still had the reputation of not having enough power "to break an egg"—again, credit Palomino. But he was connecting with what Ray called "some dynamite shots," one of which rocked Ray in the seventh.

And so the rounds went, Leonard using his piston-like, four-inch-longer left to perfection to pile up points, almost as if in response to my constant screams of "the left, Ray, the left," but continually missing with overhand rights to Benitez's bobbing head. Benitez was throwing fewer punches, but making Ray miss and moving inside to counter with his right. Every now and then Leonard would fire off one of his patented flurries, but Benitez would either block most of the punches or slip them. The only thing I had to tell him in the corner was "Keep it up," and that what he was doing was "beautiful." Only before the twelfth round did I feel a need to say, "Don't go to sleep on me now," as Benitez began to mount a comeback.

Fighting a three-dimensional fight—punching with accuracy, moving aggressively, and blocking effectively—Ray had opened up a wide lead through fourteen rounds. But, as he sat in the corner before the fifteenth, you could see him looking across the ring at Benitez, his eyes reading, "Oh my God, he's still standing." At the bell for the final round, with my "let it all hang out" call to arms ringing in his ears, Ray rushed out, determined to remedy that piece of unfinished business. Throwing quick-fire punches, Ray fell on Benitez, alternating his attack to the head and body. But Benitez continued to counter with his right over the top of Ray's left. Flurry followed flurry as the two put on a furious final finish. Then, with less than fifteen seconds to go in the fight, Ray caught Benitez in a neutral corner with a left jab-hook and Benitez went down. Up quickly, Benitez, with a smile on his face, this time more hurt than embarrassed, took the mandatory eight-count. Ray was on him immediately, pummeling him with rights and lefts. And with six seconds left in the fight, referee Carlos

Padilla—with the ring death of Willie Classen the previous week on his mind—stepped in and stopped the fight to prevent further damage to Benitez. Benitez seemed not to mind the stoppage. The only person in the arena who did was a bettor who had wagered $150,000 that the fight would "go" the distance, six seconds more.

But if one bettor was unhappy with the outcome, he might have been the only one who was. For, as Ray catapulted to the top of the ring ropes to celebrate winning the welterweight championship in what he called his "best performance," the crowd of 4,000-plus crammed into the Pavilion at Caesars Palace roared their appreciation for Ray. And they roared for Wilfred Benitez as well, who, after the fight, said, "Now I know I have boxer like me . . . a good champ."

FIFTEEN

Duran: "No Mas?" No Way, No Say

Sugar Ray Leonard's first title defense came some four months later against former British and European welterweight titlist Davey "Boy" Green. To those in the press who asked, "What's a Davey 'Boy' Green?" I answered, "He looks like an American fighter . . . crawls all over you. He's got real long arms and impressive upper-body strength." What I didn't tell them was that he only had a fair jab and held his hands so far apart he was open for a left hook.

And that's exactly what happened in the fourth as Ray, at the end of a left-right-left combination, hit Green with what he called "the hardest blow I've ever thrown," a left hook from hell that resounded with the noise of an explosion that would have felled five or six bystanders and that laid Green endwise. Referee Arthur Mercante only counted six over his fallen body and then waved it all over. He could have counted to six hundred 'cause it took Green that long to recover, finally wobbling to his feet after a few Leonard-induced minutes of sleep.

But if that was the hardest blow I had ever seen, the hardest blow I never saw happened just moments later. All I remember was that I was walking between two security guards with nobody in front of me on my way to the press conference one moment and the next I was lying on the floor, face-down, my glasses knocked off, totally discombobulated.

What happened? I asked myself through my haze. All I could figure out through the fog was that someone had coldcocked me with a sucker punch from behind. As I was lifted off the ground by cotrainer Dave Jacobs and carried to a nearby room, two policemen came up and asked me if I wanted to "lock him up." Him? Who the hell was *him*? In my vagueness all I could come up with was that they wanted to lock up half a set of hand towels.

As I lay there in a muddled state trying my damnedest to make some sense out of the bizarre episode, I became aware of the familiar voices of those in the Leonard camp. From the fragments of discussions I could make out, it seems that an assistant trainer named Pepe Correa had become upset at something or other I had either said or done and cowardly swatted me in the back of the head. To this day I still don't know what it was all about. Just a wannabe trainer who had trained Ray back in his amateur days and was now jealous of my position in his camp? What could have compelled him to pull a lily-livered act like that? What was he afraid of? That if he had dared to try to hit me from the front I might have slipped the punch and clocked him with a good counter?

I have always been on good terms with other trainers, going all the way back to the time when I used to sit with the likes of Chickie Ferrara, Ray Arcel, Charlie Goldman, Freddie Brown, and the rest of the old-old crowd at gatherings I used to call "Last Suppers" at the tavern known as The Neutral when I first came to New York. Through the years I was always close with other members of the training fraternity, even those I worked against. One of those was Gil Clancy. When I had the young Cassius Clay fighting against Gil's fighter, Alex Miteff, in Louisville, the night before the fight Gil invited me out to dinner. The club he was supposedly taking me to was way out of town, over the state line somewhere in Indiana. As we kept driving and driving—going through towns so quickly I almost thought their names were "Resume Speed"—Gil kept joking that he was kidnapping me and was going to keep me locked up until after the fight. Gil swears that every time he mentioned the word *kidnapping*, I would moan. But I don't remember that now, only the anxiety of not being in my fighter's corner the next night. Finally, after what seemed like a day or two, we arrived at the club, which was really a roadhouse, and the joke was on me. We had a great time. And, oh, for the record, he brought me back to Louisville where the next night Cassius won by a knockout.

Another time, when I was down in Nassau with Muhammad Ali for his final fight against Trevor Berbick, I brought along a plastic surgeon just in case. Well, Muhammad didn't need him, but Tommy Hearns, who was fighting on the undercard against Ernie Singletary, certainly did, having suffered some nasty cuts despite winning his fight. Afterward I took

Tommy along with his trainer, Emanuel Steward, to Ali's dressing room to have Dr. Julian Groff, the surgeon I had brought down from Miami, treat him, which he did by putting in 101 stitches to secure Tommy's cut. As Emanuel said, "Angelo didn't have to offer his services of his own private guy, but that's the way he was."

It was just the way I was taught from the beginning, that you have to look out for other trainers, for the trainers who might be in the opposite corner today might be working in the same corner with you tomorrow. But I never had to look behind me for a trainer working in the same corner. Which is why I was so puzzled by what had happened.

While I tried mightily to collect my thoughts, publicist Charlie Brotman came into the room. The press wanted to know what had happened. One reporter said I was hit by a member of the Leonard entourage I was arguing with; another said a trainer in Leonard's corner had coldcocked me in the face. Charlie asked how best to handle the situation, what he should tell the media.

At this magic moment in time, Sugar Ray was already a brand name, his winning record and equally winning smile and charm having won over Madison Avenue. And the advertisers had come pounding at his door, using him in 7-Up commercials and as the endorser for a line of sporting goods equipment with others lined up as well. But if there's one thing Madison Avenue cannot tolerate it's controversy—and here something about daredevil Evel Knievel having hit his promoter with a baseball bat was mentioned. So lawyer Mike Trainer, as caretaker-in-chief of Leonard's good name, in an effort to cover up the incident and protect Ray's image, told Brotman, "I don't want to get our team involved. Tell them that one of the fans hit him and ran," pointing the finger at some anonymous schmo.

Great! There I was lying on a table in the middle of the room in a semiconscious state, and they were discussing how to treat the situation. Not *me*, just the situation. Maybe it was better for all concerned that they went into damage control, otherwise there would have been more damage. For, at that moment, two friends of my son, Jimmy, having witnessed the incident, were prowling the arena looking to "Get Pepe"—and not to shake hands with him either. Lucky for him they never found him.

Somehow, someway I was loaded onto a plane, although I don't remember either getting on or off the plane. And when I landed in Miami, Ferdie Pacheco picked me up and took me to the hospital for a CAT can.

Fortunately for me, as Dizzy Dean had said many years before after being hit in the head by a baseball and taking a CAT scan to see what, if any, damage had been done, my CAT scan "showed nothing."

To this day that incident still rankles me. First it was Mike Trainer who had stabbed me in the back, and then it was Pepe Correa who had cold-cocked me from the back. I was beginning to think that nobody in the Leonard camp *had* my back.

But I had no time to look behind me for Pepe Correa. I had to look ahead to Ray's next fight, against Roberto Duran. To understand how this fight came about is a study in the mysteries of the rules of those sanctioning bodies that control boxing, the alphabet-soup organizations, with about as much chance of understanding them as cracking the Da Vinci code.

Let me explain how the Roberto Duran fight came to be, and if you understand, please explain it back to me so I will. Seems, at least according to the rules of the World Boxing Council (or WBC, which, as Teddy Atlas says, stands for "We Be Collecting"), when Ray defeated Benitez he assumed Benitez's responsibility to fight the number one contender, better known as "the mandatory challenger." At the time of signing for the Benitez fight, the number one contender for the welterweight title was Carlos Palomino. But somewhere between Ray signing to fight Benitez and beating Benitez, Palomino had lost to former lightweight champion Roberto Duran, who, by some conjuring by WBC president-for-life José Sulaiman, was immediately catapulted into the mandatory contender position. It was pointed out to Sulaiman that Duran had not, as dictated by the WBC rules, been the number one contender for a year and, therefore, could not be deemed the mandatory contender. In response, Sulaiman, making up one of those on-the-spur-of-the-moment rules, called a Leonard-Duran fight "a significant fight," which made it Ray's mandatory. Now, while Sulaiman was busy pulling rules out of his hat, or some other place, negotiations were going on with the WBA welterweight champion, Pipino Cuevas. However, those negotiations had broken down under the weight of boxing—not to mention national—politics as officials of the Panamanian government pressured the WBA president, who, not incidentally, was also Panamanian, to make Leonard fight the hero of Panama, Roberto Duran, or be stripped of his title. Then, having achieved his objective, Sulaiman came up with another seat-of-his-pants rule, giving Ray permission to have one title defense before his mandatory, that against Davey "Boy" Green. Got all that? Hell, you have to rub lemon juice on the WBC rulebook to be able to read its rules.

And so Roberto Duran it was. Duran was a fierce competitor, one who fought with street *cujones*, breathing fire and contempt for anyone who dared cross his path. His style was that of an assassin, constantly coming forward and employing three weapons—his left, his right, and his head. He attacked with the singular desire to destroy his adversary, sometimes going into a left-handed stance, all the better to get inside. And, with teeth biting into his mouthpiece in a half-sneer/half-smile, he buried his head into his opponent's chest and took him apart with body shots. Lightweight champion for nearly seven years and winner of seventy of his seventy-one fights, the man called *Manos de Piedra* ("Hands of Stone") had fifty-five KOs, sending most of his victims to boxing's home for the bewildered. (Watching one of his victims, Ray Lampkin, being scrapped off the canvas and carted away to the hospital on a stretcher, through clenched teeth Duran told his interviewer, "Next time I 'keel' him.") To him, it was less "the Noble Art of Self-Defense" than "the Manly Art of Modified Murder."

And yet, with the notable exception of Esteban De Jesús, Duran had never met anyone of Ray's caliber. During his six-plus years as lightweight champion, he had defended his title twelve times against mediocre competition, inasmuch as there were fewer top-notch fighters in the division than at any time in the division's history. Against the likes of ordinary fighters like Vilomar Fernandez and Lou Bizarro, Duran had looked so-so, both opponents almost going the distance. And the slick Saoul Mamby had given him hell. Moreover, while dominant as a lightweight, he was underwhelming as a welterweight, having gone the distance in three of his five fights at 147 pounds.

The fight seemed to shape up as a classic boxer-puncher matchup, sort of a second edition of the first Cassius Clay–Sonny Liston fight. But to me it was Leonard who was Liston, the puncher, not Duran. Ray's jab was a lot like—don't laugh, this is no typo—Sonny Liston's. He knocked people down with it. Duran's fifty-five KOs had come against smaller men, all of whom he had outmuscled. The reason Duran had problems with tall guys was because he couldn't use his head against them. His head was definitely a weapon. I knew he could use it and use it well, having seen him work on the speed bag, throwing his punches, left hand, head, right hand in rapid rhythm. He used it as a pivot in the clinches. Maybe I should have asked the officials to put a glove on it.

Ray's faster hands and angled movements as well as his cool and calm ring generalship were more than equal to Roberto's projected heat. With a 2½-inch height advantage and a 3-inch reach advantage, everything favored Ray—even the odds at 9–5.

Deconstructing the films of Duran's fights, you could see that he was a heel-to-toe guy. He took two steps to get to you. So the idea was not to give him those two steps, not to move too far away because the more distance you gave Duran, the more effective he was. What you can't do in the face of Duran's aggression is run from it because then he picks up momentum, so my guy wasn't going to run from him.

Stylistically, Duran gave you great movement of the body, as he slipped from side to side. He wouldn't come straight in. He'd try to feint you, many times just waving with his hand. And if he missed you with an overhand right, he'd turn southpaw and come back with a left hook to the body. Duran also had a unique way of throwing his right hand, left hook, and left knee all at the same time. Ray was going to move side to side, and he was going to go to the body. Nobody ever hit Duran in his weak spot where he's soft, but Ray was going to nail him. He would stop him in his tracks with that jab. My guy had so much talent they hadn't seen yet. I had seen Duran when he worked out at the 5th Street Gym, and my fighter, Doug Vaillant, had banged him around pretty good. So, if Doug could do it, Ray could, too. There was no question in my mind that Ray was going to knock Duran out.

Montreal, a city of old-world charm with streets named Rue Ste. Catherine and Rue Notre-Dame, horse-drawn carriages, and restaurants, many of which were Italian, lining the sidewalks, was the site of what they were already calling "The Fight of the Decade," only six months into the 1980s. It was also the place of Ray's greatest triumph, where he had won Olympic gold four years before, in the very ring in which he would fight Duran.

With hundreds of miles of streets, Montreal is also one of the great walking cities on the North American continent. And so it was that one lovely June evening Ray, yours truly, and our wives, Juanita and Helen, were taking our customary after-dinner walk, leisurely unwinding and looking into shop windows and chatting, when who should we run into but Roberto Duran and his entourage.

Now I have always thought Roberto could have been as popular as Muhammad Ali if he had learned to speak English. But, except on rare occasions, like the time someone asked him what would have happened if he had ever fought Ali and he replied in his characteristic macho manner, "I would have beat the 'sheet' out of him," he hadn't. But this time he wasn't using English to communicate his thoughts. Instead of merely acknowledging us with a nod or a wave, Roberto launched into a series of hand gestures indicating what he was going to do to Ray—hit him in the head, the balls, anywhere. Then, cursing in two languages, he hollered he would "keel" Ray, among other insults. Normally nothing fazes Ray who manages to stay as cool as the proverbial cucumber no matter what. But enraged at Duran's obscene gestures and taunts, Ray wanted to fight him right then and there.

That would be the beginning of Duran's campaign of psychological warfare. It would continue throughout the buildup to the fight as Roberto continued to cast aspersions on Ray's manhood (saying he would make him "fight like a man") and on his abilities (calling him a "clown"), and it reached its climax at the weigh-in. In a scene reminiscent of the one in *Cinderella Man* where Max Baer tells James J. Braddock what he's going to do to Braddock's wife after he destroys him, Roberto, in a more X-rated version, shouted at Juanita, "after fight you and me . . ." and then, with all the subtlety of a community bedpan, turned back to Ray and in Spanish screamed, "I'm going to screw your wife . . . she's a *puta*." And for bad measure accompanied his taunt with a couple of crude pelvic thrusts in her direction. That did it! He had pushed Ray's hot button. Ray went berserk and had to be forcibly held back as he tried to get at Duran.

After the weigh-in, Duran, with his typical swagger, crowed to the press, "Where I come from, in the ghetto, those that blink, blow . . . and Leonard, he was blinking." Meanwhile, back in our dressing room, the normally composed Leonard came as close as I've ever seen to losing it. I realized that Duran had really done a number on him and that our carefully laid-out plans were out the window as Ray went on and on about how he was going to avenge Duran's insults—of how he was going to prove he was the better man by beating Duran at his own game.

Before a fight Ray usually sequestered himself, almost as if he put a "Do Not Disturb" sign up, remaining unavailable to the press. He left it to his publicist, Charlie Brotman, to handle his statements. When Charlie approached him and asked for his prefight comment to relay to the media, Ray told him to tell the press, "I'm going to fight him flat-footed."

Hearing that, Duran's trainer Ray Arcel, who had been around forever and seen and heard everything, told his fighter: "You won the title right there."

Normally the dressing room before a fight is tense and expectant, waiting for what seems like hours but is only a few minutes for that inevitable knock on the door signaling the fighter to the ring. This time Ray, who usually approached every fight with a surgeon's emotional detachment, was especially edgy, anxious to get into the ring to exact his revenge on Duran for all the indignities he had suffered at his hands.

Since it was the prerogative of a champion to enter the ring last, challenger Duran would be the first to make the "perp"-like walk down the aisle and into the ring. Going back, almost to David versus Goliath, that had been the custom. The only time it was not so honored was when James J. Corbett played a game of "hokey-pokey" (you know, "you put your left foot in, then you take your left foot out. . . ."), faking his entry into the ring before champion John L. Sullivan. Thinking Corbett had already entered when in fact he was standing on the apron of the ring, Sullivan actually went into the ring first, which so aggravated the great John L. he wanted to kill Corbett on the spot.

You could hear the cheers for Duran reverberating through the hallways as he made his way down the aisle on his way to the ring—a *looooooong* walk. As he climbed into the ring, sportswriter Dave Anderson, catching sight of the scruffily-bearded Duran, almost snorting fire, his black eyes ablaze with fury, leaned over to Joe Frazier and asked the former heavyweight champion who the man alternately nicknamed "El Diablo" reminded him of, thinking Joe would answer "me." Instead, after studying Duran for a few seconds, Frazier said, "Charles Manson."

Then, uncharacteristically, Duran beamed at the crowd, evoking a great roar. And when his entourage unfurled the Quebec Liberation flag, it ignited an even more deafening din from the Quebecois in the upper reaches of the stadium who now joined the cheers of Duran's 2,000 countrymen who had flown up from Panama to cheer on their hero.

Then it was Ray's turn. As he came into view there was polite applause, but less raucous than that which had greeted Duran. Entering the ring, he bowed to the crowd from all four corners of the ring, bringing cheers of adulation—and even, incredibly, a few boos—from those in the crowd of 46,317, most of whom remembered him as the darling of the Montreal Olympics four years earlier.

As I stood in the corner with Ray, I chanced a look across the ring and couldn't help but notice my counterparts, Duran's trainers Ray Arcel and Freddie Brown, in a huddle with referee Carlos Padilla. *What the hell was that all about?* I asked myself. What I found out later was that Arcel, who knew that Padilla was famous for breaking fighters whenever they got close enough to touch, was lobbying Padilla, telling him something along the lines of: "You're good. But this is a fight everyone wants to see. I only hope you let my boy fight."

Little did I realize how well Arcel's prefight psyche job on Padilla would work when all was said and done.

From the opening bell and Duran's first bull rush, several things were obvious. One, referee Padilla had let Arcel bullshit him and was going to take a hands-off policy, letting Duran turn the fight into a wrestling match. Two, Duran had drawn an Alamo-like line in the sand, forcing Ray to fight on his territory, the ropes, rather than on Ray's territory, the middle of the ring. And three, Ray had it in his head that he was stronger than Duran and had decided to play a game of *machismo* with Duran, abandoning his prefight game plan of slipping in and out and giving Duran angles.

For the first couple of rounds, Duran charged, pushed, bulled, and punched his way inside, forcing Ray into the ropes and keeping him there—once, in the second, driving Ray across the ring and into the ropes—while referee Padilla stood by, refusing to break the two if there was anything resembling a loose hand showing. Duran mauled Ray and forced him to fight reflexively. Beginning with the third round Ray began to land some punches underneath Duran's charges, scoring heavily with his patented flurries as he caught Duran coming in. Still, Duran kept Ray pinned against the ropes, taking away his advantages of hand and foot speed.

By the middle rounds the action had heated up with both landing non-stop punches, Duran the aggressor and Ray meeting Duran's unrelenting aggression with his own furious flurries. As the two went at it toe-to-toe, the crowd got caught up in the pace and excitement of the fight—Ray's wife, Juanita, overcome with emotion, fainted. Ray closed the gap and may even have been ahead slightly, the only marks on either fighter the rope burns Ray sported on his back, compliments of Roberto having almost glued him to the ropes.

Coming down the stretch Ray landed several good shots to the untrimmed jaw of Duran, but all he got back in return was a sneer from Duran before he tore back into my guy for more of the same. The pace and noise continued unabated throughout the last two rounds as Duran, now so sure of imminent victory, virtually conceded the rounds to Leonard.

At the bell ending the fifteenth and final round, Ray extended his hands to Duran to congratulate him, but a disdainful Duran spurned them with a scornful "get-the-hell-out-of-here" wave of his glove and then threw a mock punch at the man he hated with a passion that burned deep within his *macho* heart. Walking past Ray, he jumped into the air in exultation.

The exultation was premature. But correct. For after a couple of minutes of correcting the incorrect scorecards, the decision was announced as 148–147, 145–144, and 146–144—including 19 "draw" rounds on the three cards—all for the new "Campeon del Mundo," Roberto Duran. It had been as exciting and close a fight as boxing had seen in years. Afterward Ray said, "I surprised a lot of people with my tactics. I fought Duran in a way I thought I could beat him." It was a mistake he wouldn't make again.

You never know what effect that first loss will have on a fighter. Some fighters, like Joe Louis—who coincidentally, like Ray, suffered his first loss in his twenty-eighth fight—pick themselves up, dust themselves off, and start all over again. Louis came back to fight Jack Sharkey two months after being KO'd by Max Schmeling and won. Then there was Sugar Ray Robinson who suffered his first loss in his forty-first fight against Jake LaMotta and came back just three weeks later to avenge his loss in the same ring. Others, however, have had their careers completely derailed by one loss, their surety in their invincibility and their confidence in their ability lost along with the fight itself. Now I honestly didn't know what Ray would do, come back or just pack his bags and go home.

After the fight, with Juanita's pleas for him to retire ringing in his ears and his body throbbing in pain, Ray stood in front of the dressing room mirror studying his battered features. Then, after a minute or two of contemplation, he turned around and announced, "That's it. No more. I gave it everything I had . . . but that's it!"

However, in what might be the shortest retirement in boxing history, Ray soon changed his mind. He couldn't close the curtain on his career with that ugly letter "L" following his name in the record books. More important, he wanted to avenge his loss to Duran and gain revenge against the man who had not only beaten him but abused both him and his wife.

All greats learn from previous fights. Take Sugar Ray Robinson, for example. After meeting and beating Fritzie Zivic, Robinson said, "Fritzie taught me a lot. He was about the smartest I ever fought. He even showed me how you can make a man butt open his own eye. He'd slip my lead and then he'd put his hand behind my neck and he'd bring my eye down on his head. Fritzie was very smart."

Just as Zivic had taken Robinson to school, so, too, had Duran taken Leonard. But if experience is learning from one's mistakes, then Ray had learned from his and chalked it up to experience. This time he would employ an all-new strategy, one as far removed from the one that failed in the first fight as New Orleans, the site of the second fight, was from Montreal. This time Ray knew how to solve the puzzle that only one of Duran's seventy-two previous opponents, Esteban De Jesús, had ever mastered— he knew how to beat Duran. Ray would box him in the middle of the ring, where his hand and foot speed would give him the advantage and enable him to offset Duran's attack-dog style.

He also had learned another lesson the hard way. The contest, to paraphrase Damon Runyon, is not always to the fastest or the strongest. Sometimes it goes to the more intelligent. And Roberto Duran had done a number on Ray, psychologically getting his goat. Now it would be Roberto's turn in the barrel, as Ray was determined to outpsyche the man who had taught him the very meaning of the word.

Appearances can be very deceiving, especially in the case of Sugar Ray Leonard. For behind that choirboy's face was a cunning mind, one capable of intriguing maneuvers and strategies. I've always believed Ray could whip off your underwear with his tricks. Now more than merely outboxing Duran, Ray wanted to get even with him for insulting Ray and his wife before the Montreal fight. Ray also wanted to get even by attacking him where Duran lived: in his *machismo*. There was a mystique about Duran's machismo, one built on stories that he had knocked out a horse, an opponent's wife, and a sparring partner's father. And Duran gloried in that mystique, almost as if he owned the original copyright on *machismo*, strutting and preening with an arrogance that announced to all that he possessed the biggest set of *cojones* in the world. It was that mystique Ray wanted to attack, to toy with Duran and strip away his mantle of *machismo*.

His mind working every angle, Ray knew that Duran never let success go to his training and that between his fights he would spend his time carousing, partying, and eating, so much so that he would balloon up to about 190. Ray's thinking was that he wanted a rematch as quickly as possible—the sooner the better to prevent Duran from getting into top shape. This despite the fact that several within Ray's camp didn't want him to take on Duran immediately without a "warm-up" fight. Trainer Dave Jacobs, for one, told Ray that "the system" was against him and that he couldn't win. But Ray wanted Duran now.

During the run-up to the fight, Duran was so confident in his belief that he would do to Ray again what he had done in their first fight that he told anyone who would listen that Ray was "afraid" of him and called him a "clown." But if Duran hadn't a hint of what was in store for him before, he should have had when Ray and I showed up at the weigh-in wearing fake beards to mock the stubble Duran sported to make him look malevolent. No, this time Ray wasn't the quiet, well-mannered gentleman Duran and the press had come to expect. This time it was Ray who acted as if the result of the fight was a foregone conclusion; this time, by the hair on Duran's chinny-chin-chin, he would be the victor.

To achieve that victory, Ray would have to keep the guy turning, hit him with shots coming in, pivot off the ropes, spin out, slip the jab, and move over. He couldn't go straight back, he had to push him off, and when he spun, he had to stay there and nail him.

As the fight neared, Ray's confidence continued to build. Knowing the ring in New Orleans would be four feet larger inside the ropes than the one he had been caged up in at Montreal, he felt so sure he would be able to outbox Duran that when Brotman approached him for his prefight comment to the press, unlike his comment before the Montreal fight that he would fight "flat-footed," he told Charlie to tell the press, "This time I will *not* be fighting flat-footed." And he accompanied his statement with a playful wink.

Ray's psychological battle plan continued right up to the fight itself. In Montreal it had been Duran who had captured the fancy of the crowd by unfurling the Quebec Liberation flag in the ring. This time it was Ray's turn as he had the man he was named after, Ray Charles, sing "America the Beautiful" before the fight, wowing the Superdome crowd.

Called to the center of the ring by referee Octavio Meyran, the two fighters stood there playing the stare-each-other-down game. Then Roberto's eyes opened wide as for the first time he took in a bigger Ray Leonard, one carrying more weight than he had in the first fight. Duran finally sensed that this was not the same fighter he had faced five months before.

Then the bell. Ray immediately moved to the middle of the ring and landed a get-acquainted punch, a left that caught Duran flush as a calling card for future hurts, before dancing away. For the first minute or so of the round, he threw more feints than punches as Duran stood midring almost as if planted. Duran made as if to bull-rush Ray, but backed off after Ray dug a left to the stomach and jabbed twice to Duran's face, leaving Roberto to retaliate only with a grin. It was pop-pop-pop as Ray moved in and out, landing punches before circling out of reach. Our prefight battle plan of moving in and out, sliding away and frustrating Duran was working to perfection.

The second round began with Ray continuing to move in and out, circling left and right and leaving a jab or two behind as a hint of what was to come. Midway through the round, Ray moved in and landed a solid shot to Duran's jaw, bringing a roar from the crowd and a sneer from Duran. Ray was not only setting the early pace but frustrating Duran, whose punches were falling far short of Ray, who was leaning back away from them and countering. Every time Duran tried to mount one of his bull-like rushes in an attempt to force Ray into the ropes, Ray was able to tie him up, refusing to go toe-to-toe. No fighting flat-footed this time.

By the third, it was Ray who was grinning. His cat-and-mouse game was frustrating Duran. Every time Duran attempted to get close enough, Ray would either tie him up or exchange evenly with him and then quickly move out of range. My guy was boxing beautifully, playing Duran like a fisherman would a salmon. By the end of the third, Ray looked so unconcerned that even while I was trying to talk to him in the corner he was looking at the shapely ring-card girl prancing around the ring. Now that's cool and calm while Duran was being collected.

The fourth, fifth, and sixth rounds were more of the same. Ray would decorate Duran's face with jabs and his body with flurries and then move away, dictating the pace, a matador to Duran's bull rushes, hitting and not being hit in return. For the first time in his career, Roberto was not in control. Thwarted in every attempt to make it his fight and finding he couldn't, he was becoming more and more frustrated. You could see it in his eyes and in his body movements. It was almost as if you could imagine steam coming out of his ears as time and time again he attempted to get inside only to have Ray quickly move away. The only thing that resembled a knockdown came in the fifth when Ray slipped and fell in his corner as Duran rushed in. Referee Meyran ruled it a slip over a depression in the ring where the floorboard had split. Other than that Ray was doing a number on Roberto.

Came the seventh and Ray, now completely in control, went into his taunt-and-humiliate game, first sticking out his chin and then his tongue, double-daring Duran to "come on" with his right. "Try to hit me," he seemed to be saying. The man who had been through seventy-two fights and met every conceivable challenger—boxers, runners, counterpunchers—looked at his tormentor with disbelieving eyes, unsure of how to respond, never having met a taunter before. Finally, after a few seconds, Duran rushed in, headfirst, only to receive a stiff one-two for his effort. And if that weren't enough, Duran was then to suffer one of boxing's most crushing and devastating psychological blows, sort of boxing's version of a parlor trick. Leonard, after first going into an Ali shuffle, wound up with a mocking imitation of Kid Gavilan's bolo punch, in windmill fashion, and then, while Duran stood there, staring in disbelief, Ray popped him a good one in the banana with his left. It was humiliating, like a bully having sand kicked in his face. As many of those at ringside began to laugh, all the seething Duran could do was snarl contemptuously. You almost—not quite, but almost—felt sorry for him. At the bell ending the round, Duran waved a disgusted glove in the direction of Ray and walked back to his corner shaking his head in the direction of his manager, Carlos Eleta.

At the start of the eighth Duran, still smarting from the complete dis-respect Ray had shown him in the seventh, charged out of his corner in an attempt to get at Ray. But Ray stood his ground and their heads collided. No damage. Again Duran tried to charge, but Ray caught him with a left and a right. If Ray weren't my guy, I'd begin to think this was getting monotonous. But here was Ray taunting and humiliating the street-tough kid from Panama and not only getting away with it but winning because of it. Once again Duran tried to charge in, headfirst, and the two fell into a clinch along the ropes. As Meyran broke them up, Duran turned to him and said something, but Meyran ordered the fight to continue. Duran simply walked away, saying something more to Meyran. Ray, thinking it was a trick of some kind, stood his ground for a second before racing in and hitting Duran with a bodacious shot to Duran's half-turned body. But Duran, without even flinching at the blow, merely said something again to Meyran and, with sixteen seconds left in the round, waved his right hand in an oh-the-hell-with-it gesture in Ray's direction and walked to his corner.

I couldn't believe my eyes. What in the name of the Marquess of Queensberry was going on? One minute Duran was charging in; the next he was walking away, waving his arm, shaking his head. It was incredible. The fight was over. Sugar Ray Leonard had won the strangest victory I had ever seen.

I've heard of fighters quitting in the ring, like Jan De Bruin who walked out of the ring against Sugar Ray Robinson believing that Robinson was making an exhibition of what was supposed to be a fight. Broadway Billy Smith did the same against Archie Moore, seeing no point in continuing what he thought was an "unequal" and "ridiculous" fight. But this wasn't Jan De Bruin or Broadway Billy Smith; this was Roberto Duran. And before this unmagic moment you would have thought there were four immutable laws that governed the universe: that the earth goes around the sun; that lawyers always get paid first; that every action has an equal and opposite reaction; and that Roberto Duran would have to be carried out on his shield, blood streaming out of his ears, before he would quit. Now you could scratch the last one.

One moment here was the toughest hombre on the boxing block, box-ing's noblest savage. And the next, wildly out of character, he was a beaten man, waving his hands in a cross between "get lost" and "your mother wears army boots." What had happened to turn the sneering model of *machismo*, the legendary *Manos de Piedras* into a quitter?

There were so many different theories as to why Duran had quit it is almost a case of "you pays your money and take your choice." And most of the choices were more expansive than plausible, because nothing about it was plausible. Ray Arcel, Duran's cotrainer, scratched his head and said, "This is the last guy in the world I would ever have thought this would happen to." He didn't have any reason why. One who did was Duran's cotrainer Freddie Brown, who carried blarney off its feet by venturing that Duran had stomach cramps—that it was something he ate, something he later admitted he had concocted. Baloney! To me it was a similar situation to the first Clay-Liston fight in which Ali had gotten to Liston psychologically. Ray was playing with Duran, making him look silly, humiliating him, and nobody had ever handled Duran that way before.

Duran may have explained the unexplainable years later when he said, "Leonard is from the United States . . . they let him do anything he wants. They let him clown around; they let him make a show." And to Duran that was the greatest insult, both to his *machismo* and to his sport—a sport he believed was a battle between two men for fistic supremacy, no more, no less. To Duran, Ray Leonard had demeaned the sport, not him.

As for what he said to Meyran, it definitely was not the two words he would forever be tarred and feathered with: *No mas*. That was somebody else's interpretation of what he said, probably Howard Cosell's, who was broadcasting the fight. In anguish and in English, what I heard him say was "I fight no more." That was it. Twice. But from the look on his face he probably meant those words to mean something along the lines of "I came in here to fight and if he's not fighting, then I'm not. Screw it!"

Whatever the reasons for Duran's actions, it was a shame. A shame that this living legend would forever be remembered for this one moment more than for his previous seventy-two fights. And it was a shame his *macho* image was now in tatters. For Roberto Duran was no quitter. He was a noble warrior who had been turned ignoble by someone who dared to challenge his *machismo*.

It was also a shame for Ray who, having been denied the ultimate satisfaction of destroying Duran, never getting the full credit he deserved for his magnificent performance. After all, it had been Ray who had outboxed Duran. It had been Ray who had controlled Duran. And it had been Ray who had made Duran quit. But his victory was tarnished in the minds of many by Duran's "quitting," several suspecting the bizarre way in which the fight had ended was only a prelude to a third bout between the two. Many in the press put a negative spin on Ray's win discounting it as a win over, and here I quote one, "a fat, over-the-hill Duran." Ray bristled at such criticism, feeling that it "threw all the happiness out the window."

A full appreciation of Ray's talents and achievements would have to wait until his fight with Tommy Hearns.

SIXTEEN

Hearns, Retirement—and a "Marvelous" Comeback

Three months before Sugar Ray Leonard's return-bout victory over Roberto Duran, Tommy Hearns had scored a devastating two-round knockout of Pipino Cuevas to win the World Boxing Association (WBA) welterweight belt. Now, with Ray wearing the World Boxing Council's WBC hardware and Tommy the WBA's, it was a given the two would fight a showdown for the unification of the title. Everywhere you went you could hear people talking about—no, demanding—such a showdown. But hey, I only went to places where people talked boxing anyway. It was what we call in boxing a "natural."

But even while the two camps were dotting the *i*'s and crossing the *t*'s on the contracts for the inevitable showdown, there was still some business to attend to: a defense of Ray's WBC title against Larry Bonds at the Carrier Dome in Syracuse. Now at most prefight press conferences you usually see the makings of a grudge match with the two fighters confronting one another with a lot of saber-rattling, saying something or other about how each is going to beat the other's brains out. Only this time, instead of faking a punch or spouting the usual prefight palaver, there was Larry Bonds coming over to Ray with some eight-by-ten glossies for Ray to sign. As he made his way over, publicist Irving Rudd, catching sight of him, ran over and hollered, "Bonds, put those goddamn pictures away right now! Are you crazy?" And with that Bonds, getting the message, quickly put away the pictures. Ray had only a little more trouble disposing of Bonds than Bonds had of the pictures, TKOing him in ten rounds.

Finally, after some serious pull-me-push-you negotiations, the contracts for a September 1981 showdown between Leonard and Hearns were signed with more than enough money involved to ensure that everyone who had a cut of the pie would soon have his own unlisted tax bracket. However, before the ultimate matchup the two were scheduled to fight in a double-header against different opponents in "tune-up" fights as part of the buildup for the fight itself, a calculated showcase to hype the closed-circuit gate.

Here it must be pointed out that there is no written guarantee a "tune-up" will go according to plan. Many is the time a planned-for fight has been derailed by just such a tune-up. Take Jackie Cranford who had been penciled in as a potential opponent for Joe Louis only to lose his chance when he lost a ten-rounder to Gino Buonvino. Or more recently, when Tommy Morrison, guaranteed an opportunity against Lennox Lewis, took on Michael Bentt in a "tune-up" and lost both his bout and his chance in one round.

For their tune-ups Hearns pulled nondescript welterweight Pablo Baez who possessed a somewhat less-than-sterling record of eleven wins and nine losses. Ray, having drawn the short straw, got undefeated junior middleweight champ Ayub Kalule. As advertised, Tommy did his part, sending Baez to the showers in less than his promised fifteen minutes of fame, KO'ing him in four. Ray, however, found his tune-up no such walk in the park and had to go nine hard-fought rounds before dispatching Kalule.

With the tune-up fights behind us, it was time to prepare for the fight itself, one called "The Showdown" and being ballyhooed as yet another "Fight of the Century"—as if we hadn't run out of centuries and were working on some century way into the future. Three months to train and to break down the other's strengths and weakness, although by this time each camp knew almost every little thing there was to know about the other fighter, having studied him almost every step and punch along the way.

Physically, Hearns was as tall as a church steeple, his 6'1" frame topped by a heavy upper body poised atop a 30-inch waist and spindly praying mantis–like legs with no rump to speak of, all of which gave the look of a fighting machine on stilts. But his most dominant physical characteristic was his gangly arms. With the wingspan of a small airplane, his 78-inch reach was longer than all but four heavyweight champions, with huge ham hock–like fists the Armour Packing Co. would have been proud of.

It was that reach and those fists that had produced thirty knockouts in his thirty-two fights, a 94 percent slugging average, and earned him the nickname the "Hit Man" as well as the reputation of being invincible. But scouring the list of those who stood on the side of the undertaker after having faced Tommy, you could see that it was dotted with many names that read more like toe tags than fighters except for one Class A fighter—Pipino Cuevas. And it was his two-round knockout of Cuevas that had earned Hearns his fame. But hey, my guys had faced so-called "invincibles" before. Muhammad Ali fought George Foreman, who went into the fight with thirty-seven KOs of his forty opponents. Earlier, as Cassius Clay, Ali faced Sonny Liston, who had 25 KOs in his thirty-six fights. So it was nothing new to me. I just had to devise a strategy to offset that power, a strategy that would have my guy play checkers with Tommy and keep him one move ahead of by putting moves on Hearns he'd never seen before.

Looking at films of Tommy's fights, it was evident he was at his most dangerous at long range. He mastered smaller fighters—and who in the welterweight division wasn't?—by being able to take one step back with his right leg and still set up, forcing his smaller opponents backward with that long left jab of his, keeping them at the end of his punches. He threw that left at one speed, covering his opponent's left eye, and then would come back with that grenade of a right of his at a faster speed. And sometimes he would wave that gangly left arm of his in a hypnotic movement, throwing his opponent's timing off and making it difficult, if not impossible, to step inside where Tommy's long arms put him at a disadvantage.

But Tommy was programmed. He always started his offense with the same feint. And when he did, Ray would be prepared to move inside where the balance of power was all Ray's, being better coordinated and able to get off quicker, especially with his left hook. While Tommy could hit solidly from the outside, he was always off-balance and flat-footed when he missed and could be hit, his defense not the greatest. He always fought off-balance, even having trouble skipping rope and hitting the speed bag. I fully believed that Ray could use that lack of balance to get inside and outmaneuver him.

Put it all together and I not only thought Ray would make the "Hit Man" the "Hittee Man," but that Ray would knock out the knockout puncher. And because Ray could take a helluva punch I didn't give Tommy much of a chance of KO'ing Ray.

But if I had made a study of Tommy, so too had Tommy's trainer, Emanuel Steward, made a study of Ray. Manny went back a long way with Ray, all the way back to Ray's days as an amateur when Ray had trained at Manny's Kronk Gym in Detroit for the National Amateur Athletic Union (AAU) finals. It was here that he had won the gym nickname "Superbad" for what Manny called his "dazzling speed" and "great power."

Manny also had known Tommy since he was a skinny ten-year-old fifty-five-pounder who would go on to win 155 amateur fights, only 12 of those by knockouts. As an alternate battle plan, Manny devised a strategy to use the boxing skills Tommy had shown as an amateur, long before he had taught Tommy to "set down" on his punches, and to box if he had to in order to keep Ray on the outside. It was that alternate plan Tommy gave voice to when he told the media, "It will come as a surprise when Ray finds out I can box as well as punch."

But, as I was to find out later, there was one thing Manny hadn't planned on. And that was Tommy running twice a day to make weight. Steward was now afraid that the extra roadwork would drain Hearns and that his slender, twig-like pins wouldn't hold up through the fifteen-round fight.

You could see the effects of Tommy's attempt to make weight at the weigh-in. He looked emaciated. When he stepped on the scale he came in at a surprising 145 pounds, two pounds below the welterweight limit. Taking one look at Hearns's skeletal form, Ray said, "He looks like one of those starving people you see on posters from Ethiopia." To me he looked slat-thin and gaunt, as if he had nothing.

But looks can be deceiving, as we would soon find out.

At 7:30 P.M. on Wednesday, September 16, 1981, the temperature was the usual Las Vegas hot, about 100 degrees in the desert twilight but even hotter under the lights inside the canopied ring sitting atop the asphalt paving behind Caesars Palace. (Most natives of Las Vegas try to explain away the heat by saying it's dry heat, but then again, so's a microwave.) The temperature was heated even more by Tommy Hearns's withering evil-eye "look" cast through a half-shrouded gaze in the direction of Ray as he entered the ring. It was a "look" that had cowed many an opponent even before the first punch had been thrown.

But Ray wouldn't give Tommy the satisfaction of looking his way. Instead, he was totally focused on his mission, spelled out on the back of his robe: *Deliverance*. Stripping the word of its fig leaf it was merely an expression of Ray's desire to gain what actor Rodney Dangerfield would call "respect"—not just from his hard-hitting opponent but from the hard-boiled sportswriters who had discounted his accomplishments, particularly his win over Roberto Duran. Ray had even been sold short by the betting fans who had bought into Tommy's so-called "invincibility" and made him the 6½–5 favorite. But Ray had great belief in himself and in what he had to do to prove himself to all the doubting Thomases, Richards, and Harrys, and he couldn't have cared less about Tommy's "look."

Even before the echo of the opening bell had died down, it was evident the two had read the other's playbook as they engaged more in a chess match than a boxing match. Tommy's heavyweight reach controlled what little action there was as Ray constantly moved away, slip-sliding backward—always one step in front of that jab. The closest Tommy got to Ray came at the very end of the round when Ray put his glove on Tommy's head and disdainfully pushed it, and Tommy retaliated with a crisp right to the chops after the bell. Referee Davey Pearl put a quick end to such extracurricular activities, and Ray turned to his corner, wiggling his hips as he walked back to it, while Tommy pointed a glove at Ray and flashed another malevolent "look" in his direction.

The second round was more of the same, sort of a form of fistic filibustering, as Ray circled the stationary Hearns like a mongoose in an attempt to tire out the man who had gone more than four rounds only eight times in his thirty-two-fight career—fitting, as Hearns had chosen to be introduced by his alternate nickname, "The Motor City Cobra." Partial to a single orthodoxy, Tommy just stood there throwing out his long left all the while prospecting for an opening to land that crushing right of his, which had skewered thirty previous opponents. But Hearns was unable to strike up even a waving acquaintance with Ray.

For two rounds Tommy's style made great demands on Ray. It was like trying to take cheese from a set mousetrap. Every time Ray tried to get inside Tommy's 4½-inch-longer reach, he was met with a wicked jab. And all it had gotten him was a mouse under his left eye. It was now time to step up the action.

Exhorting Ray to "go out there and get him," I pushed him out of the corner for the third. But as he went out to take the fight to Tommy, Ray stepped into the path of one of Tommy's rights. And surprise of surprises, he didn't even blink. Now Ray knew he could take anything Tommy threw and stood his ground, swapping shots. For the first time Ray scored with his own right as Hearns, momentarily confused by Ray's quick hands and agility, went into retreat. At the bell a confident Ray raised his hands over his head. He now knew he *would* win, not merely that he could.

Rounds Four and Five mirrored the first two, sandwiched around Ray's third, with Hearns pecking away at Ray's angry-looking eye, looking for a way to break Ray down. But one thing was different. Ray, unable to reach Hearns to the head, was quietly moving inside with shots to the body. Still, they were rounds for Hearns. Barely. But something had to be done to alter the course of the fight, so before Round Six I exhorted Ray, "Come on, let's get this guy."

Now for the first time Ray was crowding Tommy, moving inside, looking for Tommy to make a mistake. I shouted as loud as I could—which for those who don't know me, was not very loud because of my high-pitched voice—"Speed . . . Ray . . . speed." Ray turned it on, catching Tommy with a right over his low-held left and then a left over his equally low-held right. Now I changed my tune, screaming, "The left hook . . . the left hook." And there it was, coming abruptly out of nowhere, threading the needle over Tommy's too slowly brought back right. Suddenly, the fight turned over on its back as for the first time in his career Tommy was hurt. He reeled backward under a barrage of blows. Numbered among them was a hard left hook to Hearns's unprotected rib cage, causing him to grimace in pain, his mouth opening and closing like a fish out of water.

The dynamics of the fight had changed. Once the pursuer, Hearns was now the pursued, as well as the boxer as he tried to fend off Ray. And Ray was now the puncher as he rattled more left hooks off Tommy's jaw than Hearns had been hit with in his previous thirty-two fights combined. Throughout the seventh Ray continued to penetrate the would-be defense of Hearns, landing left hooks from in close as the crowd began to chant, "Su-Gar Ray . . . Su-Gar Ray." Unable to keep the swarming Leonard off, Hearns merely grappled to keep Ray away.

At the end of the round Hearns staggered off on legs that were strangers to each other, heading somewhere in the vague direction of his corner, much the worse for wear. Ray, too, looked weary, breathing heavily from his prolonged fungo practice and saying, "I had him. . . ."

The eighth was more of the same, but you could see Ray's attack winding down even as the crowd continued to chant and we exhorted him from the corner, "Box, Ray . . . body, Ray." Hearns, trying desperately to stem the tide that was all Ray, attempted to catch Ray with a right. But, as the round wound down to a close with Ray swarming in, he took off on his bicycle, throwing out his long left in a getaway manner.

Tommy returned to his corner just one punch away from "Queer Street," a condition hardly lost on his trainer, Manny Steward, who was doing anything and everything he could to bring his fighter out of it—including shouting at him, "If you're not going to fight, I'm going to stop it." Finally, grasping at any straw to stay the inevitable, Steward said, "Let's go back to the amateur days." And with that, beginning in the ninth, Tommy reverted to his amateur style, the style that had enabled him to win 155 fights. Suddenly gone were his attempts to gain leverage by leaning in. Gone, too, were his flat-footed attempts at a knockout. But also gone was the stationary target Ray had found so inviting for the previous three rounds. In its place was a master boxer, one who was giving Ray angles, slipping his punches, and taking advantage of his 78-inch reach to jab, jab, jab—welting up Ray's damaged eye, which was now beginning to impair his vision.

And just as the tide had turned once in the fight within a fight, it was turning again, this time in Tommy's favor as he continued to flick out that long left of his, with very few rights thrown in for good measure. In fact, there were so few rights thrown during Rounds Ten, Eleven, and Twelve, you could count them on your right thumb—with the exception of a beautiful one-two by Tommy that landed flush on Ray's whiskers in the eleventh. But again, Ray barely blinked. The fans began to stir a little impatiently at the low-contact rounds, some of the high rollers even clapping and whistling for more action. It wasn't so much that Ray was lifting his foot off the pedal as Tommy was changing the pace of the fight and the momentum with his newfound tactics.

By the end of Round Twelve Tommy's fans had worked themselves into a frenzy with Hearns himself leading their vocal chorus in chants of "Tommee . . . Tom-mee." It didn't take a brain surgeon to see that the moment had gotten away from us, that there were no more Sundays, no more tomorrows, and no title at the end of road. Something had to be done. Now there are certain rules for trainers in corners: there's no time for hand-wringing; and no time to get preachy. You've got to give your fighter stripped-to-the-bone advice, just as Manny Seamon had given Joe Louis in the second Jersey Joe Walcott fight when he told him simply, "You've got to knock him out" and Louis, heeding his advice, did. So, in order to get Ray to turn it up a notch I told him, "Nine minutes . . . you're blowing it, son. You've got to pick up your tempo. Don't fight at his tempo. If you don't pick up your tempo, you're going to blow it."

Granted, it wasn't a battle cry that would wake the echoes, but it paid immediate dividends as Ray, knowing it was "all or nothing," leaped off his stool as if it were incandescent and raced out to do battle. First he landed a left hook, snuck in over Hearns's low-held right. Then Ray followed with three more left hooks to the head. Under siege, Hearns tried mightily to hold off the swarming Leonard, but couldn't, his efforts having about as much effect as a deck chair blowing off the *Queen Elizabeth II*. Unsure of how to clinch, never having had to, Hearns threw a right in the direction of Ray, but Ray beat him to the punch, jarring him off balance. Another left by Ray, still another, and a third, and suddenly Tommy was careening around the ring, his legs spaghetti-like, having given out from his two-a-day roadwork and the twelve grueling rounds.

Ray was atop Tommy now, throwing flurry after flurry, every punch in his arsenal in rather generous servings. Finally, after too many punches to be counted—twenty-one by one count and "enough" as writer Vic Ziegel noted—Tommy, in his best imitation of an accordion, gently folded through the red, white, and blue ropes. Referee Davey Pearl watched as Tommy slowly sank through the ropes and called his exit from the ring a push rather than a knockdown. It was as much of a knockdown as I had even seen, and I was now up on the ring apron yelling at poor Davey, "Count . . . count, dammit. It's a knockdown." As Hearns slowly regained his feet, Ray was on him again, raking him with yet another volley of punches. Again Hearns went down, this time not so much falling through the ropes as getting entangled in them, and this time Pearl called it a knockdown. As Pearl tolled the count, Tommy tried to haul himself up to his full 6'1" height, giving the impression of a balloon slowly inflating. Finally, at the count of nine Hearns made it to his feet just as the bell ending the thirteenth sounded.

There seemed to be no doubt as to the outcome now. At least not in the minds of the 23,615 fans. Nor in Ray's mind. He jumped off his stool for the fourteenth round and went right at the damaged piece of goods once thought to be invincible, throwing everything in his arsenal. Hearns tried to avoid the incoming fire by twisting his body back and forth from a right-handed stance to that of a southpaw. It was all to no avail as Ray kept throwing lefts to the body that made the exhausted Hearns wince and rights to the head that made him blink. Then Ray caught him with his hay-maker—call it his "Suzy-Q" or his "Maryanne" or whatever you want, but a haymaker pure and simple—landing a straight right to the chops, which he followed by throwing up his hands in his traditional victory signal. However, Tommy didn't fall, instead sliding backward along the ropes, his legs barely holding him up. Ray wouldn't let him off the hook now. After waving for referee Pearl to stop the fight, mimicking a move he had seen Muhammad Ali make, Ray stalked the now all-but-defenseless Hearns to the ropes, strafing him with right uppercuts, left hooks, and hard rights. Still Hearns wouldn't go down. But even if Hearns hadn't had enough, Pearl had. He pulled Leonard away from the beaten Hearns as all Tommy could do was look in his direction as if to ask, "Wha' happened?"

It was all over. Ray had won in a comeback so late it usually would be noted by an asterisk placed on train schedules for late trains. He had won "The Showdown" and was now the unified welterweight champion of the world. Lesser mortals couldn't have done it, but then again Ray Leonard was no lesser mortal.

As I stood there watching all the well-wishers jump into the ring to share in Ray's victory celebration, I thought to myself that for someone who had been told he had "no credibility" and that he hadn't been doing his job, I must have been doing something right.

I recall a little ditty we used to chant back in my youth about a character known as "On-again-off-again-Finnegan." I know there was some sort of verse that used to go with the name, but I've forgotten that, recalling just the name, "On-again-off-again-Finnegan." Anyhow, the next seven years of Sugar Ray's career after the Hearns fight reminded me of that guy, on again and off again.

The "on" portion of Ray's post-Hearns career began just five months afterward with a defense of his newly unified welterweight crown against

Bruce Finch. Three rounds and out. Next up on his dance card was a scheduled defense in May 1982 against Roger Stafford. However, one week before the Stafford fight, Ray began experiencing blurred vision, flashes of light, and floating dots—the same kind of "floaters" he had suffered after his fight against Marcos Geraldo three years earlier and again after being hit in the eye with an elbow by a sparring partner before the Hearns fight.

Using the pretext of visiting his wife and mother on Mother's Day, Ray left training camp and returned to Baltimore to see one of the best retinal surgeons in the country, Dr. Ronald Michels of Johns Hopkins University. Examining the same eye that had been damaged in his fight with Hearns, Dr. Michels told Ray that his blurriness could be traced to a loss of peripheral vision in his left eye and that he needed surgery to correct his partially detached retina—and the sooner the better to ensure complete recovery. Obviously there would be no fight against Roger Stafford. Nor any other fight—including a potential blockbuster rumored to be on the drawing board against middleweight champ Marvin Hagler—until Dr. Michels had given Ray a clean bill of health.

Six months after the operation and with Dr. Michels's go-ahead to resume his career, Ray hosted a massive gala, fittingly held in the same Baltimore Civic Center where his pro career had started. However, instead of it being the "coming out" party all had expected, Ray announced that "it wasn't worth risking my sight" to continue his career. Then, turning to Hagler, who was in attendance expecting Ray to announce a fight with him, he said, "Unfortunately, it will never happen." And with that Ray retired. Again.

But the name Sugar Ray Leonard and the word *retirement* didn't go together, not even belonging in the same sentence. I mean here was a kid who loved the ring, loved the action, loved the challenge—or, as he freely admitted, "I miss it. I love to fight." And he was going to retire, at the age of twenty-six, in the prime of his career, turn out the lights, close the door, and walk away from it all?

Come on! Some writer once said "short retirements urge sweet returns," and I fully expected Sugar Ray to make that sweet return sooner or later.

And so it came as no surprise when, after two years of inactivity, I got a call telling me that Ray had yielded to the siren call of the ring and was coming back. Now it was my job to find a suitable opponent for him from the list of eligible candidates submitted by Ray. Out of those I selected Kevin Howard, a fighter of some distinction but, more important, a fighter schooled in those tough Philadelphia blood pits that were more zoos than gyms and where they held wars, not sparring sessions. Howard's straight-ahead style coupled with his toughness would provide Ray with a true test of his skills in his first comeback fight.

The fight, a tune-up over the welterweight limit, originally scheduled for Worcester Centrum in Massachusetts for February 1984, had to be postponed when Ray had to have some additional nonsurgical retinal repairs done, this time to his right eye. The fight was rescheduled for May. The Centrum was crowded to capacity—and among those 10,000 fans anxious to watch Ray's comeback was one more-than-interested spectator, Marvelous Marvin Hagler. Licking his lips at the prospect of meeting Ray somewhere down the line, Hagler was heard to exclaim, "I can hardly wait."

Ray had opted for thumbless gloves, concerned about potential damage to his eye. Now I'm not a big fan of thumbless gloves. In fact, I think they stink. The original ones were too bulbous and the later editions were, too. But more important, the newfangled gloves affect such boxing niceties as spinning an opponent, grabbing him, or clutching him. I mean where would Willie Pep—who one time complained about them by saying, "How can you pull your trunks up with thumbless gloves?"—have been with thumbless gloves? Nevertheless, Ray liked them, so thumbless gloves it was.

But thumbless gloves weren't going to help him in there. Especially in the early rounds when he looked apprehensive, out of synch, and rusty. One ringside reporter described Ray looking "as if he were fighting under-water" while another said he was "exceedingly mortal." And then in the fourth, for the first time in his career, he was knocked to the floor as Howard came over with a straight right—Boom!—over Ray's lazily held left. Up quickly, Ray stood there, taking the mandatory eight-count with an embar-rassed grin on his face. Now there's one thing about boxing that's not true about any other sport. When you're embarrassed or humiliated there's no place to hide, no dugout, no bench, you're just there, standing all but naked, except for your trunks, for everyone to see. Sort of like a fly in coffee, the focal point of attention but hardly enjoying it. When he returned to his corner at the end of the fourth he knew his comeback had been a mistake, that it was all over, saying, "I can't go on humiliating myself."

And although Ray would come back to stop Howard in the ninth, within seconds of returning to the dressing room he announced, "It's just not there. . . . I retire for good."

The boxing world and Marvelous Marvin Hagler would have to wait another three years before boxing's Finnegan was "on" again.

By now Ray had retired so many times his picture was next to the word *retirement* in Webster's tome. And when he said he was retiring again after the Howard fight, I said, "Amen," thinking maybe this was it, his final-final retirement.

But he was still at that intersection where he had something to prove, an intersection he acknowledged after the Hearns fight when he said, "History is what drives me. I don't want to be remembered as just another champion. I want to be remembered as one of the greatest fighters of all time."

Above all else Ray was a pride fighter as much as a prizefighter, and he harbored ambitions to be included on that small island called "all-time greatness" with the likes of Sugar Ray Robinson and Muhammad Ali. He somehow felt he hadn't yet attained that exceptional status that would gain him inclusion—something more was needed to put a flourish on his career.

The man who said "I like to fight" was hardly resigned to the life of leisure and of being a celebrity. He hungered for something more, a challenge. It was in his boxing DNA. And what better challenge than the man who stood astride the middleweight division, the man who now called himself Marvelous Marvin Hagler?

As Ray played should-I-or-shouldn't-I with thoughts of coming back to challenge Hagler, two incidents pushed him to his ultimate decision. The first occurred after the Hagler–Roberto Duran fight, won by Hagler in the closing rounds. After the fight, Ray's one-time fistic foe came over and in broken English Duran told Ray, "Box him. You can beat him." The second incident happened two years later when Ray, seated ringside, watched John "The Beast" Mugabi, a slugger and hardly a Nureyev in boxing trunks, actually outbox a listless Hagler. Turning to his seatmate, actor

Michael J. Fox, Ray said, "Mike, I can beat this guy." Fox, echoing the thoughts of skeptical boxing fans everywhere, pooh-pooh'd him, saying, "Yeah, sure . . . have another beer!"

But Ray's mind was already made up. He needed just one more piece to the puzzle to confirm what he sensed. And so, in sort of a fact-finding mission, he invited Hagler down to Maryland for the opening of a restaurant he was part owner of. Sitting at a table drinking champagne, the two discussed (what else?) boxing—and Marvin's future. Ray broached the subject by asking, "So, Marvin, who are you fighting next?" Perhaps affected by the brew of the night, Marvin answered, "Ray, I'm just not as motivated anymore and I'm starting to cut real easy."

That did it! A week after their meeting I got a call from Ray telling me he had to do it, he had that itch again. He wanted to fight Hagler. I said "Amen" to that, too.

Usually all I need is three weeks in camp. Hey, I'm no sweat wiper. My job is to put myself into the body of my fighter in order to study his opponent and figure out how he's going to offset that guy, how he' s going to beat the sucker. That means sitting at home for hours going out of my mind analyzing and reanalyzing tapes, breaking them down frame by frame and studying the sonuvagun my fighter is going to be fighting until I come up with that slap-to-the-head "eureka" moment that tells me I've found a way to win. Then I build a better mousetrap to do it.

Never one to duck a challenge, this time it looked like Ray had pulled the short straw in selecting one of the most fearsome fighters in the whole of boxing, Marvelous Marvin Hagler, made all the more menacing by his evil-looking shaven bullet head. Hagler, the current middleweight champion for the better part of six years, had gone undefeated for eleven and had won his last thirty-seven fights. In the process, he had acquired the label of "invincible." Even his name was troublesome, tending as it did to obscure a full appreciation of his talents, sounding less terrifying than the hard-hat fighter who spat on his hands, rolled up his sleeves, and put in a good day's work at what he called "his office," that area inside the ring.

Hagler came by the name "Marvelous" somewhat dishonestly, having dubbed himself on the shoulders with his own gloves, giving himself the adjective meaning "awe-inspiring," almost as if with that name he could make it so. He insisted on being introduced as "Marvelous" Marvin before every fight. But when he demanded the name be used before his title fight with Caveman Lee, one of the ABC-TV directors overseeing the fight snapped, "If he wants to be announced as 'Marvelous Marvin,' let him change his name." And so, in less time than it took him to score a 67-second knockout of Lee, Hagler hied himself down to the Newark, New Jersey, registrar's office to officially change his name to Marvelous Marvin, without any quote marks surrounding the adjective.

Whether it was Marvelous Marvin or just plain ol' Marvin, or, as he called himself, a "bad dude," Hagler presented problems. His style was uniquely his own. A natural right-hander, Hagler fought left-handed, all the better to position his power hand, his right, closer to his opponent. Fighting in a straight line, his hands and his feet alternated with splendid timing and changes of pace as he crossed over from his left to his right side and back again with all the precision of a Hollywood production number, never losing a beat. And he could alternate his offense as well, interchanging his finesse for power and boring into his opponent with a bewildering variety of punches thrown from both sides of the plate.

Southpaws can give you all kinds of hell, their left-handed stance making their natural skills all the more baffling to their orthodox right-handed opponents. They come at you from a different direction with a different balance, a different flow, and a different blend of punches. And you've got to fight them differently. There was a fighter many years ago named Knockout Brown who not only was a southpaw but cross-eyed to boot. After he fought lightweight champion Ad Wolgast, an exasperated Wolgast was ready to swear off southpaws, mumbling something to the effect of: "How in the hell are you gonna fight him when you think he's looking out the window, but he's looking at you and hitting you from all angles?"

Back in the 1950s I had a southpaw kid named Andy Arel who gave the legendary Willie Pep fits with a cap *F*. And even though Pep won a close battle, I learned several things then that would now give Ray the edge and enable him to lick Hagler. You see, Pep used to circle, but you don't make circles with a southpaw. If you circle, you give a southpaw momentum. You've got to be first with everything you do, throwing him off his rhythm.

But Marvin was a completely different cat. He was a right-hander masquerading as a southpaw. Having done my homework by sending a kid over to get his autograph and watching Hagler sign it right-handed, I knew. It was that "aha" moment I had been looking for, the moment when I had to turn logic on its head and change all the standard rules about fighting a southpaw. For Hagler's strength, as I now saw it, was not in his left, but in his right. You had to respect that right hand, the hand he starched Tommy Hearns with, not so much his left, his supposed power hand.

Because every fight was different, requiring different plans and different strategies, I had to look at Hagler differently, not as a normal southpaw but as a turnaround southpaw. Now normally when you move away from a southpaw, you move to your left, away from your opponent's left hand. But with the naturally right-handed Hagler fighting southpaw, human algebra told me it was just the reverse—you had to move away from his right hand, moving right as Duran did in his fight with Marvin, and nail him with a right hand.

Studying films of Hagler's previous fights—especially those against Duran and Juan Roldan, both of whom had given Hagler trouble—I saw little things, things poker players would call "tells." For instance, Marvin was what I called a two-stepper, a hopper who had a sort of Lawrence Welk a-one-and-a-two-step cadence—he took a step or two before throwing a punch. And once thrown off his rhythm he would be a sucker for a right-hand counter. Moreover, when he threw a double jab he slid to his right, so Ray would have to slide to his right so as not to be there for Hagler to hit.

There were other things, too, little things that didn't show up on film but I thought would play an important role in the fight. One such thing was the so-called "rust" factor. While most of the writers were busy filling space writing that Ray hadn't fought in almost three years and only once in five, very few, if any, mentioned Marvin's having fought only once in two years—and that, in a less-than-memorable fight against John Mugabi, his once "marvelous" skills showed signs of erosion. Add to that the fact Ray was the only fighter in recent memory to come back as the younger fighter against an older one, and all of a sudden Ray's chances looked a helluva lot better than the 3–1 odds favoring Hagler.

There was also the question of Marvin's confidence. Or should I say Marvin's *overconfidence*? Just to get Ray into the ring, Marvin had readily agreed to all of Ray's contractual demands. Ray wanted a twelve-round, not a fifteen-round, fight to ensure he wouldn't get fatigued. He also preferred lighter Mexican Reyes gloves for speed. And he wanted a 20-foot ring, all the better to maneuver in. It made no difference to Marvin who agreed to all of Ray's requests, probably thinking what difference would the ring size make, Ray wasn't that tall and would fit into any size ring when he fell. And Hagler probably thought he wouldn't need twelve rounds anyway. And, oh, one more thing! Marvin and his promoter were already looking past Ray to another fight, this one tentatively planned against welterweight champion Donald Curry.

Call me a cockeyed optimist if you want, but after connecting all the dots and adding everything up, I left for training camp believing not only that Ray would win but that he would catch Marvin with a punch and knock him out.

When I arrived at the Hilton Head (South Carolina) training camp three weeks before the fight, I found Ray in great physical condition, fantastic shape, ahead of schedule. I never had to worry about him being in shape because he was always in shape. And ever since his compass needle had started pointing in the direction of Hagler, he had been working out three or four times a week. Now, here at the training camp, under the watchful eye of trainer Janks Morton, that great physical shape had been converted into great fighting shape. Just looking at him, it looked like he was ready to jump into the ring right then and there.

I say it "looked like" because something didn't feel quite right. I wasn't the only one to get those vibes. Within minutes after my arrival, publicist Irving Rudd came over to me and greeted me with, "Ang, this guy doesn't look good. He's gonna get the shit kicked out of him."

It was almost a case of "if you don't know where you're going, you can't get lost." While Ray was in terrific shape, he wasn't in shape to fight Hagler. I've always been able to see if I know what I'm looking at, and it took me only a minute or so to see that everything was moving in the wrong direction.

You see, coming up with a strategy is not a paint-by-the-numbers process, but one sketched out differently for each and every opponent. And apparently zilch attention had been paid to showing Ray how to fight Hagler. Take, for example, one of the first things I saw him try to do was get out of a clinch by moving to his right. "No . . . no . . . no," I hollered. "Go to the left." Ray didn't seem to understand, saying, "But I'll be going into his left hand," thinking Hagler's left was his power hand. "Yeah," I answered, "but his strength is in his right because he's a converted right-handed fighter." Now that I had Ray's attention I told him, "When this guy leans on you, make sure you not only slide to your right side but always lean on his right shoulder, not his left."

Ray had also flirted with the idea of going toe-to-toe with Marvin, to attack him. I had to put a stop to that nonsense. I hollered at him, "What? Are you nuts?" His game plan was to move, then move some more, not get into a battle with Marvin. Moreover, I told him to break up Marvin's rhythm. When he took that one-two step of his, preparatory to throwing a punch, pop him, then get the hell out of there. Ray listened. You see, he was different than Muhammad. With Muhammad I'd have to go around the mulberry bush, make him think he was the one who came up with the idea. But Ray was different. He listened. Especially after one of his sparring partners, Quincy Taylor, had put him on his duff while he was going toe-to-toe with him preparing to take on Marvin in, as he originally planned, a toe-to-toe battle.

Now he started implementing the fight plan I laid out for him in every sparring session, working against the grain to negate his left-handed sparring partners' right without concentrating on their left.

And when we watched films of Hagler's fights looking for flaws, it was like Max Schmeling looking at films of Joe Louis before their first fight and saying, "I 'seed' something . . ." as we continued to pick out Hagler's fault lines.

Despite his inactivity, Ray was now brimming with confidence, looking and sounding like a man who knew all the headwaiters in all the best places in town and knew he could get a table anytime he wanted. His table was now set for Marvelous Marvin Hagler.

Trainer Al Silvani once said that no fighter was truly calm before a fight, that "all have some fright inside." I'm not sure I'd call it "fright," preferring instead to call it being "nerved up." But basically Al was right, all boxers, in varying degrees, are "nerved up" or "antsy" before a fight.

Even Muhammad Ali, who looked so calm during a fight, tended less to "float like a butterfly" before fights than have butterflies floating in his stomach. Before his first fight with Sonny Liston, he was a boundless mass of energy, restless and unable to sit still. Instead of resting in the dressing room, he went out and watched his brother fight a prelim match against

Levi Forte. Then he returned to the dressing room and, after having his hands wrapped, spent several minutes slamming his wrapped fists into the metal lockers. It got so that Sugar Ray Robinson almost had to sit on him to keep him from expending all of his energy before the fight.

Leonard was no different. To say he was on edge before the fight would be an understatement. He was a bundle of nerves, almost a nervous wreck, unsure of what five years with only one fight had done to his ring skills, uncertain of his stamina, and unconfident of his ability to contend with Hagler.

Ray's crisis of confidence would last less than three minutes—or one round. For at the opening bell, Hagler came out of his corner in an unconventional, at least for him, right-handed stance. *What the hell was that?* I thought. I could only guess that Marvin was so dismissive of Ray—even having mockingly called him "pretty boy" at the prefight press conference—that he wanted to show him up, outbox him, convinced he'd catch him sooner or later and knock him out whichever way he was fighting. But, hey, you don't take nobody cheap. You never give anything away. And by fighting right-handed, not left-handed, Marvin was not only giving Ray an inviting target, one Ray took advantage of, peppering the advancing Hagler with flurries from the outside then moving away before Marvin could set himself to retaliate from the right side, he was also giving away rounds. And allowing Ray to gain confidence.

Ray's confidence was further buoyed when, near the end of the first round, Ray feinted and Marvin overreacted, throwing up his hands. Coming back to the corner Ray said, almost as if breathing a sigh of relief, "Shit, he's scared, too."

Fueled by his own arrogance and stubborn machismo, Hagler continued to fight right-handed long after its ineffectiveness had become apparent to everyone but Marvelous Marvin himself. Fighting from the right side, Marvin was forced to wage battle on unfamiliar terms and was being maneuvered by Ray into positions where he couldn't throw punches. Even when he changed back to his normal southpaw stance, it looked like he was more concerned about looking bad than fighting good as he remained hopelessly polite, allowing Ray to dictate the action, biding his time between flurries, circling out of reach, and walking Hagler around.

Joe Liebling once wrote "tactics are merely executions of strategy." And as Ray continued to execute our strategy to perfection, I got caught up in the action, hollering at Ray, "Box . . . box . . . dip and slide." And at Hagler, "Hey, Marvin, where did he go? There he is, Marvin. Look behind you, Marvin."

But our "coaching" from the corner took on other forms as well. With Charlie Brotman at my side holding up a stopwatch, I'd continually ask him, "How much time? How much time?" And when he told me "thirty seconds," I'd pound the mat, telling Ray the time left in the round, enough time to begin one of his late-round flurries. And then, as the clock ticked down, I'd have Ollie Dunlop, who had a much stronger voice than my squeaky one, shout out "ten seconds," and Ray would turn it up a notch. Through the years several people have claimed that Ray "stole" rounds by responding to our timing cues with end-of-the-round flurries. But I prefer to call it "one-upsmanship," the kind practiced by great fighters like Sugar Ray Robinson and Barney Ross, all the better to capture the attention of the judges who seem to be impressed by such end-of-round activity. That's their last look. Whatever you call it, Ray's flurrying at the end of every round and his tactics of staying away from Marvin combined to carry the first four rounds on two of the three judges' scorecards and three of the first four on the other.

Whenever Hagler developed a disliking for an opponent—as he did with Mustafa Hamsho, wanting to "wipe that shitty grin off his face," or Wilfred Scypion, wanting "him at my feet because he's got a big mouth"— he made them pay for their real or imagined disrespect. For Ray that disrespect took the form of his not fighting Marvin's fight in the trenches where Marvin wanted him. Now, after spending four rounds of calling Ray a "wuss" and a "sissy" for fighting "like a girl," Marvin was determined to make Ray pay the price for showing such disrespect.

At the bell signaling the start of the fifth round, Marvin came out like a raging bull, intent on exacting that price. For the first time he forced Ray into the ropes and landed a left to the head, a right to the body, and another short left to Ray's face. Ray came back with a left to the head, but Hagler got in a left to the head as well and then a right and a left. With less than thirty seconds to go in the round, Hagler landed a bodacious right uppercut that caught Ray flush. Ray was in trouble, but somehow Marvin didn't realize it.

As Ray plopped down on his stool, he said, "He had me and didn't know it" as if *he* now had Hagler. But you sure couldn't prove it by seeing what happened at the end of Round Five. So, rather than giving him hell about getting his butt kicked, in words as concise as a ten-word telegram, I calmly told him, "Look, I know he's not hitting you on the ropes. I know you're blocking those punches. But when you stand on the ropes, it looks like you're getting hit. So make sure you move off the ropes so he can't steal rounds."

If Marvin was laboring under a delusion that Round Five was the turning point in the fight, he didn't labor long. Things reverted back in Round Six with Marvin slowly following Ray around the ring, gloves held high, and Ray repeatedly stepping to one side and catching the incoming Hagler with a combination before moving quickly away. Still, by Round Eight Hagler's constant aggression had brought him back to about even on the judges' scorecards, even though Marvin was missing most of his punches. Taking note of Hagler's efforts to air-condition the ring, closed-circuit commentator Gil Clancy said, "Leonard's not doing anything to make Hagler miss, he's just missing." If that was an example of the so-called "effective aggression" judges are supposed to reward in their scoring, then they probably would have given the fight to Goliath for falling forward dead.

The ninth was one of those white-knuckle rounds that give trainers *agita*. Ray's legs, which had taken him out of trouble time and again, suddenly deserted him, and Marvin, forcing the action, cornered him against the ropes and landed several hard rights before Ray managed to escape with a flurry of his own, landing more punches but getting much the worse of the bargain. Moments later, with signs of fatigue setting in, Ray was again forced to the ropes and made to stand and deliver. This time Hagler landed a hard right before Ray, in a furious give-and-take, came back to close out the round with several crisp punches.

At the bell an exhausted Leonard staggered back to the corner and fell heavily on the stool with a puff of relief. Having worked with many champions over the years, it has always been my belief that what separates great fighters from the rest is that little extra something, call it their hidden reservoir of inner strength if you will. It was now time to summon up that strength of character, so I asked him to "suck it up." I also told him, "Don't trade shots with this sucker . . . that's a no-no."

At the bell for the tenth, Marvin came out hell-bent on following up his Round Nine assault, stalking Ray with the intent of breaking him up into smaller pieces. Somehow Ray dug deep and found that inner source of strength I knew he had, managing, although by now totally exhausted, to evade Marvelous Marvin's punches, which were coming one at a time and missing completely. It was almost as if when Marvin knocked, nobody was there. His inability to get to Ray so frustrated him that Marvin was reduced to hollering at his tormentor, "Come on, bitch, fight like a man . . . you little bitch."

Round Eleven was more of the same, Hagler coming in and Ray moving away, leaving a flurry or two as a reminder of where he had been. Several times the two fell into a clinch, where Ray, as per our strategy, leaned on Marvin's right shoulder and, on the break, exited left, completely offsetting Marvin's right hand. One of those times, as Marvin's head came dangerously close to butting Ray, I hollered up at referee Richard Steele, "Watch that bald-headed sucker's head!" But the round was mostly one of Ray staying out of Marvin's wheelhouse and frustrating his every attempt to lure Ray in.

It was now Ray's fight to win. And as the bell for the twelfth and final round rang, like Paul Giamatti in *Cinderella Man*, who hollered out to the cinematic James J. Braddock, "Last round . . . that's right . . . new champ," I tried my own form of cheerleading, hollering, "Three more minutes . . . three more minutes and you're the new champ of the world!" I not only wanted to exhort Ray to close the show, but I also wanted to sell the idea to the judges. I don't know what effect my hollering had, but I felt in the pit of my stomach that Ray soon would be crowned the new champ. He had dominated the action, fought his fight, and imposed his will on Hagler. And the fans knew it, too, standing up and shouting, "Su-gar Ray . . . Sugar Ray."

As the seconds wound down to the one-minute mark, instead of waiting for the "thirty-second" signal, Ray hollered over, "How much time?" Told "one minute," Ray began his victory dance, waving his fist in the air to spur on the crowd. Marvin, too, went into a two-step as the round came to a close, and the Caesars Palace crowd rose as one to cheer on the two.

In what seemed like an eternity but was really only a couple of minutes, the official decision was announced: judges Lou Fillipo and Dave Moretti both scored it 115–113, but each for a different fighter, and judge Jo Jo Guerra scored it an improbable 118–112. There was a pause and a pants-wetting second before ". . . for the winner . . . and NEW world middleweight champion . . . Sugar Ray Leonard."

The improbable had happened. Sugar Ray had turned conventional thinking on its ear with his comeback after a layoff of three-plus years and only one fight in five to best the man thought to be unbeatable. It was one of my most satisfying moments in boxing.

Unfortunately, it would also be my last with Sugar Ray Leonard.

After the fight Marvin complained he had been robbed. But, hey, he wasn't the only one. Here I was, having just pulled off one of the greatest tactical successes of my career and somehow my efforts had run afoul of the economics of Sugar Ray Leonard Inc., most notably attorney Mike Trainer who had rewarded me—if that's the right word—with substantially less than what I had expected.

I never had any problems with any of my fighters. When Herbert Muhammad became the manager of Ali he told me, "You'll be with this guy as long as he fights" and treated me fairly. And the year after the Hagler fight, Pinklon Thomas, after losing to Evander Holyfield, made sure that when the purse was divided I got my fair share, saying, "I don't care if I get a dime, Angelo's got to get paid." Unfortunately, it didn't work that way with Sugar Ray Leonard Inc.

Oh, how I tried coming to terms with Trainer. I had written letters and my lawyer had even tried calling Trainer's office leaving word that I wouldn't be going anywhere until I had a contract and knew what I was going to get paid. But there was no response. I had even written Ray himself, but again no response.

Jump-skip about a year and a half after the Hagler fight and Ray, who never met a challenge he didn't like, was considering fighting Donny LaLonde for his WBC light-heavyweight championship. I didn't like the fight, thinking LaLonde was "too big" for Ray. But Ray, salivating at the challenge like one of Pavlov's experimental dogs, decided to take it anyway, especially after the accommodating WBC, making up its rules on the fly, made the fight for two championships—the WBC light-heavyweight and the WBC super-middleweight titles, giving Ray a chance to add two more pieces of hardware to his growing list of belts.

A day before the press conference announcing the LaLonde fight, I got a call from Trainer telling me to be at the press conference. I told him I wouldn't attend until I knew where I stood, contract-wise. No answer to that, just be there.

That did it! I was tired of being run around and had had my fill of Mike Trainer and his manipulations. A light switch went on, and in one of those "you-can't-fire-me-I-quit" moments we all dream about, I decided enough was enough and that I was no longer interested in being trotted out and put on display like the Queen of England's ceremonial jewelry. I was not going to be at the press conference.

Ray would go on to stalk his own youth, always looking for that challenge at the end of his tunnel. But he would have to do it without me. I know Ray would say my absence had no effect, but fighting with all the frequency of Halley's Comet he would fight five more times over the next nine years, winning only two of them. Still, had he said something, anything, telling me he wanted me in his corner, I would have been there for him. I cared for him and still do. In my mind Ray Leonard will always be a champion. He was born a champion and will be a champion until the day he dies.

But I wish, just wish, Ray would have said something.

SEVENTEEN

The Second Coming of George Foreman

If déjà vu is the illusion of having experienced something before when it's actually being experienced for the first time, what do you call it when the future enters and carries you along toward some experience way before it actually happens? Maybe just "Angie's luck," because it had happened before and was about to happen again—just as working with Willie Pastrano had helped me get Muhammad Ali and working with Muhammad had helped me get Sugar Ray Leonard. The "it" in this case was the return to the ring after a ten-year absence by George Foreman just twenty-eight days before the Ray Leonard–Marvin Hagler fight.

How was I to know then that somewhere down the line, somewhere in the future, George Foreman and I would hook up and become part of boxing history? Forget 20/20 rearview vision, to even think about that happening sometime in the future would have been nothing more than wishful thinking, sort of like looking for a needle in the haystack and finding the farmer's beautiful daughter instead.

Let me backtrack a little here . . .

I almost lost track of George after Zaire. Almost, but not quite. I had heard rumors, confirmed by his trainer, Dick Sadler, that George had been devastated by his humiliating loss to Ali and had descended into what Dick called "a deep funk." Occasionally I would catch sight of him on TV. His first TV appearance after his loss to Ali was a circus-like exhibition against five of boxing's bowling pins that was something of a public mortification—made all the more so by one of the five trying to plant a big wet kiss on him during the prefight instructions. The next time I saw him was nine months later when he traded punches and knockdowns with heavy-hitting Ron Lyle, finally knocking Lyle out in an if-you-hit-me-again-and-I-find-out-about-it-you're-in-big-trouble donnybrook called by Red Smith "one of the best two-sided fights in recent boxing history." Four more fights, four more KOs in wham-bam-thank-you-ma'am fashion before he showed up one last time to fight the crafty Jimmy Young on St. Patrick's Day in 1977. Losing for only the second time, George claimed after the fight that he had had an apocalyptic experience in which he encountered God and that God had told him he would now be fishing for men's souls rather than fighting for boxers' bodies. And with that George sank from sight to answer "the call."

For ten long years George turned his massive back on boxing—reading no newspaper columns, watching no TV, and paying no never-mind to the sport. He devoted himself to tending to his parishioners at the First Church of the Lord Jesus Christ and to the Houston youth at the George Foreman Youth and Community Center. In order to support himself, his church, and his youth center, he began to accept outside speaking engagements, including appearances at other churches in the evangelical community. But sitting there listening to other clergymen use his presence to fill their collection plates, George began to think to himself, "I know how to make money."

And so it was that long past the age when most heavyweight champions have ridden off into the sunset, the thirty-seven-year-old Foreman embarked on a second career. He began "moonlighting" as a boxer to underwrite his church and youth center while continuing to spread the Gospel of Jesus Christ.

F. Scott Fitzgerald wrote "there are no second acts in America." But obviously F. Scott Fitzgerald had never met G. Edward Foreman, whose second act was far greater than his first. Beginning with his first comeback fight in March 1987 against Steve Zouski, far from boxing's spotlight in Sacramento, George bowled over twenty-two heavyweight tenpins, working his way backward through the alphabet from Z (as in Zouski) to A (as in Adilson Rodrigues, my fighter). Most of the fighters he met entered the ring looking for the first train going south and were sent packing so quickly that, as one writer put it, "the crowd got refunds on their hot dogs."

But while George was laying opponent after opponent endwise, and the fans, many of whom had cheered him at the beginning of his career in anticipation, in the middle in acceptance, and now at the end in appreciation, were applauding his efforts, but the press was hardly giving him a ticker-tape parade of praise. Instead of celebrating his achievements, they dismissively derided his efforts as those of an old has-been with the body of a pot roast—the *New York Daily News* calling him "a fat cartoon character." Sportswriters ridiculed his opponents as nothing more than "bums"; one writer commenting they were "only slightly livelier than Joe Louis's statue."

Granted, some of those on George's catalog of opponents were about as unknown as the second man to fly across the Atlantic Ocean. Still it was much the same cannon fodder other heavyweights had met, and stepped over, on their way to the top. The names Bobby Crabtree, Manny Almeida, and Rocky Sekorski also dotted Michael Dokes's résumé. And David Jaco, Steve Zouski, and Max Young could be found on Mike Tyson's hit list. Then there were J. B. Williamson and Dwight Muhammad Qawi, both former light-heavyweight champs, and Bert Cooper, a heavyweight perennial. To call these repeating decimals "bums" when they fought George but "worthies" when they fought others was much like examining a wine bottle but not tasting its contents.

Knowing that even kinder words than those the press had lavished on George and his comeback had closed many a Broadway show, George decided to beat the sportswriters at their own game. He deflected their scoffs and critiques with good-natured, self-mocking humor. To questions about his age he replied, "I'm going to fight to pass a bill that would force a mandatory retirement age on boxers . . . sixty-five." And in response to critics that he only fought fighters on respirators, George said, tongue planted in cheek, "That's a lie . . . they've got to be at least eight days off the respirator."

It got so that those who had wondered whether George and his comeback weren't all a big joke had to wonder whether the joke wasn't on them. George took their jabs and stabs in stride, disarming writers with his mother wit, delivered with a twinkle in his eye and a smile on his lips. Emphasizing his 43-inch waistline and love for food, George would answer questions like "How far do you run every morning?" with "Depends on how far my refrigerator is." Responding to "When do you think that you'll fight for the title?" he laughingly said, "Today, the biggest decisions I'll make aren't related to the heavyweight title, they're whether I visit McDonald's, Burger King, Wendy's, or Jack in the Box." By displaying the most spontaneous wit since Muhammad, George left every interview and press conference the better for his presence and left the press laughing with him, not at him. But while the press was entertained by George himself, calling him "Captain Cheeseburger," they didn't entertain any realistic thoughts that he would achieve his fistic goal of rewinning the championship, labeling his quest, in food talk, "pie in the sky."

In order to validate his credentials as a possible title contender, George would now have to face a top-ranked contender, not another "opponent" from the lower precincts of the division. He found one in the person of Adilson Rodrigues—who, not incidentally, was my fighter.

Just as in the days of my youth back in South Philly when I'd sneak into the movie, coming in halfway through, and after having seen the entire movie, from middle to beginning, then back to middle, get up and say, "This is where I came in," this is the place where I came into the picture with George.

For George, the Rodrigues fight was the culmination of the long road back, a three-year, twenty-one-fight barnstorming campaign he called "puddle jumping" that had seen him travel the highways and byways of America to such outlying boxing outposts as Anchorage, Orlando, Galveston, Fort Myers, Springfield, Bakersfield, and other places mapmakers would have had trouble finding on the boxing map. He did so at the cost of big purses; his goal was not the money but winning back the heavyweight title. He gave as his reason for taking the long road round: "I had seen others, like Muhammad Ali and Joe Frazier, fail in their comeback attempts because they were looking for overnight success. I knew it would take a long period of time to do it right, so I started from the bottom and worked my way up and that took three years."

But if George had been fighting those the press labeled as qualifiers for the "tomb of the unknown boxer" thus far in his comeback, he was going to find his first real challenge with my fighter. Rodrigues was a hero in his native Brazil where he was called "Maguila"—as in the cartoon character "Magilla the Gorilla." He had put together a formidable record of 36–3, with 26 KOs. However, it wasn't his knockout prowess I thought that would enable him to beat George, but his boxing ability, having already outboxed and decisioned another big knockout puncher, James "Bonecrusher" Smith. Because George had averaged less than four rounds in his twenty-one comeback fights and had gone past five rounds only four times, our strategy was to force him to use his aging legs in order to extend him into the later rounds where it would be Rodrigues's fight.

Early on in his comeback George had learned the importance of the press saying, "I'm only a product of the media. They made me. I'd be eating hard corn bread and red beans today if it hadn't been for the media deciding to write about me. They made the people so curious they started filling arenas." Now, with the press converging on Las Vegas for George's fight against Rodrigues—as part of a doubleheader with Mike Tyson sharing the bill in his first appearance since losing his title—their presence provided the preacher man with a bully pulpit.

Crowding around the man they viewed as having taken Ali's place as boxing's resident philosopher, the press wore their pencils down to the nubs recording George's every note and quote. Channeling his "inner Ali" the man they now referred to as "Big" George first patted his stomach, calling it his "investment." Then, mixing humor with a little self-deprecation, he told them to "stop calling people old . . . old is 102. I'm here to show people that being over forty isn't a death sentence." His strategy for the fight? "To try to hit Rodrigues before he can duck." Then he added one quote that had me scratching what hair I had left, saying, "Now Rodrigues has hooked up with Angelo Dundee. Dundee has always been successful against guys of my nature who are punchers. That's enough to know right there." What the hell did he mean by that? George might have known then, but I wouldn't know until after the fight.

Come fight night I needed some help in the corner, so I called upon my son, Jimmy, who had accompanied me to Vegas, to help bring the stool in, carry the buckets, that sort of stuff. As we stood there, awaiting George's arrival in the ring, which took ten minutes or so, George "icing" Rodrigues by deliberately coming in late, I turned to Jimmy and told him that from what I had seen on TV George was "in bad shape" and that this wouldn't be a tough fight. Or something like that. Suddenly there was Big George, up in the ring, scrunched over under his hooded white terry-cloth robe and skipping around. Jimmy and I were leaning on the ropes looking out at the

Caesars Palace crowd when George came over to our corner and gave me a forearm shiver right in the chest. Straightening up to his full 6′3″ size, he greeted me with, "Hi, Angelo, how are you?" Suffering a sudden seizure of *agita*, I gasped to Jimmy, "Oh my God, we're in trouble!" I wished I could be anywhere else in the world but in that Caesars Palace ring with George at that moment.

However, my fears seemed unfounded, at least for the first 2:40 or so of the first round. For there was Rodrigues, moving in and out—although the padding under the canvas had softened in the hot Vegas sun, making it harder for him to backpedal—tattooing George with jabs, some of them belly punches. All George was doing was moving constantly forward, his few jabs so slow they looked like they had tin cans tied to them. Then, in the closing seconds of the first round, he threw a jab that came out of nowhere and landed with all the force of a two-by-four being shoved through a wall, bloodying Rodrigues's nose. Back in the corner Rodrigues said, "That hurt." Unlike Paddy Flood who, when told by his fighter Bobby Cassidy that his eye ached, candidly said, "Yeah, I see . . . and the ache is getting purple," I tried to gloss over Rodrigues's anxious comment with a "No, it didn't." But I knew then that the outcome was written in stone. And about two minutes later George confirmed my worst fears by staggering Rodrigues with a left-right combination and following that up with a vicious wait-here-until-the-stretcher-comes left hook—BAM! BAM! BAM!—sending Rodrigues down and out at 2:39 of the second round.

I was now sold on George. What I didn't know then was that George was sold on me, too. I would find that out later that night when, at the airport waiting for the red-eye back to Miami, George plopped down in a seat next to me and said, "Angie, I've always admired you, the way you take care of fighters." Then he told me he remembered how, back in Zaire, when he had Ali cornered in the sixth round and was thinking "I finally got him," I had shouted up to Muhammad, "Don't play with that sucker!" and Ali had covered up quickly, ending any chance George had of winning. George went on to add that he also respected the way I protected my fighters. When Ali fought Larry Holmes, when everybody else was, in his words, "deciding to let this tough man keep getting a beating," George remembered my pushing Bundini away and saying, "I'm boss here and I say it's over." Now George said to me, "I've always wanted you to work with me . . . will you?" What else could I do but answer, "Yes." And so the chain of events that had begun with my being in Muhammad's corner in Zaire had come full circle.

The George Foreman I knew was the 1974 version, the George Foreman of Zaire. That George Foreman was hardly a Prince Charming, having wrapped himself in the cloak of his first role model, Sonny Liston. Small wonder then that, like Liston, he was, by turns, sullen, distant, and rude; someone who, in his own words, "would offend anybody."

However, when I arrived at his training camp to help prepare him for his fight with Evander Holyfield, what to my wondering eyes should I find but an all-new George Foreman, no longer the 1974 model. In effect he had reinvented the George wheel, turning from a Sonny Liston growl-alike into a nice, round-faced, warm, cuddly teddy bear. Replacing his early guardedness with openness, he was garrulous, amusing, almost touchy-feely. Maybe a little of Muhammad Ali had rubbed off on him. But most probably it was those ten years away from the ring, ten years that enabled him to come to grips with himself and be who he wanted to be, just plain ol' George—not the person others wanted him to be. If so, his ten years away had been one helluva career move.

If ten years had brought about a change in the internal George Foreman, it had wrought a change in the external one as well. Now he looked as big as the proverbial barn, almost as if each added year had also added to his middle, like rings around a tree. From the somewhat lithe 220 pounds he had weighed in Zaire, he had ballooned up to 315 during his retirement, coming back down to between 267 for his first comeback fight against Steve Zouski to a "svelte," for him, 235 pounds against Dwight Qawi. Obviously uninterested in fashioning the type of designer body that fans had come to expect in their heavyweights during his absence—bodies like those of Mike Weaver and Ken Norton—the well-upholstered Foreman was comfortable fighting somewhere in the 250- to 260-pound range.

When sportswriters would make jokes that he looked like a parade standing still and press him on whether he was satisfied with his weight, George would parry the interviewer in kind. He would resort to shtick, joking that he had gone on a cheeseburger diet, that he was the prodigal son of boxing looking for the fatted calf, that his training camp was right next to the local ice-cream store. He added several other one-liners that sounded as if they had come right out of a Milton Berle joke book. Then, without missing a beat, he would answer, "Satisfied? No, I'm not satisfied. I want to be BIGGER! I'm a lion, not a pussycat. I don't see why I have to lose weight just so I can fight like a kitty cat." And that would answer that. Sort of.

But if the boxing press saw a body of great acreage, one that looked pulpy with a kind of aging massiveness, then they didn't know what that body contained. For this George Foreman was nothing like the first George Foreman, the "new" Foreman having little in common with the "old" model. This George Foreman's style also bore little or no resemblance to the style of the "old" George Foreman. The George Foreman of Zaire would spend his time winding up and flailing away, much like an axe man trying to fell a tree, almost as if the draft of a punch might give his opponent pneumonia if he missed. Instead, this second coming was of a man who had matured, who had acquired the patience of age, the savvy of an old pro, and the wisdom of thoughtful exploration. Not only that, but George had developed a jab that could break tall buildings in a single shot, one that landed with all the force of a wrecking ball. Someone once asked me who was better, the young George Foreman or the older one, and after giving it some thought I told him that George was "smarter" the second time around and would have handled Zaire better; he wouldn't have been tricked by that rope-a-dope stuff nor Ali's psyche job.

Sure, this new version of George Foreman was s-l-o-w-e-r. But while speed is the first thing a fighter loses with age, George never had any in the first place, his movements were always −10 on the Richter scale. What George had was overwhelming power, many considering him the greatest hitter since axe-wielding Lizzie Borden took out two in one night up in Fall River, Massachusetts. And power is the last thing a boxer loses. For references just ask George's 23 KO comeback victims who had felt it.

Watching George train was a revelation. Unlike almost every other fighter in boxing history, George did little of his training in the gym. It was almost as if he was allergic to it. Instead he cut logs or ran along behind a slow-moving pickup truck equipped with a heavy bag dangling from the rear throwing punches as he plodded along—first all lefts and then all rights. It was a rare exhibition of a man programming himself to move constantly forward throwing punches. No turning, no moving sideways, just chugging forward. Me? I was trailing along behind him, riding in a car, watching. Whatever worked for George, worked for me. Hey, I try to blend as best I can with my fighters. And with twenty-four wins and twenty-three knockouts in his comeback—counting two more KOs after Rodrigues, Ken Lakusta and Terry Anderson—who was I to argue with George and his training habits?

George was as ready as he'd ever be for his Ahab-like quest to recapture the heavyweight title. His mental state, his stamina, and, yes, his weight were exactly what we wanted them to be. All that stood in his way was the champion: Evander Holyfield.

Almost from the moment George decided to return to the ring, he had told anyone who would listen that his dream was "to become the heavyweight champion of the world." Further, he told those who hadn't thrown their backs out trying to hold in their laughter that he had the perfect style to beat the then-champion, Mike Tyson. But, as so often happens in boxing, being a champion is subject to immediate revocation and Tyson, who had won the World Boxing Association (WBA) version of the crown a scant two days before George had started his comeback, was now no longer the heavyweight champion, having lost his belt to Buster Douglas who, in turn, had lost the valuable bauble to Evander Holyfield. And so George now set his sights on Holyfield.

The man who stood between George and his fistic dream was an undersized overachiever. Called "The Real Deal" by his promoter, Holyfield might better be described by his alternate nickname, "The Warrior," for, to use an old boxing phrase, "he came to fight." Possessing the arms of a village smithy and a steel-tough anvil body, Holyfield was a one-man strong-arm crew who more than compensated for his lack of size and poundage with a heavyweight heart. He also had a heavyweight punch, one he was able to deliver from both inside and outside. If Holyfield had one flaw, it was his propensity to get hit. He admitted as much, saying, "I don't try to get hit . . . it just happens." And even though he had a great set of "whiskers," George would test them, the same way he had tested his comeback foes, reducing twenty-three of the twenty-four to resin dust.

This being my first fight in George's corner, I really didn't know what to expect. Would it be the same George Foreman I had seen in Zaire, the George Foreman so stricken by self-doubt that even as he entered the ring he would be saying to himself, "You shoulda worked in this. You shoulda worked on that"? No this time around the "new" George Foreman was "loose as a goose," supremely confident in himself and in his mission to win the heavyweight title. Again.

And when I say "loose as a goose," let me tell you how loose that was. The eve of the fight I dropped into the pressroom to visit with some of my old friends, newspapermen like Pat Putnam, Eddie Schuyler, and Mike Katz. And what to my wondering eyes should I see but George holding court with the press. In all my years in boxing, I had never seen a fighter the day before a fight in the pressroom. Almost to a man they were up in their rooms resting, the way Willie Pastrano was that day in Louisville when a young kid named Cassius Clay called up to the room and asked to visit Willie and yours truly.

But there was George in all his glory, surrounded by hordes of writers, playing them like a musician would a keyboard, with an assortment of smiles, sermons, and plain ol' shtick. And he wasn't talking about his chances in what was being called "The Battle of the Ages" nor his place in boxing history. Instead he was making fun of his size and age, telling them he didn't mind being called "big," "fat," "old," or even "late for dinner." But few thought he could beat Holyfield, most wondering how in the world he had ever maneuvered himself into a position to fight for a title he had won some eighteen years before. There were even some who thought he was on a suicide mission—including my friend Ferdie Pacheco, who worried that a man Foreman's age could suffer a heart attack, and Evander's trainer, Lou Duva, who said, "It's going to be stopped by the referee or the Red Cross." Despite the skeptics George continued to play to them, knowing that through them he was reaching the fans who had adopted him as a folk hero.

Now you know me, I'm the guy who gets up to speak at the sight of half a grapefruit. But not around George, who not only commanded attention but center stage as well, allowing nobody, me included, to upstage him. One time during the preparations for the Holyfield fight, while George was in the locker room resting after his workout, several members of the media approached me for comments. Well, wouldn't you know it, but the next thing I heard was George's thundering voice hollering from the back, "There goes Angie again, you got to watch him!"

From that point on I let George do all the talking for the both of us. It was his pulpit and by talking to the press he was, in effect, talking directly to his fans. And I sure wasn't going to get in his way. After all, it was his show. Still, I was able to be of help by giving him one small piece of advice. Watching him give out his homespun philosophy and what had become known as "sound bites," I couldn't help but notice that he was chewing gum about as fast as he was talking. So, calling him aside I said, "Look, George, never let the media take pictures of you chewing gum. It doesn't look nice in the papers, you moving your mouth all funny." And wouldn't you know it, he stopped chewing gum from that moment on. Of course, his mouth never stopped moving as he continued to talk . . . and talk . . . and talk.

And talk on he did, right up to fight time, telling one and all, "I'm going to show the whole world that forty is not a death sentence." And, "When I win it's going to be a compliment to the earth itself. It's proof that the water supply is just fine, that the fish in the sea are multiplying, and that acid rain didn't bother the food at all." Boy, was the Reverend George ready to go to battle.

George's one-man promotional campaign had worked. The Atlantic City Convention Center was jam-packed with eighteen thousand cheering fans, and early reports indicated his ballyhoo had generated over a million buys on HBO's first-ever pay-per-view boxing telecast. Hard as it was to believe, the champion, Evander Holyfield, was but the party of the second part, merely a bit player in this drama called "George."

To say that the night belonged to George would be an understatement as celebrity after celebrity—including Donald Trump, Jesse Jackson, and several other uninvitems—dropped into the dressing room before the fight to wish him good luck. Not since the days of Ali had I seen anything like it, not even with Sugar Ray.

And then came the walk to the ring. This time there was no dash down the aisle as in Zaire, but a slow deliberate walk, almost a processional, led by co-trainer Charley Shipes and myself to a chorus of "George . . . George." This time George wanted to conserve his energy knowing there would be no early knockout, but, as he told me, he "would get him sometime before the tenth round." This was all fine with me; I was too old for that running stuff anyway.

From the very first second of the fight, those doubting Thomases, Jerrys, and Marks posing as savvy newspapermen who had thought the fight was a joke—some called it a "flimflam"—were proven wrong. George, after blocking several of Evander's right-hand howitzers, began to land his jab with metronomic repetition, beating Evander to the punch time and again. In the second, George, after patiently waiting for Evander to throw his hook, countered with a hard left hook of his own and then caught the champion with a ponderous right, snapping Evander's head back and stunning him. All of a sudden the crowd, now believers, began chanting, "George . . . George" and the echoes in the cavernous convention center came back, "George . . . George." No, this fight was anything but a joke. This was for real.

Between rounds I told George to continue using that jab whenever Evander made as if to throw his hook and to look for a place to drop that powerful right of his over the top. All of which wasn't easy to convey inasmuch as George was standing between rounds, refusing to use the stool since he thought that sitting down and then standing back up took more physical exertion than merely standing for the entire one-minute rest period. (And, not incidentally, standing gave him a chance to sneak a peak at the opposite corner to see what was going on over there.) As short as I am, I was getting a kink in my neck looking up somewhere in the direction of George's ear to talk to him.

And then in the third, in what Charlie Goldman would have called an "Oy vey!" moment, Evander got through George's cross-armed "armadillo" defense with an overhand right from hell, catching George flush—the same overhand right that had knocked out Buster Douglas and Michael Dokes. It was one of those moments that causes you to question your faith in Gibraltar as the 207-pound Holyfield shifted the 257-pound Foreman's center of gravity. But unlike the Foreman of Zaire, who would have submitted to the punch, the "new" George showed his thoroughbred heart, willing himself to remain upright. He not only survived the right but also Holyfield's follow-up assault to last out the round.

The fourth, fifth, and sixth rounds were give-and-take violence with the two standing mid-ring on a square of canvas no bigger than the biggest white napkin swatting away at each other. Evander's punches were more frequent and more surgically precise, while George's were more ponderous but fully capable of bisecting his opponent if they had landed. The only problem was every time George tried to throw his power right over the top, the quick-footed Holyfield would move back out of the way and then come back in with a countering punch.

And then came the seventh, the most savage two-sided round since the first round of the Hagler-Hearns all-out war five years before. George started the action with a huge right that sent Evander reeling backward. Then he reverted to the George of old, throwing punch after punch, most of which were either deflected by Holyfield or missed. Evander then returned the favor, responding in kind. But even though winded by his efforts, George never budged and traded combination for combination and punch for punch in a "take that" exchange as the two fighters took turns beating the bejabbers out of each other. The punches were so brutal that after the round Evander returned to his corner and asked, "Are my teeth still there?"

Two rounds later, there was none of the give-and-take of the seventh, as Evander rattled punch after punch off George's head—one ringside observer counting twenty in a row. Later, Evander would say, "I hit George with everything I had." They were blows that would have felled buildings, blows that would have felled the Foreman of old, the Foreman of Zaire, but George, calling on a will and determination he didn't have then, took them all, proving that, contrary to Bob Fitzsimmon's famous line, the bigger they are the harder they *don't* fall.

You could see that Evander was exhausted by his effort, and Charley and I, figuring it was now George's turn, told him to throw his right hand more during the closing rounds. And throw it he did, finally catching Evander with one perfectly placed right hand in the twelfth and final round. A hurt and tired Evander fell into a clinch and held on . . . and on . . . and on . . . even after referee Rudy Battle had warned him several times to break. I'll never understand why Battle, who had deducted a point from George on a questionable low blow, didn't penalize Evander for holding. But them's the breaks. Anyhow, the fight ended with an exhausted Evander grabbing George in a bear hug.

Then came the damnedest thing I had ever seen in all my years in boxing. George walked over to Evander's corner to thank Evander and his trainer, Lou Duva, "for the opportunity."

The decision came moments later, a unanimous decision for Evander. But the real winner was George, who, having established the improbability of the calendar, said, "We didn't retreat and we kept our dignity. So everyone at home can take pride that while we may not have won all the points we made a point."

And he had, proving to all that while Evander Holyfield may be called "The Real Deal," Big George was "The Real-Real Deal"

Many are the fighters who have been defined more by their losses than by their wins. Take Billy Conn, for example. Conn's gallant but losing effort against Joe Louis completely obscured the rest of his great career, which included a light-heavyweight championship and sixty-three wins. Or Tommy Hearns, more remembered for his losses to Ray Leonard and Marvin Hagler than for his forty-eight KOs and seven titles.

Determined that he would not be one of those seen through the wrong end of boxing's looking glass, George viewed his loss to Holyfield merely as a dream deferred. There was no reason not to continue. He wanted one more chance at the brass ring, one more opportunity to climb his Mount Everest, one more shot at the heavyweight championship. And he didn't care *which* heavyweight champion it was, saying, "The heavyweight championship is a mountain I consider the top and I've been climbing that mountain so long they can call it the WBO, the WBC, the WBA, or the WBwhatever, but I'm going to win it."

With no unconditional surrender to the undeniable fact that time might be running out on him, George soldiered on, refusing to take no for an answer to his dream. And after three more wins, he finally got his second chance at one of those alphabet soup group's titles, a fight for the vacant World Boxing Organization's (WBO) heavyweight championship versus Tommy Morrison.

We didn't think that Morrison would be all that difficult. After all, he had been brutally knocked out two years earlier by Ray Mercer, and Ray's punches were nothing like the bombs George threw. But rather than standing and fighting, Tommy came in with an all-new battle plan and won going away. And I mean *going away*. Admittedly, I was never a good scorekeeper, but I really didn't think he deserved to win since all he did was run. But you know what? The more I looked at the tapes of the fight, the sharper he looked. He fought a good, smart fight. He had a good jab, and by coming in and landing and getting away before George could retaliate, he might have won. I say "might have won" because I still think George won, but I'm willing to give Tommy the benefit of my doubt.

Whatever, here it was seven years and twenty-nine fights into George's comeback and he still had no championship belt to show for his efforts. Nor for his dream. But in one of those little tricks history continually plays on us to make sure we are paying attention, despite his loss to Morrison, George was once again given a chance at the heavyweight title, this time by the International Boxing Federation (IBF) and WBA champion, Michael Moorer. In a scenario not unlike that followed by the man he had beaten for the title, Evander Holyfield, Moorer and his handlers decided he could make the most money with the least risk by making his first title defense against the same man Evander had made his first defense against: Big George.

But a funny thing happened on the way to the fight that almost derailed George's dream of making fistic history. Seems that the WBA, in their classic nonwisdom, citing something or other in their rules about their champion having to face a top contender, refused to sanction the fight. They even threatened to strip Moorer of their title if he went forward with his plans to fight George. Nonsense, said George, who was having none of such tomfoolery. He had hoped for this fight, trained for it, even prayed for it. Now he would sue for it. Believing that this was his last shot at the WBO, the WBC, the WBA, or the WBWhatever championship, George, after consulting with his attorney, Henry Holmes, and his promoter, Bob Arum, determined to fight the WBA ruling and filed a suit against them, along with Michael Moorer, his handlers, and the Nevada State Athletic Commission.

During the trial it was shown that the WBA had more than occasionally gotten caught in their own mental underwear and hadn't exactly followed their own rules, especially the one about their champions fighting a "top contender." Moreover, in keeping with the longtime tradition of alphabet groups not only taking money under the table but over the table, around the table, and even taking the table itself, some of the testimony concerned someone associated with the WBA trying to get a piece of the action for gaining a sanction for a title fight between Moorer and Joe Hipp. Joe Hipp, for crying out loud!

Finally, after hearing from everyone, including George himself—who testified, "I've wanted to be heavyweight champ ever since I entered the ring in 1987. I wanted to fight for the title to show the world not only that I can win this thing, but that age forty is truly not a deficit"—the judge, Ronald Mosley, ruled in George's favor, holding that the WBA rules weren't worth the paper they were written on and that the organization had violated their own rules in the past.

George's win over the WBA was merely the appetizer. Now it was on to the main course: Michael Moorer.

One of my favorite words is *blend*, a word I tend to overuse. Just ask Helen. To me it means to mix, to harmonize, to bond, something I tried to do with all my fighters so that the two of us became comfortable with one another. By "blending" with my fighter, I was always there for them, to hear them out, to do what was best for them—or as Ray Leonard once said, "I knew I could ask Angie anything, and I knew he would always tell me the truth."

"Blending" was a matter of mutual trust, and having been in George's corner for five fights, I had earned enough trust from George to be able to "blend" with him. He trusted me enough to look for me to come up with a winnable battle plan for his fight with Moorer.

At our first meeting, we discussed the fact that since Moorer was left-handed—the first southpaw heavyweight champ in history—we had to come up with a strategy that would enable George to counteract Moorer's most effective punch, his right jab. Since George's jab was much stronger than Moorer's, the plan was to put it to good use, sometimes just sticking it out when Moorer leaned forward to throw a punch and touching Moorer's face with it and other times countering whatever Moorer threw with a jab. The only times George would throw his right would be whenever Moorer started to throw his straight left. Then, with Moorer's body crossing over in front of him, George would unload that atom-smashing right of his, a right called by Teddy Atlas, Moorer's trainer, "a sneaky right." It was made all the sneakier by George frequently pawing out with his jab, almost like a shot across the bow, then coming across with what I would call a "stealth right" right behind it. It was a simple strategy, but one I thought would work, even if George had to take three punches for every one he landed.

But strategy wasn't the only thing George and I talked about. During one of our daily discussions, George unburdened himself, confiding that he was still, as he called it, "haunted" by Zaire. He had, he said, never even tried to get up after Muhammad had knocked him down and "for years couldn't live with that." For twenty years he had lived with that mental scar, spending every waking hour obsessing over his failure. Now he had, in his words, "a chance to exorcise the ghost once and for all."

While divulging his innermost secrets, George also said that he thought he had been drugged before the fight in Zaire, that the water he had been given before the fight had "medicine in it." But if he had taken anything before the fight, it must have been steroids judging from those home run shots he was throwing for the first six rounds. No, it wasn't "medicine" that did George in, nor loose ropes, which he first claimed. It was that one-two Ali hit him with in the first round, the "rope-a-dope," and any one of a hundred other things Ali did to beat him. Ali hadn't needed any help from any "medicine."

As the countdown to the fight neared, just days away, George was in "trim" fighting shape—if 250, his lightest weight in three years, could be called "trim"—and more than determined to win back his heavyweight championship. He felt destined. All he had to do to achieve that dream and "exorcise the ghost" of Zaire was beat Michael Moorer.

The scene in the dressing room before a fight, far away from the television cameras, is an elaborate piece of theater. Fighters of all sizes, shapes, and kinds, all sniffing the promise of the night, try to work off their nervousness, each in his own distinctive way. Some will be going through a normal workout routine, stretching, exercising, and shadowboxing, working up a sweat. Others will be throwing punches in the air or into their trainers' hand pads. A few will be standing in front of a mirror, studying their stances, their punches, or themselves. More than a few will be listening to music to soothe themselves. And still a few others will go into the bathroom relieving themselves or spitting and blowing their noses to clear their respiratory tract while others dance their butterflies away. The styles may vary, but all are trying to work out their nervousness and get their minds set for the fight.

Not so Big George. Convinced he was on a mission and would once again be heavyweight champion, he came into the dressing room radiating a hard glow of high purpose. With all the coolness of the proverbial cucumber, he began unpacking his bag and, after rummaging around in it for a minute or so, came out with a pair of trunks. The trunks, once bright red, had now faded to pink. But you could still read the lettering on them: "George Foreman, Heavyweight Champion." They were the same trunks he had worn in Zaire twenty years ago.

Going all the way back to about the first decade of the twentieth century when the current style of boxing trunks replaced the skin-tights worn by John L. Sullivan and his successors, boxing trunks are about the only thing besides paper clips that haven't changed. Essentially men's underwear with "Everlast" or "Ringside" imprinted on the waistband, they occasionally sport a legend, usually the fighter's name or some advertisement, like the one Nino Benvenuti sported advertising an Italian restorative. The trunks George now put on were his advertisement that this "old geezer," as he was called, just two months short of his forty-sixth birthday, intended to put to rest the slander that the contest always belonged to the young. More important, those trunks were a sign he intended to exorcise the "ghost" of things past.

Singing "The Impossible Dream," he told everyone within earshot, "I'm fighting for every guy who ever got told to act his age." Instead of warming up in the dressing room, George stepped out into the hallway to do a little shadowboxing. But when an HBO camera crew came into view, George, without even the slightest trace of nervousness, broke into a loud laugh, not wanting anyone watching to think, as he put it, that "I was having anything but fun."

An HBO producer asked George if he had any special music he would like played when he entered the MGM Grand arena. George, never having had a musical accompaniment for his entrance, hadn't given it any thought. He paused for a second and then, without saying a word, quickly turned and went back into his dressing room to fish out of his bag the tape he had jumped rope to, Sam Cooke's "If I Had a Hammer." Returning, he handed it to the producer.

Moments later we were on our way into the arena. As soon as George heard "If I Had a Hammer" blaring over the P.A. system, he burst down the aisle, all pumped up. Suddenly the arena took on the look of a giant psychiatric ward as almost twelve thousand fans, all partial to George and his comeback, greeted his entrance with a deafening roar, collectively maltreating their lungs by repeatedly shouting his name. The cheering suddenly stopped, almost as if the choirmaster had waved off the choir, and was replaced by booing when rap music began playing. For here came Michael Moorer down the aisle. George, standing in the corner, cloaked in a sweatshirt with the hood up, knew what Moorer was going through. He had been there before, in Zaire.

Even before the echo of the opening bell had died down, Moorer had begun landing his right jab, pumping it into George's face two and three times in succession. George was content to just stand there, arms crossed in front of him, occasionally throwing his left, more a pawing motion than a punch, with a right thrown in every now and then for good measure. And every so often he would deliver a long looping left, less as a scoring punch than as a range finder to keep Moorer from moving to his right, away from George's lethal right. It was almost as if George was playing "rope-a-dope" without the ropes, waiting Moorer out just as Ali had waited him out twenty years before in Zaire.

As the rounds continued to mount and those keeping score continued to write "ditto" on their scorecards next to Moorer's name—with the exception of the fourth round, won by George on the strength of his body attack on all three scorecards—it was becoming painfully evident that George's strategy of waiting for Moorer to throw his straight left so that his body crossed over in front of George, creating a target for George's "sneaky" right, was not going to happen soon enough.

Like a watched pot that never boils, we needed something to bring George to a boil. I tried to provide that something before the tenth round when I told him, "Look, George, you're kind of behind on points." Hardly on par with my exhortation, "You're blowing it, son" to Sugar Ray before the thirteenth round of his fight with Hearns, but words I thought would make the point that George now had to "dig deep" to win. George didn't want to hear any such words and in an agitated tone snapped back, "Don't come with that stuff."

Angry at me, George went out for the tenth round intent on taking his anger out on Moorer. But Moorer, convinced the lion known as George Foreman was asleep just because he hadn't heard him roar and paying no heed to trainer Teddy Atlas's warning to move away from George's right, stood in front of George, peppering him with jabs and punctuating each jab landed with a verbal "pop, pop, pop." All the while George stood his ground, looking—through horizontal slits that had once served as eyes— for Moorer to cross over in front of him. About two-thirds of the way through the round, George threw a sharp left jab and followed with a strong right, catching Moorer on the forehead. Moorer stood there, stock-still, right in front of George, right where George wanted him. This was the chance he had waited for, and like a bird dog spotting a wounded pheasant, George was quick to jump on his stricken prey. Throwing a left, he then threaded the needle's eye with a powerful right, catching Moorer on the sweet spot of his chin. Suddenly Moorer collapsed to the canvas like a balloon whose string had been detached.

As referee Joe Cortez tolled the count over the soon-to-be-ex-champ, twelve thousand fans in the MGM Grand arena jumped to their feet screaming with all the wild joy of prisoners on the announcement of their release. At the count of "ten," George, too, felt some of that same release, freed of the ghost that had haunted him for two decades. His prayers answered, he fell to his knees to give a prayer of thanks, saying simply, "Thank you, Jesus."

One reporter at ringside, then in the process of giving a running commentary, was asked by the voice on the other end of the phone whether Foreman's victory was "a bad day for boxing." The writer merely held up the phone and said, "Bad day for boxing? Listen to the cheering."

While all this was happening I was thinking to myself much the same thing. When miracles like this happen, how can it be bad for boxing? This was the greatest thing that had ever happened in the sport. And it had happened in the MGM Grand, which seemed appropriate since the lyrics to one of the greatest songs in one of MGM's greatest movie went "Somewhere over the rainbow . . . ." As in the song, the dreams George had dared to dream had come true.

George Foreman's long pilgrimage was over. George would have four more fights left in him, but they were mere footnotes to the greatest comeback in sports. For when history revisits the career of this time traveler whose career had spanned four decades and twenty years between championships, it will pause longer over the name of George Foreman than any other great.

If there was a fitting tribute to this man who had triumphed twenty years after having been beaten by Muhammad Ali and after twenty years of hiding his pain behind a big smile and thousands of one-liners it came from Muhammad himself who sent George a letter after his win reading, "Congratulations, Champ, you had the courage and the guts to go out and do it." Those words were worthy of being lettered on all the white ribbons all over the world to honor the accomplishment of Big George Foreman.

EIGHTEEN

The Last Chapter: Memories Are Made of This

I t's been said that life is not measured by the number of breaths you take but by the moments that take your breath away. And, boy, over the past sixty years have I had my share of those breathtaking moments.

When you're aging, time goes by at a fairly accelerated clip—or as someone once said, "When you're over fifty, every fifteen minutes is breakfast." It's been that way for me, too. And looking back over those years is almost like opening an old trunk and having the dusty memories come billowing out, filling the air with reminders of people, places, and friends of the past.

Just reminiscing (a ten-dollar word), there are so many I'm grateful to who made those breathtaking moments happen. First there were the many trainers who lit the way for me and on whose shoulders I stood, from Chickie Ferrara, who took me under his wing at the very beginning, to Ray Arcel, Charlie Goldman, Freddie Brown, and so many others who guided me when I was the new kid on the boxing block.

Larry Holmes was once quoted as saying, "Angelo Dundee never took a right hand or a left hook in his life, but he had somebody in front of him that did." And Buster Douglas Sr., along the same line, was once heard to say, "Where did they get that 'we' shit? When the bell rings, I go out into the ring; they go down the stairs." But to Larry and Buster, and all those who have no idea of what a trainer does or how valuable he is, I say you don't have to be a hen to know how to make an omelet. And we're in the omelet-making business, so to speak.

As a bona fide member of the trainers' fraternity, I can tell you that every trainer I have ever known is there for his kids, helping to give those with

God-given talents a better chance of doing what they do best. And any-one who doesn't understand that doesn't understand just how complex the game of boxing is. We have a list of a thousand to-dos to help our kids. It's a mixed bag combining certain qualities belonging to a doctor, an engi-neer, a psychologist, and sometimes even an actor, in addition to knowing your specific art well. In short, whatever we can do to give them an advan-tage in the ring, we do. And if you don't think we care for our fighters, let me tell you about Charlie Goldman, who was found sleeping the deep sleep, dead in his bed, wearing the championship robe of his fighter, Rocky Marciano.

I know that whatever help I can give my fighters ends at the sound of the bell for the next round. Then he's on his own, out there in the loneli-est spot in the world, the center of the ring, just him, the other guy, and the ref. And that other guy is there to hurt him and the ref can't help him—although Randy "Tex" Cobb tried to enlist the aid of the referee in his fight with Larry Holmes when, unable to get to Larry with a taxi cab, he hollered over to referee Steve Crossen, "You're white, help me!" But for three min-utes it's up to the fighter—and the fighter alone.

When the bell rings ending the round, that's when the trainer takes over. That's when, with our minds working at computerized speed, we com-municate with our fighter, telling him what to do for the next three min-utes. That's when something like "You're blowing it, son" to a Sugar Ray Leonard can turn around a fight. Or when a push in the back or fiddling with a torn glove in the corner of a fighter named Cassius Clay can avert a defeat. That's our time to win or lose a fight for the fighter. And know-ing how and when to do that voodoo that trainers do so well comes only with experience, for experience counts for everything in this business. That's why I'm grateful to all those trainers who came before me, handing down all their experience and advice, like old clothing, and teaching me to become a trainer. Or, in the words of Yogi Berra, to all those who "Learned me all their experiences."

Then there were the fighters, those great athletes I had the pleasure of working with, starting with my first champ, Carmen Basilio, who proved that a good little man can beat a good big man, as he did in beating Sugar Ray Robinson. And to my three Cuban champions, Luis Rodriguez, Sugar Ramos, and José Napoles, who not only gave me so many great moments in the ring but also taught me "Spanglish" so I could communicate with the many other Latino fighters I was fortunate to have been associated with. And, of course, Muhammad Ali, who never made me a millionaire but made me rich in so many other ways during the most fun years I've ever had. And Sugar Ray Leonard, who was always a ball to be around and took up the slack both for me and for boxing after Ali's retirement. And George Foreman, who showed me the meaning of perseverance and determination. And so many others, those less-than-boldfaced fighters I had the pleasure of working with over the years.

These were the best athletes in the world. And if you don't believe me when I say that, then maybe you'll believe ESPN.com, which conducted a poll of trainers, coaches, sports scientists, and medical professionals who ranked sixty-four sports in terms of "athleticism." Based on strength, speed, agility, quickness, courage, stamina, and decision-making under pressure, the pollsters ranked boxing number one—with fishing number sixty-four. So, is it any wonder why I've enjoyed working with the best athletes in the world? They're number one in my book, too.

Then there were the members of the media, friends who were always "there" for me, like Budd Schulberg, Bud Collins, Dave Anderson, Mort Sharnik, Lim Kee Chan (my writer friend from Singapore), Steve Ellis, and Howard Cosell.

Speaking of Cosell, who was always speaking of anything and everything, he was what you might call a real "beaut," bombastic and full of himself—Jimmy Cannon once saying of him, "If Howard Cosell were a sport, he'd be roller derby." What I could never understand was Howard's constant boast that he "made" Muhammad Ali when, if truth be known, it was the other way round, Muhammad the one who made Howard.

Muhammad might have "made" me, too. For just being associated with Muhammad, I was more than just a trainer; I was a "famous trainer."

As "a famous trainer" I was able to get gigs announcing fights with Howard Cosell and Tim Ryan. I could never understand why Cosell—who was quoted as saying, "Angelo Dundee is the only man in boxing to whom I would entrust my own son" (which was easy for him to say, Howard never having had a son)—would never entrust me to say anything on the air, almost always saying what I told him during the commercial break and incorporating it into his own observations. Ryan, on the other hand, let me have my say. Maybe too much as occasionally, with my scanty knowledge of Spanish, I would correct his pronunciation of Latino fighters' names.

And Tim would always tell me he was "using the King's English." Well, I might not have known "the King's English," but I knew the king was now a queen and besides names like "Cuyo" were pronounced "Cujo" in Spanish, with a *j* sound for the *y*. Anyway, my biggest contribution to the telecast with Tim came during the second Michael Dokes–Mike Weaver fight when I said, "Weaver's jab is more perceptive than Dokes's." So maybe announcing wasn't my bag. But recently I've made somewhat of a comeback, appearing on ESPN Classic's "Ringside" show as a commentator. Everybody thinks I have hair, so it's a great show.

Then there were the movies. And here I didn't have to speak. I remember my first movie part. And when I say "part," I'm not kidding because it was a part of my arm. The movie was *Requiem for a Heavyweight*, back in 1962, and the producer, David Suskind, was looking for a heavyweight to fight Anthony Quinn, who was playing the part of a well-worn fighter named Mountain Rivera. Well, they cast Cassius as the heavyweight and along with Cassius they cast that "famous trainer" as (guess what?) his trainer. In the movie Cassius KOs Mountain in the seventh round, and if you look closely you'll see my hand and part of my arm holding up Cassius's hand in victory after the fight. For that "part," I received residuals of about eight or ten dollars a year for the longest time. Or rather my arm did.

The part of that "famous trainer" was later played by Ernest Borgnine and Ron Silver in films about Muhammad. Silver played me in Michael Mann's 2001 picture *Ali*, and although I didn't appear in the picture, I trained Will Smith to imitate all of Ali's moves in the ring. Here let me tell you that until I worked on *Ali* I thought boxers were the hardest workers I'd ever seen. But I soon found out that actors work as hard, if not harder. They're as dedicated and disciplined as fighters, working from early in the morning till late at night. And no one worked harder than Will Smith, a great athlete and an excellent learner, who worked at it until he had all of Ali's moves down pat. He even loved to spar, going through several great workouts with James Toney, who played the part of Joe Frazier. I can't begin to tell you how much fun I had just being a part of *Ali*, even though I didn't have a "part" in it.

Then came *Cinderella Man*, the title coming from the nickname given to James J. Braddock by writer Damon Runyon. Here was a guy going nowhere, fighting for food on the table. He was on welfare and working on the docks—that kind of guy. Then, against all odds, he won the heavy-weight championship of the world, beating Max Baer in one of the biggest upsets in boxing history. I was fortunate to work in the picture training one of the nicest guys and best actors I've ever met, Russell Crowe, who played the title role. Russell was a great athlete who was easy to train, and by the time our training sessions were over, he not only looked and moved like Braddock, but in the film he *was* Braddock.

Besides serving as a Boxing Consultant or Technical Advisor (or some other lofty-sounding "Wizard of Oz"–like title), director Ron Howard gave me a small part in the movie. So small in fact that I had more lines in my face than I had in the picture. However, that didn't stop me from inadvertently enlarging my part. I would get carried away, the "reel" action looking so real that several times during the filming I'd forget myself and start screaming instructions up at Russell from the corner for him to do something or other. And every time I did, Ron Howard would come over to calm me down, telling me, "Angie, that's not in the script." At the end of the film after Russell, as Braddock, defeated Baer, Russell leaned over and planted a big kiss on my bald head as a gesture of "thanks." That wasn't in the script either.

Cinderella Man was a stirring, uplifting, feel-good movie, one that won critical acclaim across the board. And yet I have one small quibble with it. I have nothing but the utmost admiration for director Ron Howard and the job he did—especially keeping in the shot of Russell kissing me on the forehead—but I also have respect for historical accuracy. And I felt that the writers didn't have to "Hollywoodize" Max Baer, making him a villain. For Max Baer was anything but a villain. In fact, if anything was a villain it was the Great Depression. Alternately known as "Madcap Maxie" and "The Magnificent Screwball," Baer was a happy-go-lucky guy who once said he "just wanted to have a barrel of fun." Here was a guy who dedicated him-self to a life of wine, women, and song, with emphasis on the former two, a hint of which you saw in the movie and which he gave voice to after losing to Braddock, saying, "I'm happy for Braddock . . . he has three kids. I don't know how many I have."

One story told around the trainers' table at The Neutral early on in my New York days had it that one of those connected with the Braddock camp, "Dumb" Dan Morgan, who was anything but dumb, put a beauti-ful bleach-blonde Venus in a ringside seat before the Braddock-Baer fight.

Her "job," if it can be called that, was to raise her skirt, spread her legs, and wave at Maxie all fight long. And as she kept at it, Maxie responded in kind instead of paying attention to Braddock's left.

Nah, that was no villain.

Quibbling aside, I've got to tell you I've never had as much fun and still remained conscious as I had on the set of *Cinderella Man*, thanks to Russell and Ron.

But a Robert De Niro I'll never be.

I know I've been on longer than Oscar Award winners, giving thanks to all those whose paths I've had the pleasure of crossing during my fistic travels of the last half-century, but wait!, as they say in those Ginzu knife commercials, there's more. There's my brother Chris, Gene Kilroy, Michael Mann, and Bert Sugar, who gave me a better view from my corner. And so many others I owe a debt of gratitude to I'll have to write another book to include them all. But the ones I owe my most heartfelt thanks to are the family Dundee, to my bride of more than fifty years, the lovely Helen, who claims we've only been married for twenty-five or so of those years since I've been gone over half the time pursuing my dream, and to my kids, Jimmy and Terri, for their understanding of the time I took away from them to spend it with my "other" family, my colleagues and boxers in my boxing family.

Regrets? I have a few. My biggest heartbreak came back in 1963—a double heartbreak, really. Luis Rodriguez, my fighter, had been promised a big story in *Sports Illustrated* after his victory over Emile Griffith for the welterweight title. But Luis had fought in the cofeature that night at Dodger Stadium on the same card headed up by Davey Moore, who was defending his featherweight title against another of my fighters, Sugar Ramos. In a rock-'em-sock-'em fight, with each fighter giving as much as he got, Ramos knocked out Moore in the tenth round, Moore's head whiplashing off the bottom rope and then bouncing on the floor. After a few frightening moments, Moore finally regained consciousness, slowly opening his eyes and talking to those around him. Thinking everything was okay, I went back to visit Moore in his dressing room. We talked for a couple of minutes, he asking for "a return bout" and me saying "sure." Then he said, "I'm tired. I'm gonna lie down." He never woke up, dying two days later.

Because of the tragedy, *Sports Illustrated* ditched the story on Rodriguez. My heart went out to Moore and his family, but I also felt a little for Luis who never got the recognition he deserved for being a great fighter.

I also regret not being there for José Napoles when he lost his welterweight title to Billy Backus. You see, as a trainer with more than one fighter in his so-called stable, you're always juggling assignments. And because I couldn't be in two places at one time—Napoles's defense in Syracuse being just four days before Muhammad Ali was to fight Oscar Bonavena in New York City—I had to make a choice and the choice was Muhammad in his second comeback fight after his three-and-a-half-year layoff. If I had been there for Napoles, I would have been able to save his title. Instead, after he was cut along the right eye by a head butt in the second round and along his left eye by a Backus hook in the third, the replacement cutman couldn't stop the flow of blood. At one minute of the fourth round, the referee called in the doctor who took one look and waved it off, Napoles losing. Six months later Napoles regained his crown from Backus, with yours truly, the man a younger Cassius Clay had called "Mr. Cutman," there to take care of Napoles's brittle scar tissue.

But my biggest regret is the state of boxing today. It's hurting. Once one of the three major sports—along with baseball and horse racing—commanding headlines not only on the sports pages but the front pages as well, today it's charitably number 11 on the list of Top Ten sports, tucked somewhere under the shipping news.

How did boxing ever lose its place in the pecking order of sports? Part of the reason is that the sports world has changed. Today fans are given more choices, a greater variety of sports, and there's been a seismic shift in the sports fans' preference, with better-marketed sports taking away our fans. Look at ESPN and you'll find so-called "sports," such as Texas Hold-'Em, being televised and watched by millions of eyeballs.

And then there's a new entry on the list of sports offered to sports fans, what the *Washington Post* calls "that gruesome junk," ultimate fighting. Some call it "human cockfighting," others "bar fights without the beer bottles." But whatever you call it, this new phenomenon has captured the imagination of young fans who have exchanged the cartoon violence of pro wrestling for the real violence of this so-called sport.

Now they're even planning to televise the "Rock-Paper-Scissors" championship! I can't wait until they begin to televise topless volleyball, maybe then I'll be interested. But put them together and you begin to see boxing's problem. It has trouble shoehorning its way onto television and into the consciousness of fans, thereby preventing it from recapturing the glory of yesteryear.

The biggest reason for the sport's decline in interest, however, can be found by looking in the mirror, for the biggest enemy is ourselves. When I first entered the sport—granted, that was just after the Great Flood—there were eight divisions and eight world champions. And you could name every one of them, from the heavyweight champion all the way down to the flyweight champion. Today we have seventeen—count 'em, seventeen—divisions and the four alphabet-soup sanctioning bodies (a four-ring circus made up of the WBC, the WBA, the IBF, and the WBO) can't even get those straight, one group calling those halfway houses between the eight traditional divisions, like welterweight or middleweight, "junior" something or other and other groups "super" something or other. And I never could figure out what a "cruiserweight" was. I know it's bigger than a breadbox and smaller than a battleship, but what's the weight limit? Again, the sanctioning bodies disagree. And with the four major sanctioning bodies each crowning their own divisional champions, today we have as many as sixty-eight champions in all. (And that's not even counting their made-up boutique-y titles, such as "interim," "super," "continental," "whatevers." That's still more champions—and more sanctioning fees.) No wonder the hard-core boxing fan has trouble naming as many as half of them. So why should the peripheral fan be interested? Hell, it's easier to ace a college entrance exam than name them all!

As my old friend Pat Putnam once wrote: "It's a good thing we only have twenty-six letters in the alphabet or we'd have more of these clowns." And more champions! And what are these clueless sanctioning bodies, who probably would only be charged half-price by a mind reader, doing for the sport? They charge outrageous sanctioning fees for championship bouts, some even taking money for ranking fighters. (Dare I call them "bribes"?) And then they give their champions belts that look like they were made out of broken beer bottles found on the San Diego freeway.

And now the head of one of those sanctioning bodies is running around peddling an idea called "Open Scoring," an idea whose time should never come. The idea is to let fans and fighters alike know the round-by-round scoring during a fight. But Open Scoring is a concept that cheats the fans. I know, having "worked" an angle on Open Scoring myself. During the Muhammad Ali–Earnie Shavers fight, knowing we were ahead by four rounds with but three left to go by virtue of NBC posting the round-by-round scores, I told Muhammad the only way he could lose was by getting knocked out. So I instructed him to go into a safety-first shell rather than risk being knocked out, which he did, winning the fight. But even though that worked for me, it didn't for the fans at Madison Square Garden that night who got less than they paid for. And what about the most dramatic phrase in all of sports: "and the winner is . . ."? That, too, would be lost with Open Scoring, since we'd probably already know who "the winner is." No, little would be gained by going to an Open Scoring system, except maybe having riots at the end of every round instead of just one at the end of the fight.

These alphabet soup groups probably think their purpose in life is to lose fans, not gain them. Why not just have the fans vote for the winner of every round, à la "American Idol"? That way the sanctioning bodies could sell *that* on pay-per-view and even charge a sanctioning fee.

But it's not just the sanctioning bodies that are responsible for boxing's current state. It's also the promoters. They're constantly bashing and slashing and trashing one another. Some aren't above spreading rumors about a competitor's promotion or telling fans not to watch another's fights. And sometimes they even schedule their own cards against another's on the same night.

It would be too easy to say that what the sport needs is another charismatic fighter like a Muhammad Ali or a Sugar Ray Leonard. No, what boxing needs is some organization for a totally dysfunctional sport—like one alphabet soup organization; one champion in each division; or one central office to market the sport like other sports. Only then can our once-great sport rightfully take its place back amongst the top sports. Otherwise, those who call themselves boxing's caretakers might well turn out to be its undertakers.

Back in the late 1950s, just after the mob scandals first came to light, I remember Dan Parker of the *New York Mirror* writing: "I've been at its bedside for forty years waiting for boxing to die." Well, here it is a half century later and the patient is still there. Hanging on assuredly, but still there. And just as boxing survived the mob scandals, it will continue to survive. It's too great a sport not to.

Time, like taffy, tends to stretch out, leaving me time to count my blessings as well as my memories. Looking back, I'm grateful to those many organizations that have recognized my work. The Boxing Writers named me Manager of the Year twice and even honored me with an award for "Long and Meritorious Service." I've been inducted—or is that indicted?—into the International Boxing Hall of Fame, the World Boxing Hall of Fame, the National Italian-American Sports Hall of Fame, the Florida Sports Hall of Fame, the Pennsylvania Sports Hall of Fame, and the UNICO National Hall of Fame. The Touchdown Club of Washington, D.C., presented me with their prestigious Timmie Award, and a permanent plaque bearing my name was placed on South Beach to commemorate the 5th Street Gym. The boxing club of Florida State even named their team the Angelo Dundee Boxing Club in my honor. Not bad for a little kid from South Philly who got into boxing almost by default.

But recently, when I was given a Lifetime Achievement Award by a local organization, I told them my lifetime was far from over, that I still had several miles left on my odometer. For far from retiring, I am still involved in boxing, working with fighters like Tommy Zbikowski, the Notre Dame safety whom I've known since he was about ten or eleven years old; Jimmy Lange, a local fighter in Virginia, who is a great local attraction; and several kids from Nassau, like Jermaine Mackey.

I remember once when Muhammad Ali was in a small town outside of Louisville he met a man who asked, "Are you Muhammad Ali?" After he answered yes, the man asked, "Do you know the Dundees?" And Muhammad answered, "Yes, Chris and Angelo." The old guy said, "Good hustlers." And for years afterward, whenever Muhammad would see me he would always say, "Still hustling."

Well, I'm still hustling. I have so many wonderful memories from the past sixty years—people I've known, places I've been to, breathtaking moments I've experienced. But there's still room for more . . . much more.

Afterword

George Foreman

On the night before Super Bowl VI in New Orleans, I happened to be at ringside for the Joe Frazier–Terry Daniels heavyweight championship fight, seated next to famed sports artist LeRoy Neiman. Just before the fight, *Boxing Illustrated* editor Bert Sugar came running over to us shouting something through his clinched cigar that sounded like, "Seeing you two guys together, the world's number-one heavyweight contender and the world's number-one boxing artist gives me an idea." Pausing to take a puff on his cigar, he hurried on, "Why don't you both do a story for the magazine? LeRoy, you can do the sketches, and George, you can write a commentary on the fight." I looked up at Bert and said, "What should I write?" With that Bert answered, "Write anything you want," and hurried away.

Well, the fight was something less than a classic, Daniel lasting all of four rounds in a one-sided fight. So when Bert came rushing back to pick up our "story," all we had was an uninspired effort to go with the fight. LeRoy handed over a couple of sketches that were, at best, preliminary, and I handed Bert a page torn from LeRoy's sketchbook on which I had merely scribbled down something. What I had written was simply, "Anything you want." Needless to say, our "story" never made it into the magazine.

Jump-skip three-and-a half decades later and again Bert, along with his book-writing partner, Angelo Dundee, has asked me to do a piece for their book *My View from the Corner*, both telling me to "write anything you want." This time I won't let them off the hook so easily.

When I came back in 1987 to fight Steve Zouski in Sacramento for $21,000, spare change compared to what I once had made, I didn't come back to make big money. I came back to be champ again. Many thought my comeback at the ripe old age of 37 seemed like an act of inspired pointlessness, labeling me as a fistic Don Quixote tilting at windmills. And those laughing loudest were the sportswriters.

Fighting in small arenas for small bucks, I won fight after fight, gaining confidence and even losing weight—trimming down from 300-plus pounds to a "svelte" 250. But it seems that early on the only people paying much attention to my comeback were the members of the media who looked at me as a time-traveling relic who represented the golden age of heavyweights and viewed my comeback as nothing more than a long-postponed victory lap for an almost forgotten era. Still, they were paying attention, even if they were making jokes about both me and my comeback.

Now you may call it "ballyhoo" or just plain ol' marketing, but in the face of such ridicule I found myself following the advice of Sammy Davis Jr. who once said, "Ya gotta make 'em love ya," and subtly stoked the fires by reaching out to the press and building on their humor as a starting point and turned it to my advantage.

When some reporter asked me if I was concerned about brain damage, I'd reply, "I already have that, I've been married four times." Or when questioned about my age, I'd say, "I'm gonna pass a bill that would force a mandatory retirement age on boxers . . . sixty-five." The old-timers who had covered me the first time 'round were amazed by my change in attitude; the younger members of the press, who had only heard about me, were amused. And when asked about my weight, I'd begin by joking that my training camp was "right next to a Baskin-Robbins" and that "I'd gone on a cheeseburger diet." So the press began calling me "Big George" and "Captain Cheeseburger." You see, all those years of preaching had taught me how to please an audience.

By the end of 1989, with a record of 19 wins in 19 comeback fights, 18 by knockout, the boxing press had begun to take my comeback seriously. One magazine, *Boxing Illustrated*, even featured me on its front cover with a headline reading: "Who to Look for in 1990 . . . George Foreman????" I had had enough wins to get everyone talking about George Foreman.

Two fights and two knockout wins later, I was in Las Vegas to fight my first top-ten heavyweight, Adilson Rodrigues. And it just so happened that Rodrigues was trained by none other than Angelo Dundee, the same Angelo Dundee who had been in Muhammad Ali's corner lo those many years before in Zaire. Over those 16 years since "The Rumble in the Jungle" I had constantly thought of Dundee and how, to my way of thinking, he had saved Ali that night when, in the sixth round, as Ali was jawing away at me and grandstanding to the crowd, I thought to myself, "I've finally got him!" and loaded up with my best right hand, ready to fire. But even before I had finished that thought, a little squeaky voice came from Ali's corner yelling, "Don't play with that sucker!" And Ali moved off the ropes, out of danger. That little squeaky voice had belonged to Angelo Dundee and I never forgot it.

Later that night, after dispatching Rodrigues in two rounds, I found myself at the Vegas airport waiting for the red-eye to take me back to Houston for Sunday's church service. And what to my wondering eyes should I see but Angelo waiting for his flight back home. Now, ever since that day (really, early in the morning in Zaire) when he had yelled, "Don't play with that sucker" at Ali, I had wanted him in my corner. And without any ado, I went over to him and asked a straight-forward question: "I've always wanted you to work with me. Will you?"

Angelo was quick to respond, answering with just word, "Yes!" He didn't have to say any more. No contract, no handshake, Angelo's word was as good as gold. For here was a man whose work spoke for itself. He had that Midas-touch reputation, having guided such greats as Carmen Basilio, Muhammad Ali, and Sugar Ray Leonard, along with many others, to championships. To be associated with Angelo Dundee would add further credibility to my comeback. Besides which, unbelievably, he was older than me.

Angelo was one of a kind, always with a twinkle in his eye and a smile on his lips, he was a trusted link to the old school, someone who could connect with the writers, young and old alike. He was always there for the writers, usually letting me handle the interviews, but in my absence working the press himself. I remember one time, after taking a shower, I came out of the door to see Angie surrounded by a mob of writers and shouted over to them, "Watch that Angie!" But I appreciated his keeping the George Foreman bandwagon going. Between us we must have conducted enough interviews to fell a forest of trees just to print the papers they ran in. And, amazingly, the writers were now laughing *with* me, not *at* me.

Not only did Angie give me instant credibility, he also gave me invaluable advice and helped me, as one of the writers said, "re-invent the George wheel," for Angie was one of boxing's best strategists and his every helpful hint made me a better boxer. So much so that he told me that I was now steadier and more patient and took advantage of everything and that I was a better fighter this time around than I had been in my first career.

Because I did all my training behind closed doors—Angie kidding me that until he trained me he thought Ali was the worst gym fighter he had ever seen—the only time Angie could be seen giving me advice came during our between-rounds discussion, which became a source of great amusement for the press. Figuring that it was a waste of energy sitting down and getting up instead of just standing for the one-minute between-rounds intermission, I stood in my corner for that one minute. And there was little Angie, in a Mutt-and-Jeff scene, standing on his tip-toes to reach up to my six-foot-three ear in order to whisper something or other so that it wasn't picked up by the corner microphones. His whispered advice came in short, cryptic messages like, "he's dropping his hands" or "watch out for his left," but was all-important no matter what it looked like.

There was only one time I paid no-never-mind to his advice and that came in my fight against Michael Moorer for the heavyweight championship. I had had a shot at the brass ring three-and-a-half years earlier against Evander Holyfield and although few had given me a chance—some even calling it a "farce" when it was first announced—I had given as good as I got for most of the fight and come up short. Now the planets had re-aligned again and I had my second shot at the title. This time I was determined not to come up short again. And so, when I hit him with a wicked body shot in the ninth and saw him drop his hands a little to protect his body, I decided to do something you're never supposed to do against a southpaw: move to my right, right in front of his power. And although Angie pleaded with me between rounds not to do that, I decided to stand right in front of him and go to his head, which I did, throwing a left jab followed by a thunderous right that froze him and then threw a second right, coming up from the hip, that knocked him down. And out!

As I said in my book, *By George*, that victory over Moorer belonged to all of those who had helped me achieve what I had set out to do—win back my heavyweight title. And one of those who had been so important in helping me was Angelo Dundee, who was always there for me. So this time I didn't want to write, as Angelo and Bert asked me to, "Anything you want." This time I wanted to write everything, as in "Thank you, Angelo . . . for everything."

Index